THE BRITISH GENERAL ELECTION OF 1979

THE BRITISH GENERAL ELECTION OF 1979

By

David Butler

Fellow of Nuffield College, Oxford

and

Dennis Kavanagh

Senior Lecturer in Government, University of Manchester

First edition 1980
Reprinted 1983

Published by
THE MACMILLAN PRESS LTD
London and Basingstoke
Companies and representatives
throughout the world

Printed in Great Britain by
Woolnough Bookbinding
Wellingborough, Northants

British Library Cataloguing in Publication Data

Butler David, *b. 1924*
   The British general election of 1979
   1. Great Britain.   Parliament – Elections, 1979
   I. Title II. Kavanagh, Dennis
   329'.023'410857   JN956

   ISBN 0-333-26934-9

Contents

List of Illustrations

List of Tables and Diagrams

Preface

This is the eleventh in the series of general election studies which Nuffield College has sponsored since 1945. It is the sixth which has a change of government to record. It will take time to decide whether the newcomers' inevitable promise to change the nation's course will be more fully realised than those of their predecessors in the post-war period. Our story here ends with Mrs Thatcher moving into Downing Street on May 4, 1979. It seeks to assemble the evidence on how this came about and to offer some tentative explanations. Elections can be turning points in history, or trifling interruptions; but as political events they are always worthy of investigation. Elections represent a multitude of individual decisions combined into one collective verdict. These decisions stem from the years which have gone before rather than from the weeks of the campaign. In 1979 it may be said (for the first time since 1966) that the outcome was so definite and expected that the events of the formal contest could not have been critical. Yet, on the evidence of the opinion polls, the number of voters changing their minds during the 1979 campaign was not far below the record levels of 1970 and 1974.

This book, like its recent predecessors, is as much concerned with the antecedents to the election as with the election itself. One virtue of elections as a focus of academic study is that they encapsulate so much of an entire period of political history; another is that they involve so many aspects of political institutions. To engage in writing a book such as this is to explore the whole situation of Britain in the late 1970s, as well as the structure and ethos of each of the parties, the current operation of the media, the working of the market research industry and a lot else besides.

Much has been written about these matters, but much remains undocumented. We are aware how abbreviated our treatment of many important questions must be — but we have done our best to supplement the obvious sources of information. We owe a great deal to the press (though, after November 1978, we greatly missed *The Times* and the *Sunday Times*), to writers of specialist articles and to pollsters. But we owe even more to the participants, to those on front and back benches, and to those in the offices of all parties, who gave so much of their time to talk to us. Our notes on almost 400 interviews contain a generous record of information, insight and indiscretion. We hope that no one looking at the pages which follow will feel we have betrayed their confidence, but equally we hope that no one will feel that our judgments on the general scene have been inhibited. In this kind of contemporary study it is frustratingly impossible to footnote evidence for all one's assertions. But we can at least claim, as a safeguard, that every chapter which follows has been read in manuscript by quite a few of those actually involved, as participants or as privileged observers — even though we have at times had to stand by our judgment against their's.

General elections develop their own myths. The 1979 election was, more quickly and more comprehensively than its predecessors, surrounded by its own controversies with devil-figures, heroes and grand theories. Later research and memoirs will undoubtedly yield new insights and a different perspective. But it might be worth drawing the reader's attention to our treatment of a number of disputed features surrounding the election: the circumstances which led up to Mr Callaghan's decision not to dissolve in the autumn of 1978 (Chapter 2); the tensions within the Conservative leadership for much of the parliament (Chapter 4); the writing of the manifestos (Chapter 6); the thinking behind the parties' strategies (Chapter 7); and, perhaps, the meaning of the election (Chapter 17).

Our profound thanks must as ever be extended to the Warden and Fellows of Nuffield College, not only for formal sponsorship of the project, but for much personal help; to the Social Science Research Council for its generous financial grant; to the many participants in, and observers of, the political scene who went so far out of their way to assist us in interviews and in correspondence; to the patient contributors whose names appear in the table of contents; to Brian Gosschalk, the most dedicated and perceptive of research assistants; to Audrey Skeats, the perfect secretary; to Craig Charney, Mary Bull and

Clive Payne for their diverse services; to Hugh Berrington, Vernon Bogdanor, Richard Rose, Anthony Teasdale, Paul McKee and Philip Williams, among those who read manuscript or proofs; and, above all, to our wives and children, for their support.

DAVID BUTLER
DENNIS KAVANAGH

October 1979

1 National Uncertainties

Successive British elections resemble each other to a notable degree. In spite of the development of television, opinion polling and the party press conference, the ritual in the constituencies, and even at the centre, changes slowly. Party organisation and party argument tend to follow standard forms. Nonetheless, an election can be very different in essence from its predecessors because the atmosphere has changed. Certainly the picture that the electorate had in 1979 of the country's status, and of what could be expected from the political system, was far removed from that of twenty years earlier. The rules of the political game had evolved, and the internal mood and general state of the national economy contrasted sharply with the years of Macmillan and Gaitskell.

Before plunging into an analysis of the events leading up to the 1979 election, it is worth pausing to consider the new setting in which it took place. Developments in political behaviour, in political machinery, and in the state of the economy over the 1970s seemed linked to a growing sense of national self-doubt.

In 1979 people are still not sure what decides elections. Indeed, since the electorate has become so much more volatile, it may actually have become more difficult to account for the diverse movements in party allegiance which cause one election result to differ from another. In the elections between 1945 and 1970, Labour's share of the vote varied only between 43% and 49%, and the Conservatives' between 40% and 50%. There was of course more instability at the individual level; one survey in the 1960s found that only just over half of the electorate cast positive votes in the same way in two successive general elections. But the February 1974 election saw a jump of 12% in the Liberal share of the vote, by far the biggest single change in percentage for a party between one election and another since 1945. It also saw the Scottish Nationalists suddenly rising to a leading position within one segment of the United Kingdom. It was

1

understandable that commentators focussed on the growth of a third force among the electorate. But the bases of support for the other parties differed: for the Liberals, it was mainly disillusionment with the two larger parties; in Wales, Nationalist strength was largely confined to rural, Welsh-speaking areas; in Scotland, the SNP vote represented in part a positive and pervasive interest in nationalism; Ulster remained, as ever, *sui generis*.

The old certainties of a two-party system were threatened, and extensive analysis was made by party officials and pollsters, as well as by academic students, of what affected voting behaviour. Conservative support in October 1974, at 36% of the vote, was an all-time low, while Labour's 37% in February 1974 was their post-war low. The evidence of a long-term decline in strength of partisanship was substantial. In 1964 44% of people said they were very attached to one of the two main parties. By 1974 that figure had dropped to 27%.[1] The status of politicians had fallen too. People were ready to vote for the lesser evil, in a sceptical mood, with a new cynicism about the outcome.

This could be explained partly in terms of general disillusion with the performance of the economy and a sense that no improvement in the national situation had been achieved by the successive alternations of government in 1964, 1970 and 1974. The opposition's panaceas had, time and again, proved no better than the muddles being made by those in power. Indeed, once in office, the new party invariably took up some of the most criticised policies of its predecessors, notably in measures against inflation. As far back as 1967 Mr Maudling, the deputy leader of the Conservative party, was suggesting that the Labour government had 'inherited our problems. They seem also to have inherited many of our remedies'. The tit-for-tat arguments between bland and often similar spokesmen for the rival parties presented in 'balanced' television programmes may have helped to confuse the public's sense of the differences between the parties, and to add to their cynicism about any party's claims to have a monopoly of wisdom. The idea that one party represented the working class and the other the middle and upper class hardly fitted the predominantly middle class university

---

[1] For full discussion, see Ivor Crewe, James Alt and Bo Sarlvik, 'Partisan Dealignment in Britain 1964–1974', *British Journal of Political Science*, (July 1977).

graduate character of the two front benches. A further element in the explanation may lie in the progress of education, and the increased sophistication of an electorate which could see both sides of the case in a grey area where there were few heroes and few villains.[2]

The decline in the fortunes of the two main parties coincided with a decline in class voting. After 1959 many commentators speculated that increased prosperity and social mobility would weaken the class basis of the two-party system, and encourage the drift of affluent workers to the Conservative party. In fact until 1970 a growing number of people voted with their natural 'class' party, though with a weakening allegiance. The sharpest decline occurred in the February 1974 election which, ironically, was to a unique extent dominated by class conflict. One main change was the rise in middle class support for the Labour party, based especially on the growing ranks of teachers and social workers, groups who tend to be more 'left wing' in outlook than Labour manual workers. At the same time issues such as race and law and order attracted a right-wing response from many working class voters. Social class itself became a more complex category, as fewer voters tend to be 'pure' middle or working class in their social backgrounds. By 1974 little over half of the electorate voted with its natural 'class' party. The weakening of such alignments in turn increased the scope for the parties which were not class-based.

The declining attachment of voters to the parties increased the potential for election campaigns to change votes. For long it had been assumed that campaigns made little difference to the outcome because of the commitment of most voters to one or other of the parties. But now short-term factors — specific issues and events, as well as the personalities of the leaders — became more important. From 1966 onwards general elections saw massive shifts in support during the campaign itself and ended with unexpected outcomes.

But it was not only the electorate which had altered. The politicians, too, had changed. Only 164 of the 635 members elected in October 1974 had served in parliament before October 1964. The new breed of politicans was appreciably different in

[2] See D. Butler and D. Stokes, *Political Change in Britain*, 2nd ed. (London, 1975), pp. 193–200.

its motives and values from the older generation. On the Conservative side it was said that the knight of the shire who had blocked R.A. Butler from the premiership had disappeared from the scene, to be replaced by an identikit young merchant banker. On the Labour side it was said that the working man or trade union official had been ousted by the polytechnic lecturer. This is to caricature the transition to a ludicrous extent. As we show in Chapter 13, the Conservatives remained as Oxbridge and public school as ever. Nonetheless, the party led by Mr Heath or Mrs Thatcher, both educated at grammar schools, looked different from that led by Mr Macmillan or Sir Alec Douglas-Home. The 'products of opportunity', in Mr Heath's phrase, were self-made professional politicians from the city and suburbs. On the Labour side the proportion of graduates grew from 33% in 1945 to 57% in 1974. By the 1970s, MPs appeared far more full-time, far more ambitious for office, and far harder to discipline than twenty years earlier.[3]

The disappointments of the 1960s dented the optimism manifest in the 1959 election and sharpened the disagreement between the parties. The Conservative government in 1970 (like Labour in 1974) set about reversing its predecessor's measures, while the opposition disowned many of the policies it had pursued in office. Mr Jenkins after 1971, on the EEC, and Mr Heath after 1975, on incomes policy, did argue for continuity and some measure of support for the government of the day, but they appeared beleaguered spokesmen for a middle way. In each party there was a growing body of opinion which spoke either of a crisis of capitalism or a crisis of socialism. One demanded more 'socialism' (more state ownership, public expenditure and protectionism, as well as minimal co-operation with the EEC) the other a 'social market' approach (less government intervention in industry and collective bargaining, a greater reliance on free market mechanisms, and strict control of money supply). Tony Benn and Sir Keith Joseph emerged as forceful and articulate spokesmen for rival but symmetrical diagnoses of what had gone wrong and what should be done.

Many Labour party and trade union spokesmen convinced themselves and their audiences that the return of Mrs Thatcher

---

[3] See P. Norton, *Dissension in the House of Commons* (London, 1975).

would mean the coming of the most reactionary government since the war. At the same time Conservatives argued, with equal sincerity, that Mr Benn and the 'wild Left' were on the brink of taking over the Labour party.

Hyperbole is the stuff of political debate, and there is nothing new about presenting one's opponents as devil figures, preparing to lead the country to disaster. During much of the parliament the gulf between the parties was presented to the public in more spectacular terms than at any time since the war. And yet, it could be argued, the true gap was as small as in the most Butskellite period, a generation earlier. Mr Callaghan could be seen as the most conservative Prime Minister since Baldwin, cautiously pursuing consensual policies and presenting himself as a kindly uncle, responsible and firm. Mrs Thatcher equally eschewed any radical policy commitment. *The Right Approach* of 1976 was a moderate document. Both parties were agreed on a firm monetary policy to limit inflation. Neither party wanted statutory control of incomes and (despite a lurch at the 1978 Conservative Conference) both sides endorsed a responsible voluntary control of incomes. Both accepted state intervention in industry, giving subsidies to depressed areas and giving transitional aid to major companies (such as British Leyland) which fell on hard times. The referendum on the EEC had seen the centrist leaders of the main parties crush the anti-Europeans. There was general front-bench agreement that membership of the EEC was a fact of life, but there was no enthusiasm for moves to integration, unless they clearly benefited Britain. On immigration and law and order, on Rhodesia and Ireland, and on many areas of the economy, the real differences in policy between the two big parties were remarkably small.

For much of the period the situation was confusing. Policies on the economy, particularly, gave rise to strange alliances across the two main parties. The social democratic wing of the Labour party together with Mr Heath and Mr Prior supported an incomes policy, cash limits in the public sector and intervention in industry. The left wing of the Labour party and the free market wing of the Conservatives agreed on free collective bargaining, while disagreeing on the government's role in managing the economy.

Labour ministers would ridicule the strict monetarism and free market views of Sir Keith Joseph and Sir Geoffrey Howe and reject Sir Keith's appeal for government to abandon the post-war commitment to full employment. But Mr Healey himself kept strict control of the money supply and presided over record levels of unemployment. Conservative critics of the consensus would argue that Labour's conversion to sound monetary and fiscal policies was only skin deep, forced by events and the IMF. They would point to *Labour's Programme 1976* and the TUC-Labour party document, *Into the Eighties*, as evidence of the party's longer term commitment to more state intervention and an expansion of the public sector, and of its yielding to the left wing advocacy of a siege economy. There were also differences of emphasis between the parties on how they should spend the fiscal dividend of the royalties from North Sea oil; the Conservatives favoured a reduction in direct taxation, while Labour wanted public investment to restore the country's industrial strength. As we show in Chapters 2 and 4, it was remarkable how centrist were policy thinking and electoral calculations in the higher councils of both government and opposition. But the voter who just listened to the politicians and read the papers would never have received that impression.

This party debate occurred against a growing and more public scepticism about the capacity of governments to solve the major problems of the day. Few voices expressed optimism about the beneficial consequences of state action. The short-comings of government and the non-fulfilment of election promises had an educative effect on most voters. They did adjust to the economic recession, perhaps faster than the politicians. Every year since 1961 Gallup polls showed that a plurality of British people expected that the economy would be in difficulties. Surveys also showed that a large majority were satisfied with most aspects of life, and this was independent of economic circumstances. But where there was dissatisfaction it was concentrated on government and those areas for which it was responsible — the economy, education, health and the like. The new scepticism about big government, ambitious spending programmes, and Keynesian economics was not confined to Britain. Tax backlash movements appeared in Denmark, California and elsewhere. Some observers feared that competitive party politics spurred the inflation spiral. Others pointed out how overloaded governments could actually go bankrupt; if present trends in spending commitments continued the sum total would soon exceed what could be raised in taxation.[4]

The shortcomings of the parties and the leaders can provide only a part of the answer to those who ask why things were turning out so badly. Britain has become a more difficult country to govern in recent years. Governments appear to be beset by more intractable problems. The effectiveness of their policies is now more dependent on the co-operation of other groups and the actions of other governments; vested interests are better organised to refuse compliance; and economic recession has limited the possibility of increasing both take-home pay and state-financed benefits. Complexity and resource constraints are universals of politics; but they seemed to be more acute in the 1974 Parliament than before.

During the 1970s the established rules of British government were not, in the main, changed. But almost all of them came under challenge and some were significantly modified.

A singular feature of British government is the absence of a written constitution. Alone among the major democratic countries, Britain has no document or clearly written set of principles that describe the institutions of government and their interrelationship. However, when Britain adhered to the Treaty of Rome in 1972 she became subject, over substantial areas, to written rules of procedure which it was outside her power to alter. Devolution of power to Scotland and Wales promised to take Britain further in the same direction. Quite independently of these developments, however, voices were raised for a written constitution which would establish limits to government and be a bulwark against revolutionary change and, perhaps, against arbitrary government interference with civil liberties. Lord Hailsham and Lord Scarman were particularly prominent advocates of a written constitution and a bill of rights, and in June 1977 the House of Lords established a Select Committee

---

[4] See e.g. R. Rose 'Ordinary People in Extraordinary Economic Circumstances', *Strathclyde Occasional Papers in Politics*, 1977. See also the contributions of P. Jay and S. Brittan in E. Tyrrell ed., *The Future That Doesn't Work* (New York, 1977); R. Rose and G. Peters, *Can Government Go Bankrupt?* (London, 1979); A. King, 'Overload: Problems of Governing in the 1970s', *Political Studies*, 1975; J. Douglas, 'The Overloaded Crown', *British Journal of Political Science*, 1976.

which narrowly voted in favour of a bill of rights.[5] There was no likelihood of early action on these proposals, but that they aroused serious discussion was a new phenomenon.

The basic British doctrine of the absolute supremacy of Parliament also came under challenge. Obviously the idea that no Parliament can pass an act that binds its successor was hardly compatible with Common Market rules, or with the proposals for devolution. Another new challenge to parliamentary supremacy came with the 1975 referendum on the Common Market, and the 1979 referendums on Scottish and Welsh devolution. Although these referendums were advisory only, they did represent a substantial derogation from the idea that the decision of parliament was final. It is hardly conceivable that parliament would ever reverse a clear-cut referendum verdict.

Collective Cabinet responsibility is another doctrine that had to be reassessed in the light of the events of the 1974—79 parliament. The 1975 referendum saw the waiving of collective responsibility over a central issue of policy for the first time since 1932. Seven members of the Cabinet openly campaigned against a basic government recommendation. The convention was again relaxed in 1977 in the vote on the method of election to the European Assembly. But collective responsibility was also under assault from a distinct increase in the number of government leaks, and the questioning of the principles of secrecy on which collective responsibility depends.[6] One more challenge to collective responsibility came with the Lib-Lab pact and the system of consultation under which ministers sounded out official Liberal spokesmen on proposed policies in advance of announcing them to parliament or to their party. As with the referendum, the forms of collective responsibility were maintained, but something departed from its substance.

The most obvious threat to the established certainties of British government came with the decline of the two-party system. From 1950 to 1970, 98% of MPs were Conservative or Labour, and 92% of all votes cast were for candidates of the two big parties, but in 1974 the proportions fell to 94% of MPs

---

[5] Lord Hailsham 'Elective Dictatorship', *The Listener*, (October 21, 1977); Lord Scarman, *English Law — The New Dimension*, (London 1975); Select Committee; *House of Lords Select Committee Reports* H. L. 176, 1978.
[6] This was best illustrated in the lawsuit over the publication of R. H. S. Crossman's diaries. See H. Young, *The Crossman Affair*, (London 1976).

and only 75% of votes. Ulster loyalists and Scottish Nationalists accounted for most of the growth in third party MPs, while English Liberals accounted for most of the growth in third party votes. It is the MPs who make the difference to the working of government, and the Ulster members had plainly come to stay as an independent force. Assuming even a modest Scottish and Welsh nationalist presence it seemed that in the future 25 minor party MPs would be the minimum likely complement in any parliament; and 25 would have been enough to hold the balance of power in five of the nine parliaments elected since 1950. With proportional representation a multi-party system would be almost inevitable, together with minority or coalition governments. In the event, from 1974 these 'unthinkables' were produced under the established first-past-the-post system. It was generally realised that single party government could no longer be taken for granted, any more than the other features of British government which hinged on it.

Because of this development, doubts arose about the first-past-the-post electoral system which used to be as totally accepted as the two-party system in parliament. The snags in the voting system (particularly its unfairness on the Liberals) were thought to be a small price to pay for the responsible one-party governments it produced. Under the winner-take-all system the major parties secured full power for some of the time and full powerlessness for some of the time, instead of suffering the compromises of coalition. Most MPs still supported the *status quo*, but the question ceased to be a closed one. Critics fastened on the power that could be wielded by a single party majority in the Commons. There was growing criticism of the adversary style of politics in which increasingly a party taking over government busied itself with reversing its predecessor's policies.[7] Some measures, if they are to be beneficial, have to be maintained beyond the lifetime of a single parliament.

The reversals are not an inevitable outcome of two-party competition. Many notable reversals occurred within the lifetime of a single parliament. However the search for continuity between governments, or at least a reduction in the abrupt

[7] For the full argument see the contributions to S. E. Finer, ed., *Adversary Politics and Electoral Reform*, (London, 1975).

reversal of policies, led reformers to look to the electoral system. Since 1970 parliament had imposed proportional representation in two elections in Northern Ireland and in 1977 the government recommended PR for the European Parliament and left the question of the method of election for the Scottish and Welsh Assemblies to a free vote. The same change was also actively considered for Westminster. Not only Liberals were shocked in 1974 when almost 20% of the vote gave them only 2% of the seats. The real driving force for change, however, came from those Conservatives who minded more about preventing Labour from getting full power (on perhaps 38% of the vote) than about attaining full power for themselves. Money was easily raised and an impressive list of supporters assembled for the National Campaign for Electoral Reform, launched in 1977. Liberals had some short-term success in their attempts to persuade companies to make their donations to the Conservative party conditional on support for proportional representation and in 1978 the CBI Conference endorsed PR. There was also widespread publicity for the report of the unofficial Hansard Society Committee under Lord Blake which recommended a German-style additional member system of proportional representation.[8]

Britain still has a very centralised system of government, unfettered by judicial review, a written constitution, a powerful second chamber or any regional authorities. But in the 1970s the complete dominance of London came under challenge. Federalism entered the political scene in two obvious ways — in the outward merger into the European community and in the inward complications of Scottish and Welsh devolution (and even some demands for English regionalsim). The centrifugal forces showed themselves to be strong and it seemed that the country would never again be so London-focussed as it once was.

Britain continued to have a unitary system of government. The confrontations between executive and legislature, and the judiciary's disallowance of the acts of one or other of them on the American model, were still absent. But, once again, Community membership and internal devolution began to change the British scene, opening up the possibility of formalised conflict between the separate institutions of government. More-

---

[8] *Report of the Hansard Society Commission on Electoral Reform*, (London 1976).

over, quite independently of such developments, the courts were becoming more active in political affairs. In the 1950s and 1960s the number of lawsuits which had a significant bearing on the political process were very few, but in the 1970s the High Court rebuffed the Education Secretary over the Tameside Council's comprehensive schools scheme, the Environment Secretary over cheap flights across the Atlantic, and the Attorney-General over the citizen's access to the law in an industrial dispute. The litigation over the Newham Labour party opened the possiblilty of a massive intrusion of the law into party affairs. Further loopholes in the law were likely to be found. Citizens, aggrieved by some action of an ever more complex state machine, of a trade union or a political party, would discover legal grounds to overrule the juggernauts and perhaps would be sustained by the judges. But it was not only through the judiciary that a separation of powers began to become more significant.

The fusion of legislature and executive (through a Cabinet answerable to, but in control of, the Commons) also came under challenge. The government lacked an assured majority and as it suffered defeats on key measures, parliament began to come into its own. The wheeling and dealing between government whips and the minor parties was probably not what the proponents of a more independent House of Commons had hoped for. But it was possible to sense in the tugs of war between Downing Street and the Palace of Westminster an echo, albeit a very faint one, of the continuous battle fought between the White House and Capitol Hill.

A few falling stones do not necessarily presage a landslide, and it would be wrong to suggest too dramatic a change in the rules of the game of British politics. Some of the consequences of the reforms might be unpredictable and not entirely to the liking of their advocates. Nonetheless the 'old' or normal model of British politics lost much of its validity, and reforms received a more attentive hearing. The later 1970s did place most of the established certainties of the British system of government in a far less positive light then they used to appear. Most threatened, perhaps, was the centralised, hierarchical style of government, so long aided and abetted by single-party government, a unitary state, and the sovereignty of Parliament. The impetus behind many of the proposed reforms — devolution, a bill of rights, proportional representation, a written constitution — was for more checks on the central government. This development was a major break with those qualities of flexibility that had long been admired by foreign observers of the British system as much as by the British themselves.[9]

Economic problems continued to plague the country. Indeed the underlying economic crisis fuelled the disappointment with the main parties and political institutions. A number of commentators in the 1970s saw Britain's economic decline as part of a more general social, political and cultural malaise.[10] In the 1960s, politicians had offered their diagnoses and prescriptions with some confidence. The theme then was of modernisation and getting Britain moving again. After 1974, however, politicians had been soured by their experiences of the previous decade and particularly by the events of 1974/1976 — the rise in oil prices, the miners' strike, 25% inflation and the collapse of the pound. They were increasingly aware of the intractable nature of the problems facing British governments. A new theme in the mid-1970s was national decline and what, if anything, could be done to reverse it.

The consequences of failing to arrest this country's economic decline are likely to become more pressing and more obvious as time goes on. Now condemned to very slow growth we might later even have to accept, if present trends continue, declines in real living standards.

This observation in the *Bank of England Quarterly Bulletin* in Spring 1979 had been foreshadowed by Peter Jenkins, in a series of articles in the *Guardian* in September 1978. Instead of growing more slowly than other countries, he argued, Britain could actually become poorer. This could come about through labour costs increasing while output remained low; British manufacturing, therefore, would become less competitive and export markets would be lost. Such a decline was already visible in such industries as shipbuilding, cars, steel and transport equipment, where Britain had lost markets and her share of

[9] See D. Kavanagh, 'New Bottles for New Wines: Changing Assumptions about British Politics', *Parliamentary Affairs*, (Winter 1978).
[10] For example see G. Allen, *The British Disease*, (London 1977).

world output. Economic difficulties had political repercussions because economic matters so dominated the political agenda in Britain.

Historically, Britain's post-war rate of economic growth compared favourably with that earlier in the twentieth century. What fuelled the sense of disappointment was partly the promises of politicans, partly the expectations of voters and partly the much better performance of other countries. The vast foreign investments and the imperial structure which had cushioned undulations earlier in the century were no longer there. It could always be said that GNP was not everything, but the fact remained that any indicators of the quality of life, such as education and health care, depended upon economic growth. The recession, following the five-fold increase in oil prices in 1973/4, heightened perceptions of Britain's economic weaknesses.[11] Whereas Britain's record on most economic indicators had been poor before the oil crisis, the uncomfortable fact remained that in the recession she continued to perform worse than other countries. Between 1973 and 1976, for example, output per head grew by only 1.2% compared with 9% in France and 10% in West Germany. The pound lost over one-third of its value against a basket of international currencies between 1972 and 1978. The inflation record was markedly worse than that in other leading Western countries, except Italy. The increase in real wages, averaging 1.5% in the years between 1963 and 1973, had been less than half that in the rest of the European Community. There was a fall of 1.5% in living standards between the middle of 1975 and the middle of 1977 (though this was followed by a 6% increase in the twelve months to October 1978).

The 1970s also saw a sharp challenge to the neo-Keynesian assumptions which had long prevailed among leading civil servants, front-bench spokesmen and most economists. That consensus assumed that policy-makers would and could keep the economy roughly in balance by increasing demand when economic activity and unemployment fell below the 'natural' levels, and restricting demand when inflationary tendencies appeared. Prices, interest rates, wages and unemployment were

[11] See R. Bacon and W. Eltis, *Britain's Economic Problem*, (London 1976).

thought to be related in a predictable manner. Inflation and unemployment had been seen as competing elements, with an increase in one being traded off against a decline in the other. In the 1970s, however, unemployment and inflation increased in tandem, and it was widely acknowledged that governments could not spend their way out of a recession without producing a further increase in inflation. By the first quarter of 1972 unemployment had reached 4%, or nearly 900,000, and the Heath government was panicked into reflation. Unemployment passed a million in the third quarter of 1975 and the powers that be came to accept the new high level as more or less inevitable.[12] Inflation, which had averaged a little over 3% annually between 1952 and 1957, averaged 20% for the first three years of the Labour government.

Economists fashioned new theories, and the politicians developed their own 'alternative' right- and left-wing strategies. A growing body of opinion, influenced by commentators such as Samuel Brittan, Peter Jay and Alan Walters, insisted on the importance of money supply in creating inflation. Before 1974 the money supply figures had not even been published. After 1975, Mr Healey's strict control of the money supply and the intellectual ascendancy among Conservatives of Sir Keith Joseph and Sir Geoffrey Howe created a new front bench consensus on the importance of money supply as an instrument for combating inflation.[13] It became even more important for the government when the incomes policy broke down in 1978. There was of course a big distinction between the pragmatism of monetarists like Mr Healey and the almost theological advocacy of free market economics by certain Conservatives who drew on Hayek and Friedman for inspiration. But strict Conservative monetarists such as Sir Keith Joseph, John Biffen and Nicholas Ridley could feel more sympathy with the economic management of Mr Callaghan and Mr Healy than with that of the Heath-Barber regime.

There was also a growing debate over the role of public expenditure. As in other countries public expenditure had

[12] See P. Jay, 'Ending the age of full employment', *The Times*, (April 10, 1975).
[13] See the essay by John Biffen, 'The Conservatism of Labour' in M. Cowling ed. *Conservative Essays*, (London, 1978). The money supply was increasing at 27% per annum in 1973 but only at 8% in 1977.

grown steadily as a proportion of GNP since 1945, with particularly steep surges in the first years of the Labour governments in 1964 and 1974. If transfer payments are included, public expenditure as a proportion of gross domestic product increased from 44% in 1965 to 60% in 1976 — a level that the Nobel-prize winner Milton Friedman and his disciples stigmatised as a threat to freedom. The contrast between Labour as a party of high public expenditure and commitment to the soeial services on the one hand, and the Conservatives as a party of restricted public expenditure and lower rates of income tax had been muted in the past. As a result of economic growth the Conservative governments after 1951 had maintained the Welfare State, and sustained a high level of public expenditure, while actually cutting direct taxation.

By 1975, however, Labour itself moved some way to checking public spending. In the spring of 1975 cuts were made and cash limits imposed on government departments; further cuts followed in July 1976 and, after the sterling collapse and the intervention of the IMF, still more cuts were made. The public sector deficit, though not appreciably out of line with that of other countries hit by the recession, required overseas loans for its funding, and its size was a target of criticism. Labour's left wing exaggerated these events, describing them as a betrayal of the Labour commitment to a high level of public expenditure. But the real take-home pay of the average worker was influenced by public policy, and levels of direct taxation were biting at a lower level. The inevitably escalating claims of the welfare state, combined with the workers' pressures to increase their take-home pay, were overloading the economy at a time when there was little or no growth in national wealth.

The book *Britain's Economic Problem*, first published in 1976 by Robert Bacon and Walter Eltis, was influential in focussing discussion on the economy and the role of public expenditure. The authors showed how the balance of the work-force was gradually moving from the production of market goods and services (largely in manufacturing) to the supply of non-market goods and services. Between 1961 and 1974 the number of local authority employees increased by 54% and those in central government increased by 9%. The decline in the numbers in the manufacturing sector was sharper than in most other industrial countries. Another way of expressing the

economic significance of the trend is to note that in 1966 there
were 4.79 workers in the market sector to support each worker
in the non-productive sector, while in 1975 the number had
fallen to 3.18. Consequently a larger total of public expenditure
had to be financed by a smaller private sector. At a time of slow
economic growth the public sector's expansion occurred at the
cost of take-home pay, profits, exports and investment in
industry.

Conservatives seized on these findings as their explanation of
de-industrialisation and inflationary pressures in the economy;
Bacon and Eltis seemed to confirm the wisdom of their policies
for holding back the public sector, reviving private enterprise,
and cutting direct taxation. The gradual change in direction of
the Labour government's economic policy also appeared to
heed this analysis. As the Public Expenditure White Paper of
1976 (Cmnd 6393) commented on the growing public sector
borrowing requirement:

> In the last three years public expenditure has grown by
> nearly 20 percent in volume while output has risen by less
> than 2 percent. The ratio of public expenditure to gross
> domestic product has risen from 50 percent to 60 percent . . .
> As recovery proceeds we must progressively reduce the
> deficit . . . more resources . . . will be needed for exports and
> investment.

A more general shortcoming was what some analysts termed
'residual efficiency' — those cultural, social and political factors
of long standing which affected the level of skills, managerial
initiative and workers' effort. The government's 1975 White
Paper on *An Approach to Industrial Strategy* (Cmnd 6315) had
this in mind when it mourned the 'generalised inefficiency' of
British industry.

This book focuses on the 1979 general election in its immediate
context. But the events of 1979 must be seen in a wider frame
of reference. Popular judgments were conditioned by longer
term factors. The pessimism that prevailed was not just a reaction to immediate circumstances: what had happened in the
1970s had, to a growing extent, forced the nation to recognise
a situation that had long been developing. Our story is largely

the story of how politicians, parties and communicators responded, or failed to respond, to a change in mood.

Nonetheless social conditions and even national moods alter
slowly. Continuities are more important than changes. Despite
hyperinflation and all the economic malaise of the 1970s, life
went on much as before. The international league table might
be depressing and the pound might be worth only two thirds of
its 1972 value in the markets of the world, but the average
Briton still had slightly more disposable real income in 1979
than 1974. The essential props of civilised life, in economic
underpinnings and social values, might be slowly eroding but
most of the voters in 1979 were, most of the time, enjoying
their customary way of life. The electoral pressures of 1979
were much the same as a decade earlier. So were the politicians,
even if the challenges they faced were more stark.

2 The Course of Government 1974-8

The October 1974 election, unlike its predecessor, produced a clear result — though not a very decisive one. The Labour government secured a majority but only just. Against all expectation, the Conservatives held on in many marginal constituencies and Mr Wilson came back to Westminster with only 319 seats, three more than all other parties combined. Only once before, in 1922, had a party won a clear majority with under 40% of the votes cast.[1]

Few people would have expected a government with so small a majority to last into the fifth year of the parliament. In 1951 a majority of six had led Mr Attlee to dissolve after nineteen months, and in 1966 Mr Wilson decided that seventeen months was long enough with a majority down to three. But in 1974 the situation was different. The government's majority might slip away through defections and by-elections, but the balance of power rested not with a single handful of Liberals, as in 1950 and 1964, but with a miscellaneous group of some 40 MPs from five distinct camps: the Conservative opposition would find it difficult to shepherd them together into the lobbies on a vote that would bring down the government. Individual measures or clauses might be lost, either by direct votes or for want of a guillotine majority, but the moment never seemed to come when it was simultaneously in the interest of all the non-Labour parties to combine on an issue of confidence.

The Labour government was not prevented by its limited majority from implementing most of its fairly radical programme, foreshadowed in White Papers during the short parliament of 1974. The nationalisation plans, the changes in labour law, and the devolution proposals were substantially carried through

---

[1] And in 1922, if the Conservatives had fought every seat (as in 1974) instead of only 483, they would certainly have got a good deal more than 40% of the total vote.

Chronology of Events, 1974–9

1974

Oct 10	General Election (Lab. 319, Con. 277, Lib. 13, Others 26)
Nov 29	Prevention of Terrorism Act passed following Birmingham pub bombing
Nov 21	J. Stonehouse MP disappears (found in Australia on December 24 and resigned seat Aug 27, 1976)
Dec 2	Manifesto Group established

1975

Feb 11	Margaret Thatcher elected Con. Leader
Feb 18	Industry Bill gets second reading.
Mar 10–11	Dublin Summit clears way for EEC referendum
Apr 26	Special Lab. Conference advocates 'No' vote in referendum
May 8	Ulster Assembly elections (Assembly dissolved without results May 1976)
Jun 5	EEC referendum (67.2% 'Yes' vote)
Jun 10	Reshuffle switches A. Benn from Industry to Energy
Jun 26	Lab. lose Woolwich West by-election
Jul 3	British Leyland Act passed
Jul 7	Lab. party delegates take up seats at European Parliament
Jul 11	Pay policy Phase I announced
Jul 14	Unemployment passes 1 million
Sep 20	Formation of Tory Reform Group
Sep 30	D. Healey voted off Lab. NEC
Dec. 16	Chrysler rescue announced

1976

Jan 18	Formation of Scottish Labour party announced (with 2 Labour MPs)
Mar 5	£ falls below $2
Mar 11	Ending of direct grant schooling announced
Mar 16	H. Wilson announces resignation
Apr 5	J. Callaghan becomes Prime Minister; A. Crosland moves to Foreign Office
May 10	J. Thorpe resigns as Lib. Leader
May 26	Wilson's Resignation Honours List
July 7	D. Steel elected Lib. Leader
Sept 9	Unemployment reaches 1,588,000
Sept 10	Cabinet Reshuffle; M. Rees succeeds R. Jenkins at Home Office
Sept 28	Callaghan speech demanding financial prudence
Sept 29	Healey cancels trip to Hong Kong and calls on last $3.9 billion of current IMF credit to save £
Oct 3	Cons. publish *The Right Approach*
Oct 21	M. Foot elected Deputy Leader of Lab. Party
Oct 27	£ reaches its lowest level ($1.56)
Nov 4	Lab. lose Workington and Walsall North by-elections
Dec 15	D. Healey announces letter of intent for IMF loan and drastic cuts
Dec 21	R. Prentice resigns from Cabinet (takes Con. whip in Oct. 1977)

1977

Jan 3	R. Jenkins resigns as MP to preside over European Commission
Jan 26	Bullock Report on industrial democracy published (Cmnd. 6706)
Feb 19	Campaign for Lab. Victory announces its formation

Feb 19   A. Crosland dies. D. Owen becomes Foreign Secretary (Feb. 21)
Feb 22   Government defeated on devolution guillotine
Mar 17   Aircraft and Shipbuilding Act finally passed
Mar 23   Lib—Lab pact saves Government in confidence vote
Mar 31   Lab. lose Stechford by-election
Apr 28   Lab. lose Ashfield by-election but hold Grimsby
May 2   Abortive 11-day loyalist strike begins in Ulster
May 5   Lab. lose Greater London Council and other local election contests
May 11   P. Jay appointed Ambassador to USA
Jun 9   Silver Jubilee of Elizabeth II
Jul 15   D. Healey outlines Phase III of incomes policy
Jul 27   *The Next Three Years* and *Into the Eighties* published by Government
            and TUC
Aug 13   National Front march provokes clash at Lewisham
Aug   Unemployment peaks at 1,636,000
Sep 14   Mrs Thatcher suggests referendums could be used in industrial con-
            frontations
Dec 13   Proportional Representation for European elections rejected by Com-
            mons

1978
Jan 4   £ touches $2
Jan 12   Firemen's strike ends
Jan 21   Special Lib. Assembly conditionally endorses pact
Jan 23   Government defeat on Green Pound devaluation
Jan 30   Mrs Thatcher speaks of 'swamping' by immigrants
Mar 2   Lab. lose Ilford N. by-election
Apr 3   Regular broadcasting of parliament begins
May 5   European Elections Act receives Royal Assent
May 25   Announcement of forthcoming termination of Lib—Lab Pact
May 31   Lab. holds off S.N.P. challenge in Hamilton by-election
Jul 31   Royal Assent to Scotland Act and to Wales Act
Aug 4   J. Thorpe accused of conspiracy to murder
Aug 10   Peugeot buy Chrysler
Sept 7   Prime Minister announces 'No election'
Sept 19   Bingham report on Rhodesian sanctions-busting published
Sept 21   Ford strike against 5% offer begins
Oct 2   Lab. Conference rejects 5% wage limit
Oct 9   Con. Conference sees Thatcher-Heath rift on pay policy
Oct 26   Swing to Lab. in Berwick and East Lothian by-election
Dec 5   Britain opts out of European Monetary System at Brussels Summit
Dec 13   Commons votes 285—283 against government sanctions on employers
            breaking 5% pay policy

1979
Jan 3   Lorry drivers' strike begins (made official Jan 11)
Jan 10   Callaghan returns from Guadeloupe Summit
Jan 22   Public employees' 'day of action', followed by widespread strikes for
            next six weeks
Feb 14   Concordat announced between government and TUC
Mar 1   Devolution referendums in Scotland and Wales
Mar 28   Government loses confidence vote 311—310
Mar 29   Election announced for May 3

even after April 1976, when by-elections and defections had deprived the government of its majority.

By the end of the parliament the only major measures promised in the 1974 manifesto but not completed were devolution for Scotland and Wales, a wealth tax, reforms of the laws on nationality and citizenship, the replacement of the Official Secrets Act with new rules for open government, and the withdrawal of tax relief and charitable status from public schools.

It is hard to select from the many political events of the period those which shaped the attitudes that politicians and voters brought to the 1979 election. In the history of the 1974—9 parliament six distinct but overlapping phases can perhaps be distinguished: the referendum; the realisation of an incomes policy; the acceptance of monetarism, public expenditure cuts and the IMF conditions; the preparation and passage of devolution legislation; the Lib—Lab Pact; and the final manoeuvring over pay and industrial confrontation. A simpler division might be between the Wilson phase (triumph and decline) and the Callaghan phase (decline and triumph — and, in the last lap, decline again). As usual, the government's morale and election prospects fluctuated according to the state of the economy.

There was, however, a quite separate curtain raiser. The Labour Manifesto of October 1974 had promised that the issue of Britain's membership of the Common Market would be decided within twelve months by the British people. The 'renegotiations' over Britain's entry were completed at the Dublin summit conference in March 1975. Although many observers saw them only as a charade, obtaining no substantial gains for Britain, the Cabinet recommended continued adherence to the Market on the new terms. On June 5, 1975, in its first national referendum, the country voted two to one in favour of Community membership. Probably the vote was in some measure an expression of preference between the leading figures on the pro- and anti- side, between 'moderates' and 'extremists'; but it principally reflected a feeling that in a hostile economic climate it would be even colder out of the Market than inside it.

The campaign had a remarkable feature. The government agreed to differ; 16 cabinet ministers argued for membership and seven against. Under the pro-Market umbrella there devel-

oped close co-operation betwen Mr Jenkins, Mr Whitelaw and
Mr Steel, and other leading front benchers (although Mr Wilson,
Mr Callaghan and Mrs Thatcher kept clear of the formal 'Britain
in Europe' campaign). Some saw in this a rehearsal for a government of national unity to overcome the national crisis. The
Labour party was deeply split. A special conference in London
on April 26 voted by two to one to support a 'no' vote. But in
practice the party organisation lay low. The battle, perhaps
because its outcome was so decisive, left remarkably few scars.
One anti-Market minister could describe it as 'an election that
the Labour party lost but the Labour government won'. Yet a
few months later both sides seemed to want to forget it: neither
in styles of campaigning nor in new alliances had it left a mark
on British politics.[2] Its most obvious consequence was to
establish the idea of referendums as a constitutional possibility.
Within three years the government was to accept referendums as
part of the devolution proposals and the Conservatives were to
advocate them as a regular constitutional device.

But there were those who believed that the referendum cost
the government dearly in a critical period by diverting ministers
from the underlying economic problems. The industrial strategy
—the establishment of a National Enterprise Board and of a
system of planning agreements between government and large
companies — had been launched by the Industry Secretary, Mr
Benn, in a strident way that frightened the business community,
but Mr Wilson felt unable to move him away from his sensitive
post until the referendum was over.[3] Negotiations with the
largely anti-Market trade union leaders over a wage policy were
also held back until the referendum had taken place.

On June 10 Mr Wilson switched Mr Benn and Mr Varley
between the Departments of Industry and Energy. In Energy,
Mr Benn had some scope, as North Sea oil flowed in, but a less
central influnce on business confidence. The quieter Mr Varley
implemented the government's industrial policy less abrasively.

The government's strategy in the 1975 Industry Act and in
the 1975 White Paper (Cmnd 6315) was elaborated at a meeting

---

[2] For a full discussion see D. Butler and U. Kitzinger, *The 1975 Referendum*, (London,
1976), and A. King, *Britain Says Yes*, (Washington, 1977).
[3] For a fuller discussion of this see Michael Hatfield , *The House the Left Built*,
(London, 1978).

of the National Economic Development Council (NEDC) at Chequers on November 5, 1975. The government explicitly recognised that growth and investment must take precedence over individual consumption and over 'social objectives', and it set out stern criteria for allocating assistance to individual companies. The compulsory planning agreements envisaged by the Industry Act 1975 were allowed to drop and no further workers' co-operative ventures of the sort which Mr Benn had sponsored were pursued. But vigorous intervention in industry continued, largely through the new National Enterprise Board under Lord Ryder. The motor industry produced the greatest problems as the imported share of the market rose from 30% in 1973 to 48% in 1978.

In the autumn of 1975 the American-owned Chrysler factories were threatened with closure unless a massive government subsidy was forthcoming. Mr Varley resisted the demands but, in a much publicised Cabinet struggle, his colleagues overruled him and guaranteed up to £162 million to underwrite the firm. The fear of lost jobs prevailed then — as it did three years later, when Chrysler sold off its British interests to the French Peugeot-Citroen firm. British Leyland, with its 200,000 employees, provided even more problems. In March 1975 the Ryder Report recommended the nationalisation of the country's only large home-owned car-producer, and by July the British Leyland Act had been passed. But strikes and falling production kept British Leyland at the forefront of politics throughout the parliament, as it drew on new tranches of government loans and shed its senior executives. Michael Edwardes, who took over the chairmanship in November 1977, gave stark warnings about the company's future.

The problem of how far to go in propping up ailing industries troubled the opposition as well as the government. Some Conservatives, as well as all Labour MPs, enjoyed the spectacle of Sir Keith Joseph, the advocate of free enterprise, endorsing the government guarantee of funds for British Leyland; too many Conservative MPs and candidates from marginal seats in the Midlands had an interest in continuing to appear as the friend of British Leyland. Financially, British Leyland's performance was not as disastrous as that of another nationalised industry British Steel. Under the impact of a world slump in demand, the corporation was by 1978 losing £500m. a year and was only

Table 1. *Economic and Political Indicators, 1974—9*

		1 Real personal disposable income	2 Index of weekly earnings 1970 = 100	3 General index of retail prices 1970 = 100	4 % of Labour force unemployed	5 Working days lost in stoppages (000's)	6 Gross domesti product at facto cost at 1970 = 100
1974	I	117	148	139	2.5	6,494	106
	II	116	159	147	2.5	2,361	110
	III	120	174	151	2.6	2,018	112
	IV	123	188	158	2.8	3,876	110
1975	I	123	196	167	3.1	1,438	109
	II	119	204	183	3.6	2,467	108
	III	119	220	191	4.2	1,400	107
	IV	118	229	197	4.8	707	107
1976	I	120	235	205	5.1	876	110
	II	118	242	212	5.3	722	110
	III	121	250	217	5.4	940	110
	IV	118	256	227	5.5	769	111
1977	I	118	263	238	5.5	2,257	109
	II	115	267	249	5.6	1,811	110
	III	115	270	253	5.8	2,444	112
	IV	120	281	255	5.9	3,630	114
1978	I	119	288	261	5.9	1,810	113
	II	124	305	268	5.7	1,540	114
	III	126	312	272	5.7	1,737	117
	IV	128	319	278	5.5	4,196	116
1979	I	128	344	286	5.6	5,442	113
% change 74/I—79/I		+9%	+132%	+105%	+124%	—	+7%

Sources: *Economic Trends* for Columns 1, 2, 3, 4, 6, 8, 11; *Financial Statistics* for colum

belatedly closing down its obsolete plants and tackling its problems of overmanning.

In July 1975 Mr Wilson announced Phase I of his pay policy. The unions had shared in the general dismay as the year-on-year inflation rate rose from 8% in October 1974 to 26% the following July. The TUC instructions to members to restrict their wage demands to the level needed to protect living standards

7 Money Supply (MS) £ bn.	8 Balance of payments on current account £m	9 FT ordinary industrial share index April 1962 = 100	10 Exchange rate US S	11 World commodity prices 1968—70 = 100	12 Gallup Poll Con % Lead	13 Gallup Poll Lib %
32.2	−927	313	2.28	298	−2	14
327	−932	275	2.40	287	−11	14
33.3	−784	227	2.35	292	−3	16
35.3	−922	180	2.33	303	−10.5	13
34.9	−565	246	2.39	287	−3	9
35.8	−333	326	2.32	284	2	9
36.8	−620	310	2.13	306	0	12
37.6	−153	359	2.04	324	0	10
37.3	−90	402	1.81	338	2	9
38.7	−390	397	1.81	381	0	8
40.2	−511	365	1.77	395	1	8.5
41.2	−413	308	1.65	423	20	9
40.2	−505	397	1.71	440	13	10
41.8	−364	441	1.72	450	13	7.5
42.9	+522	481	1.73	432	10	7
45.3	+501	491	1.81	413	2	7
45.4	−341	465	1.92	393	5	7
48.1	+146	468	1.83	414	1	6
49.4	+51	499	1.93	401	3	5
52.1	+398	486	1.98	403	−2	5
51.7	−787	482	2.01	419	13	6
+61%	−	+54%	−12%	+41%	−	−

7, 9 and 10; *Monthly Digest* for column 5; and Gallup Poll for columns 12 and 13.

were themselves inflationary; there was no possibility of absorbing the jump in world oil and commodity prices without a decline in living standards. But even those instructions were ignored and the union leaders publicly acknowledged that wage increases were contributing to inflation. Inflation left its mark. Between February 1974 and the end of 1978 prices rose by over 100%, a record markedly worse than other Common

Market countries and other industrial competitors. The value of large wage increases was wiped out by equally large price increases. In July 1975 worried union leaders accepted the need for a wages policy, albeit a voluntary one. They agreed to a £6 limit on all pay increases over the next year, coupled with further measures to keep down prices and limit dividends. Jack Jones of the Transport and General Workers was a particular sponsor of this measure which inevitably helped his own lower paid workers most, although, by reducting differentials, it sowed the seeds of later troubles.

In July 1976 Phase II was agreed with the TUC and CBI — a 5% limit on pay increases up to a maximum of £4. But the anti-inflation strategy was undermined by the collapse of sterling in 1976 and by a renewed rise in prices. There was a steady decline in living standards during 1976 and 1977, as the rise in prices outpaced the increase in wages (See p. 24). By December 1977 the take-home pay (gross earnings less income tax and national insurance deductions) of a family on average earnings with two children under 11 was worth £4.30 less in real terms than it had been four years earlier (*Hansard*, March 3, 1978, Col. 429)

In 1977 it became obvious that there could be no formal agreement on Phase III of Incomes Policy — yet in July the government set a target of 10% for wage increases, and largely imposed it throughout the public sector. In the private sector sanctions were imposed on firms which exceeded the guide line — government contracts and government assistance were withheld. Although earnings rose by 14% over the year, the policy worked far better than many expected.

Under the 'Social Contract' with the Labour Government, the unions secured much more than the repeal of the hated Conservative Industrial Relations Act. The Trades Union and Labour Relations Acts of 1974 and 1976, and the Employment Protection Act of 1975, considerably extended job security and redundancy rights, though not without controversy. The Closed Shop provisions of the new legislation in relation to journalism and its implications for freedom of the press provoked a running dispute that lasted throughout the Parliament. A Dock Work Regulation Bill produced one of the government's most spectacular setbacks in November 1976, when the well-advertised abstention of Brian Walden and John Mackintosh led to the loss of a clause that would have given dockers a monopoly of cargo-handling for five miles inland.

Few would question that Labour's greatest asset at this period was seen as its ability to work with the unions. But doubts persisted about the price to be paid for this co-operation, and the unions remained unpopular with the public. Hugh Scanlon and Jack Jones – 'the terrible twins' who had helped to frustrate Labour's proposed union reforms in 1969 – now proved strong defenders of the government and of the pay policy which they saw as essential to its survival. The TUC did protest about the unacceptable levels of unemployment[4] but calls for import controls, reflation and the restoration of public expenditure cuts went unheeded. Regular informal contacts with ministers and formal consultations in the NEDC and the TUC–Labour Party Liaison Committee gave the union leaders the appearance of a Praetorian guard, defending ministers against the criticism of the NEC. In 1978 Mr Jones and Mr Scanlon retired, to be replaced by Moss Evans at the TGWU, and the 'right-wing' Terry Duffy at the AUEW.

The period was presented in the press as one of growing industrial trouble, although, particularly during Phase II of the pay policy in 1976–7, days lost through stoppages were at the lowest level for ten years. The strike that drew most attention was at Grunwick, a North London film processing plant, where some workers, mostly Asians, were dismissed over the issue of union recognition: the trade union movement as a whole took up the strikers' cause, and later there were ugly scenes around the factory gates as massed pickets tried to stop workers and supplies from entering. George Ward, the head of the factory, with support from the National Association for Freedom, fought a determined campaign and ultimately triumphed. The TUC drew back from supporting the secondary boycotts – of electricity, water and posts – which alone could have ensured victory. The violence on the picket lines, vividly recorded in the television news, excited distaste for the militants drawn to the struggle from far and near. The strike provided the Conservatives with a dilemma over how far to go in support of what seemed like an intransigently anti-union management. The

---

[4] Unemployment in the 1950s ranged between 210,000 and 620,000. In 1975–9 it ranged between 1,220,000 and 1,635,000.

problem was seen in a different light by Mr Prior, trying to build a bridge to the unions, and by Sir Keith Joseph, defending free enterprise against union power. It was also seen in a different light by Mr Rees, the Home Secretary charged with maintaining law and order, and by most of the more left-wing MPs, suspicious about police impartiality.

Another type of strike that caused increasing anxiety was in the public services. In March 1975 the government called in troops to deal with the health hazards of a prolonged dustmen's strike in Glasgow, and in 1977—8 troops were again called in to provide emergency cover during a nation-wide strike of firemen. In hospitals a number of disputes over the ideological issue of pay-beds within the National Health Service, as well as over more mundane issues of pay and grading, led to much disquiet as patients were turned away and lives perhaps put at risk by this spread of militancy to new areas.

On the industrial front the continued troubles in Fleet Street and throughout the motor industry provided staple material for headlines. In 1977 much of British Leyland was shut down for several weeks by a strike of toolmakers, worried at the way that incomes policy had eroded their differentials and at the failure of the Amalgamated Engineering Union to take up their case.

Immigration and race continued to prove contentious, even though the numbers entering the country had declined to less than 20,000 a year. In January 1978 Mrs Thatcher revived controversy with her statement on television that 'people can feel rather swamped' by immigration; but her subsequent remarks and the official Conservative policy, while calling for stricter controls, contained reassurances to immigrants already settled in Britain. In April 1978 an all-party Parliamentary Select Committee called for stricter controls on entry, as well as internal controls, and a quota for the Indian subcontinent; but this was disowned by the Home Secretary. The polls suggested that immigration was far less salient for voters than the traditional bread-and-butter issues. The National Front, apart from beating the Liberals into fourth place in the Stechford by-election, attracted slight support at local and by-elections.[5] Its marches and meetings were often attended by

[5] See M. Steed, 'The National Front Vote', *Parliamentary Affairs*, (Summer 1978).

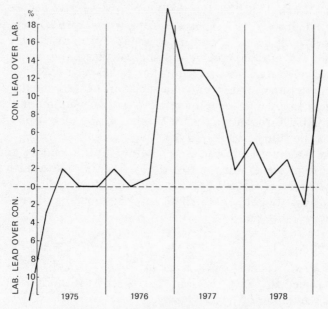

Diagram 1. Party Support 1974–9

ugly violence. The Anti-Nazi League, formed in December 1977 to combat racialism, met with some success as an umbrella for anti-Front groups, though some suggested that it was under control of the far left, and others that its activities were counter-productive.

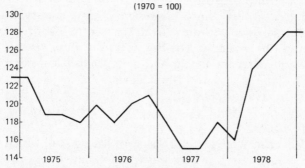

Diagram 2. Real Personal Disposable Income

On March 16 1976 Harold Wilson announced his intention to resign from office. It was a complete surprise, even to his Cabinet colleagues. Speculation about his motives was widespread, but nothing emerged to suggest that it was other than a long-planned decision to retire when he reached sixty. Nonetheless his reputation fell under a cloud in his retirement, partly through the names recommended in his resignation honours list and partly through successive revelations or allegations about his premiership of 1964–70.

The Labour party had never before had to choose a leader while in office. It was the first time a British Prime Minister had been directly elected by his parliamentary colleagues. The battle was fought out in three successive ballots of the Parliamentary Labour party.

22 March		29 March		5 April	
M. Foot	90	J. Callaghan	141	J. Callaghan	176
J. Callaghan	84	M. Foot	133	M. Foot	137
R. Jenkins	56	D. Healey	38		
A. Benn	37				
D. Healey	30				
A. Crosland	17				

The affair was conducted without rancour. Although Mr Benn issued a manifesto identifying himself as the left-wing candidate, most of the votes of the left went to Michael Foot, whose new moderation and loyalty in the Cabinet won him a broad base of support. Mr Healey was criticised for forcing a third ballot instead of withdrawing gracefully like Mr Jenkins and Mr Benn. There was some surprise at the poor showing of Roy Jenkins. He had lost ground since his resignation as deputy leader in 1972, and he soon withdrew from the centre of British politics to take up the presidency of the European Commission. In the new Cabinet Barbara Castle and Bob Mellish lost their posts, Tony Crosland succeeded Jim Callaghan at the Foreign Office for a brief 10 months, and Shirley Williams moved to Education. In March 1977 David Owen followed Tony Crosland at the Foreign Office.

Mr Callaghan won partly because of his age, 64, which meant that he would not too long block the channels of promotion, but mainly because his style and affability made him the most acceptable, middle-of-the-road candidate. He was the first non-Oxbridge Prime Minister since Churchill – or on the Labour side, since MacDonald. In public he was firm but avuncular, free from the 'too clever by half' image of his predecessor and clear in his intention to be more than a caretaker. In private, he was a tough but fair chairman of Cabinet. He let discussion range freely but he made his own position clear and, when a decision was reached, he would not let the matter be reopened. He never fostered a kitchen cabinet and, though he relied a lot on Michael Foot and Denis Healey, he seems to have had no inner circle of ministers. He was more involved in the party, but less in governmental detail, than Harold Wilson. He made an immense impact on his colleagues and on the country; by the end of 1978 most members of the Cabinet were ready to say that no one else, and certainly not Harold Wilson, could have got them through the hazards of the period without disaster.

Mr Callaghan faced an extraordinarily tough first twelve months. Unemployment rose from 1,200,000 to 1,500,000. The pound, which was worth $1.93 when Mr Wilson resigned, dropped to $1.56 by September. Cuts in public spending were found to be necessary even before the IMF crisis, the first turning point in the government's fortunes. With the British government as well as the British currency at stake, the Americans were concerned for Western stability. The collapse of sterling brought to a head several fears about the management of the British economy. Financial opinion at home and abroad expressed alarm at the growth of public expenditure (up from 51% of GNP in 1973 to 59% in 1975) and the mounting public sector deficit. In 1975 Mr Healey had already made substantial reductions and imposed cash limits in the public sector. Pressure in the Treasury for more deflation and for expenditure cuts to reassure financial opinion was always baulked by fears of the reaction from Labour back benchers and the trade unions. But on June 22 there were further cuts of £1 billion in spending plans and a 2% increase in the employers' national insurance contributions.

What had begun as a Treasury-managed devaluation in the summer quickly got out of hand. On June 7, with the pound at $1.71, the government was forced to arrange a standby loan of $5.3 billion from American and West European central banks. To the dismay of most ministers, however, the loan was to last for only six months; further appeals for help would have to be addressed to the IMF which would impose strict conditions.

When Mr Callaghan faced his first Labour Party Conference at Blackpool in September, Mr Healey was already in urgent negotiation for a new IMF loan; the amount of $3.9 billion was the largest loan it had ever been asked for. He was forced at the last moment to turn back from his flight to the Fund's conference in Manila in order to devise measures to check the continued plunge of sterling. Mr Callaghan's speech, widely thought to bear the imprint of his economist son-in-law Peter Jay,[6] was a very firm exposition of the need to stop living on borrowed money and to face up to whatever cuts might be needed. In fact the speech was drafted by his staff, though Mr Jay suggested one widely quoted passage: 'Quite unequivocally, [unemployment] is caused by paying ourselves more than the value of what we produce . . . The option [of spending yourself out of a recession] no longer exists . . . We must get back to fundamentals.' He went on to preach the need for profits, for investment, and to restrain the rise of public expenditure and the printing of money. His speech was heard for the most part in sullen silence. The Conference proceeded to pass resolutions calling for massive increases in public expenditure, showing just how far apart were ministers and delegates.

Over the next months the Cabinet discussed at length the measures required to meet the IMF's conditions for a new loan, in particular the need for a reduction in the public sector borrowing requirement of £1.5 billion to restore international confidence. Tony Benn and Peter Shore had the chance to expound different versions of the 'alternative strategy' which the left and some Cambridge economists had been advocating, a 'Fortress Britain' policy of import controls. But such a strategy flew in the face of EEC commitments as well as of the received wisdom of Whitehall and the City, and had no hope of being accepted by the Cabinet.[7]

The Social Democrats were divided: some, such as Tony Crosland, Roy Hattersley, and Shirley Williams, agreed with the left in resisting public expenditure cuts, and were prepared to

---

[6] Later in May 1977 Mr Callaghan drew much criticism for accepting Dr Owen's nomination of Peter Jay as Ambassador to the United States.
[7] S. Fay and H. Young, *The Day the Pound Nearly Died*, (London, 1978).

accept a scheme of import deposits or even import controls. They were opposed to further deflation at a time when unemployment was already high. There was, therefore, a potential Cabinet majority in favour of some protectionism and resistance to IMF demands. In the end Mr Callaghan, who had been scrupulously neutral throughout the discussions, decided to back the discomfited Chancellor. Both the Americans and West Germans had made clear their unwillingness to support the loan application without the cuts. Mr Crosland and his allies then withdrew their opposition. Mr Crosland's view of the package was, 'It's nonsense but we must support it', (because of fears for the currency if the Prime Minister and the Chancellor were repudiated). But one left-wing colleague termed the abandonment of public spending policies 'the death of Croslandism'. On December 15 Mr Healey announced in the House of Commons that the public sector borrowing requirement would be reduced by £1.4 billion in 1977–78. This would be achieved by cuts in planned public spending, the sale of shares in British Petroleum, and increases in the excise tax.

Mr Callaghan seems to have felt the need for a tighter grip on public expenditure even before the IMF intervened. The episode reminded ministers, in spite of the success on the pay front, that the economy was still in a fragile state and that the British government was dependent on outside forces. The episode also set the scene for the main planks of subsequent economic policy — strict control of money supply, pay policy and tax cuts. Of longer term importance was the achievement of Mr Callaghan, no doubt reminded of his harrowing experiences as Chancellor between 1964 and 1967, in securing American and West German support for funding the sterling balances. His own reputation was greatly enhanced among ministers; 'He dissipates the air of conspiracy,' said one. The government had also stolen some of the Opposition's clothes. Conservative spokesmen welcomed the package but, naturally, gave the credit for it to the IMF.

In 1977 the tide turned. The IMF loan was never fully drawn upon. As North Sea oil flowed in with the prospect of self-sufficiency by 1980, the economic indicators changed. The balance of payments moved from a deficit of £511m. in the third quarter of 1976 to a surplus of £483m. a year later. The pound rose from $1.56 to $1.86 between October 1976 and October 1977, and a year later stood at $2.01. The gold and dollar reserves jumped from £2.4 billion in December 1976 to £10.9 billion in March 1978. The sense that the country had touched bottom and was climbing up grew as the year advanced.

But it is no wonder that the government did not want to face the electorate in early 1977. The economy was in poor shape and legislation for devolution and for direct elections to the European assembly had bogged down and was causing division in the Labour party. When Mrs Thatcher suddenly tabled a motion of no confidence in March, after the government had dodged a vote on its public expenditure plans, there was a danger that for the first time since 1924 such a vote might succeed.

Labour had only 310 members in a House of 635. As Diagram 1 shows, Labour's standing with the electorate was low. It could not survive except by courtesy of the Liberals, the Scots Nationalists or the Ulstermen. The SNP were too angry at the failure to get a guillotine on the devolution bill to be willing to vote for the government, and the price for support from the Ulster Unionists was almost bound to be too high. But the Liberals did not want an election or a Thatcher government. They had fared disastrously in by-elections, and their support in the opinion polls was heavily down. During 1976 press head-lines about Jeremy Thorpe's involvement with the male model Norman Scott had further damaged the party. Mr Thorpe's resignation and the election of David Steel as Liberal leader had failed to restore the party fortunes.[8] Two days of knife-edge negotiations between Mr Callaghan and Mr Steel finally produced 'the Pact', a public agreement on the terms on which the Liberals would guarantee to back the government on any con-fidence issue up to the end of the summer. The Liberals were to be consulted in advance on all major policy initiatives; and legis-lation for European elections and devolution was to go ahead with free votes on proportional representation.[9] For the first time since 1931, Britain had a government explicitly dependent on an understanding with a party not in government.

Mr. Callaghan and his colleagues were not really paying any price for Liberal support; they were not giving up any policy

---

[8] David Steel's succession meant that between February 1975 and June 1976 each of the three main parties had chosen a new leader.

[9] For a full account of the negotiations see Simon Hoggart and Alistair Michie *The Pact*, (London, 1978) and David Steel's own account *A House Divided*, (London, 1979).

that they had any chance of implementing in the present parliament. The only really contentious issue for Labour was proportional representation for European elections, which was opposed in Cabinet and in the House by Mr Benn, Mr Booth, Mr Orme, Mr Shore and Mr Millan. Most ministers realised that, in exchange for the mere promise of consultation, they were being given a guarantee of survival. It was a guarantee of survival for the Liberal MPs too; and they were being given a chance of national prominence, a sniff of power, a potential veto on government action. They did actually block an increase in petrol duty, change the arrangements for the Post Office Board, and secure some small advances towards industrial co-partnership. Liberal links with ministers were varied in closeness and importance. David Steel got on excellently with the Prime Minister, but John Pardoe was usually at odds with the Chancellor. The party in the country was suspicious of its MPs being too involved with Downing Street and, with some encouragement from three MPs, Cyril Smith, Jo Grimond and David Penhaligon, moves were made against the pact, especially after it was renewed for a further year in July. At the Liberal Assembly in September 1977, and at a Special Assembly in Blackpool in January 1978, motions repudiating the pact were defeated by a 3 to 1 margin. Finally in May 1978 David Steel announced that in no circumstances would the pact be renewed after the end of the session. It had served its purpose of enabling the country's economic recovery, and the time had come for a new parliament.

The pact does not seem to have cost the Liberals many activists, but the Conservatives reported that many 1974 Liberal voters had turned to them in disgust at the Liberals actually keeping in power a discredited Labour government. In fact, Liberal support in the opinion polls had already drifted down from the 19% of 1974 to 10% at the time the pact was made, and it fell only slightly in the ensuing 15 months. But deposits were lost in all but one of the by-elections of the period and, inevitably, Liberal morale was depressed.

The issue of devolution for Scotland and Wales permeated the Parliament. (The Scottish dimension is elaborated in Chapter 6 by William Miller.) The SNP's achievement in getting 30% of the Scottish vote and 11 seats in the October 1974 election convinced the government, with 41 of its 319 seats coming from Scotland, that something must be done to meet the Scottish urge for self-government. There was no enthusiasm among English MPs or in the Cabinet. But Edward Short struggled to produce a White Paper (Cmnd 6348), and then a Bill, to set up Scottish and Welsh Assemblies. The first Bill ran into increasing trouble. The Conservatives drew back from their Heath-inspired commitment to devolution (losing their Shadow Secretary for Scotland, Alick Buchanan-Smith, in the process) and many Labour MPs made their unhappiness manifest. Tam Dalyell, the Labour MP for West Lothian, was particularly determined in his efforts to point out the inconsistencies in a measure that, by transferring responsibilities to an Edinburgh Assembly, would leave Scottish MPs at Westminster voting on English but not on Scottish measures. In the 1976—7 session the Bill failed because on February 22 the government was defeated by 312 to 283 when it sought a guillotine (22 Labour MPs voted against and 25 abstained). However in 1977—8 separate measures for Scotland and Wales were introduced, with conciliatory modifications including referendums before they took effect. These, together with the Lib-Lab pact and the efforts of the whips, secured a guillotine by 313 to 287 on the Bills on November 16, 1977, with only 9 Labour MPs opposing. Ministers frankly acknowledged an unintended by-product of the devolution legislation; it cemented the Lib-Lab pact and kept MPs busy in the 1977—8 session, allowing time for consciousness of the economic recovery to seep through to the public. Labour, which was 15% behind in the polls in March 1977, was on equal terms with the Conservatives by July 1978.

The 1975 referendum and its decisive result was seen by most people as closing the European issue. But the pinpricks of Brussels bureaucratic decisions, and in particular of the successive crises over the Common Agricultural Policy, together with the general sluggishness of the British economy, led to a resurgence of anti-Market feeling. The Gallup poll, which in May 1975 had shown a 26% majority for the proposition that British market membership was a good rather than a bad thing, revealed a 9% majority in the opposite direction by May 1978. Within the Labour party, the anti-Market forces became more vocal, and the 1977 Conference passed overwhelmingly a motion condemning the Common Agricultural Policy. Mr Benn at Energy and, even more, Mr Silkin at Agriculture and Fisheries proved doughty spokesmen for national views, and irritated their European ministerial counterparts. As the issue of direct elections to the European Parliament loomed up in 1976 the NEC, together with many MPs and some ministers, expressed their hostility to the idea. The Labour Conference at Blackpool in September voted 2 to 1 against it. The government moved slowly and secured the agreement of the European Council of Ministers to the postponement of the elections from 1978 to 1979. The European Elections Bill, with its provision for a regional list system of PR, was an essential point in the Lib-Lab pact, but when it came to the crunch in Novermber 1977 Mr Callaghan could not get more that 147 out of 308 Labour MPs to cast a vote for the system. Indeed he could only handle the whole issue of direct elections by resurrecting the agreement to differ employed in the referendum. Collective responsibility was suspended: 6 Cabinet Ministers were among the 126 Labour MPs who voted against direct elections on July 7, 1977 (128 voted in favour). The NEC stalled till September 1978 before it endorsed Labour participation in the elections.

In November and December 1978 Mr Callaghan's main concern was how to react to the European Monetary System which Chancellor Schmidt and President Giscard were promoting. The large body of anti-EEC Labour opinion was activated by the possibility of what was seen as a further move towards integration. Mr Callaghan found little enthusiasm in the party, and indeed, on this issue, Whitehall itself was divided. Although he was concerned that Britain's generally negative attitude to EEC initiatives was taxing the patience of other Prime Ministers, in the end he had to tell the December summit of European Heads of Government that Britain must stay out. He argued that until the richer countries were prepared to take measures which produced an economic convergence and a transfer of resources, then EMS would be self-defeating.

During the 1974 to 1979 parliament, public opinion on issues was more stable than on voting intention. As usual issues affecting the economy and strikes concerned most voters. Prices declined in salience as the rate of inflation was lowered. But law and order was seen by many voters as a growing problem. The Gallup poll found that the proportion mentioning it as a failure of government doubled between 1975 and 1978 and by 1978 it was ranked fourth. Conservatives tried to brand the

*Table 2.   Government failures as seen by the electorate
              1975—78*

Which of three or four of these items are the biggest failures of the present
government?

	Sep. 1975	Sep. 1976	Sep. 1977	Sep. 1978
Prevent the rise in unemployment	56	63	59	50
Stop strikes	54	39	53	48
Keep down prices	60	60	64	43
Maintain law and order	18	24	27	36
Make British industry efficient	40	38	31	30
Provide an efficiently working health service	14	20	24	29
Develop our education system properly	12	23	28	28
Maintain Britain's military and naval power	9	13	15	21
Stop wages rising too fast	43	23	18	15
Build enough houses	15	14	14	11
Make money easily available to buy one's own house	11	11	9	9
None of these	5	3	3	4

government as 'soft' on crime (*Table 2*). In two free votes in
December 1974 and 1975 the House of Commons handsomely
rejected the restoration of the death penalty for terrorist
crimes, although many more Conservatives voted in favour than
did Labour MPs. The police attracted sympathetic headlines,
as they coped with the Grunwick situation and the National
Front troubles. Police unrest over pay and threats of a strike
late in 1977 were averted by the reference to a Committee
under Lord Edmund-Davies which recommended increases of
29%—45%.

The three successive Education Secretaries found their service
under a cloud. Public expenditure cuts, falling school rolls,
heavy teacher unemployment and mounting concern over
educational standards made for difficulties. A long-running
enquiry at the William Tyndale school in London brought to a
head worries over teaching standards. Mr Callaghan launched a
euphemistically titled Great Debate and encouraged moves to a
common-core curriculum. The efforts of Mr Mulley, Education
Secretary in 1975, to compel the Tameside authority to introduce comprehensive secondary education were rebuffed when

the Law Lords upheld the authority's appeal that the Minister was exceeding his powers.

The memories of 1974 hung heavy over the parliament. The changes in the Conservative leadership in February 1975 did not eradicate the confrontationist image which had been pinned on Mr Heath's government in the winter of 1973. Mrs Thatcher, having gained the title 'the Iron Maiden' for her blunt speeches about the Soviet threat, also acquired (rightly or wrongly) a general reputation for intransigence. Indeed by the end of the parliament, her ungracious rival, Mr Heath, came to be seen, even more than the union-sympathising Mr Prior, as the apostle of moderation. By 1978 polls were suggesting that more people would vote Conservative if he were again the leader; perhaps he was now regarded as a figure above party politics.

Three major reports from Committees set up by the Labour government conspicuously failed to lead to action during the parliament. In August 1976 Lord Houghton's Committee on Finance for Political Parties (Cmnd 6601) recommended by a majority a system of state subsidies for routine activities and for election costs. The public reaction was not favourable and the hostility of the Conservative party and of a few Labour MPs prevented action. In January 1977 Lord Bullock's Committee on Industrial Democracy (Cmnd 6706) recommended by a majority that workers in plants with over 2,000 employees should appoint a number of trade union directors equal to the shareholder directors. In March 1977 Lord Annan's Committee on Broadcasting (Cmnd 6753) recommended new bodies to run the fourth television channel and to manage local radio. In each of these three cases divisions within the Labour party (and sometimes between departments) as much as the lack of a parliamentary majority inhibited the government from following up its own initiatives.

In June 1975 there had been a brief experiment in broadcasting the proceedings of parliament and, after unexpected delays, a permanent system was introduced in April 1978. The barbaric noises accompanying question time excited much adverse comment but the broadcasts were thought on balance to favour the government, always having a well-briefed last word, against an opposition that necessarily appeared captious. They also favoured Mr Callaghan, relaxed and avuncular, as against Mrs

Thatcher, who could not help sounding shrill as she raised her voice to be heard above the din.

The problems of Northern Ireland continued to provide a focus for debate. Direct rule of the province from Westminster was suspended on January 1, 1974 but it was restored after the strike of May 1974 had brought the experiment with power sharing to an end. Once the Constituent Assembly elected in May 1975 had reached its inevitable failure to agree, the British government found no alternative solution and continued with direct rule. Violence declined slowly. The death toll, which had reached 468 in 1972, averaged only about 200 per year in 1975–8. The Ulster Unionist members demanded stronger policy and army measures and at times it seemed that the hard-line attitude of Airey Neave, the Conservative spokeman, might break the broad bipartisanship of the Westminster approach. But Roy Mason, the Northern Ireland Secretary from 1976 onwards, though he produced no new political initiatives, was firm enough to mute serious criticism. Mr Powell remained a formidable obstacle to a rapprochment between Unionists and Conservatives, and Mr van Straubenzee's speech in September 1978 firmly ruled out the restoration of a Protestant-dominated Stormont Parliament.

The nearest that Northern Ireland came to affecting British politics was just after the October 1974 election when an IRA bomb outrage in a Birmingham pub led to the hasty passage of the Prevention of Terrorism Act with its minor but unwelcome breaches of traditional civil liberties. A number of small bombs went off in London and the public, especially around Westminster, had at times to put up with security restrictions and even body-searches of a sort long familiar in Belfast. The IRA violence in Britain died away (until a slight resurgence at the end of 1978) but occasional atrocities, mainly among visitors from the Middle East, kept alive the notion of political violence, to add to the normal and growing worries about law and order.

The world setting for the Wilson and Callaghan administration was one of economic depression and of political moderation. President Carter, who took office in 1977, failed to do much to speed American recovery. Chancellor Schmidt and President Giscard continued to dominate the West European scene and their governments each won re-election on centrist policies. The candidates for EEC membership, Greece, Spain and Portugal, which had shrugged off dictatorships in 1974–5, managed to stay on their democratic course. But Britain in its post-imperial phase was very introverted. The troubles in the Middle East were no longer her problems any more than those in Indo-China. Only the intrusive demands of European involvement and of the interminable Rhodesian tragedy made major claims for attention.

Mr Callaghan and Mr Healey were much involved in EEC and OECD summit politics. Their attempts to encourate reflation by the stronger European economies made little progress. The Prime Minister clearly enjoyed his own camaraderie with the major Western leaders. The fact that Helmut Schmidt and Giscard d'Estaing provided strong national leadership while heading coalitions was not lost on him.

In Rhodesia settlement attempt followed settlement attempt and, with atrocities on both sides, the situation deteriorated. But, although Ivor Richard's 1976 pilgrimage in search of a solution, and David Owen's more extended efforts in 1977–8 excited critical Conservative comment, Rhodesia never became a dominant issue in British politics. The Conservative leadership refused to follow the eager backbenchers who wanted a unilateral endorsement of Ian Smith's attempt at an internal settlement. 116 of the Conservative backbenchers defied the leadership and voted for an end to sanctions against Rhodesia on November 10, 1978. A fortnight later there was general support for Mr Callaghan's move in sending Cledwyn Hughes, the Chairman of the Parliamentary Labour Party, on a mission to Southern Africa to get everyone involved to the conference table, but the move achieved little.

It was not a period in which new personalities apart from Mrs Thatcher made much of a mark on politics. Michael Foot was transformed from a stormy petrel into the key man of the government. Reg Prentice and George Brown were notable defectors from the Labour party. Reginald Maudling failed to make an impact and was sacked from the front bench in 1976, slightly marked by the Poulson scandal that drove one Conservative backbencher, John Cordle, from the House of Commons.

From the nature of their jobs some Cabinet ministers made news: Roy Jenkins (until his departure in 1976), Tony Crosland (until his death in 1977), Merlyn Rees, Roy Mason, Shirley Williams, Eric Varley, David Ennals, John Silkin and

Peter Shore. But Denis Healey and Tony Benn alone were continually in the headlines, until in 1977 the photogenic David Owen leapt into globetrotting prominence. Mr Healey followed his extended stint at Defence in 1964—70 by becoming the longest serving Chancellor of the Exchequer since Neville Chamberlain in the 1930s.

The Liberals got a fair share of personal publicity, with Jeremy Thorpe and David Steel deploying their media-drawing talents, and with Cyril Smith and John Pardoe commenting quotably on the party's leadership troubles in May 1976; but as events drew towards the indictment of Mr Thorpe for conspiracy to murder, the publicity was not all of a sort they would have wished.

The government suffered a loss of support in mid-Parliament which matched that of 1967—8. Up to 1978, it lost only six seats in by-elections, but the defeats in Workington and Walsall in November 1976, and in Stechford and Ashfield in April 1977, were in seats that had been held by Labour since the war and which were regarded as utterly safe. The Gallup poll showed Labour 10% behind throughout this period and in local elections Labour lost control of the great majority of the cities it had governed in 1974. However, at the end of 1977 the party's fortunes improved. The Conservative lead fell to single figures and disappeared altogether in the latter half of 1978. The swing in by-elections was much reduced and to Labour's surprise they were able to hold off the Scottish Nationalists first in Garscadden in April 1978 and then in Hamilton in May (Hamilton had seen the first SNP breakthrough in a 1967 by-election, and the redoubtable Margo Macdonald was the SNP candidate). Labour also held Berwick and East Lothian in November with a progovernment swing (the first since January 1966).

Shortly after the 1977 party conference the Prime Minister told Tom McNally, his political secretary, to make arrangements for an election which might come at any time from spring 1978. He did not think it was possible or desirable to continue the Lib-Lab pact to the end of the parliament. He asked Mr McNally to establish an informal group of advisers for him and to liaise with the party's General Secretary, Ron Hayward, so that Transport House would be aware of his plans. In the early months of 1978 a group of media advisers (see p. 132), political

journalists and a campaign team for Mr Callaghan were established. In March 1978 Mr Callaghan told his staff that he had
a date in mind for the General Election and that, while he
would not reveal it to anyone, he would listen to advice. He also
asked for a 'calendar' of autumn Thursdays, noting the problems
that any of them would pose for an election. One aide had the
impression that Mr Callaghan's mind was moving to October 12
as the likely election date. At the same time, however, Mr
Callaghan asked aides to think about possible items for the
1978/79 Queen's Speech and to write to Joan Lestor, voicing his
disapproval of the 'farewell' party she had arranged for retiring
MPs. 'Tell her this parliament still has over a year to run', he
said. His staff and colleagues acted on these instructions 'without
believing a word of it!'

During the summer it was generally assumed that there would
be an autumn election. Indeed some Conservatives thought he
would dissolve in June. The termination of the parliamentary
pact with the Liberals in the summer made the government's
position in parliament even more parlous and it was expected
that the economy would worsen at the turn of the year.

But by October the figures showed an annual advance of 6%
in living standards, the largest single increase for 20 years. As Lord
Kaldor advised 'It is a peak. Maybe a submerged peak, but a peak
nevertheless.' Other countries expected a slowdown in growth
and there was another troublesome wage round ahead. The
1979 calendar was already congested with local elections,
devolution referendums and assembly elections, and the direct
elections for the European parliament. Arrangements in all major
parties proceeded on the assumption of a late September or
early October poll. The Conservative and Liberal parties added
the finishing touches to their manifestos. Mr Callaghan's coy
remarks to the TUC Conference at Brighton and his promise of
a statement to the nation on September 7 all seemed to set the
scene for the announcement of a dissolution. In the event the
Prime Minister informed his Cabinet colleagues at their first
meeting since the recess that he had already told the Queen of
his intention to carry on, and that therefore there was nothing
much to discuss. In his broadcast later that day Mr Callaghan
expressed the view that an election at this time was not in the
national interest. The decision surprised most Cabinet ministers,

amazed Transport House officials, and gained him a scathing press from journalists and editors who felt he had made fools of them.

In retrospect the Prime Minister's decision was understandable. The probability of parliamentary defeat was less than popularly supposed — the Nationalist parties wanted devolution on the statute book and neither they, nor the Liberals, could go to the country in a confident mood; the economic prospects, at least for the first half of 1979, were better than generally supposed, and this was confirmed by the economic indicators in subsequent months; the electoral prospects for Labour in early October were worse than generally supposed, and this was confirmed both in the private polls and public polls taken at the time he was making up his mind. Mr Callaghan assured those close to him that delay was in the national interest; he calculated that the unions would be anxious not to damage Labour's election prospects and would be moderate in their wage demands.

Mr Callaghan apparently arrived at his decision in August. He had long been saying that he wished to stay in office until 1979 if he could. During the June and July meetings of the Campaign Committee in Transport House, he had gone out of his way to correct officials who had spoken of an autumn election. There is no evidence that he had ever decided in favour of an autumn election, 'but he jolly nearly had' commented one aide. He had not sought advice at all widely in the party. His TUC speech of September 5, 1978, with its music-hall allusion to leaving the bride waiting at the church, was ambiguous, but he certainly succeeded in leaving Transport House officials, most Cabinet colleagues and his immediate staff guessing about his intentions. Some union leaders felt they had been belittled. On the day of the speech Mr Basnett had briefed industrial reporters about plans for union assistance in the imminent campaign. Mr Callaghan informed Mr Foot and Mr Healey of the way his mind was moving on August 17. Mr Foot was optimistic about the parliamentary situation and Mr Healey asked for time to think over the decision for delay. It is difficult to identify an influential lobby on the inside that argued for October. Mr Rees, Mr Foot and Dr Owen all seemed to have communicated their pro-1979 views. Mr Healey was a late convert on the ground that it was not worth having an election that would result in a hung parliament. The pro-Octobrists — Bill

Rodgers, Roy Hattersley and Shirley Williams — were less weighty, and few seem to have expressed their views to the Prime Minister, most of them assuming that an autumn election was inevitable.

The summer had not brought the swing-back in support to the government that had been manifest in 12 of the last 18 years. In early September all the polls showed Conservative leads of between 2% and 7%. The government's failure to advance was attributed in part to the skill of the large-scale Conservative advertising campaign, 'Labour isn't working', in August mounted by their new advertising agents Saatchi & Saatchi (see p. 139).

Some commentators quickly, but probably erroneously, identified Robert Worcester, the Labour party's private pollster, as the key influence. His public MORI poll in the *Daily Express* on September 4 was carried only two days before Mr Callaghan's announcement and showed a Conservative lead of 2 points. But a more important factor was Mr Worcester's private poll of the 70 marginal seats in England. He presented this in July and Mr Callaghan considered it over the summer. The results were profoundly depressing for Labour. As he compared the findings with the *Times Guide to the House of Commons,* Mr Callaghan was unable to see where the necessary Labour gains would come from and was aware that the Liberal collapse increased the likelihood of Conservative gains. The danger from his point of view was that the most probable result would be indeterminate. If Mrs Thatcher won by a narrow majority then she could dissolve again at a time of her own choosing. But a confirmation of the *status quo* would worsen his position. As he commented to a colleague, 'I can only ask for a mandate once.'

In the end, however, Mr Callaghan decided on delay because his assessment was that he would not win a clear victory in October and that he stood a better chance in 1979.[16] Regional organisers presented gloomy reports from the grass roots, confirmed by Merlyn Rees who had toured the country in August. Another factor making for delay was the belief that the new register coming into effect on February 16 would be worth an extra six or more seats to Labour. Mr Callaghan was also attrac-

[16] Two polls published after Mr Callaghan's announcement, but based on interviews before it, showed Conservative leads, MORI by 6% and Gallup by 7%.

ted by the notion of 'allowing the money to jingle in the voters' pockets' as the lower tax rates and higher child benefits came into effect in November. There was also the attraction of delivering devolution to the Scots before an election and waiting for the economic recovery to be more fully appreciated by voters.

What was never persuasively explained, however, was why the electoral prospects for Labour would actually improve in 1979, and why the unions would go along with the government's target of 5% wage settlements: there seems to have been a delusion that fear of a Thatcher government would induce them to cooperate through the winter. Whatever Mr Callaghan's logic, however, there was satisfaction in Conservative Central Office at the postponement of the election.

3 Labour in Office

All parties behave differently in government and opposition. The balance of power in the party is transformed as the leader becomes prime minister and as his front bench colleagues acquire ministerial position and become obsessed with decision-making and day-to-day business. The contrast between opposition and government has always been most marked in the case of the Labour party. The role of the National Executive and the Annual Conference in the formation of party policy provides constant opportunities for the activist to press for bolder socialist measures. But Labour ministers after 1974 were increasingly aware of the limitations of the real world. In this case they had to live with a narrow and then a non-existent parliamentary majority and under severe economic constraints. The Labour government in 1974–9 was far more obviously at odds with the party machine than it had been in 1964–70. It was as if there were two Labour parties, one with the voice of the NEC and Conference and the other with that of the parliamentary leadership.[1]

The origins of this tension could be traced back to 1970. While the Heath government was in power the Labour movement shifted to the Left, and the National Executive of the party fell into the hands of the left wing. There were two activist Chairmen, Ian Mikardo and Tony Benn, in the years 1971–3. The party moved to a position demanding far greater state intervention in industry and more public expenditure. In the 1974 elections the party offered its most left-wing programme since 1945. At the same time the party's right or social democratic wing was much weaker. Disappointment at the record of the Wilson Cabinet was visited on the right wing; that government's version of planning had failed to promote more economic growth or more social justice. An additional factor which undermined resistance to the left was the split in the party over

[1] See L. Minkin, *The Labour Party Conference*, (London, 1978).

membership of the EEC. The resignation of Roy Jenkins from the deputy leadership in 1972 signalled the disenchantment of the more intellectual moderates with the direction the party was taking and also their weakness. By supporting the Conservatives' terms for membership of the EEC, a large section of the right aligned itself against the sentiment of the Labour movement and was forced onto the defensive on many other issues as well. The Labour party has always been less embarrassed by its quarrels than the Conservatives. Nontheless the disunity expressed within the Labour movement over one major issue after another during the Wilson and Callaghan administrations of the 1970s was spectacular.

There was a great difference in the style of party management displayed by Harold Wilson and by James Callaghan. In some measure it was the difference between the fox and the hedgehog, the man who knows a lot of little truths as against the man who knows just one big truth. Harold Wilson showed all his skills of political timing and management in 1974 in parleying the party from a minority position to the victory of October 1974. He showed it still more in leading the country up to the European referendum and forcing on a reluctant party an overwhelming popular verdict which flew in the face of so much that it had said over the previous three years.

Then, as the social contract was shown to be the flimsiest of shields against inflation (and indeed was used as a pretext for massive wage claims), the party was persuaded to accept an incomes policy. Defenders of Mr Wilson would point to the skill in his timing of these issues and to his success in preserving party unity. Yet Mr Wilson's style produced increasing criticism and seemed somewhat tarnished, even before he left office and had to face up to the revelations of the Crossman Diaries and the memoirs of friends and enemies alike. Jim Callaghan, who took over from him so unexpectedly at the age of 64, assumed the leadership of a Britain suffering from hyperinflation and a collapsing pound. Mr Callaghan made plain that, as so often with a new leader, he was determined to differentiate himself from his predecessor. He had, of course, publicly disagreed with Mr Wilson over *In Place of Strife* in 1969; and in 1972 he was prepared to abandon politics for the World Bank. Jim Callaghan, a cautious and conservative man, was totally of the Labour movement; he was a former trade union official and a dedicated constituency MP; he had always worked within the party. Once a naval petty officer, he had a patriarchal image of himself as a Moses leading Britain to a promised land. He was prepared to be quite firm in expressing disagreements with the Labour party, but he was never going to part company with it.

An intuitive politician, Mr Callaghan had until October 1978 demonstrated a sure touch for what the Labour party would stand. His main interest was on the big issues, foreign affairs and detente (colleagues noticed how proud he was of his reference group of Jimmy Carter, Helmut Schmidt and Giscard d'Estaing). His conservatism was shown in his initiation of the education debate and his frequent references to the importance of law and order. But his most cherished goal was to keep inflation well down into single figures. It was widely understood that he was simply not prepared to continue as Prime Minister while inflation raged out of control. People believed he would be quite happy to retire to his farm. As Prime Minister he appeared more at ease with himself because he had long since abandoned hope of achieving the job.

In Cabinet Mr Callaghan had a happier time than Mr Wilson. On the one side Roy Jenkins, and on the other Barbara Castle, were missing and Cabinet discussions were far less polarised than before. Mr Callaghan, unlike Mr Wilson, did not try to fix things in advance. He allowed an open discussion and on issues such as Chrysler, public expenditure cuts and the IMF negotiations, he usually gave a clear lead. But when a decision had been reached it was final. Cabinet disagreement continued, of course. It had been brought into the open in an unprecedented way during the referendum when the agreement to differ publicly had shown sixteen pro- and seven anti-Europeans. The anti-Europeans continued to be recognisable but, except on Europe, they did not act as a group and their most vehement spokesman, Tony Benn, was in many ways isolated and even counter-productive to the causes he espoused.[2] The absence of a really vocal pro-European made Cabinet management much easier for Mr Callaghan. In any case his force of personality and his close alliance with that loyal ex-member of the left, Michael Foot,

---

[2] Mr Benn stretched the concept of Cabinet responsibility to the limit in abstaining from supporting government policy in NEC votes and in encouraging NEC initiatives and policy papers which were plainly at variance with government policy.

and with the formidable Denis Healey, made him very much master of the situation.

However, neither Mr Wilson nor Mr Callaghan could control the National Executive Committee or, indeed, the Conference. In the period from 1974 all but one of the seven constituency members of the NEC were patently representatives of the left; in 1976 Mr Healey was voted off it and in 1977 and 1978 over 80% of the votes cast by the constituency parties went to left-wing candidates. Four out of the five of the women's section of the NEC were also from the left. The twelve-member trade union section was more evenly divided and hard to classify, but it certainly could not counterbalance the others. Basically, the government had reliable support from little more than 10 of the 29 members of the National Executive. The referendum exposed the conflict. The NEC by 18 votes to 11 recommended that the Labour party Special Conference in April 1975 advocate a 'No' vote and the Conference by 3,724,000 to 1,986,000 endorsed the NEC view. A motion by Ian Mikardo to campaign against the EEC and the Cabinet majority attracted 18 NEC signatures. But, after a bold statement by the General Secretary that Transport House would remain neutral during the referendum, the motion was not put.

The NEC also opposed the government's decision to support direct elections to the European parliament and vehemently opposed any scheme for linking European currencies. Some compromise between the two wings was reached in Mr Callaghan's long open letter to Mr Hayward of September 30, 1977 which, while pointing out the disastrous consequences of withdrawal from the EEC, accepted the need for its reform. He stressed in particular the urgency of changing the Common Agricultural Policy and of maintaining the authority of national governments and parliaments. The NEC also opposed the government's expenditure cuts and the later stages of incomes policy. It merely 'noted' the Lib/Lab pact, treating it as a matter for MPs. This phlegmatic attitude contrasted with the agonising at the Liberal Party Conference.

At the same time the NEC resisted investigations of alleged left-wing infiltration of the party. It decided not to publish a report on Trotskyist entryism which had been prepared by the national agent, Reg Underhill, and by Ron Hayward, the general secretary of the party. The NEC also endorsed the choice of a declared Trotskyist, Andy Bevan, as youth officer for the party. This was passed by 15 votes to 12 in spite of a personal appeal by Mr Callaghan and vigorous opposition from the National Union of Labour Organisers. In re-selection contests in Newham North East,[3] Hammersmith North and elsewhere, the NEC was thought to be taking sides against the right wing. The organisation sub-committee also upheld the selection of Jimmy Reid, who had stood as a Communist in 1974, as prospective candidate for Dundee, even though he had been a member of the Labour party for only eight months. Traditionally the NEC had acted as a support for MPs who faced trouble with their constituents. In the 1970s they became more concerned to see whether the technical rules had been observed. (See p. 280ff).

The party's left wing was rebuffed in two areas, however. The Campaign for Labour Democracy worked to make MPs and the leadership more accountable to the membership. A working party was set up in the wake of the 1976 Labour Conference to define the office of the Labour leader and also 'consider appropriate means of widening the electorate involved in the choice of the leader'. In the event the 1978 Conference left the choice with the MPs. Pressure for mandatory reselection of MPs was also rebuffed. MPs, not only on the right, feared the greater insecurity and the potential witch-hunts which might follow such a move. Trade unions also feared for the prospects of their sponsored members. The 1978 Conference, thanks to a disputed AUEW vote cast by Hugh Scanlon, left constituency parties free to decide mid-way through each parliament whether or not they wished to consider changing their MP.[4]

Relations between the NEC and the government became very strained and Mr Callaghan accepted a suggestion put forward in a February 1977 policy paper of Geoff Bish, the Research Secretary of the party, for regular meetings between members of the NEC and the Cabinet. These meetings were only a partial

[3] The Newham dispute led to repeated court actions in the climax of which the constituency moderates sought a High Court order nullifying actions of the NEC. Lord Denning and the Court of Appeal rejected this, which could have set a precedent for almost unlimited litigation in party disputes. But the action did bring out grave defects in party rules and led to frantic activity in the National Agents' department. See Lord Denning's judgement, *The Times*, February 8, 1978. See also P. McCormick, *Enemies of Democracy*, (London, 1979).
[4] At the October 1979 Conference memories of this vote contributed to the question being reopened and to a system of compulsory reselection being approved.

success; attendance was poor and members could not commit either side, but the informal contacts did something to smooth relations at a difficult time. Mr Callaghan withheld approval from establishing an economic strategy committee until the summer of 1978 and even then the group contained no Treasury minister. Geoff Bish's initiative had been taken with a view to preparing the way for a manifesto. But Mr Callaghan was determined to keep this firmly in his own hands. Mr Benn and Transport House, on the other hand, looked back to the policy exercise following 1970. The February 1974 manifesto bore the heavy imprint of the work of those years. Transport House continued to act as 'a ginger group for socialism' and the flow of policy proposals continued. Indeed, tensions between the government and the NEC stemmed largely from the behaviour of Mr Benn and his Home Policy Committee. The contents of the NEC's *Labour's Programme 1976*, with its proposals for the nationalisation of banks and insurance companies, compulsory planning agreements and a wide range of welfare benefits, was clearly anathema to most of the Cabinet. Although the document was overwhelmingly endorsed by the 1976 Conference, the ill-tempered and left-wing tone of that gathering provoked a hostile reaction within the party and still more outside it. It was difficult to achieve cooperation between the government and the NEC when the latter body pushed policies that were so contrary to the central thrust of ministers' economic strategy.

Partly because of the changes in government policy at the time of the IMF loan in December 1976, and partly because of conciliatory and educative measures by Jim Callaghan and his colleagues, the Labour party drew back a bit. However, ministers continued to be embarrassed by the pressure for more reflation, higher levels of public expenditure, demands for more state control, all at a time when the government was adhering to the IMF guidelines and trying to restore the confidence of industry. Mr Callaghan took the NEC more seriously than his predecessor. Mr Wilson had become so disenchanted with the NEC that, over the year preceding his retirement, he rarely attended. But Mr Callaghan had encouraged ministers not to neglect NEC meetings and also to consult with the policy groups. At the same time he vigorously warned the NEC against policies that he did not like. This did not prevent the NEC assuming to itself full authority for the preparation of a manifesto for the Euro-elections, or from adopting, in January 1979, a document that departed from government policy in its criticism of the Community and its threat to withdraw if certain, politically impossible, demands were not met.

The government's relations with the Parliamentary Labour party were much easier than with the NEC. In 1974 the PLP had moved somewhat to the left; the *Tribune* group had increased from 47 to about 80 members between 1973 and 1975, but in the process it had been somewhat diluted.[5] Some MPs joined the *Tribune* group as a sort of insurance policy against the left-wingers in their constituency parties. In 1976, a rival Manifesto group of right-wing MPs was set up and some 80 MPs joined it. The Executive of the PLP was consistently drawn from the right and centre of the party and Cledwyn Hughes, as a sympathetic pro-government chairman, was able to avoid significantly adverse votes at PLP meetings.

In 1977 members of the Manifesto group together with survivors from the old Gaitskellite Campaign for Democratic Socialism formed the Campaign for a Labour Victory but, except perhaps in Scotland, it had limited impact. A Social Democratic Alliance was formed and supported the embattled Mr Prentice in Newham, but it overreached itself and became discredited within the party even before the desertion of Mr Prentice.

The moderate stance of the PLP leaders did not save the government from trouble with the parliamentary party. The Whips were by no means always able to marshal their full strength in the division lobbies, and there were some notable defeats, particularly on devolution. There were also embarrassing revolts on defence and on the civil list increase of funds for the Royal Family. On July 22, 1975, 37 Labour MPs voted against a motion approving the White Paper *The Attack on Inflation* (Cmnd. 6151). There were also damaging abstentions over public expenditure cuts.

But it is important to stress that in general the government could rely on the support of the bulk of the PLP. Most notably, when the pact with the Liberals was negotiated, it was meekly accepted by MPs who, unwilling to face an early election, seemed to feel that parliamentary tactics were best left to Jim

[5] See C. Hitchens, 'The Tribune Group goes missing', *New Statesman* (July 21, 1978).

Callaghan and his parliamentary manager, Michael Foot, whose past left-wing credentials were impeccable. Only in connection with a few limited measures such as parts of the Dock Work Regulation Bill and, more seriously, in connection with devolution was the Labour government's programme frustrated by its own backbenchers.

The key relationship for the government was with the unions. Mr Wilson was determined to avoid a repetition of the rift over *In Place of Strife*. He wanted to maintain a firm alliance with the unions and Mr Callaghan, who had stood by the unions in 1969 against Mr Wilson, persisted in this policy. The great triumph of the Labour government was to get *de facto* union co-operation in an incomes policy over the years from 1975 to 1978. The disagreement with the majority of the unions over the EEC referendum was not too serious since several influential unions were on the government's side and there was a general determination not to let this extraneous business interfere with good relations.

Labour's ability to get the consent of organised labour was, until the final winter, its strong card against the Conservative party. It was also useful in showing opinion leaders at home and abroad that Britain was still governable. The key figure was Jack Jones, the prime author of the 'social contract'. Mr Jones and his colleagues on the TUC General Council wanted some major legislation from the government. It was not only the repeal of the hated Industrial Relations Act, which was carried out speedily in the 1974 parliament, but further amendments to union law in the Trade Union and Labour Relations Act (1976) and the Employment Protection Act as well as in the Dock Work Regulation Act. The unions did not get quite all they wanted. There were troubles over proposals for the closed shop in journalism, and the reservation of jobs near the docks to dockers was defeated in the House. Nonetheless, as they co-operated with the government in 1975 and 1976, the unions could see themselves gaining some long-term advantages. They were, moreover, not disinclined to help with an incomes policy because they, like everyone else, had been frightened by the wild inflation of 1975 and the consequent escalation of unemployment. The unions' influence in the Labour party was also increased by the party's even more complete dependence upon them financially. As individual membership went down and costs went up, the party had repeatedly to turn to the unions for financial support which was given in a relatively ungrudging way.

The dominant figures in this period were Jack Jones of the Transport and General Workers and Hugh Scanlon of the Engineers, together with David Basnett of the General and Municipal Workers. In 1977, however, the first two approached retirement. The election of their successors and their subsequent behaviour placed a question mark over the whole future management of the party. The T & GWU and the AUEW between them deployed almost 30% of the vote at Conference and they were in a position to determine the composition of the National Executive and the outcome of almost any controversial issue. Hugh Scanlon, who had moved from the left to a more moderate position, was replaced by Terry Duffy, a little-known figure who was explicitly the candidate of the right wing; Jack Jones was replaced by Moss Evans, who continued to be an unknown political quantity, and was in no position to exercise the strong leadership traditional in the T & GWU since the days of Ernie Bevin. Neither of the new men made much of an impact. Certainly at the 1978 Conference their unions cast their votes no differently in the NEC elections. In the subsequent disputes at Fords and in the transport industry, Moss Evans was considered by ministers to be 'most unhelpful to the cause' and even 'pathetic'. During the winter he did not use his weight in the TUC General Council to moderate the damage to Labour's prospects inflicted by the public sector employees in NUPE and COHSE even more than in his own union.

Liaison between the leading members of the TUC and the government was maintained in various ways. They encountered each other at the monthly meetings of Neddy; they also had regular private dinners at 10 Downing Street. In addition there was the TUC/Labour Party Liaison Commitee which met several times a year to discuss current issues. This was an important body which consisted of six Cabinet Ministers, nine members of the NEC and six representatives of the TUC. The Social Contract which was drawn up each year covered a wide range of government policies. As long as the TUC accepted incomes policy and also acquiesced in public expenditure cuts, then the left-dominated NEC was outflanked. On a number of occasions, NEC members protested at being presented with a *fait accompli* and TUC leaders, in turn, resented the sniping from NEC critics. The alliance between the left of the NEC and the big trade union leaders which dated back to 1968 gradually broke down. Trade union leaders resumed their traditional role as defenders of the parliamentary leadership. The tensions came to a head at the Blackpool Party Conference in 1976. At the *Tribune* rally Mr Mikardo returned to the theme, claiming that the unions had given way too easily to the government: an incensed Jack Jones charged to the microph'one accusing Mr Mikardo of behaving like a Tory in his attack on the unions. In November 1976 the NEC supported a parliamentary lobby against the government's economic policy, organised by the left-wing trade unions, but ignored by the TUC. On a number of occasions the Liaison Committee proved more effective than the NEC in advancing the NEC's own policies. For example, in 1976 Jack Jones revived interest in the wealth tax, and the Liaison Committee worked out a compromise over child benefits.

Mr Wilson and, even more, Mr Callaghan, took considerable trouble to inform themselves of the views of Len Murray and his senior colleagues, and a large number of potentially fraught issues were settled privately. On July 26, 1978 the TUC-Labour Party Liaison Committee approved a new policy document, *Into the Eighties*, which boasted of recent achievements. However, it gave only three of its 45 paragraphs to pay policy which was: 'one of the most difficult fields of our national economic life. We have still to reach a national consensus on the overall distribution of income... We do however believe that there must each year be a thorough discussion with the trade union movement.' Behind these bromide phrases was an acknowledgement that the strains over incomes policy could no longer be reconciled by private understandings between Downing Street and Congress House. The block votes at the September TUC Conference were cast overwhelmingly against a policy of restraint even when union leaders had been led to think that they were within days of an election. At the Labour Party Conference they repeated their votes; Jim Callaghan accepted the snub in a graceful speech but the rot had set in. Cabinet members approached union leaders to work out a new agreement. On November 14 the General Council on a tied vote rejected a revised and limited proposal for moderating wage claims. But it was not until the shock of the winter's troubles that the Liaison

Committee was driven to work out a new Concordat which was signed on February 23 (see p. 122).

The party had its financial troubles. It did benefit from trade union help, particularly after the foundation of Trade Unions for a Labour Victory in May 1978. This was largely the brainchild of David Basnett, that year's chairman of the TUC, and was set up when it was already clear that there would be no agreed fourth phase of the incomes policy; the major union leaders were anxious to demonstrate their goodwill to the party. But its achievements were limited and it was regarded by some in Transport House as 'a rival show' diverting resources that would have been better used going directly through party hands (see p. 181).

The party's income rose from £0.8m. in 1973 to £1.3m. in 1975 to £1.7m. in 1978 (excluding special funds).[6] But as Norman Atkinson, the Treasurer, told the 1979 Party Conference the party was fast overspending its income.[7] A deficit of £77,000 in 1978 was turning into one of £300,000 in 1979. One particular financial shadow hung over the party. The Transport and General Union which had given them house room for fifty years wanted to repossess their premises. Some houses bought by the party in Walworth Road, south of the river, proved unexpectedly difficult to redevelop, but in late 1978 it was finally agreed that a trade union consortium would build and lease premises to the party for occupancy in 1981.

The Labour party machine continued its decline. The number of individual members of the party stayed nominally just above 650,000. The Houghton Committee in 1976 reckoned the individual membership to be no more than 300,000. *Labour Weekly*

---

[6] An appeal for £1m. was launched at the 1978 Trade Union Congress. Some cheques had already come in when, two days later Mr Callaghan announced there would be no election. The appeal was rejuvenated in March 1979 and by election day between £800,000 and £1m. had been gathered. The main contributors were

	£		£
TGWU	150,000	NUPE	50,000
GMWU	150,000	NUR	40,000
AUEW	102,000	UPW	35,000
NUM	100,000	Boilermakers	25,000
ASTMS	50,000	SOGAT	10,000

[7] For a full discussion of party accounts, see M. Pinto-Duschinsky, *British Political Finance*, (Washington, 1980) and for further detail on the 1979 election, see M. Pinto-Duschinsky's chapter in H. Penniman, ed. *Britain at the Polls 1979* (Washington, 1980).

(September 27, 1979) arrived at a similar estimate (284,000). And the activists were a small and increasingly middle class fraction of that number, who were demanding a greater share in the running of the party. There were only 25 constituencies with a declared membership of over 1,500. Some of the other constituencies, all of which were listed as having 1,000 members, had a mere handful of subscribers (one had 14). The number of full-time agents fell to the lowest level since 1918. The 296 agents of 1951 had declined to 115 in 1974; by 1979 there were only 70, and these were not particularly concentrated in marginal areas. An agent's salary in 1978 (£3,070– £3,430) was certainly not attractive to would-be party organisers.[8]

In Transport House there were no radical changes. A proposal from the General and Municipal Workers for an overhaul of the party's organisation at the 1977 Conference was remitted. Sceptics might point to the minimal reforms which followed in the wake of the Wilson (1955) and Simpson (1968) enquiries. Ron Hayward continued as General Secretary to act as spokesman for the party in the country, while trying to smooth the rough edges between government and party. Reg Underhill presided over his decaying organisation. Percy Clark served out his last years as Director of Publicity. Geoff Bish, twenty years younger than these, was an activist research officer.

But the standing of Transport House was not high. A group of candidates in marginal seats established a ginger group to press for improved organisation and the campaign brought forth plenty of complaints about the party machine. During the winter party morale sank, as the strikes had their disastrous impact on public opinion and as the local activists occupied themselves with what was for most of them the uncongenial task of preparing for the June 7 Euro-elections. Between November and March they met together at ward, constituency and Euro-constituency level to choose 80 candidates. In some cases the struggle between left and right, overlapping with the struggle between

---

[8] See T. Forester, 'Labour's local parties' *New Society*, (September 25, 1975); C. and D. Martin, 'The Decline of Labour Party Membership' *Political Quarterly*, (October 1977); P. Seyd and L. Minkin, 'The Labour Party and its Members', *New Society*, (September 20, 1979) and M. Linton, 'The Membership Mystery' *Labour Weekly*, (September 28, 1979).

pro- and anti-Europeans, added to internal tensions, besides fully involving the understaffed Regional Officers, who would have preferred to focus on the coming struggle for Westminster seats. As one organisation man said 'We've never gone into an election in worse shape.'

4 Conservatives in Opposition

The Conservatives did not find the transition to opposition in 1974 an easy one. Previous defeats in 1945 and 1964 had followed long spells in office; they provided the opportunity for digesting the lessons of government and of defeat; policy could by rethought and organisation revamped. But the events of 1974 had been singularly demoralising; the party could not feel self-righteous about what it had done in government; it had lost power in an ill-judged confrontation which damaged its reputation as a national party representing all the people. The sense that the Conservative party was the natural party of government was severely shaken. Since 1964 Labour had emerged successful from four out of five general elections and had been in office for all but three and a half of the subsequent years. Conservatives were confused and uncertain as to the future of the party and of the country. In using the time in opposition as an opportunity to re-think policy and reorganise the party, the Conservatives were somewhat constrained by the fact that the government's majority was so narrow that the parliament could surely not live for very long. In fact it lasted for five years.

After October 1974 the party faced major problems. Firstly, it had to resolve the leadership issue, either by confirming Mr Heath or by ousting him and selecting a successor. Secondly, it had to re-establish unity and recreate a consensus on policy. Thirdly, it had to regain the voters' confidence by establishing rapport with the public and convincing the electorate that the Conservatives could solve their central dilemma of dealing with the unions without a disastrous repetition of the 1974 confrontation. Fourthly, it had to work out a strategy which would win the next election and provide future ministers with practicable policies. The way in which these problems were tackled provides a fascinating insight into the modern Conservative party.

Mr Heath's leadership came under question immediately after the February defeat. But criticism of his record and personality could not be much voiced while another election was pending. During the October campaign Mr Heath's friends pressed him to strengthen his appeal for national unity by offering to stand aside should his personality be regarded as an obstacle to forming a coalition; but after some thought he refused to volunteer what insiders called 'the supreme sacrifice' (See *The British General Election of October 1974*, pp. 124—9). Looking back on the October election, Mr Heath could feel some satisfaction at having held Labour to so narrow a majority. He appears to have entertained the hope that his call for a coalition would be vindicated by the coming economic crisis. His friends however, more aware of his weak position among Conservative backbenchers and knowing how much he was regarded as an electoral liability, urged him to resign quickly or at least to declare his willingness to stand for re-election. Without such action they feared that he might alienate support from the obvious heir-apparent, Mr Whitelaw, who was politically close to him. Critics of this line of thinking feared that it smacked of a 'magic circle' trying to fix the succession.

This uncertainty meant that for four months after the election there was a vacuum in the Conservative leadership. The first move came quickly when the Executive of the 1922 Committee met on October 14 at the home of the chairman, Edward du Cann. It was unanimously agreed that there should be a leadership election in the new parliamentary session and Mr du Cann was asked to convey this message to Mr Heath. Unfortunately the relations between the two men had been cool since Mr du Cann's time as Party Chairman under Mr Heath in 1966—7. The consequent tension was increased by speculation that Mr du Cann himself was a contender for the leadership, and by press talk of a 'Milk Street Mafia'. Mr Heath refused to discuss the leadership issue with the 1922 Executive until the election for new officers had been held.[1] He had misread the

---

[1] The 1922 Committee once met privately at the Milk Street offices of Keyser Ullman, the merchant bank of which Mr du Cann was Chairman, and were photographed as they left. The Executive of the 1922 Committee consists of a Chairman, two Vice-Chairmen, a Treasurer, two Secretaries and twelve members elected at the beginning of each session to serve for one year.

mood of the party. If he would not resign he would have to stand for re-election.

A committee under Lord Home was convened to consider changes to the rules established in 1965 for the first parliamentary election of a Conservative leader. The three main proposals for change were accepted:

1. There should be an annual election of the leader.
2. A candidate, to be elected on the first ballot, required not only an overall majority but also a lead over the runner-up equal to 15% of those eligible to vote (it had previously been 15% of those who actually voted).
3. Though only MPs had votes, the views of the Conservative peers and of the party in the country should be conveyed to them.

Margaret Thatcher's name occurred to very few people as a likely candidate. She was a supporter of the claims of Edward du Cann and Sir Keith Joseph. It was only after these two declined to be considered that she decided to oppose Mr Heath. Airey Neave, who was to be her campaign manager, originally offered his services to Sir Keith and Mr Whitelaw. When they refused, he turned to Mrs Thatcher. Other Shadow Cabinet ministers, apparently feeling bound by ties of personal loyalty and collective responsibility, refused to stand against him. Mrs Thatcher had been Secretary of State for Education in the 1970–74 government and therefore had not been closely involved in the main strategic arguments of the Conservative government and she had not been near to Mr Heath's entourage. She took a prominent part in the October campaign with her promise to peg the mortgage rate on houses to 9½% or less, and she had impressed her colleagues when leading the opposition to the Finance Bill in the winter of 1974 (just as Mr Heath had done a decade earlier). Inevitably she drew support from diverse quarters, from those who had felt slighted by Mr Heath, from those who were critical of the U-turns made by his government, and from those who simply felt it was time for a new leader. Because she was the only serious candidate to oppose Mr Heath it was necessary for MPs to vote for her if they wanted a change. This was a decisive consideration: 'There were never 139 votes for Margaret' said one MP.

The result on February 4 was a surprise to many outside the immediate Thatcher camp. Airey Neave, her campaign manager, deliberately understated Mrs Thatcher's strength, whilst Mr

February 4		February 11	
Mrs Thatcher	130	Mrs Thatcher	146
Edward Heath	119	William Whitelaw	79
Hugh Fraser	16	James Prior	19
Votes not cast	11	Sir Geoffrey Howe	19
		John Peyton	11
		Votes not cast	2

Heath's managers made over-optimistic sounds. Mr Heath had the support of most of the senior figures in the party and of the press and he was heavily backed among the peers and the constituency workers, but MPs did not share their reaction.

Mr Heath resigned immediately he heard the result. A second ballot was necessary because Mrs Thatcher had not reached the target figure of 139, and the way was clear for a larger field. Mr. Whitelaw's belated candidature was weakened by his identification with the rejected Mr Heath and by his earlier reluctance to stand. Unknown to him, a few acknowledge Heathmen had voted for Mrs Thatcher on the first round. There was a surge of support to Mrs Thatcher who had been courageous enough to oppose and topple Mr Heath. The candidatures of Sir Geoffrey Howe and Jim Prior, who were laying 'markers' for the future, may also have fragmented Mr Whitelaw's support. The second ballot on February 11 proved decisive and Mrs Thatcher became the first woman leader of a British political party.

The Conservative party had changed in the decade since the resignation of Sir Alec Douglas-Home. Although the front bench MPs remained almost uniformly upper middle class products of public schools and Oxbridge, Mr Heath and Mrs Thatcher represented a more meritocratic strain. Both came from modest backgrounds, both had won scholarships to grammar schools and Oxford and both were self-made professional politicians. Although he was the first leader chosen by MPs in a contested election, Mr Heath had long been at the centre of the party, had ascended the ministerial hierarchy, and might well have 'emerged' under the old system of informal consultation. He represented continuity with many of the principles associated with Harold Macmillan and R. A. Butler. Mrs Thatcher, however, had to overthrow the established leader; she had not previously served in any of the major offices of state; she was the product of a backbench rebellion against the leadership and, apart from Sir Keith Joseph, lacked front-bench support on the first ballot. She was very much an intruder.

Mr Heath's visible disenchantment with his successor and his rare but powerful interventions in defence of his 1970—74 record, and its U-turns, discomfited some frontbenchers. He was angry at what he saw as attempts, chiefly by Sir Keith Joseph,[2] to disown or even to denigrate the party's recent policies. However, his continued refusal to make conciliatory gestures to the new Conservative leader gradually lost him support. Critics contrasted his conduct with Sir Alec's loyal behaviour after 1965. But his presence in the shadow cabinet, together with that of Sir Keith, would have hindered the achievment of agreement on policies. Some of his friends both in and out of the shadow cabinet grew increasingly frustrated by his conduct. 'Look, he threw it all away', said one shadow minister. 'He could now be the major voice in Britain had he only resigned after October. But he created the opportunity for Margaret and Keith and now he is undermining the position of moderates.' Any pro-Heath noises or expressed doubts about the new leadership and policy were condemned as 'treason' by more militant supporters of Margaret Thatcher.

Mrs Thatcher's election was widely represented as a shift to the political right, by supporters and opponents alike. It reflected a reliance on market mechanisms rather than government intervention in the economy and on individual self-help rather than state-provided welfare benefits. However, the record of her leadership defies simple analysis because she was in practice caught between her own free-market instincts and her natural caution on matters of tactics and policy. The tension was manifested in a militant tone of speaking and a fierce style of debate which was not always matched by the content of her policy pronouncements.

---

[2] One of Sir Keith's more remarkable statements was that, although he had been a member of the Conservative party for years, 'it was only in April 1974 that I was converted to Conservatism. I had thought that I was a Conservative but I now see that I was not one at all'. *Reversing the Trend*, (London, 1975) p.4.

The suspicion of her right-wing political outlook was encouraged by her reliance on Sir Keith Joseph. Sir Keith was determined to roll back what he called 'the vast bulk of the accumulating detritus of socialism', and the ratchet-like way in which policy was levered ever more leftwards. She gave him overall charge of policy. His speeches on the importance of monetarism and his calculations about the modest impact it would have on unemployment excited controversy across the political spectrum and particularly aggravated Mr Heath. Mrs Thatcher in turn was protective towards Sir Keith. A critic of one of his suggestions met with the retort, 'Instead of criticising other people's ideas, why don't you have one of your own?' The monetarist and free market statements from his Centre for Policy Studies and from the Institute of Economic Affairs tended to be visited on Mrs Thatcher and were constantly criticised by supporters of Mr Heath. On a personal level people such as Nigel Lawson, George Gardiner and Norman Tebbit were part of the misleadingly named 'Gang of Four', who appeared to have her ear on matters of political tactics and on preparations for Prime Minister's question time. Jock Bruce-Gardyne and Alfred Sherman were among those who helped with speeches. Some of these were abrasive in personality and outspoken in the way they criticised the Heath record. The choice of these associates entailed some political costs as senior colleagues doubted her judgment in relying on advice from such quarters.

Perhaps the primary explanation of her image as a strident seeker after confrontation lay in her position as one of the few major politicians to think that British politics was based on an important, even a decisive, battle of ideas. Mrs Thatcher took pride in stating her political convictions and insisted that policies should derive from a coherent set of principles. Without such a starting point, she felt, a leader is at the mercy of events and unlikely to produce coherent policies. She also felt that the time had come to attack Labour's assumption of moral superiority and what she saw as its fallible premises. Some belligerent right-wingers agreed and used her approach to criticise her predecessor's.

Her attitude of certainty could make her overbearing in discussion. More than one sceptical senior colleague was admonished, 'Don't tell me *what*; tell me *how*. I know *what*.' Even friends acknowledged that she approached conversations as an intellectual exchange rather than as an opportunity to empathise; her invitations to colleagues to define terms and to explain 'precisely' what was meant often disconcerted the unprepared. Her frequent denunciations of high levels of taxation and public expenditure and of big government and the diminution of individual freedom and choice were passionate and deeply felt. Her ideal society was one in which the market would underpin personal choice and freedom and in which people would spend more of their rising incomes on better services than the state could provide. The Welfare State would operate as a safety net and more people would turn to private health insurance rather than the National Health Service and to independent education rather than the local comprehensive school. The economic growth which would be required for the realisation of this vision must depend on more incentives, lower taxes, fewer government controls, and the opportunity for people to accumulate capital of their own.

She was not a conciliatory leader; in this regard Labour and Liberal MPs compared her unfavourably with her predecessors and colleagues. She dismissed woolly talk of 'consensus' policies, complaining that there could be no compromise with the Labour party which she considered to be a captive of the left, with policies that were only a staging-post on the way to a fully planned society. There was, she believed, a fundamental divide between socialism and freedom, and people must be made aware of this. She was outspoken in her disapproval of the 'me too-ers' who wanted proportional representation, or a deal with the Liberals, and of those who, because of 'bourgeois guilt', did not stand up against abuses of power by the left. Such appeasement could result in the ultimate abandonment of freedom itself. She frequently made clear that she, at least, was not going to be intimated as others had been by charges of seeking a 'confrontation'.[3]

Some of her senior colleagues grew seriously worried by her view of politics as an ideological battleground and by her disavowal of many cross-bench attitudes. They feared that she

---

[3] Among the biographies of Mrs Thatcher see P. Cosgrave, *Margaret Thatcher, a Tory and her Party*, (London, 1978); G. Gardiner, *Margaret Thatcher: From Childhood to Leadership*, (London, 1975); R. Lewis, *Margaret Thatcher: A Personal and Political Biography*, (London, 1975); T. Murray, *Margaret Thatcher*, (London, 1978).

was seen to be, and was, too abrasive and lacking in compassion. Some were also worried about her administrative inexperience and her style of committee chairmanship. 'Too much preaching of the gospel and not enough of a managerial politician' said one colleague. Certain quarters in industry and the City feared the instability that might come with a return of Conservative government. Peregrine Worsthorne expressed these fears in an eloquent article (*Sunday Telegraph*, May 14, 1978). Mrs Thatcher's partisanship, he suggested, betrayed an unfortunate inflexibility and an intolerance of the views held by many people in the country. The Conservative tradition was one of tolerance. As a potential national leader Mrs Thatcher needed to demonstrate a greater sympathy and understanding with the views of ordinary people, even if she disagreed with them.

Yet, despite the ample evidence that she was a radical Conservative and on the right wing, the image of divisiveness was not borne out by her actions. Her Shadow Cabinet continued to be dominated by Mr Heath's former colleagues. A group that contained such political heavyweights as Willie Whitelaw, Jim Prior, Lord Carrington, Ian Gilmour and, for a time, Reggie Maudling, could counter any swing to the right in the Shadow Cabinet. Although Robert Carr and Peter Walker were not there, her new appointments did not mark any sharp change of direction; they were made with an eye to healing past wounds. The official strategic party document, *The Right Approach*, was moderate in tone and content and even earned the approval of Mr Heath at the 1976 Conference. In parliament the front bench abstained on the £6 pay limit; it did not oppose the rescue of British Leyland and of Chrysler; and it did not wage war against the closed shop. Mrs Thatcher's caution and her concern for party management were everywhere evident in her appointments and in the fine print of Conservative policy statements.

Mrs Thatcher's main strength, unlike Mr Heath's, lay with the backbenchers. She was accessible to them and took care to demonstrate this accessibility. The weekly meeting of the Business Committee — consisting of elected officers of back-bench committees and all front-bench spokesmen not in the Consultative Committee — became more important. Mrs Thatcher regularly briefed it on shadow cabinet decisions and insisted that other spokesmen kept in touch with it. But this diplomacy did not still criticisms. Some back-benchers expressed concern at her tone of speaking and at the performance of some shadow ministers. In early 1977 the officers of the 1922 Committee took the almost unprecedented step of expressing dissatisfaction with the shadow cabinet and suggesting a reshuffle.

There also were a number of complaints that Mrs Thatcher was not a good chairman. Though she was less forceful than Mr Heath, critics still complained that she spoke too much and interrupted too frequently. Her caution was seen in her reluctance to move shadow spokesmen except when circumstances forced her hand. The continuous possibility of an early dissolution, did of course mean that a shadow minister might be just learning a portfolio as an election was sprung. Michael Heseltine, to his own regret, was moved from Trade and Industry to Environment: he had upset some colleagues who were embarrassed by his eagerness to promise a complete repeal of the 1975 Industry Act. But apart from the dismissal of Reginald Maudling, the only reshuffle followed John Davies' resignation from Foreign Affairs in November 1978. Francis Pym took over the Foreign Affairs portfolio, with Norman St John Stevas replacing him as Leader of the House of Commons. Mark Carlisle, formerly a junior minister at the Home Office, took over Education and John Biffen assumed responsibility for Small Businesses.

Airey Neave was in charge of her private office although his increasing involvement with Northern Ireland meant that day-to-day management was in the hands of Richard Ryder. Her parliamentary private secretaries, Adam Butler and John Stanley, assisted with speech writing, and Chris Patten and Adam Ridley from the Research Department and Ronald Millar, the playwright, helped out on major political and economic statements. She did not have close political cronies and some colleagues regretted the lack of an equivalent to Douglas Hurd who, as Mr Heath's secretary from 1967 to 1974, had effectively known the leader's mind. Although Margaret Thatcher was strongly supported on the back benches, the lack of expressed enthusiasm among front-bench colleagues was noticeable. They did not excuse her shortcomings or her poor standing in the opinion polls by saying 'But she'll be a fine prime minister', as they had with Mr Heath in similar circumstances before 1970.

But there was no challenge to her position. Everyone accepted that she was leader, at least until she lost an election.

Spells in opposition have usually coincided with far-reaching reforms of the Conservative party's organisation. Under Mrs Thatcher the structural changes were minor, although staff alterations excited controversy. At the end of 1974 the key appointments at Central Office and the Research Department reflected Mr Heath's preferences. However, two election defeats in a year, followed by the dismissal of Mr Heath, meant that morale was understandably low. The top offices in the organisation are held at the leader's pleasure and changes in personnel, if not in direction, were inevitable under Mrs Thatcher, particularly as some of her more zealous advisers claimed that Central Office had unfairly leant towards Mr Heath during the leadership contest.

Mr Whitelaw quickly resigned the chairmanship which he had assumed twelve months earlier. He had been the fifth chairman to serve under Mr Heath. All had been active, sometimes prominent, politicians. Mrs Thatcher's surprise choice as successor was Lord Thorneycroft. He was 65 years old, and he had last held political office in 1964; in recent years he had been more involved in City and industrial affairs than in Conservative politics. But though he had refused her request to express public support for her on the eve of the first ballot, he enjoyed Mrs Thatcher's confidence. The offer was conveyed by his cousin, Mr Whitelaw, the retiring chairman, who had been scrupulous to see that Central Office was neutral in the leadership fight. One other departure meant that the Conservative party could fight the next election without the services of an official who had been at the centre of the party's thinking on policy and campaigning since 1950. Lord Fraser of Kilmorack, Director of the Research Department (1957–64) and then Chairman of the Department and Deputy Chairman of the party, retired in 1975. Lord Butler wrote of him as 'the best adjutant the party has every had'.

A key figure in any Central Office re-shuffle was Michael Wolff. In April 1974 he had been appointed to the new post of Director General, in full charge of Central Office, with a remit to coordinate the work of the different departments (see *The*

British General Election of October 1974, pp. 38—9). In playing this role he was to act as the equivalent of Permanent Secretary to the Chairman, who was inevitably a part-time functionary. Michael Wolff, however, was seen as irrevocably Heathite. He had had a long association with Mr Heath as speechwriter and adviser. Moreover, he had not overcome his lack of experience with the work of the party organisation and the agents. There was also resentment by at least one departmental head at the new line of command. Relations were difficult with Sir Richard Webster, the long-serving Director of Organisation, who could count on some voices in the Executive of the National Union being raised on his behalf; the situation became increasingly difficult after the departure of Mr Heath.

After only six days in office as Chairman, Lord Thorneycroft dismissed Mr Wolff on March 1975. Mr Prior, among others, protested at the abrupt manner of the sacking, going so far as refusing to vote in an important division on the Finance Bill. Some critics regarded the action as a politically motivated revenge on Mr Heath. *The Times* termed it 'the act of a downright fool' in an editorial, and thought that the new Central Office leadership suffered from a narrow political outlook and an average age of over 60.[4]

'The right concept but the wrong man', was one authoritative Conservative assessment of Mr Wolff's brief record. He was not formally replaced; however, Sir Richard Webster was obviously the senior paid official, although he was formally on the same level as the other departmental directors, and he enjoyed wide support in the National Union. Ironically, Mr Wolff's original job specification and the general re-organisation that accompanied his appointment had presumed Sir Richard's retirement in 1974. Both Mr Heath and Lord Carrington (then Chairman) wanted improvements and mistakenly thought that Sir Richard would acquiesce in an early departure. In the event he outstayed both. But, after repeated differences of opinion with Lord Thorneycroft, Sir Richard abruptly cleared his desk in January 1976. The anticipated explosion from the National Union did not occur[5] and he was replaced as Director of Organisa-

[4] Lord Thorneycroft was 65, and Sir Richard Webster 61. Angus Maude, Deputy Chairman and Chairman of the Research Department, was 62 and William Clark, Deputy Chairman and Joint Treasurer, was 57.
[5] But forceful complaints from agents were expressed in the February 1976 issue of the *Conservative Agents' Journal.*

tion by Anthony Garner, the Area Agent for the North West. In the case of the two dismissals of key officers in Central Office Mrs Thatcher appears to have left the initiative to Lord Thorneycroft, though inevitably some of the resentment was directed at her.

Lord Thorneycroft proved almost a full-time chairman. He was a compelling platform speaker in the constituencies and at conferences, and a direct and influential voice on matters of strategy, although illness kept him away for lengthy spells in 1975 and 1977: a central role fell to his assistant, Alan Howarth and, in 1977, to Lady Young. Mrs Thatcher relied on him, and in time he exercised a powerful influence on matters of strategy in the steering committee and on the final manifesto.

The party's finances were in a desperate state after the two 1974 elections. In the year ending March 1975, expenditure exceeded receipts by £1.2 million, and the party's reserves were depleted. This was turned into a small surplus in the next year.

A basic change under the Thorneycroft regime was the separation of fund raising from budgetary and financial control. As far as boosting the party's income was concerned a key role was played by Alistair McAlpine, who became Treasurer in 1975. The quota payments theoretically expected from the constituencies to Central Office were doubled in the course of the Parliament. Business donations recovered after the squeeze on profits in 1974–5, despite Jeremy Thorpe's efforts to persuade companies to make their contributions conditional on Conservative support for proportional representation (see p. 96). Mr McAlpine was very effective with smaller businesses whose donations, frequently channelled through industrial councils, averaged around £250.[6] Contributors were impressed by the need for advertising and appreciated the flair of Saatchi and

[6] According to a Labour Party Research Department study of large company reports in the year ending March 1979, 358 firms gave £1,721,000 to political causes. £951,000 went directly to the Conservatives; £450,000 went to British United Industrialists and £144,000 to Industrial councils (which presumably passed almost everything on to the party centrally or in the areas). £34,000 went to Sir Keith Joseph's Centre for Policy Studies. The Economic League received £117,000 and Aims (formerly Aims of Industry) received £18,000 but these bodies followed their own anti-Socialist lines: a further £6,000 went to other organisations – but none of the large companies in the survey reported any gifts to the Liberal or Labour parties – though one donation of £500 to the Liberals was reported later. Taylor Woodrow with £34,000 to the party and £30,000 to B.U.I. was the largest contributor. Allied Breweries with £53,000 to B.U.I. came second.

Saatchi's campaign. Mr MacAlpine was usually accompanied by Jock Bruce-Gardyne, an ex-Conservative MP and leader writer on the *Daily Telegraph*, who reinforced the political argument for making contributions. Expenditure was reduced on private polling, on staff (by not replacing vacancies due to retirements), and by the termination of the scheme for the central employment of agents. This innovation in 1972 had been welcomed by some as a means of placing professional agents in the marginals where they could be electorally most effective. In the event, however, even before the financial axe fell, few were prepared to be transferred to critical seats. At the same time, modest sums were found for the Conservative Trade Union organisation under the new Community Affairs Group. Its Director, Andrew Rowe, was charged with dealing with groups not amenable to more traditional organisational approaches such as racial minorities and Conservative Students as well as the new Small Business Bureau. A fully-fledged Local Government Department was also created with larger responsibilities. The number of agents increased from 306 in 1975 to 346 by July 1978, and each of the 97 'critical seats' had the services of a full-time agent. The critical seats selected for special treatment were selected on aggressive assumptions. Only 14 were Conservative-held in October 1974: the other 83 would represent gains.

Mr Clark's economy measures inevitably made him unpopular among the agents. His somewhat brisk manner of announcing cuts and dismissals caused further offence. His request for greater control of the budget was refused and he resigned in November 1977. His successor, Lady Young, took firm and less abrasive control of organisational matters.

Publicity, as so often, caused difficulties. The party was unable to match the higher salaries available in private industry. When Alec Todd, the Director of Publicity, left to join ICI in 1975 there was considerable delay before Tom Hooson was appointed. He failed to make much impact and he in turn was replaced by Gordon Reece in March 1978. Mr Reece had helped Mrs Thatcher during her leadership campaign and worked in her private office in 1975 before returning to EMI. His professional advice on publicity matters was greatly respected by the leader and she responded to suggestions for adjustments to her personal appearance and style of speaking.

In the Research Department, Mrs Thatcher replaced Ian Gilmour as Chairman with Angus Maude. Sir Keith Joseph took overall charge of policy and research. The retention of Chris Patten, who had been made Director of the Research Department in 1974 at the age of 30, and was a pronounced moderate, supplied some political balance to the new team.[7] The scale of Research Department activity was not cut although much less was spent on opinion polls than in 1966–70.

After the election of Mrs Thatcher the party in the country was reasonably quiescent. She had no rival. Both Mr Powell and, gradually, Mr Heath, lost support. Strong statements on immigration and law and order were predictably welcome but the party leadership enjoyed a free hand on policy. The only difficulty with the National Union occurred when the executive insisted on making an appointment to serve on the Joint Committee Against Racialism, notwithstanding the leader's wishes to the contrary.

In so far as the Conservative party has been in office for two-thirds of the period since 1885, it is understandable that commentators have regarded it as the natural party of government in Britain. Surveys in the 1950s and 1960s showed that many voters saw the party as more national in its outlook and more administratively competent than Labour. But this advantage in terms of party image was dissipated by the circumstances of the February 1974 election; then a majority of voters saw the Conservatives as being more divisive and sectional.[8] The removal of Mr Heath and his replacement by Mrs Thatcher did not erase

[7] It was announced in May 1978 that Mr Patten would be replaced as Secretary to the Shadow Cabinet by David Wolfson who had recently joined Mrs Thatcher's private office. The Secretary's task is to prepare the agenda and circulate the minutes of meetings. The Times reported the suspicion among some senior figures that Mr Patten was being replaced because of his moderate views. Mrs Thatcher took the remarkable step of writing to the paper on May 31, 1978 claiming that the change was being made solely to relieve the workload borne by Mr Patten. The affair was a storm in a teacup. There had been earlier moves to appoint Mr Wolfson to the post of Director-General in Central Office. But after the experience with Michael Wolff (see p. 70), the idea was not welcome to senior figures in Central Office. An appointment to the post of Secretary to the Shadow Cabinet was therefore proposed as an expedient. In the event, Mr Wolfson gained the title but Mr Patten continued to take the minutes.

[8] J. Alt, I. Crewe and B. Sarlvik, 'Partisanship and Policy Choice' British Journal of Political Science, (July, 1976). The findings contrast with those from the 1950s. See M. Abrams, R. Rose and R. Hinden, Must Labour Lose? (London, 1960).

the memory of that election and the fear of the disruption
which would follow another confrontation between a Tory
government and a powerful union. The final package of policies —
particularly the retreat from the Industrial Relations Act and a
statutory incomes policy — could hardly be considered provocative to the unions. Most Conservatives thought they had done as
much as was politically possible to reassure voters on this
question, without surrendering totally to the unions.

At the same time, and conflicting with the above objective, a
number of Conservatives felt that they had lost intellectual
ascendancy to 'progressive' opinion-formers promoting collectivist and egalitarian values. There was a series of internal debates,
sometimes coded, sometimes explicit, about the nature of
'true' conservatism and what the electorate 'really' wanted.[9]
One group could point out that on a number of issues, such as
immigration, capital punishment and trade union power, the
views of most voters were well to the right of the leadership in
both parties. But though there was probably some vague shift
in the public mood, it is well to remember that trade unions had
been unpopular for many years and that resentment against
high taxes was nothing new, any more than the desire for a
tougher line on immigration and law and order.

The inevitable call in opposition for a return to 'true' Conservative principles was not primarily motivated by calculations
about electoral mood, though its spokesmen were confident
that it would win votes. What they wanted was for the Conservatives to stand for a distinctive set of values and policies rather
than appearing to react to the initiatives of their opponents.

The debate could easily be portrayed as one between left and
right-wing versions of Conservatism, or between the personalities
of Mr Heath and Mrs Thatcher. It was as much a rivalry between
tough and tender-minded attitudes. The tough-minded became
more vocal in opposition; they usually favoured monetary
discipline, drew on the views of the *Black Papers* on educational
matters, and wanted stricter measures to combat crime and
immigration. They were opposed to socialism and to the concil-

[9] See for example: I. Gilmour, *Inside Right*, (London, 1977). P. Walker, *The Ascent
of Britain*, (London, 1977). R. Boyson, *Centre Forward*, (London, 1978). Lord
Hailsham, *The Dilemma of Democracy*, (London, 1978). W. Waldegrave, *The Binding
of Leviathan*, (London, 1978). T. Russel, *The Tory Party*, (London, 1978).

iatory character of Conservatism over the previous decade and a half. They believed that a fundamental change was necessary and possible, given the political will.

Sir Keith Joseph was the chief spokesman of the tough-minded. He frequently distinguished between the *common ground*, the area on which there was general agreement between the parties and which most voters accepted, and the *middle ground*, a point mid-way between the policies of the two main parties. His complaint was that Labour gave a turn of the ratchet to Socialism each time they were in office and that this was then accepted by the next Conservative government with the new position being enshrined as a 'consensus'. As each Labour government moved to the left, enacting collectivist and egalitarian policies, and Conservatives moved to the centre, so the middle ground increasingly moved away from them. This line of analysis certainly impressed Mrs Thatcher and emboldened those who looked for a more radical Conservatism.

Other self-styled middle-of-the-road' voices, predominantly in the upper reaches of the party, doubted the electoral wisdom and political possibility of such policies. The electorate, they believed, had become used to high levels of public expenditure and high rates of taxes to provide the welfare services and employment; most uncommited voters were indifferent to ideological appeals. It was all very well to strike postures in opposition, but the constraints of government limited the possibilities of a sharp change in direction. One pragmatic shadow minister commented: 'I think it is more important to keep the country together, to conciliate and have continuity of policies than to have "big C" conservatism.'

Campaigners usually distinguish between particular issues as 'ours' or 'theirs'; the former are those issues on which their own party's stand is preferred by most voters to that of the opposite party. Private and public polls confirmed that, once the Labour government started to roll back the rate of inflation, the Conservatives were at a disadvantage on the main socio-economic issues of prices, and of handling the unions and unemployment, as well as on welfare questions. A 'winning' electoral strategy in these areas would involve acceptance of the views of the moderates in the shadow cabinet. On the other hand the Conservatives were thought to be the best party to handle immigration and law and order, although the polls suggested that these last issues were less salient to voters. But some Conservatives noted that the polls also showed a large majority of voters thinking that not enough was being said about law and order, and that Mrs Thatcher's remarks on immigration in February 1978 preceded an impressive, if short-lived, Tory gain in the polls. They believed that there were potentially rich electoral dividends to be won by distinguishing the party's harder line from the Labour position.[10]

All politicians are to some extent cocooned in their own Westminister nest of like-minded people. They may go out into the pubs and shopping centres in their constituencies, but they come back to shape policies among their fellow politicians and inevitably they fall into the language and thought patterns of that group. Yet those around Mrs Thatcher did make an effort to identify target voters and to reach out to them: there was an awareness that if large numbers of votes were to be won, they would be found primarily among the wives and families of well-paid workers; there was a very conscious attempt to speak to women in Labour-voting households and to *Sun* and *Mirror* readers. Mrs Thatcher in her Conference speeches deliberately skipped some of the traditional *tour d'horizon* and aimed at 'gut' issues.

Conservative policy is made in a more restricted and private way than that of the Labour party. In the end, policy is what the leader says it is. Policy is, of course, made under the pressure of deadlines imposed by parliamentary debates and external events. While it has to be framed with due regard to the party's past record and commitments, it must demonstrate a willingness to learn new lessons. A particular problem during the 1974—9 parliament was the danger that too explicit a repudiation of the previous Conservative government's record might embarrass the many members of the shadow cabinet, Mrs Thatcher among them, who had been members of Mr Heath's administration. Nonetheless the leadership was free to make policy without major pressures from the rank and file. Their problem was to formulate viable solutions to the national dilemmas which would not frighten the electorate unduly nor perpetuate divi-

[10] See I. Crewe, 'Popular Attitudes and Electoral Strategy' in Z. Layton-Henry ed. *Conservative Party Politics*, (London, 1980).

sions within the party leadership. In contrast to the earlier post-war policy exercises, the party was now more concerned to articulate a philosophy and to set out an indication of the kind of society it wished to encourage. After 1945 the groups under R. A. Butler produced the *Industrial Charter* which symbolised the party's acceptance of the mixed economy and the welfare state. After 1966 a number of policies were worked out in detail, particularly for industrial relations and tax reform. In part this approach reflected Mr Heath's temperament and his belief that people were so cynical about politics 'that detail is needed to convince them that you really intend to carry out your promises.' In retrospect, however, the Conservatives came to realise the disadvantage of committing a government to policies for circumstances which could not be predicted or on which, as with industrial relations, negotiations might be desirable once in government. They were clear that they had neglected the relationship between money supply and inflation and that they had failed to anticipate the strength of trade union opposition to their reform of industrial relations. In the late 1970s avoidance of detail fitted in with a new modesty about what government could actually do to solve problems; on balance such attitudes limited argument and kept the party together. In this Mrs Thatcher's caution was due less to revulsion from the pre-1970 exercise than to her concern to reach agreement on a set of basic principles from which the 'correct' line of policy would then follow. *The Right Approach* was deliberately presented as 'a strategy document'.

There was a familiar pattern to the formal organisation of policy-making. Some 60 policy groups, composed of MPs and outside experts, were chaired by the relevant Shadow minister or his nominee, and serviced by a secretary from the Research Department.[11] The Advisory Committee on Policy, chaired by Sir Keith Joseph and drawn from MPs, peers and the party in the country was consulted as a formality. Decisions about official party policy were taken in the inner Steering Committee and in the full Shadow Cabinet. At one point so many reports were being presented that Sir Keith formed a small policy sub-committee of Shadow ministers to filter proposals before their submission to the Committee.

[11] See C. Patten, 'Policy Making in Opposition' in Z. Layton-Henry (ed.) *Conservative Party Politics*, (London, 1980).

Sir Keith Joseph failed to wield the expected influence on specific policies although he had a major part in shaping the intellectual atmosphere. His Centre for Policy Studies was an irritant rather than a rival to the Research Department. There were conflicts between personalities but the roles of the two bodies were very different. Sir Keith had set up the Centre in April 1974. Its original brief was to draw lessons from the successful social market economies, but its main activity was to assist in preparing the speeches of Sir Keith and, to some extent, of Mrs Thatcher. Its tone and particularly the views of its Director of Studies, Alfred Sherman, were viewed with suspicion by a number of 'moderate' Conservatives. Certainly its firmly monetarist standpoint was at variance with the blander productions of the Research Department.

The official policy groups were guided by their ministerial chairmen, and the centrist majority in the Steering Committee and the Shadow Cabinet meant that radical departures were unlikely. Events also shaped policy. For example, although the party was generally opposed to statutory controls on incomes, it was difficult for it to oppose the concept of a pay policy as such, having just fought an election on one. Conservatives, particularly those in the West Midlands, were not enthusiastic about closing down British Leyland and explaining the consequent unemployment. Sir Keith Joseph found himself defending the £400m advance to British Leyland.

The balance of forces in the leadership group was also reflected in the tone of the two main mid-term strategy documents, *The Right Approach* (1976) and *The Right Approach to the Economy* (1977). Both conveyed the style of R. A. Butler's *Industrial Charter*. The party manifesto drew heavily on the broad principles laid down in these documents. *The Right Approach* reflected the writing skills of Chris Patten and Angus Maude; it was characterised by an emphasis on getting value for public money, on 'balance' and on 'cautious realism'. Early drafts were checked with Mr Heath to ensure that he would not repudiate what was proposed. Specifics were avoided, apart from the promised abolition of the Industry Act and the National Enterprise Board, together with the repeal of the Community Land Act and the 1976 Education Act. Future policy commitments were cautiously worded with due reference to their dependence on adequate resources, parliamentary time, further study and the like. Emphasis was placed on the approved themes of enterprise, wider ownership, better educational standards and the rule of law. The economic policy document brought together the work of groups on public expenditure, taxation, industrial subsidies, and industrial relations. It made obeisance to the importance of money supply and the role of responsible wage bargaining. The fact that it could be signed by men as diverse as Sir Keith Joseph, Sir Geoffrey Howe and Jim Prior indicated that a truce had been reached in this area, one to be broken temporarily in October 1978 at the Conservative Conference.

The Conservatives were troubled by the leaking of policy documents to the press. 'We're getting as bad as Labour', said one official; but it also indicated a fraught mood in some quarters. Lord Carrington's report on how a government might cope with an economic emergency similar to the miners' strike was predictably attacked as 'confrontation' by critics. The same fate befell Nicholas Ridley's leaked report on the finances and labour problems of the nationalised industries in May 1978.

But Mrs Thatcher's off-the-cuff announcements, frequently in television interviews, could take her shadow ministers unawares. In September 1977 she suddenly proposed that a referendum might be invoked in strike situations and in February 1978 her remarks on the problems of immigrants 'swamping' upset some colleagues. Teddy Taylor's advocacy of a referendum on capital punishment was seen as an attempt to seize the initiative before the policy group completed its deliberations; he was put down by Mr Whitelaw.

The three main areas of prolonged argument in the shadow cabinet concerned incomes policy, industrial relations and immigration. On these, at least, genuine disagreement was voiced (by contrast Mr Heath's teams had been more like-minded and he had dominated debate, particularly after the death of Iain Macleod and the withdrawal of Reginald Maudling). Sir Geoffrey Howe chaired the key economic reconstruction group which decided economic policies. The conflicting views of Sir Keith Joseph and Mr Heath were not reconciled, but the shadow cabinet achieved some agreement, partly because the differences were transmuted into more bargainable differences of emphasis by Jim Prior and Sir Geoffrey Howe. *The Right Approach* indicated a willingness to use any instrument, short of a statutory incomes policy, to combat inflation. Most of the party, however, were bored by the technical disputes between monetarists and advocates of incomes policy. The Labour government's adherence to the IMF guidelines at the end of 1976 helped to take the issue away from the centre of the party battle. 'We are all monetarists now,' said a minister. The Conservatives were clear about the need to cut public expenditure as a prerequisite to the reduction of direct taxation, though they were reluctant to publicise the areas to be cut.

Senior shadow ministers spent a lot of time working out a coherent policy to curb public expenditure. The Labour argument that the 1975 level could not be significantly pruned was punctured by the government's own IMF-induced cuts of £4 billion in December 1976. The Conservative goal was to get back to the 1976 level of public expenditure in real terms and eventually to the 1973 level. The routes to this goal would be (a) cutting waste, (b) cutting housing subsidies and selling council homes, (c) selling off some nationalised firms, (d) reducing financial aids to industry, and (e) other cuts all round, except in a few priority areas.

Industrial relations has been a long-standing source of turmoil in the party. 'Doing something about the unions' was important if the goals of industrial peace, more efficient work practices, and cutting back of inflationary wage settlements were to be continued. But how was it to be done? The strict monetarists wished to face the unions with the consequences of free collective bargaining, namely a choice of moderate settlements or loss of jobs. Their free-market principles were offended by restrictive work practices and the closed shop. Jim Prior, by contrast, represented a more conciliatory strand. He was more concerned with the problems of gaining the consent of the union leaders and hoped to avoid any major legislation such as the Industrial Relations Act.[12]

Mr Prior's task of keeping open lines to the trade unions was hardly helped by the penchant of his colleagues for expressing their own views, particularly on the Grunwick affair and on the

[12] For a valuable discussion of the different strands in Conservative thinking about the unions and their implications for policy, see M. Moran, *The Politics of Industrial Relations* (London, 1977), and 'The Conservative Party and the Trade Unions since 1974', *Political Studies*, (1979).

operation of the closed shop. Sir Keith Joseph had earlier
objected to informal meetings with the economic committee of
the TUC. In the end Mrs Thatcher came down firmly on Mr
Prior's side and at one point admonished Sir Geoffrey Howe for
speaking out of turn on Communist influence in the unions. Mr
Prior's emphasis on the practical 'problems' of dealing with the
unions and avoiding another 'Who governs?' conflict appealed
to her own caution. The party was prepared to accept the
closed shop where it was established practice, but it wanted new
safeguards for individuals as well as postal ballots for union
elections and a code of practice that could if necessary be based
on legislation.[13]

Mr Whitelaw's official policy statement on immigration at
Leicester on April 7, 1978 promised a quota system to reduce
immigration and a compulsory register of dependants. But a
number of senior Conservatives feared that the whole episode
had been mishandled from Mrs Thatcher's 'swamping' remarks
onwards (see p. 28); the party had managed to alienate the
immigrants in inner-city marginal seats without appeasing the
anti-immigrants. In July 1978 Enoch Powell scornfully pointed to
the contrast between the leader's earlier call for an end to immigration and her more recent promise to 'control the rate of
immigration'.

Constitutional matters came up repeatedly in Parliament and
the party was forced to rethink its line on a number of issues.
Lord Hailsham was a powerful voice for wide-ranging institutional reform as a means of limiting the sovereignty of parliament and the role of government, though his arguments were
heard less as the election approached. A growing number of
Conservatives, including some shadow cabinet spokesmen, also
supported the principle of proportional representation, in spite
of Mrs Thatcher's strong opposition. On March 1, 1978 over
a third of Conservative MPs voted for PR in the Welsh Assembly.
Her own view was that a clear Conservative majority was the
best way to reverse socialism. Moreover, the Lib-Lab pact confirmed her own fears that a small Liberal party would gain
great power with PR and would also lean to Labour. The party's
report in September 1978 on the referendum eventually recom-

---

[13] For further developments on the party's trade union policies see below, Chapter 7.

mended its use for entrenching changes in the Constitution.[14]

A major difficulty arose over the government proposals for devolution in Scotland and Wales. The Conservative party, already dominated by English MPs, became increasingly negative towards the Labour government's proposals. Though Conservatives differed about how best to proceed there was widespread agreement on the shortcomings of the government's bill. Most Scottish and Welsh Conservative MPs were pro-union, and gradually the party moved into a strong anti-devolution mood. In December 1976 a three-line whip opposing the Scotland and Wales bill led to the resignation of the Scottish spokesman, Alick Buchanan-Smith, and his replacement by Teddy Taylor. In contrast to previous ministers for Scotland who had been pro-devolution, Mr Taylor was an outspoken opponent of any form of it. The party abandoned its previous commitment to a directly elected Scottish assembly, and now called for a constitutional conference to examine the various options. However, the leadership was prepared to allow the referendum to go ahead and abide by the results. Francis Pym, though personally sympathetic to devolution, skilfully kept the party together while not entirely ruling out that solution.

Conservative morale in opposition ebbed and flowed according to by-election results, opinion polls and the progress of government business in the Commons. Mrs Thatcher's standing with her party was similarly affected. During the first six months of 1978, as Mr Callaghan outscored her in Parliament and the polls, living standards improved and the government recovered its popularity in the opinion polls, so Conservatives became more critical. The government had survived public expenditure cuts, the IMF package, defeats on key parliamentary votes and the loss of its assured majority in the Commons. In spite of having presided over a record combination of soaring inflation and soaring unemployment, its political position had improved. Yet on many issues of policy, public opinion had either moved to, or remained on, the right. This was true of immigration, crime,

[14] A small committee under Nicholas Edwards had been appointed to study this subject, in the wake of Mrs Thatcher's suggestions to hold a referendum in the case of strikes against government policy. For further examples of Conservative thinking on constitutional matters see Lord Hailsham, 'Elective Dictatorship' *Listener* (October 21, 1977); and I. Gilmour, *Inside Right*, (London, 1977).

tax reductions and an assault on 'waste' in the public sector. 'What puzzles me,' said Geoffrey Howe, 'is that, when we are so obviously right, we have had such limited success in getting our case across. We are puzzled by our failure to do better in such circumstances.'

But translating a mood into votes requires, among other things, a measure of political skill and an ability to communicate. Unfortunately, many of the front-bench spokesmen were not well-known to the public, and the well-publicised utterances of Mr Heath and Mr Walker did not help the shadow cabinet's efforts to purvey a concerted line. Mr Callaghan had also narrowed the target area for Conservatives. It was not just his style as, his opponents complained, 'the best Conservative Prime Minister we have'. The combined effects on the economy of incomes policy, cash limits and control of the money supply weakened the effect of Conservative charges of profligacy. The government's reliance on Liberal votes checked left-wing measures and undermined claims that the Labour government was extremist as well as impotent.

Mrs Thatcher would dismiss suggestions that there was a new consensus between the front benches on the mixed economy, Europe, monetarism, more economic incentives and higher educational standards. She stood for a different set of values and sympathies and her goal was, in her own words, 'a change of direction without extremism'.

Looking back on the Conservatives in opposition one is impressed by the divergence between image and substance, by Mrs Thatcher's ability to mould the image without actually dictating specific policies. She appeared as a more ideological, aggressive leader than the post-war party had known. Yet the fine print of party policies suggested the durability of the *One Nation* group's thinking. The image was hostile to comprehensive schools (but they would be retained and 'improved'), to the closed shop (but it was accepted), and to intervention in industry (but British Leyland would survive). This tension mirrored the position of Mrs Thatcher herself: her instincts and intellect pulled her to the right, but her assessment (reinforced by senior colleagues) of what was politically acceptable pulled her another way.

There was some relief when Mr Callaghan decided against an

autumn election, as there had been when he did not call a snap
vote in June 1978, and some self-congratulation at Central
Office among those who had sponsored the Saatchi and Saatchi
advertising which perhaps had checked any adverse tide during
August and September. Their prospects, they felt, were bound
to improve over the winter. But the improvement came about
only gradually. At first confidence grew in the party at the way
that Mr Callaghan had apparently funked calling an election.
Morale was further boosted by the spectacle of the central
economic policies of the government being so decisively repudiated at the Labour party conference. This confidence was
quickly dissipated, however, by the Conservative party's internal
wrangles at its own party conference over its rival form of
incomes policy.

The immediate problem for the opposition was what to do
about the government's 5% incomes policy, already running
into opposition among trade unions and many Labour backbenchers. Mrs Thatcher saw these developments as a vindication
of her own claims that incomes policies gradually broke down
under their own rigidities. By contrast, Mr Heath, in his conference speech and in frequent television interviews, called for
the party to support the government's line. The dispute harked
back to Sir Keith Joseph's speech in Preston in September 1974
on the importance of monetarism which had opened divisions in
the party on the eve of the election. This widely publicised rift
between the leader and her predecessor reopened the wounds
which had been delicately bound over in *The Right Approach*.

Mr Heath could fairly point out that it was Mrs Thatcher
who had abandoned the agreed ground spelt out in the document. Of more immediate importance was the disaster of the
Berwick by-election and the finding that opinion polls had also
turned sharply against the Conservative party and reflected
greater support for Mr Heath's policies and personality. 'Supporting a free-for-all looks like favouring a wages explosion',
said one influential strategist. 'Callaghan at least will get credit
for trying to do something about it.'

It was Lord Thorneycroft, the Party Chairman, who took the
initiative in settling the simmering dispute. At a shadow cabinet
meeting on October 31 the 'peace treaty' embodied in *The
Right Approach to the Economy* was restated as official party
policy. Although the eventual collapse of the 5% norm eased

the Conservatives' position, the official party line faithfully emphasised the importance of 'responsibility' in free collective bargaining and Mrs Thatcher refused to exclude a statutory policy in the case of an 'emergency'.

There were further difficulties for the leadership over Rhodesia. Conservative activists in the constituencies were a powerful lobby for ending sanctions against Rhodesia. In the vote on sanctions in the Commons on November 8, 1978 116 Conservatives defied the whips' instructions to abstain. Two front-bench spokesmen, Winston Churchill and John Biggs-Davison, were dismissed following their votes against sanctions.

The main boost to the party, and to Mrs Thatcher personally, came with the rash of strikes, unruly picketing and well-publicised suffering of the public during January and February of the new year. The government's claim that it alone could work with the unions was shown to be hollow by the spectacle of union members openly contemptuous of agreements and spurning the instructions of leaders and the exhortations of Labour ministers. In her party political broadcast on January 17 Mrs Thatcher was able to capture the headlines with her proposals for trade union reform. The only new proposals covered her suggestions for no-strike agreements in essential industries, and the taxation of supplementary benefits for strikers. As public resentment over the trade unions mounted, so Mrs Thatcher's standing in the opinion polls and support for the Conservative party rapidly improved. Colleagues were impressed at how she had seized the initiative and also at her performances in the House of Commons and on television. There was still widespread scepticism, however, among her colleagues about what sort of a prime minister she would make.

5 Liberal Frustrations

The Liberal party has consistently challenged the view that Britain has a two-party system. But when in 1974 the party system suddenly appeared at its most fragmented and unstable, the Liberals found that they were not the key group in British politics. There was now a third force of almost 40 MPs unattached to Conservative or Labour — a body of members large enough to have held the balance in all the parliaments since the war, except those of 1945, 1955, 1959 and 1966. However, this residue was divided between Liberals, Nationalists and Ulstermen. The Conservative/Labour hegemony in votes might be breaking down, but the Liberals had not yet reaped a sizeable harvest of parliamentary seats. There was no clear majority in parliament, but there were others besides the Liberals who could determine the balance of power.

The 1974—9 parliament proved a disappointment for the Liberals. The failure in October 1974 to build on the February break-through was the first disappointment: the party's new found strength seemed a wasting asset. The failure to profit from power sharing with the Labour government proved an equally unpleasant surprise. The Liberal upsurge had posed a number of awkward questions about the party's political strategy. Before 1974 arguments about joining coalitions or choosing which large party to support had been largely academic debates; thereafter they had some practical urgency. In February 1974 the party had been taken by surprise by the result and even by October it was still not clear what Liberal MPs would do if no party gained an overall majority. Some optimists aimed for a Liberal government and dismissed any talk of inter-party arrangements. MPs themselves discussed co-operation with another party, though they disagreed whether this should take the form of a coalition or just support on key votes, and they also disagreed on the price that Liberals should seek for their support.

Notwithstanding its small size, the parliamentary group proved a difficult body to weld together. The MPs themselves were colourful individualists, often representing far-flung constituencies and commanding large personal votes, and the Liberal party disliked whipping on principle. Yet because of the novel parliamentary situation, Liberal MPs had increasingly to act collectively and to weigh the likely political consequences of their votes in the division lobbies. Five of the thirteen MPs were from Scottish and Welsh constituencies, and this gave the devolution issue an extra urgency for them. A further three were from remote parts of Devon and Cornwall, giving the party a Celtic and agricultural complexion in Parliament. (All but three of the Liberal-held seats were in the hundred most agricultural constituencies in the country.) By contrast most of the Liberal activists and the bulk of the Liberal voters were drawn from the English suburban and rural areas.

Academic surveys have suggested that the partisan commitment of most of the 6 million Liberal voters in 1974 was slight. The Essex study pointed out that Liberal appeal lay 'in the areas of personality and image as opposed to issue-based preferences'. This did not augur well for a break-through. Between the two general elections the party lost some 2½ million votes and gained almost 2 million new ones.[1] The problems were to retain the attachment of fickle voters and to persuade potential supporters actually to vote Liberal. This was always going to be difficult after 1974. By tradition Liberals do worse under Labour governments, as refugees from the Tory party go homing back to cast a more effective anti-socialist vote. After 1974 the Liberal collapse was particularly noticeable at by-elections in the blue-chip Tory seats such as Bournemouth East, Epsom and Wycombe.

Liberal voting strength depended upon two factors. First, there was the anti-system, protest-oriented Liberal, a group which has tended to grow under Conservative governments. Second, there was a centrist type of supporter who voted Liberal because of his dislike of class conflict, his dislike of the other two parties and his perception of the Liberals as being less divisive than the other two parties.[2]

[1] See J. Alt, I. Crewe and B. Sarlvik, 'Angels in Plastic; Liberal Support in 1974', *Political Studies*, (September, 1977).
[2] See P. Lemieux, 'Political Issues and Liberal Support in the February 1974 British General Election', *Political Studies*, (September, 1977).

The Liberal party machine has suffered long-standing weaknesses. Limited by a tiny budget, the party could not offer a career structure to first-class administrators. In 1969 bankruptcy was averted at the last moment by drastic dismissals of staff and the last minute appearance of wealthy donors. In February 1975 the executive asked Richard Wainwright to chair a committee to review how the Liberal Party organisation should operate within a budget of £80,000—£100,000. Richard Wainwright was an influential figure because of his chairmanship of the Standing Committee, and his membership of the Rowntree Trust, which was a major contributor to the Liberal party. A number of Liberals thought that the continuation of Rowntree aid would be conditional on acceptance of the Wainwright proposals. The report's main recommendation was for a fragmentation of the headquarters and a decentralisation of its work to the regional offices. This recommendation was an implicit acknowledgement of the impossibility of reforming the central headquarters. Extra funds would be channelled to the regional offices, and constituencies would be encouraged to take their problems there rather than to London. The report made clear the general belief that the LPO, as presently constituted, deterred potential donors. Some of the larger donors insisted that their money went to special projects.

The report was turned down by the National Executive in March 1975, on the vote of the chairman, Ken Vaus. In fact, however, many of the recommendations — except for the main one, decentralisation — were carried through. Ted Wheeler, the head of the LPO, was given twelve months' notice and the party agreed to look around for a Secretary General. Though the post carried a new title, it was clearly understood that the new appointment would be as head of a revamped LPO.

In December 1976 Hugh Jones, an ex-civil servant who was Director-General of the English Speaking Union, was appointed; he took up his duties in March 1977. Though a long-standing Liberal, his appointment was a surprise to many activists. He was chosen over two other well-known contenders, John Spiller, who had been in charge of the marginal seats operation since 1973, and Lord Beaumont who was a former head of LPO. Mr Jones's asset was not only his administrative background but the fact that he presented the opportunity for a clean slate.

Hugh Jones had to work with a miniscule staff which actually declined during 1975—6. He was supported by five executives and twelve other (mainly clerical and secretarial) staff, and five professional regional organisers. In the constituencies there were only about seventeen full-time professional agents. All told the party had no more than 50 full-time employees (including those employed by the semi-autonomous Scottish and Welsh Liberal parties).

After 1974 the Liberal party income declined at a time of roaring inflation. This problem affected the other parties, but because the Liberals started from such a small financial base, the impact was felt more strongly. Jeremy Thorpe had been a remarkably successful fund-raiser, securing large amounts from Jack Hayward, a Bahamas-based millionaire, and others for his special seats fund which bypassed the official party accounts. Mr Thorpe refused to disclose his sources, citing the donors' wish to remain anonymous. However, this sort of financing was wound down after 1974, and the whiff of scandal attached to it as the Thorpe affair became public, together with the police investigations into the Hayward money, further handicapped the party's tasks of raising funds. In fact, as a special party committee appointed in 1978 duly reported, these funds had been largely spent on advertising and installing the TV link to Barnstaple. But by 1978 the party was only raising around £100,000 per annum for its central operations. In addition the Rowntree Trust gave substantial sums to various organisations, officers and organisations of the party. In early 1977 Hugh Jones, together with Clement Freud, who had just become chairman of the Finance and Administration Board, began a concerted effort to pull the party back from bankruptcy, and by tight budgetting and energetic fund-raising they succeeded.

The party did have one infusion of funds. In 1975 the government arranged for some money to be allocated to the opposition parties in parliament for research and administrative purposes.[3] The £30,000 at the disposal of the Liberal MPs strengthened their hand in relation to the rest of the party. Although the

[3] This 'Short money' (as it was known after the Lord President who introduced the scheme) substantially added to the influence of the parliamentary element in all the minor parties. A parliamentary question on February 6, 1979 revealed that a total of £813,660 had been paid to opposition parliamentary parties. This sum was divided: Conservatives £615,000; Liberals £136,259; SNP £39,762; Plaid Cymru £9,557; UUUP £7,875; SDLP £5,207.

party never wavered from a broad front strategy of fighting elections, and aimed at contesting over 500 seats, the Rowntree money was extremely important in making possible the assurances that the 100 or so most struggling associations needed to field a candidate.

The Liberals, with their traditional emphasis on participation, had set out to be pioneers of community politics and in a few places, notably Liverpool, they continued to be in the forefront of the movement. As Diagram 1 shows their one advance in a by-election in 1975–8 was in Newcastle Central, where an activist local councillor raised the party's vote from 12% in 1974 to 29% in November 1976. But community politics became less fashionable and earned the party fewer and fewer headlines. In another direction they were relieved to get less publicity: the Young Liberals made less stir, especially after Peter Hain finally switched from Liberal to Labour.

Between 1974 and 1976 Jeremy Thorpe's fortunes fluctuated wildly. During 1975 there were several muted complaints about his failure to provide leadership and a clear sense of direction. Cyril Smith resigned as Chief Whip in protest. But two revelations on January 29, 1976 seriously undermined his position. The long delayed Department of Trade and Industry report on the collapse of the London & Counties Securities fringe bank, of which he had been a director, was published. Its criticisms of the company's malpractices cast doubts on his judgment. More sensationally, the male model, Norman Scott, used the cover of the courts to allege that he had had a homosexual relationship with Mr Thorpe. This charge had circulated in senior Liberal quarters for a number of years but it had not been believed. Mr Thorpe promptly denied the allegation.

In the following months, however, there were further allegations of hush money, and even murder attempts. Press interest in the case was intense and in May Mr Thorpe reluctantly resigned. It was later revealed that he had promised parliamentary colleagues in 1971 that he would resign if the Scott charges were made public and embarrassed the party. Unfortunately the affair hung fire for a further 2½ years. It reached a further stage in August 1978 with the former leader and three others being charged with conspiracy to murder Norman Scott. To the chagrin of parliamentary colleagues he remained a candidate for parliament, and even visited the September party conference,

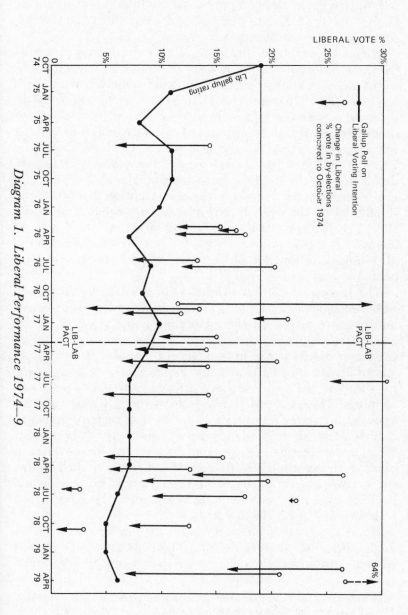

Diagram 1. Liberal Performance 1974–9

stealing the headlines. On December 13, 1978 he was committed for trial at the end of a prolonged and fully-reported hearing in the Minehead Magistrates Court, during which many sensational and lurid allegations were made.[4]

The party was, by coincidence, already considering proposals for the election of the future leader by the whole membership of the party. A hastily convened Special Assembly in Manchester on June 12, 1976 approved a new system under which candidates, who had to be MPs, were to be nominated by at least three other Liberal MPs, and constituencies would cast a vote weighted for the votes gained at the last general election. Given the nature of Liberal electoral strength, the voting was heavily dominated by the south of England. The Liberals were the first major British party to break with the convention that MPs alone should decide the issue of the leadership, though between 1975 and 1976 the three main parties had either reformed or were about to re-examine their system for electing the party leader. Mr Grimond returned as an acting leader while the election was held.

The leadership contest offered a constrast of styles, though not of ideology or even political strategy. John Pardoe promised an aggressive attack on the established political system, while David Steel emphasised his willingness to co-operate with one of the major parties in the hope of getting desirable reforms. John Pardoe had a firm base with the activists, and was supported by most of the regional party officers and leading executive members. However, his penchant for striking phrases and his knockabout style (referring to himself as a bastard) added to doubts about his political judgment. David Steel had been Chief Whip under Jeremy Thorpe, and had shown his qualities in piloting the Abortion Law Reform Act of 1967. Though lacking the campaigning braggadocio of John Pardoe, his serious and cautious tone impressed the bulk of the party. He beat Pardoe by a majority of 12,546 to 7,032.

David Steel was a political 'loner'. In this he resembled his predecessor. But whereas Mr Thorpe tended to surround himself with an entourage (a colleague compared him to a medieval

---

[4] The full trial of Mr Thorpe and three others did not begin until May 7, 1979. On June 22 they were all acquitted on all charges. See L. Chester et. al, *Jeremy Thorpe*, (London, 1979), for a description of the trial and its background.

monarch practising court politics with access depending more upon flattery than upon formal position), Mr Steel was prepared to consult with elected office holders. Gruffydd Evans (Lord Evans of Claughton) and Geoffrey Tordoff were listened to and some formerly influential figures such as Lord Chitnis and Richard Holme became important again. But there was never any doubt that David Steel made his own decisions. He was less exciting as a leader than Jeremy Thorpe or Jo Grimond, but he proved a more skilful committee man and he did supply a clear and consistent sense of direction. Mr Steel had never disguised his impatience with those Liberals who refused to countenance coalition or co-operation with another party. He regarded it as a logical outcome of electoral reform and multi-partism, and his willingness to make a deal with another party in suitable circumstances had long been clear. This had been a major theme of his leadership campaign in 1976 and he could, with justice, regard his election as a mandate for attempting a pact.

Liberal MPs felt some relief that the party did not embark on enlarging its array of policies as it had under Jo Grimond. David Steel was more concerned with influencing the government of the day than with acting as a brains trust for other political parties. The main policy body was the Standing Committee, elected by the Council, MPs and Liberal candidates. Its constitution gave it more of a parliamentary than an activist orientation. By tradition the chairman was a Liberal MP, elected by his colleagues. John Pardoe, who had been an energetic chairman of the Standing Committee, resigned soon after his defeat in the leadership contest. He was succeeded by Richard Wainwright who proved less interested in pushing particular issues.

During the early stages of the parliament the Liberals opposed much of the Social Contract legislation in parliament. They voted against the Employment Protection Act, the Dock Labour Bill, the Trade Union Law Reform Act and other measures. But once membership of the EEC was settled and the Labour party had an incomes policy, there was little doubt that the bulk of the MPs were more sympathetic to the Labour party and wished to help it to bring devolution into effect.

However, there was no doubt that the Lib-Lab Pact of March 1977 came as a surprise to many in the party (see p. 35). In return for consultation with the government the Liberal MPs agreed to support ministers on confidence votes. The pact was agreed with little opposition in the party. The extra-parliamentary organisation voiced no strong objections when presented with a *fait accompli*. The consultative machinery which consisted of three ministers (Mr Foot, Mr Rees and Mr Cocks) and three Liberals (Mr Pardoe, Mr Hooson and Mr Beith) came into operation when ministers and their Liberal shadows could not agree, with a Callaghan/Steel summit occasionally invoked as a final court of appeal. It certainly gave Liberal MPs a taste of government and most of them enjoyed it. Serious difficulties only arose between Mr Benn and Mr Penhaligon over energy questions and, still more, between Mr Healey and Mr Pardoe over a wide range of economic issues. In July 1977, the MPs renewed the pact with little consultation with the party in the country. By the autumn Assembly, however, dissatisfaction over the meagre legislative product and over the mounting disasters in by-elections led to attacks on the continuation of the pact, and Cyril Smith resigned as a parliamentary spokesman.

Critics of the pact — as well as some supporters — insisted that a substantial majority of Labour MPs should vote for the regional list system at the forthcoming vote on the direct elections bill, as a condition of continued support for the government. On December 15, 1977, the day after the defeat of the regional list system, the Liberal MPs only agreed, on a straw poll, to continue the pact by a 6–4 majority. Had the MPs voted to withdraw from the pact it was understood that David Steel would resign, because his strategy had been disowned. The special assembly which met at Blackpool in January 1978 accepted this decision, but made clear its opposition to continuing the pact after the summer of 1978 unless much better terms could be delivered. David Steel wanted either PR for the Scottish Assembly elections or a referendum on PR for Westminster. Mr Callaghan was unable to deliver either, and the pact was terminated in August 1978. The Liberals then had a minimum period to detach themselves and to regain their independence with a view to fighting an autumn election.

The Liberals could boast of some gains from the pact, though it could be argued from a Labour standpoint that nothing had been conceded that would not have been done anyway. Some Labour ministers expressed their surprise that the Liberals had allowed themselves to be bought off so easily. The Liberals could point to profit sharing and help for small businesses as a furtherance of Liberal ideals, though the 5½p reduction on petrol and the 1p off income tax both flowed from the government's minority position in parliament. The Liberals did not get proportional representation or tax powers for the Scottish assembly. It is true that David Steel himself rarely pointed to the specific measures; he preferred the loftier argument that the pact had come about because the national interest required a stable government which would allow the reduction of inflation. He also boasted of having done more to ensure Labour moderation than the Conservatives had ever done.

Yet the pact had tested the party; it had remained fairly united, although Cyril Smith voiced eloquent opposition to the pact at the 1977 Assembly, Mr Grimond remained a ruminative sceptic, and a minority throughout the party continued to express disapproval. By the summer of 1978 there was no incentive for Liberals to maintain the pact, given Mr Callaghan's understandable inability to deliver proportional representation.

The endless Liberal argument over political strategy was settled only briefly by the situation that the MPs found themselves faced with in March 1977. Thereafter the debate centred on three elements. First, the party had to decide whether it was going to be even-handed between the Conservative and Labour parties. It was difficult to do this because of the strong anti-Conservative feelings of many of the party's activists. These were fuelled by the Conservatives' increasingly explicit rejection of devolution, their encouragement of free collective bargaining, and some of their leader's statements on Ulster and immigration – as well as by Mrs Thatcher's abrasive style. At the same time there were those like Jo Grimond who believed that any serious prospect of realignment depended on a break-up of the Labour party, and that the Liberals had to conduct themselves in such a way as to expedite this. In retrospect, Mr Grimond and others doubted that the pact had actually helped this long term goal.

A second factor depended upon electoral reform. Traditionally electoral reform had been advanced by Liberals in the interests of providing a more representative parliament, and strengthening the Liberal party. By 1974, however, a wider body of opinion objected to the adversary politics of the two-party system and came round to favour electoral reform in the interest of better government. Critics pointed to the way in which one-party governments, with a shrinking minority of votes, enjoyed full power to enact and repeal their predecessors' legislation. It was now being argued that moderate policies would be encouraged by electoral reform and coalition government.[5] The 1974 parliament saw five votes on the principle of proportional representation (two on the electoral system for the Scottish and Welsh assemblies, one on the direct elections to the European parliament, and two on the Lords' amendments to the two assembly bills) and ironically more Conservative MPs proved themselves consistent supporters of electoral reform than Labour MPs.

Finally the party had learned something from the experience of the pact. The 1978 Conference agreed on the party's strategy for future pact or coalition occasions: the party would only enter an agreement if the governing party gave cast-iron guarantees about electoral reform (a promise of legislation, not just a promise of a Speaker's Conference) and the arrangements must be endorsed by the MPs, as distinct from the leaders, of both parties.

In common with the other parties, the Liberals were surprised by Mr Callaghan's decision not to have an election in 1978, but at least the delay gave them a further chance to distance them-

---

[5] S. Finer, ed. *Adversary Politics and Electoral Reform*, (London, 1975) and *Hansard Society Commission on Electoral Reform*, (London, 1976). See the *Economist*, (May 13, 1978), for an ORC poll conducted for the Campaign for Electoral Reform.

The strategic position of the Liberals was nicely illustrated in a letter from Jeremy Thorpe to Jack Hayward, written on November 28, 1974, and quoted in full during the Thorpe committal hearings on November 24, 1978:

'As you know in February we soared from two million to six million and last time, albeit on a smaller turnout, held at 5¾ million. On a proportional representation system that would have given us 116 MPs.

'The hopeful thing is that we have (except for Ted, who is going anyway) convinced some Tories [in the margin Mr Thorpe sketched the names of Edward du Cann and William Whitelaw] that we are here for good and many accept (a) that the Labour Party will never and has never polled 50 per cent or more of the votes but (b) under the present electoral system 39 per cent of the votes can and has given one party a majority. Ludicrously, Labour polled 29 per cent of the total electorate, had they all turned out. We now have a group of prominent Tory MPs in favour of announcing it well before the next election. Eight of us (i.e. Liberals) are going to see those companies who have been the Tory Party's chief backers financially and suggest that they pressurize the Tories to come round in favour of electoral reform by the next general election since (a) it would mean that there would never again be a socialist majority in its own right and (b) it gives Liberals next time a powerful incentive to return a Tory MP where no Liberal was standing or where his chances were remote.

'Marks and Spencer are the first converts!'

selves from Labour. In the first three months of 1979, as the government's anti-inflation policy and its support in the country collapsed, it was the Conservatives, not the Liberals, who profited from the public anger. Mr Steel devoted a widely-acclaimed television broadcast to the industrial relations chaos on January 31, and it prompted a brief Liberal upsurge in the polls. But the Liberal appeal to let them exercise a moderating influence on the other parties showed small sign of taking hold. In the winter of 1978–79, the Liberals had little to encourage them as they pursued their declared policy of bringing about an election as soon as possible.

6 The Scottish Dimension

by William Miller[1]

In recent years politics in Scotland and England have developed along different paths. While Labour and the Conservatives have remained major parties in Scotland, their hegemony has been challenged and the balance between them has shifted radically. The SNP took over 30% of the vote in 1974 before falling back to 17% in 1979. But in another respect 1979 represented a major extension of Scottish/English differences for there was a 21% gap between the Conservative/Labour margin in Scotland and England.[2] From 1945 to 1955 the Labour/Conservative balance had been much the same on both sides of the border and, although Labour enjoyed a modest advantage in Scotland from 1959 to 1974, 1979 was quite unlike anything that had gone before.

At Westminster, the 1974–9 parliament was dominated by efforts to come to grips with the Scottish problem. London politicians who came north of the border quickly sensed a different political climate in Scotland. However, the Scottish dimension remained elusive, ignored by the English electorate, recognised but scarcely understood by English politicians, and perhaps something of a mystery to the Scots themselves.

The basic problem was that Scottish politics were not purely Scottish in the sense that politics in England are almost exclusively English and politics in Ulster almost exclusively Irish. The Scottish dimension coexisted rather uneasily with a British dimension. With some variations in attitude or emphasis, Scots worried about the same issues and personalities as other Britons:

---

[1] The author wishes to thank Kevin Allen, Hugh Berrington, David Martin, Kate Stephen, David Simpson, Richard Rose and Alf Young for their comments on earlier drafts of this chapter. For a fuller discussion see W. Miller, *The End of British Politics*, (Oxford, 1980).

[2]

	Con %	Lab %	Con lead %
Scotland	31	42	−11
England	47	37	+10
		Difference	21

prices, jobs, Mrs Thatcher, the unions, even Saatchi and Saatchi. So this is not the only Scottish chapter in this book; they all apply to Scotland.

When the election finally came, it was a remarkably British affair in Scotland (See p. 309–11). The April 1979 campaign was more marked by the absence of Scottish issues and personalities than by their presence. There was nothing in the campaign itself to explain the enormous discrepancy between Scots and English voting patterns.

From 1974 to 1979 the main issue on the Scottish dimension was the battle over the Scotland Act. Gone were the days when the principal Scottish issue had been the supply of 'goodies for Scotland', such as landing rights at Prestwick, the Forth Bridge, a motorway, or some special help for a factory or an industry. The Scotland Act was exceptionally Scottish; it applied to the whole of Scotland, no more and no less, and it touched what had become the nation's most significant defining characteristic – its separate system of laws and public administration. Hence it was far more of a national issue than quarrels over EEC membership or help for steel or fishing.

The Scotland Act did not represent sovereign independence. Although it offered a substantial measure of self-government by Scots elected in Scotland, many of the proposed Assembly's actions would be subject to scrutiny, veto and parliamentary tolerance. Was it devolution? At first, supporters in all parties claimed it was 'the only devolution on offer'. The argument ran, 'Support devolution and you must logically support the Act; oppose the Act and you oppose devolution.' By 1979, however, the issue was no longer devolution but the Labour government's Scotland Act, firmly established as binding Labour policy and resolutely opposed by the Conservatives: 'Support Labour and you must logically support the Act, oppose the Act and you could bring down the government.' Even so committed a devolutionist as Lord Home could bring himself to oppose the Act on these terms.

This transformation from identification with the concept of devolution to identification with the Labour party reduced popular support for the principle but increased support for the party since devolution was not only popular in itself, but Labour's struggle to enact devolution was a measure of its concern for Scotland.

Since there is a powerful British dimension to Scottish politics, much of the raw trend in Scottish party popularity must be explained by British factors. The 1978/9 'winter of discontent', for example, produced a large drop in Mr Callaghan's popularity and a large swing from Labour to Conservative on both sides of the border. Conversely, comparative measures of popularity in Scotland and England are required to gauge the significance of the Scottish dimension. Diagram 1 shows the trends in both the level of SNP support, and the difference between the Conservative lead over Labour in Scotland and England.

The 1974 elections convinced many doubters that there really was something special about Scottish politics. Even the SNP's 22% share of the vote in February could be discounted as equivalent to the English third party (i.e. Liberal) vote at that time, but in October, the English Liberal vote declined while the SNP rose to over 30%.

Monthly polls showed SNP support falling throughout 1975 but leaping to a peak of 37% in December, apparently in response to the White Paper on devolution: *Our Changing Democracy* (Cmnd 6348). After the initial explosive reaction to this document, support for the SNP subsided till the summer of 1976. Perhaps it was coincidence, but as soon as Tam Dalyell and 70 Labour MPs published their letter threatening to vote against a guillotine motion on the devolution bill, support started to flow back to the SNP and its popularity hit a second peak just after the guillotine defeat on February 22, 1977. During the passage of the second devolution bill into an Act, the SNP suffered another long decline, particularly sharp in the four months leading up to the Royal Assent on July 31, 1978. Once the Act was on the statute book SNP support stayed near to 20%.

The data appeared to fit the theory that SNP support declined when Labour fulfilled its devolution promises and increased when Labour appeared to renege. SNP leaders consciously

---

Notes: (1) The gap between Scottish and English Conservative leads is calculated from 4 statistics — the Conservative and Labour percentages in Scotland and England, and hence is subject to large sampling errors. (2) Poll estimates of this gap are underestimates since I have used the Gallup GB percentages for English party preferences. (3) Scottish figures are from all known polls, mainly by System Three.

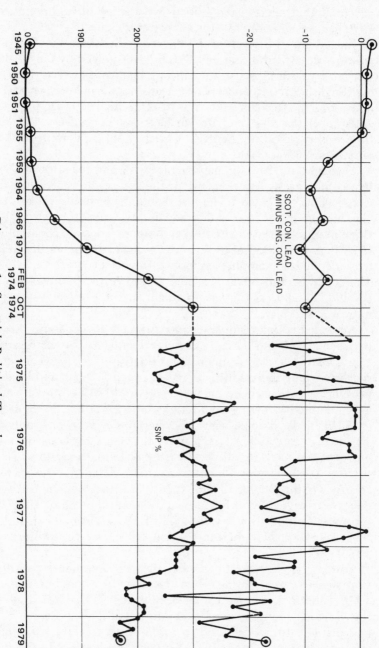

Diagram 1. Scottish Political Trends

accepted that theory and hoped for a surge of support in the 1979 general election; but the surge never came.

Judged by the level of SNP voting, Scotland moved back towards the British norm in 1979, but not judged by our second indicator of the Scottish dimension. The gap between Scottish and English Labour/Conservative leads was 6% in February 1974, and 10% in October, but up to 21% in 1979. Despite the collapse of the SNP, and British factors encouraging a swing to the Conservatives, the Scottish Tories could only improve their vote from 25% to 31%.

Throughout 1975 the gap averaged 8% and for most of 1976 it was much less than that. But at the end of the year, when the Conservatives decided to oppose Labour's devolution plans, the gap increased to 12% and gradually widened thereafter. For three months at the end of 1977 it disappeared, and in September 1978 it touched 35%; but both these departures from the trend may be due to sampling errors or imperfect synchronisation. The general trend towards a 25% gap by April 1979 was unmistakable. Finally, in the last fortnight of the campaign, the gap narrowed sharply.

Neither Scotland nor England enjoyed an economic boom between 1974 and 1979. But several indicators — car registrations, GDP per capita, unemployment rates and wage rates — suggested that the traditional gap between Scottish and English prosperity narrowed in the years up to 1976 before widening again. Publicity was given to two statistics. First, the Scottish level of male manual earnings, popularly known simply as 'earnings', rose in 1975 to 2% above the figure for Great Britain, but dropped back steadily thereafter. Second, the ratio of Scottish to English unemployment rates, the so-called 'unemployment relative': in the 1950s and 1960s Scottish unemployment had been over twice as high as in England and even at the end of 1972 the ratio stood at 1.7; but by the end of 1975 it was down to less than 1.2, though it increased again to 1.4 by the summer of 1979.

Politically, it is relevant to ask what the government's contribution was towards closing, then opening the economic gap. In 1974 Labour made two claims about jobs: it had just doubled the Regional Employment Premium (REP), which the Tories had planned to abolish, and it proposed to transfer 7,000 civil service jobs from England to Scotland. In the event the civil service jobs never materialised and REP was abolished in the wake of the IMF loan crisis. On the credit side, Labour produced a battery of Special Employment Measures (SEM). It is not at all clear whether the net effect of these changes increased or decreased the number of jobs in Scotland. Since REP statistics were given in cash terms, and SEMs in numbers of jobs affected, they were not strictly comparable. But they showed that Scotland's share of REP was two or three times as large as its share of SEM.

Sometimes election results must be explained by the events of the campaign, the few weeks or even days before the vote. But the trends in Diagram 1 show that Scotland's special political behaviour in 1979 is to be explained by what happened long before the official campaign opened. The campaign itself helped to make the Scottish results less, rather than more special.

Economic trends also fail to match the party trends in Diagram 1. In relative national terms at least, Labour scored its great gains over both the Conservatives and the SNP in 1977, and especially in 1978 when the gap between Scottish and English prosperity was beginning to open up again.

Leading politicians, usually non-Scots such as Ted Short, Michael Foot, Jeremy Thorpe or Roy Jenkins, warned of another Ireland if Westminster went back on its promise of a Scottish Assembly, but there was nothing comparable to the IRA. Reaction to the guillotine defeat in 1977 was almost reassuringly mild and, such as it was, it was expressed in opinion polls and District Council elections, not violence.

Terrorism in Scotland ran at an even lower level than in England and mainly stemmed from UVF and UDA attempts to obtain supplies for use outside Scotland. When nationalist violence did occur it was promptly and vehemently denounced by spokesmen for the SNP, and SNP members were expelled by the party if convicted by the courts. Two groups — one known as the APG (Army of the Provisional Government), the other as the Tartan Army — robbed the Royal Bank and bombed power lines, oil pipelines, the railways and the Glasgow office of the Bank of England, but their activities were on a very small scale and they were quickly infiltrated by the Special Branch of the police.

Under cover of the general battle over devolution, there was one lasting victory for nationalism. Labour's plan for devolution was to transfer powers from the Secretary of State to the new, directly elected Assembly. To justify his status in Cabinet and in Scotland, he had to have new functions. Informally he had long been regarded as responsible for all government in Scotland but he lacked the power, particularly on industrial matters, to match this responsibility. In December 1975, Harold Wilson announced that powers for selective discretionary aid to industry would be transferred from the Department of Industry to the Scottish Office. In the event the Scottish Office also acquired the whole of the Department of Industry's Office for Scotland, civil servants and all. Since Labour's devolution plans were never implemented, the Scottish Office ended by gaining new industry powers without any compensating loss.

Labour depended on Scotland. Without Scotland the party would have lost the election in 1964 and again in February 1974; and consequently have lost the opportunity to call the elections of 1966 and October 1974 in circumstances of its choosing. Many felt that, without Scotland, Labour would have been permanently out of government since 1951. Moreover, Labour's 40 Scottish seats after February (41 after October 1974) were hostages for good behaviour in a way that the party's 38 Yorkshire seats were not. The challenger in almost all Labour's Scottish marginals was the SNP, not the Conservatives, and all the evidence suggested that voters were less reluctant to switch to (and from) the SNP than between Labour and Conservative. Labour had cause both to thank and fear the Scots.

Much of the progress towards the Scotland Act can thus be seen as a dialogue between Labour and the Scottish people, in which Labour displayed a genuine sympathy for Scottish aspirations, coupled with an equally genuine fear of losing a significant part of its Westminster majority. Labour adopted devolution to appease its friends, the Scots, not its enemies, the SNP.

On October 31 1973 the Kilbrandon Commission reported in favour of some form of devolution for Scotland. A Labour government had set up the Commission but the party, in evidence to it, had advised against devolution. But within days of the February 1974 election and the SNP's leap forward, Labour's Scottish Executive and Conference had accepted a cautiously pro-devolution resolution. Then in June a sparsely attended meeting of the Executive voted 6 to 5 against devolution (the Executive had 29 members), and to settle the matter in an authoritative way the British NEC issued instructions for a special Scottish conference. It met at the Cooperative Halls, Dalintober Street, Glasgow in mid-August and voted over-whelmingly for a 'directly elected Assembly with legislative powers'. This proposal went into the UK manifesto and formed the centrepiece of Labour's autumn campaign in Scotland. Opting out of the British Labour broadcasts, the party described the Assembly on Scottish TV as a 'parliament' with 'powers of taxation' and 'control of the Scottish Development Agency'. 'Primed by North Sea Oil' it would get 'trade and industry' powers. After Dalintober and the autumn election campaign, the party in Scotland could not easily forget about devolution. Yet the topic ran to only twelve lines in the British manifesto, which omitted the term 'legislative', and the British conference had never discussed the matter.

Support for the SNP dropped to only 22% during the EEC referendum campaign, then made a modest recovery in the autumn of 1975. But the polls were eclipsed by a spectacular string of SNP victories in local government by-elections. In normal times local by-elections do not make headlines, but nationwide council elections were not due until 1977 and, as it turned out, no parliamentary by-elections came up before 1978. Regular monthly polls of Scottish opinion only began in 1974 and had not yet acquired the respect which Gallup and others enjoy as barometers of British opinion (see p. 266). At a time when public opinion was regularly quoted as the basis for con-stitutional change, any indicators of popular attitudes, including local government by-elections, were front page news.

Stephen Maxwell began the series on September 9, 1975, by taking a ward on the outskirts of Edinburgh with a swing of 22% which seemed impressive enough at the time though swings up to double that size were recorded later. A week after this SNP victory, Labour's Home Policy Committee, which included pro-devolutionists Judith Hart and Alex Kitson, declared it was 'worried sick' about Scotland. Twice in the next two months the Scottish Executive reminded Labour MPs that the Assembly was a manifesto commitment, and a meeting of the Scottish Labour group attended by 32 of the 41 MPs unani-mously reaffirmed that commitment.

Throughout 1975 moves were made within the Labour Party

to extend the devolution commitment. The Scottish Labour Conference, in March, only narrowly defeated a resolution calling for tax, trade and industry powers for the Assembly. The vote was 341,000 in favour and 353,000 against. When the White Paper, *Our Changing Democracy* (Cmnd 6348), was published at the end of November it received an almost uniformly bad press: it offered no industrial powers and no tax powers except the unusable right to put a surcharge on local rates. But its worst feature was its emphasis on restricting and confining the Assembly. Even Labour's Scottish Executive noted: 'It is unfortunate, and perhaps unintentional, that the reserve and veto powers have been apparently over-emphasised in the White Paper,' and concluded, 'we do not believe there should be any reserve powers written into the Devolution Bill and suggest that the only right of veto on Assembly legislation should be the overriding power of an Act of the UK Parliament.' Three months later this statement was adopted by the 1976 Conference.

Jim Sillars, MP for S. Ayr, suggested a separate Scottish Labour Party (SLP) as early as November 1974, and again when the EEC referendum result was declared. Now he resigned from the executive along with Dan Skene. Together with Alex Neil, the party's Scottish Research Officer, John Robertson, MP for Paisley, and a number of others they formed the SLP. Labour was not looking to make martyrs, and the two SLP MPs were left to resign the Labour whip in due course. The new party enjoyed a brief honeymoon in the opinion polls, but never made much impact in elections.[3]

The White Paper had many enemies, though they disagreed amongst themselves as to its faults. William Ross himself attacked the governor-general role assigned to him in the White Paper, while consigning the SLP rebels to a 'special hell', but he warned English Labour MPs 'you can say goodbye — if you do not agree with this White Paper — to the Labour Party in Scotland and possibly to Willie Ross as well.' From now on the plan was to make mainly cosmetic changes to the proposals to reduce the insult to Scotland, while threatening English Labour backbenchers with the wrath of Scotland should they obstruct the government. In England the air was full of talk about another

[3] See H. Drucker, *Breakaway: The Scottish Labour Party*, (Edinburgh, 1978).

Ireland, about the break-up of the United Kingdom and, far worse, the end of Labour governments for a generation or more.

When Mr Wilson resigned as leader, William Ross joined him in retirement and was replaced as Secretary of State by his deputy, Bruce Millan. Michael Foot, the new devolution minister, outlined a package of concessions designed to placate Scottish feelings, and a poll showed a swing from the SNP to Labour compared with 1974. It was the only poll between the 1975 White Paper and the passage of the guillotine on the Scotland Bill at the end of 1977 to show a pro-Labour swing. A fortnight later Tam Dalyell sent Mr Foot a letter on the devolution bill signed by 70 Labour MPs, declaring 'We could not support a guillotine motion.' The polls drifted back to the SNP.

In the autumn of 1976 Mr Millan told the British Labour Conference, 'If we were to renege on devolution now I do not believe the Labour Party would be a credible force at the next General Election.' Helped by the concession of a referendum before implementing devolution, Foot got conference to back the Assembly proposals by a majority of 6 to 1. At last the whole British Labour party was committed to Scottish devolution.

The government had a Commons majority of 45 on the principle of the Scotland and Wales Bill on December 16, 1976. 30 Labour members abstained and ten voted with the Conservatives — Tam Dalyell being the only Scot amongst them. But the bill made little headway in committee and on February 22, 1977 the government lost a timetable motion by 29 votes. Tam Dalyell and Willie Hamilton were the only Scots amongst the 22 Labour MPs who voted against the guillotine. Although 11 Liberals voted against the government, it was clearly Labour votes which defeated the guillotine. A disciplined and loyal Labour party would have had a majority of around 30. The government lacked the nerve to make devolution an issue of confidence.

Blood did not run on Scottish streets. The grim warnings by English advocates of devolution about another Ireland proved false. But at the District Council elections in May Labour lost 129 seats and the SNP gained 107. Half-a-dozen districts fell to the SNP and Labour even lost control of Glasgow.

Mr Callaghan edged slowly towards making devolution an issue of confidence. Bribes accompanied the threats. Northern

Labour MPs felt especially threatened, and were particularly well organised in their opposition to devolution; but in 1977 their region was showered with government aid.[4]

In November the government brought devolution back to the Commons, this time in the shape of two separate bills, one for Scotland and another for Wales. The Scotland Bill had a majority of 44 on principle, and 26 on the guillotine. Only 11 Labour members voted against the principle, and 9 against the guillotine. Tam Dalyell was the lone Scot amongst them.

In February 1978 exactly a year after the first guillotine defeat, the Commons approved the details and sent the bill to the Lords. Success came only just in time, for three of Labour's Scottish MPs died in 1978. A year earlier three by-elections would certainly have cost Labour three seats in parliament, and very probably induced a surge in SNP support such as followed the Hamilton by-election in 1967 and the Govan one in 1973. But in 1978 Labour won all three — Garscadden, Hamilton and Berwick — the last two with increased majorities (see p. 388—9).

The Scotland Act received the Royal Assent on July 31, 1978 and for the rest of the year monthly polls averaged Labour 50%, Conservative 26%, SNP 19% and Liberals 4%, with remarkably little month-to-month variation. John Smith, who had guided the Bill through the Commons, was appointed Trade Secretary and became the youngest member of the cabinet. Perseverance was rewarded.

Yet devolutionists praised the Labour government in 1978 for enacting something not essentially different from the proposals in the much abused White Paper of 1975. Though the Scotland Act was a significant improvement on the White Paper it did not include the tax powers, the trade and industry powers, nor the freedom from veto which had been powers demanded in 1975 and 1976. That did not mean the Act was riddled with 'design faults', as Tam Dalyell claimed, but it showed how much the balance of forces had changed since the guillotine defeat in February 1977.[5] The debate was no longer about whether to go beyond Labour's 1974 manifesto, but whether to honour it.

---

[4] For the Northern reaction against Scottish devolution see R. Guthrie and Iain McLean, 'Another Part of the Periphery', *Parliamentary Affairs*, (Spring, 1978).
[5] For a review of the provisions of the Scotland Act and the likely workings of its proposed Assembly see D. I. Mackay ed. *Scotland: the Framework for Change*, (Edinburgh, 1979). See also V. Bogdanor, *Devolution*, (Oxford, 1979).

The Conservatives were in a different position. For them, unlike Labour, the issue was symbolic, even spiritual. They were, like the SNP, nationalists; but they were British nationalists. Yet 30 years earlier their basic principles had not prevented them using a ferociously Scottish nationalist rhetoric in their attack on socialism. 'Until the Socialist government is removed neither Scotland nor Wales will be able to strike away the fetters of centralisation and be free to develop their own way of life', said their 1950 manifesto.

Edward Heath therefore had a precedent of a kind for his famous Declaration of Perth in 1968. The Heath/Home plan for devolution was included in the 1970 Scottish manifesto, but never emerged as legislation and was rejected by the 1973 Scottish Conference. In response to Labour's initiatives the 1974 Conference reaffirmed support for the principle of devolution, and the October manifesto proposed an Assembly indirectly elected by the regional councils. Shortly after the defeat in October, the Shadow Secretary of State, Alick Buchanan-Smith, issued a statement committing his party to an elected Assembly. Mrs Thatcher, the new party leader, told a rally in Glasgow City Hall that 'an Assembly must be a top priority to ensure that more decisions affecting Scotland are taken in Scotland by Scotsmen.'

But divisions gradually appeared. By November 1975 the 16 Conservative MPs were split into three roughly equal groups: one for devolution, one against, the third undecided. Scottish Conservatives held their version of Dalintober in the Music Hall, Edinburgh in January 1976. By 103 votes to 60 they approved Malcolm Rifkind's resolution accepting an elected assembly but rejecting the government's proposals as 'unworkable'. Mr Rifkind was one of the handful of leading Conservatives who actively campaigned in favour of the Labour government's Scotland Act in the 1979 referendum. A debate on devolution at the normal annual Conference in May ended in a near-riot, but the chairman declared the Music Hall policy had been carried on a show of hands.

With the party in Scotland so divided over devolution, the instincts of Unionism and the habits of parliamentary opposition produced a drift towards simple opposition to Labour's proposals; a policy defined by what it was not. At the time it appeared a weakness but it was turned into a tactical advantage during the referendum campaign.

Mrs Thatcher issued a three-line whip against the principle of the Scotland and Wales Bill in December 1976, but only 5 of her 16 Scottish MPs obeyed it. She accepted the resignations of her front-bench spokesmen on Scottish Affairs, Alick Buchanan-Smith and Malcolm Rifkind, but rejected the proffered resignations of Scots MPs who were spokesmen on other matters. Teddy Taylor became the new Shadow Secretary of State. At the 1977 Conference Mrs Thatcher avoided any reference to devolution and Francis Pym described the Assembly commitment as 'in a sense, inoperative'. After their flurry of resignations, Scots Conservatives dropped back into line and only one voted for the essential guillotine motion on either devolution bill.

The SNP accepted the Scotland Act reluctantly. After all, it had been devised to destroy them. The party stood for full sovereign independence but accepted devolution as a useful step in the right direction. Did it help or hinder the moves towards devolution? The electorate's threat of voting SNP must be seen as one of the greatest influences towards devolution, and actual SNP votes made the threat of still more SNP votes both more credible and dangerous. But did the SNP as a party achieve by its actions anything more than the electorate achieved by voting for it?

In March 1974 SNP MPs began by rejecting all pacts and forcing a vote of confidence when Mr Wilson's government was only a fortnight old. Every year thereafter they voted against the government in confidence motions. Their votes failed to carry the guillotine on the Scotland and Wales Bill. The guillotine on the Scotland Bill and the votes of principle on both bills would have succeeded even if the SNP members had switched sides and opposed them. Their difficulty was not an intransigent refusal to compromise nationalist ideology — they did that often enough — but the inevitable weakness of a party of 11 trying to manipulate a party of over 300.

There were always those within the SNP who argued that the party should reject devolution even as a first step, and insist on the 'purist' demand for immediate sovereign independence. The strength of this faction depended on one of two arguments; a high level of SNP support in the polls, or evidence that the government would renege on devolution; there was no point in accepting something that was not on offer.

In the midst of the public reaction to the 1975 White Paper, when SNP support had touched 37%, the Motherwell Conference reaffirmed the party's welcome for the Assembly proposals, but only by a margin of 594 to 425 – a victory for the gradualists, but much less decisive than they would have expected in other circumstances. Their next Conference met shortly after the 1977 guillotine defeat and even the gradualists were provoked into hard line speeches by a combination of disappointed hopes on devolution and elation over the SNP's standing in the polls. It was a natural reaction but it left Labour in an undisputed position as the only party of devolution when the government actually pushed the Scotland Bill.

Next year the SNP met shortly after the Garscadden by-election defeat and just before Hamilton. Conference pointedly ignored devolution but passed a long resolution on the structure of government. It was a multi-purpose policy, listing 16 ministries, the first 11 of which it noted would be required under devolution. Margo Macdonald's election address in Hamilton headlined the slogan 'MAKE SURE of your Assembly', and added 'the Assembly, now dangerously at risk, is essential to force Scottish unemployment down and living standards up.' After the guillotine defeat she had told the 1977 Conference that 'the only choice facing Scots is the helplessness of the *status quo* or the hope that independence will bring'.

On January 25, 1978 (Burns Night) the Commons forced on the government two amendments to the Scotland Bill. These gave Orkney and Shetland the right to secede from the area governed by the Act and imposed the 40% rule which eventually destroyed both the Act and the Labour government.

The original purpose of the government's referendum concession in 1976 was to induce reluctant backbenchers to toe the party line on the Scotland and Wales Bill. With the separation of Scotland from Wales in the 1977 bills the referendum looked like being a mechanism for dropping Welsh devolution while securing the consent of even Welsh anti-devolutionists to devolution for Scotland alone. Until the 40% rule was passed, the referendum was a London matter without any significance within Scotland.

After the Act became law, there were still two hurdles before an Assembly could be set up. If, in the opinion of the Secretary of State, less than 40% of eligible Scots voted for the Act, he was required to lay a repeal order before parliament; otherwise he had to lay a commencement order before parliament.

A System Three poll in October 1978 confirmed that there was still a 2 to 1 majority in favour of the Act, but that meant the referendum turnout would have to be over 60% and if the 'No' campaigners made any headway it would involve participation at general election level. Mr Millan could perhaps discount some names from the electoral register as ineligible to vote — the dead for example — and declare himself satisfied with less than 40% of the register but, if he appeared unreasonably lax, parliament, though deprived of the opportunity to vote for repeal, could vote against the commencement order. Millan chose to make the minimum reasonable discount, postpone the referendum until the new register came into effect in mid-February 1979, and prepare to discredit the 40% rule, so that even if he had to present a repeal order to parliament he could successfully urge its rejection. March 1 was named as referendum day.

This strategy had advantages for the Labour party, for it put the SNP under pressure to replace the Liberals as a prop for the minority Labour government at Westminster. But it split the SNP. The majority of MPs wished to keep up the momentum towards devolution with an autumn referendum, and 9 of the 11 MPs reacted by voting against the government in the autumn confidence debates. In contrast, the majority of the party leadership in Scotland considered it vital to maintain Labour in office long enough to 'manage' the referendum.

SNP votes failed to bring down the government in 1978 but provided the margin necessary to defeat the pay sanctions policy on December 13 (see p. 120). The 'winter of discontent' that followed was an unfortunate background for any cause supported by the government. Labour refused, in its own words, to 'soil its hands' with a joint Labour/SNP campaign, and the party's devolution posters pictured Jim Callaghan superimposed on a massive 'Yes'. In the three months before the referendum, Gallup showed that throughout Britain a Labour lead of 5% turned into a Tory lead of 20% and Mr Callaghan's personal popularity dropped even more: in November 18% more were satisfied than dissatisfied with him as Prime Minister, but by February there were 25% more dissatisfied than satisfied. For a critical few weeks, the Prime Minister became a negative asset.

Labour fought as poor a campaign as it had in the EEC referendum. It was not at its best when campaigning for an idea rather than a class. Two of its most eloquent and forceful devolutionists had been lost through the defection of Jim Sillars and the death of John Mackintosh, and the Scottish Executive was known to contain some ardent anti-devolutionists. Government ministers had other problems than Scotland to attend to. But sheer incompetence also played its part. Before his death John Mackintosh had looked forward to turning the referendum into the simple gut question, 'Are you for Scotland or are you a grade A bastard?' Instead Labour's campaigners allowed it to turn into another simple question, 'Do you want more government?'

Tam Dalyell, the only Scots Labour MP consistently to oppose the government's plans in parliament, showed all the tenacity and flair that the party leadership lacked. He set up a travelling 'Yes versus No' circus with Jim Sillars. Though Mr Sillars was an excellent debater, he was a notorious defector from the party. So by appearing against him Tam Dalyell looked less of a rebel than he was. Tam Dalyell formed a 'Labour Vote No' organisation in an audacious and successful bid to associate the Labour name with an anti-Labour policy. While Labour hesitated to bring in the law by taking court action against this unauthorised use of the party name, Mr Dalyell took the party to court to prevent the screening of special party broadcasts on TV. Since three of the four leading parties were pro-devolution, three broadcasts would have urged a Yes vote. Tam Dalyell got a court order requiring two on each side. This would have meant as much television time for Mr Dalyell's 'Labour Vote No' group as for the Labour Party. So all broadcasts were cancelled. He took advantage of EEC pairing arrangements at Westminster to come to Scotland, not Europe. He wrote a staggering number of letters from the House of Commons to the myriad of local weekly papers and he lobbied the national media as persistently if less publicly. It was a magnificently single-minded and effective performance.

While Tam Dalyell and the public service strikers combined to free Labour supporters from the ties of party loyalty, Thatcher and Home used their party's lack of any specific devolution policy as a means of reinforcing Conservative loyalty. It has been claimed that the Yes side suffered from the contradictory arguments put forward by Labour and the SNP in support of a Yes vote, but there is clear evidence that the No side benefited from the contradictory arguments put forward by different Conservatives. In a well-publicised speech to Edinburgh University in mid-February, Lord Home declared: 'I should hesitate to vote No if I did not think that the parties will keep the devolution issue at the top of their priorities', but went on to advocate a No vote because the Scotland Act provided no tax powers, no proportional representation and no well-defined formula for separating Scottish and English business at Westminster. BBC Scotland was forced into rescheduling its programmes to include a set-piece interview with Lord Home to give this argument more publicity, and on the day before the vote the press printed a short message from Mrs Thatcher which began with the pledge 'A No vote does not mean the devolution question will be buried.'

Obviously any Conservative anti-devolutionist would vote against any Labour devolution plan. The Thatcher/Home strategy was to get even the Conservative pro-devolutionists to vote against it also and the strategy proved unexpectedly successful.

Support for devolution appeared to decline slightly between 1970 and 1974, but with every party advocating it, support went up again between 1974 and 1975. Support dropped over the winter of 1976–7 and suffered a further decline between then and the referendum, but rose slightly just after the referendum. A detailed comparison of the first and last *Scotsman* series of questions is instructive. They were put in April 1974 and just after the 1979 referendum. The dividing line between those who wanted independence, a federal system or a directly elected Assembly and those who wanted none of these scarcely changed. But support for a federal system almost doubled, while the numbers who wanted more and less extreme change declined. Similarly the total of those who opted for either the status quo or the 1974 Conservative suggestion of a nominated Assembly also remained almost constant, but, within this total, support for a nominated Assembly declined and that for the status quo increased.

As for referendum voting intentions there were three distinct phases. Over the short interval from October 1976 to March 1977 the Yes side lost 12% as the Conservatives moved to a position of outright rejection of the Labour plan. There followed a long period of stability until January 1979, then a swift collapse in the last weeks before the vote.

On March 1, on a 63.6% turnout, Scottish electors recorded their choice:[6]

	Votes	% Electorate	% Votes
Yes	1,230,937	32.9	51.6
No	1,153,502	30.8	48.4
Did not vote	—	36.4	—
		100.0	100.0

The opinion polls show how the Scotland Act became very much a party issue but devolution did not. SNP supporters were almost unanimously in favour of both at all times. In October 1976 Conservative and Labour supporters had much the same referendum intentions, but by March 1977 there was a gap between them of 28%. In 1979 it increased steadily, from 22% in mid-January to 53% on referendum day. But even in 1979 party differences on the principle of devolution and on whether to press on with some form of devolution after the referendum stayed under 20%. The Thatcher/Home strategy worked. Pro-devolution Conservatives voted No to the Scotland Act without giving up their expressed desire for devolution.

It was, perhaps, inevitable that the referendum campaign should make the Scotland Act more of a party issue, though not to the extent that it became. But even the extreme party differences in Yes support cannot completely explain why the Yes side got only 52% of the vote. The Conservatives were enjoying an unusual burst of popularity throughout Britain, so there were an unusual number of them around. The Conservatives were also much more successful than Labour in getting their supporters to back the party line — 81% compared with 72% according to the ITN poll — and this despite the underlying and continuing popularity of devolution. If Labour had been as popular as in the general election on May 3, and if Labour rather than the Conservatives had achieved the higher loyalty rate, then even with a 53% difference between the parties a simple

[6] In Wales the figures were: Yes 243,048 (11.9%); No 956,330 (46.9%); and did not vote (41.2%); or, put otherwise, Yes 20.3%; No 79.7%.

arithmetical calculation shows the Yes vote would have been 66% rather than 52%.

Certainly the Conservatives made the Act a party issue, but they cut the Yes vote to 52% by being so much more successful than Labour in making it a party issue, despite taking the basically less popular position. Moss Evans and Tam Dalyell must, in their different ways, share some responsibility for the devolution result. In 1978 devolution carried Labour to a new height of popularity, in 1979 it sank under the weight of an unpopular and distracted government.

After the referendum several polls showed that only a third of Scots wanted devolution dropped, but relatively few expected the government to proceed as if the referendum had never happened. Some revision in the plans, if only cosmetic, was expected.

Labour had gradually been building up its Scottish staff. A research officer had been appointed in 1974, and after strong pressures from the Scottish Executive the regional organiser was replaced in 1977 by two posts — a Scottish Organiser and a Scottish Secretary. All the Scottish staff were paid by Transport House but the new post of political Secretary was intended to give the party a stronger Scottish presence. Helen Liddell, who was appointed in the gloomy spring of 1977, made a good public impact; she was young, female and articulate.

Labour adopted a new set of rules at its 1977 Conference which changed the nature of the party in Scotland. The new rules were riddled with references to the Assembly, Assembly-men and the Assembly Labour Party (ALP) which was to be an Assembly version of the PLP. Throughout, Assemblymen generally were allotted the same rights and duties as MPs. The Scottish Executive and the ALP were given the right to draw up the Assembly Manifesto and validate candidates, and the Scottish Conference would decide the Party Programme. The British NEC retained no more than the formal right to be consulted. Like the proposals for the nation itself, these changes conceded devolution within the party — not federalism or independence — on devolved subjects.

Spurred by a lack of funds, the Conservatives reacted to their 1974 defeat by combining the posts of Director of Organisation and Director of Information, and appointing the Area Agent from Yorkshire, Graham Macmillan (a Highlander), to the new single directorship. Mr Macmillan was given greater independence of action than his predecessors. At the same time they cut their total staff from 11 to 5, but later their fortunes improved. By 1979 the staff was up to 7, and constituency parties required significantly less financial assistance than in previous elections.

In 1977, prompted by a floor revolt at the 1976 conference, a committee under the party chairman, Russell Fairgrieve, produced a reform package under which the Scottish Central Office was integrated with the Central Office in London. The Scottish constituencies were now eligible to send representatives to the Conservative Conference in England on the same basis as English constituencies, though the Scottish Conservative and Unionist Association (SCUA) continued on as before.

The SNP also built up its headquarters staff to a total of 7 by 1977 and they were supplemented by a further 3 full-time officials at Westminster paid out of public funds. A legacy of over £250,000 in the summer of 1978, to be used only for general election purposes, left the party with an excess of financial resources for the 1979 election.

But the party not only suffered disappointments in by-elections; personality disputes created further problems. In Garscadden Keith Bovey lost his nationalist message in arguments over pacifism and abortion. The SNP Executive tried to avoid a repetition in Berwick by using their power to depose the local SNP candidate and imposing Isobel Lindsay in his place. This produced a string of resignations in the local party and the best, long-running SNP news-story of the campaign. While Margo Macdonald's campaign at Hamilton avoided the obvious blunders evident in Garscadden and later in Berwick, she could not prevent Labour from doubling its majority. Overall, the by-elections gave the SNP an image of a squabbling band of incompetents. At the same time success in the 1977 District elections was producing the usual crop of local government stories to tarnish the SNP image in 1978 and 1979. The party was entering the election campaign in a mood close to despair.

The House of Commons had already rejected an amendment to the 40% rule lowering the threshold to 33%. So, as soon as the result of the referendum became known, it was universally agreed that there was little chance of persuading the present parliament to implement the Act. On the very day of the result a government spokesman outlined the 'Frankenstein solution' —

neither repeal nor implement the Act until after the general election. For a few weeks the government tried exerting pressure on its anti-devolution backbenchers but it was plainly irritated by the Scots and would take no more risks for devolution. Mr Callaghan would not make implementation a confidence issue; that alone might have gained him the votes of Liberals and Nationalists on the issue and of his own rebels on the confidence aspect and so saved both devolution and his government. But, as the next chapter shows, his thinking had passed beyond that point.

A highly stage-managed Labour Conference met in Perth on March 9, 1979 and approved the Executive statement which declared devolution would 'remain at the forefront of our programme', and urged the government to do 'all in its power' to implement the Act. Significantly the final draft stopped short of demanding even a three-line whip. Aware that it would have to face an election within weeks, the party closed ranks.

SNP support was so low in the polls that it looked as though they would lose all but one of their seats if they precipitated an election; but both the Executive and the MPs agreed to end the government if it would not at least put the Act to the vote. They disagreed only on the time limit before action, and when Mr Callaghan proposed to continue discussions until the end of April, the SNP responded with a motion of no confidence. In the final vote, which ended the Labour government, every SNP member voted against it (see p. 126). If even one of them had refused to do so, as George Reid and Hamish Watt had in the autumn, Mr Callaghan would have survived through the spring and might well have won an election in the autumn. The SNP hoped that the government would be blamed for the failure to implement devolution, but Mr Callaghan's careful behaviour after the referendum made the SNP appear the most immediate cause of that failure.

In 1974, nationalism, both as a constitutional and political force, threatened to ignite British politics. It had the potential to break up the United Kingdom and to create a multiparty system with all that would involve. The 1979 referendum meant that the hopes and fears that nationalism had aroused were exaggerated, at least for the time being, in Scotland.

7 The Forcing of the Election

In the autumn of 1978 the parties all found that certain costs attended the postponement of the election. When the Liberal conference met at Southport ten days later it was dominated by the extensive coverage of Mr Thorpe's troubles with the law. Mr Steel had relieved him of his responsibilities for foreign affairs, but had no success in dissuading the former leader from paying a flying visit to the conference. The Labour party conference turned out disastrously for the government when the delegates rejected the pay policy, although Mr Callaghan salvaged some credit with a brilliant speech. Labour's special relationship with the unions on pay restraint began to seem less and less convincing. The Conservatives gathered at Brighton for their annual conference, confident that Labour support had already peaked. However, they fell into some disarray when Mr Heath gave explicit support for Mr Callaghan's incomes policy, which he thought should be pursued 'in the national interest'. His intervention reopened the old wounds, and the polls subsequently showed more support for Mr Heath's line than Mrs Thatcher's. The Conservatives failed to win the Berwick by-election; there was in fact a pro-government swing, the first in twelve years. Labour soared ahead in the October opinion polls, and Conservative morale was severely buffeted.

The government's major miscalculation about the sentiment of rank-and-file workers became apparent as Christmas approached. The ceiling of 5% for wage settlements arose firstly out of the inability to agree on a target with the TUC and, secondly, out of the need to provide a figure in August for Treasury estimates about public expenditure for the coming year. Mr Callaghan had floated the suggestion of 5% as early as January 1978 and it made sense, granted the goal of reducing inflation and the anticipation of an autumn election. The Treasury thought a 5% norm would result in an earnings increase of 9%–11%. The figure was never discussed within the Cabinet, but it gradually came to take on the tones of an immovable target. The trade union leaders remained fairly quiescent, for they were geared up for an October election, but they made it clear to the government that they could not deliver the support of their members for a Phase IV. Negotiations for some new understanding with the unions began at once, but they were hampered by the TUC leaders' feeling that Mr Callaghan had misled them and embarrassed them about his election intentions before and during the September Congress.

The first key settlement was with the Ford Motor Company. When the company made an offer in accord with the guidelines, the workers went on strike even though the existing agreement had not expired. Ford eventually gave way after a three-week strike and settled at about 15%. On December 13 parliament refused by 285 votes to 283 to grant the government the powers to impose sanctions on Ford or other firms breaking the wage guidelines. The government had not made the vote a question of confidence. Although it won a motion of confidence the next day, the defeat had shown that it lacked the wholehearted support of backbenchers and its economic strategy had been undermined. The election had ostensibly been delayed in part so that the fight against inflation could be carried on. Now the government lacked what it had proclaimed as indispensable instruments, and its strategy was coming apart. In retrospect, some ministers looked back on the sanctions debate as a possible launching pad for an election. But only on the day of the vote did ministers even consider this. An alternative response would have been to set a more generous target for wage settlements of 7% or 8%. Instead, the government soldiered on.

The main wage troubles, however, developed in the public sector. A hasty and damaging settlement of 15% was agreed with striking technicians in order to keep the BBC on the air at Christmas. As one disillusioned aide complained 'We sold our pay policy to have "The Sound of Music" on Christmas Day'. There then followed an outburst of walkouts, militant picketing and violence by oil-tanker drivers, lorry drivers, ambulance drivers and local government manual workers. All this coincided with the worst winter weather in decades. Demands for comparability by public sector workers handsomely exceeded the 5% norm as settlements in the private sector rose into double figures. On January 22 a day of action by over 1 million local government workers was the biggest one-day stoppage since the 1926 general strike. The government was prepared to bend the guidelines for the low-paid workers, but it was also determined to set a new lower norm after the lorry drivers' settlement.

It was unfortunate that Mr Callaghan and Mr Healey were off form during these weeks. On his return from the Guadeloupe Summit on January 10, 1979, Mr Callaghan was 'badly briefed' about the situation, and he appeared lighthearted in an airport television interview. His irate reply to one questioner was mercilessly satirized by the press and by the Conservatives in the following weeks.[1] Guadeloupe in January 1979 was for a politician 'The wrong place and the wrong time.' Any hypothetical benefits from Mr Callaghan being seen as the world statesman were soon dissipated by the strikers. The government seemed to be dithering. Ministers made discordant remarks — that there was or was not a crisis, that a state of emergency would or would not be declared, that there was or was not room for flexibility in settling particular wage disputes. Colleagues were very critical of the way the ministers most concerned, David Ennals, and to a lesser extent Peter Shore, handled the dispute. Throughout this time, Mrs Thatcher was gaining headlines with her proposed initiatives for trade union reform.[2]

So much political capital had been invested in the special relationship between the Labour party and the trade unions that these events obviously damaged morale. 'Labour's trump electoral card is turning into its Achilles heel,' one observer remarked. In 1968–9 Mr Wilson had tried to curb the powers with his proposals in *In Place of Strife*. These were abandoned after Mr Callaghan had led the opposition within the Labour party. Mr Heath's reforms, embodied in the Industrial Relations Act, passed through Parliament in 1971, had been effectively abandoned because of trade union opposition, and quickly repealed by the Labour government in 1974. The unions had gained many concessions from the government but, throughout the winter disturbances, union leaders demonstrated their powerless, to manage the situation.

[1] He never actually said 'Crisis? What crisis?', but only 'I don't think that other people in the world would share the view that there is mounting chaos.'
[2] On January 17 Mrs Thatcher used a party political broadcast to publicise the reforms. Ministers were aghast to learn that Labour's broadcast on January 24 concentrated on developments in council house building in Manchester.

Ministers were bitter as they saw the political and economic gains of the previous three years dissipated. The much-prized record on inflation was threatened; wage increases would feed price-rises. They identified the major culprits as Moss Evans, the new leader of the Transport Workers, and Alan Fisher, the Secretary of the National Union of Public Employees, who seemed unable to control their members; and they lamented the departure of Jack Jones and Hugh Scanlon. As one commentator noted, 'With friends like this, Jim needs no enemies'. But for all Mr Callaghan's distaste for free collective bargaining — 'free collective chaos' he called it — he was determined not to confront the trade unions or get into a 'Who governs?' election. Both Mr Wilson and Mr Heath had come to grief through confrontation; cooperation and consent was the only way.

In fact, the government managed an orderly retreat of sorts. On February 21 local authority manual workers settled for 9% on account pending an investigation into pay comparability by a commission. On March 7 the unions accepted a similar deal for the hospital workers, though NUPE held out for more. After elaborate negotiations a 'Concordat' with the TUC was reached on February 23. The TUC agreed to draw up a voluntary code covering picketing, the closed shop, strike ballots and resort to strikes. But few ministers had much faith in it as an answer to the problems that had arisen during the winter.

Mrs Thatcher seized the initiative with her proposals for trade union reform. The tougher line she now voiced was put forward before the shadow cabinet had defined its stand and was a setback for Mr Prior. But even he admitted that the recent events had changed his mind about the desirability of legislation. One Labour strategist noted how the Conservatives, aided by the disruption, had transformed the trade union question from one about inflation and incomes policy to one about industrial relations and strikes. This redefinition of the issue decisively affected the politics of the coming months. For the remainder of the winter the Conservatives had only to be patient and project their main themes while events worked for them.

During these weeks, colleagues found it difficult to read Mr Callaghan's mind. He was depressed; he had been shocked and even hurt by some of the excesses he had witnessed on the picket lines. His inscrutability, already apparent in the decision not to hold an election in the autumn, was more pronounced than ever. He refused to go on television and make a speech about the situation because, in his own words, he had nothing to say. Some ministers wrote him memoranda about strategy. But he did not invite a Cabinet discussion on general political matters or hold meetings with individual ministers. Some colleagues grew concerned at the lack of opportunity for talks on political strategy. In fact Mr Callaghan was his own strategist, though the strategy appeared to be limited to reducing inflation. Everything else was subordinate to that goal.

It was inevitable that the problems facing the minority government were caught up with speculation about a 'snap' election. Since October 1978 Labour ministers had looked to spring 1979 as the next possible election date if they could survive until then; they would have the benefit of fighting on the new register which would come into effect in February. Survival depended on avoiding a defeat on a confidence vote in the House of Commons. In fact, the government had policies in hand which reduced the incentive for either the Ulster MPs or the Nationalists to turn it out. The Nationalist parties wished to see the devolution referendum held on March 1 and a date fixed for setting up the new assemblies. The Ulster MPs wished to see the bill creating additional seats for Northern Ireland carried through.

But the orderly approach to a spring election was abandoned amid the ruins of the pay policy. The government's main concern throughout the first three months of 1979 was to postpone an election for as long as possible, or at least until the memories of the winter strikes and the helplessness of the government had evaporated in the public mind. Already it was plain that the Prime Minister had miscalculated in his two gambles — that he could avoid defeat in parliament on a major issue of confidence, and that the trade unions would cooperate with the government. Mr Callaghan's strategy for conquering inflation and thereby strengthening his political appeal had collapsed. Transport House officials and some ministers saw June 7, the date already assigned for the European elections, as the likely target in spite of objections from the Home Office. It would at least save the party the expense of fighting two separate contests. Although David Owen was briefed to make sure that the European election avoided May in case a Westminster election was held then, Mr Callaghan never responded favourably to the idea. It was generally

SECONDARY CANVASSING!

assumed that he would go on for as long as possible — and to the autumn if he could.

The immediate cause of the government's parliamentary difficulties was the referendum in Scotland. Ironically, the policy had originally been developed to save the party in Scotland. The polls showed that devolution was approved there by a large margin in 1978. Unfortunately for the government, support collapsed in the few weeks before the referendum. As William Miller showed in Chapter 6, the Conservative opposition gradually made devolution into a party issue. Although the Scotland Act was supported by 52% of the voters this figure amounted to only 33% of the eligible electorate, far short of the 40% required.[3] There was never any possibility of the government proceeding with far-reaching proposals on such a narrow basis of support, especially in the face of strong opposition within the Labour party.[4]

On March 21 Mr Callaghan asked for a 'short interval' to allow party talks to be held to see if agreement on the next stage could be reached. He also offered a vote on the repeal of the devolution orders by the end of April. This approach was spurned by the SNP who proceeded to table a motion of no confidence. Mr Callaghan likened their action to that of turkeys voting for an early Christmas. Since the Liberals were also committed to forcing an election, the Conservatives now had the opportunity to table their own motion of no confidence on March 22. Their bruising experience with such votes in March 1977 and December 1978 had made them more cautious of taking initiatives alone.

Perhaps the government had conducted the affair clumsily. By allowing two weeks to elapse before declaring their intentions, they had fuelled the suspicions of the Scottish Nationalists. One minister thought the referendum result the worst possible; had the proposals been defeated, the Scottish Nationalists might have feared an election; had the margin of victory been a little higher, the government would have been tempted to proceed. The Nationalist MPs, feeling cheated by the delay, decided by a

---

[3] Under the Cunningham Amendment to the Scotland Act, the Secretary of State was required to lay an order for the repeal of the Act if it did not in his opinion secure the support of '40 percent of those entitled to vote'.
[4] In Wales, the proposals were defeated by 956,000 votes to 243,000, on a turnout of 59%.

narrow majority, to seek an election as soon as possible, while the devolution issue was still fresh in the public mind.

In the confidence debate on March 28, Labour managed to attract the votes of the three Welsh Nationalists and the two Scottish Labour members, as well as persuading two Ulstermen to support them. The other 32 minor-party MPs joined Mrs Thatcher in the opposition lobby. Had Labour managed to poll its full strength by bringing the sick Alfred Broughton down from Yorkshire, then they would have tied with the opposition. In that event the Speaker would have cast his deciding vote with the government. The debate was belligerent and lively, and set against an undercurrent of rumour and counter-rumour. There was a sense of enormous drama as the division came at 10 p.m. Only when the tellers formed up before the Speaker was it clear that the government had lost. The margin was only one — 311 to 310.

A more determined or desperate Prime Minister than Mr Callaghan might have won the confidence vote. Already the Welsh Nationalists had been conciliated with the promise of early action to compensate Welsh slate-quarrymen suffering from lung disease, an offer matched by the Conservatives. The two Irish Catholic MPs, usually well-disposed to Labour, had been alienated by the granting of extra seats to Ulster (which were thought to favour the Protestants). But Frank Maguire was certainly open to persuasion, and Gerry Fitt sought out Michael Foot on the Tuesday night; the latter, however, was unavailable, giving precedence to a speaking engagement at the Edge Hill by-election. Ulster MPs openly offered their votes for the speedy installation of a gas pipeline. There were rumours that Clement Freud could be persuaded to miss the vote by the promise of parliamentary time for his Freedom of Information Bill, or even that an offer of a peerage could secure a convenient absence from a retiring Conservative. Sir Alfred Broughton could have been brought to the precincts of the House and nodded through the lobby. The whips and some ministers were prepared to be ruthless. Michael Foot wanted to outflank the Conservatives by tabling a confidence motion, so worded that it would attract Liberal and Nationalist support.

If they found Mr Callaghan slow to focus on their concerns and strategems it was because he had already decided to let events take their course. There had been enough wheeling and dealing; if the government were defeated, so be it. It is not clear that, even had the government managed to win the vote, the election would have been long delayed. Some advisers in Number 10 wanted to have an election on May 24, and would have pressed Mr Callaghan to announce it that week. Mr Healey would have been able to introduce his budget, though there would have been serious problems getting a finance bill through parliament without wrecking amendments. But the problems of running a minority government were such that a number of ministers did not think that an election could have been delayed beyond June 7.[5] Mr Callaghan had no majority for his policies on wages or devolution, and the performance of some ministers over the winter had turned his mind to a reshuffle. He was thinking aloud about May 3, May 10 or June 7 as election dates even if he won the vote.

Mr Callaghan's government was the first to be defeated on an issue of confidence since Ramsay MacDonald's minority Labour government in 1924; the examples previous to that were in 1886 and 1895. It was therefore the first government in 55 years to have no control over the decision to dissolve. Yet, what was really remarkable was that the minority government had lasted so long.

Though Mr Callaghan offered the Cabinet a discussion on election timing, there was little debate about having the election on May 3. The only difficulty about May 3 was that the date was already assigned for local elections for all authorities outside Scotland and Greater London: under existing law a polling booth could be used for only one election at a time. The Conservatives' preference for April 26 would have required a speedy dissolution of Parliament and prevented Mr Healey from introducing even a care and maintenance budget on April 3. It would also have prevented the passage of several bills already in the pipeline. By choosing May 3, the government was able to ensure the enactment of laws on merchant shipping, banking deposit protection and the promised compensation of Welsh quarrymen.[6]

---

[5] However, one group, including Bill Rodgers and Roy Hattersley, would have argued for a delay until October.

[6] But the dissolution involved the loss of an Education Bill, a Housing Bill, and measures providing for the compulsory wearing of seat belts and the public lending right for authors.

After the Cabinet meeting Mr Callaghan went to see the Queen. He then announced to the House of Commons that Parliament would be dissolved on April 7, the election would be on May 3, and the new Parliament would assemble on May 9.

8 Central Preparations

For more than two years the parties had been aware of the possibility of having to cope with an election held at short notice. Apart from the dissolution of February 1974, British general elections have been widely anticipated in the post-war period. Choosing the time for a dissolution is a prerogative of the prime minister of the day. Yet prime ministers are constrained by the limited number of available dates and, when they take account of economic indicators and the trends in opinion polls, the date usually appears to be an obvious one. Certainly the party organisations, though theoretically always supposed to be on a war footing, expect some advance warning that an election is imminent. But once Mr Callaghan had passed by the opportunity for an autumn election, a forced dissolution was always on the cards. The shift to the government, reflected in the Berwick by-election and the opinion polls in October and November, combined with the open divisions in the Conservative party, doubtless made a number of Labour candidates in marginal seats wistful about the missed opportunity.[1] But since the summer of 1978 preparations for publicity, tactics and private polling in all parties had reached an advanced stage. The parties, except for Labour, had complete drafts of their election manifestos ready for an early contest.

Indeed it could not be said that Transport House was any better prepared for the election than it had been the previous autumn. It was 'in its usual state of unreadiness' as one jaundiced minister commented. Since the new year, the party machine had been occupied with the selection of European candidates. Organisers were worried about the response of local activists; there were reports of grass-roots disillusion with both the 5 % pay policy and with the strikes and picketing which followed.

The Labour party's position in the country had crumbled in the previous three months and Mr Callaghan was calling an

[1] In October Gallup reported a Labour lead of 5½%; in November the lead was 5%.

election at a time which he would never have chosen freely. The weakness of the government's position at the outset of the campaign is conveyed by a reading of the opinion polls. As recently as December 1978, NOP had registered a narrow Labour lead in voting intentions. But Gallup showed the Conservative lead bounding up from 7½% to 20% between January and February: by March it was 14½%. This represented a two-party swing of nearly 10% since October 1974, and was closely echoed in the Knutsford and Clitheroe by-elections. Such a swing in a general election would produce a Conservative landslide.

The industrial troubles damaged Labour credibility in the area of handling the economy and trade unions and, as usual, weakened the government's position in many other areas as well. Table 1 shows the general dissatisfaction with the government's handling of problems. Other indicators of party support also turned sharply against Labour. Mr Callaghan, who had enjoyed a commanding lead over Mrs Thatcher during the previous three years, fell behind her, and his own rating sank to an all-time low. Between November 1978 and March 1979 his 2-to-1 advantage over Mrs Thatcher collapsed into a deficit of 32% to 41%. The Conservatives were also thought to have the best policies and the best leaders, again a sharp reversal from the findings in November.

Table 2 shows that on the main issues Labour's position had worsened considerably since the summer of 1978. On the key issue of industrial relations a large minority of Labour voters

Table 1.   Approval of Government's Handling of Main Issues

	(% approving minus % disapproving)		
	%		%
Common Market	−19	Cost of Living	−51
Immigration	−28	Economy	−48
Law and Order	−21	Strikes and Labour relations	−62
Education	− 9	National Health	−23
Employment	−48	Old Age Pensions	9

Source: Gallup, March 1979.

Table 2.   Which Party has the Best Policies?

August 1978—April 1979

	Aug '78	Feb '79	4—6 Apr '79	Change Aug—Apr
Prices/Inflation				
Con	31	39	36	+5
Lab	40	27	33	−7
Industrial relations/strikes				
Con	32	39	35	+3
Lab	41	26	36	−5
Unemployment				
Con	36	39	37	+1
Lab	29	24	28	−1
Law & Order				
Con	42	NA	49	+7
Lab	24	NA	19	−5
Taxation				
Con	NA	NA	48	
Lab	NA	NA	24	
Common Market				
Con	32	NA	34	+2
Lab	28	NA	22	−6

Source: MORI, *New Statesman*, April 27, 1979.

agreed with Conservative proposals for reforming trade unions; the polls also revealed that there was little confidence in the recent Concordat between the government and the TUC. Yet Table 2 also shows that by April Labour had recovered half the ground lost; everything was to be gained by hanging on.

Over the years opinion polls have shown a strong relationship between expectations that people will be better off personally in the next twelve months and a willingness to vote for the government a month or two later. During 1978 growing optimism among voters accompanied the recovery in Labour's support (see p. 29). Once again, however, this indicator went wrong for

Labour. Gallup's survey into economic expectations in March found that only 18% expected the economic situation to improve in the next twelve months while 52% expected it to worsen. Wages still ran well ahead of prices, but there were doubts about future prosperity.

Labour's campaign was to be a No. 10 affair. Mr Callaghan made it clear to Transport House officials that he would run his own show and select his own team. In the previous summer Derek Gladwin, a Southern Area official with the GMWU, was selected by the Prime Minister to be his campaign manager. Roger Carroll, a political reporter with the *Sun*, who had offered suggestions for Mr. Callaghan's speeches in the past, was recruited to help with speech-writing.

Arrangements for the party's use of media and publicity created tensions before and during the campaign (see p. 225). In May 1977 Edward Booth-Clibborn was asked to organise the publicity. Mr Booth-Clibborn is Chairman of the Designers & Art Directors Association of London (D&AD), a charity set up to encourage high standards in visual communication. He had worked occasionally for the party in the past, publishing reproductions of early Labour Party posters to raise funds, and the 'Yesterday's Men' poster in 1970. He recruited other sympathetic advertising, marketing and research people, including a creative director, Tim Delaney, Managing Director of BBDO Ltd.; Trevor Eke, Managing Director of Playtex Ltd., to cover marketing; and Ivor Crewe from the academic world. Their understanding was that not only would they control advertising and political broadcasts, but also that they would not be encumbered with Transport House committees and 'interference'.

On February 14, 1978, the first meeting took place of a group of people the Prime Minister had selected to be the publicity and 'think-tank' team for the election. The meetings at No. 10 were known as the 'White Drawing Room' meetings, and were supposed to be secret. Those attending the meetings, besides Mr Callaghan, were Derek Gladwin, Michael Foot, Merlyn Rees, Edward Booth-Clibborn, David Lipsey, Tom McNally, Ron Hayward, Percy Clark, Reg Underhill, Norman Lewis (from the TUC) and Mike Molloy (editor of the *Daily Mirror*). After August 1978 meetings became more frequent and additional

attenders were Tim Delaney, Trevor Eke, Roger Carroll and
Michael Callaghan.

At these meetings Mr Callaghan talked freely about the
government's policies and his thinking on the issues of the day.
The sessions provided the creative team with a chance to understand his political values and take them into account in preparing
their material. During the 1978 meetings Mr Callaghan was
interested in tapping traditional Labour ideals; 'We must have
some Jerusalem,' he said. Later on this element became less
pronounced in his campaign discussions. Another purpose of
the meetings was to get reactions to the team's suggestions for
campaign strategy. Some participants saw the White Drawing
Room meetings as a device to outflank Transport House (even
though party officers were present). Mr Callaghan at the time,
however, hoped that the ideas would be conveyed to the
Campaign Committee.

Many people inside and outside politics have a misleading
picture of Transport House as an electoral force. In recent years
headquarters had become entangled with matters of policy and
the manifesto; the organisation and the party's popular base
had been somewhat neglected. In the past, Mr Gaitskell and
Mr Wilson, as party leaders, had felt the need to go outside the
party machine to seek expertise in winning elections. In 1979,
however, ministers and advisers were openly despairing and even
contemptuous of Transport House as a vote-winning organisation,
and of the policies emanating from the NEC. Volunteers from
the advertising world were dismayed at the time taken in making
decisions and at the general inertia and apparent naivety about
effective means of communication with ordinary voters. On the
other hand, the Labour party takes the idea of accountability
seriously and many officials and activists were deeply suspicious
about professional communicators. Their outlook was expressed
in Nye Bevan's complaint in 1959, 'You are taking the poetry
out of politics.' Members of the Executive and party officers,
who were paying the bills, wanted a say in decisions.

Inevitably, there were conflicting lines of authority between
the creative group and the official party machine. Tensions
centred particularly on the preparation of posters and television
broadcasts. Transport House decided that there should be a
strong poster campaign in January 1979, and that the group

should use an idea that had been produced for a possible October 1978 election. The poster selected featured two dragons, one rampant and the other peaceful, representing Labour's conquest of inflation. Unfortunately the artwork was not very strong, and some people did not like it very much. The group also used the slogan 'Keep Britain Labour and it will keep on getting better', which had been created for the October 1978 campaign. The timing was disastrous, for the poster's appearance in January 1979 coincided with the lorry drivers' strike. The slogan remained on sites throughout the subsequent disputes.

At a Campaign Committee meeting held on February 15, 1979, in the House of Commons, a layout was shown for the next poster. This featured a candle and the headline 'Remember the last time the Tories said *they* had all the answers.' This poster was originally agreed by the White Drawing Room Committee, but, since the committee was secret, posters had to be shown to the NEC and Campaign Committee for their formal approval. The poster was hurriedly prepared, in advance of the Campaign Committee meeting. On March 5 the majority on the committee, angry at the *fait accompli*, requested that the candle poster should be stopped. In the meantime, however, *Tribune* had reproduced the poster on its front page on March 2, 1979, saying:

> Our picture shows a new Labour Party poster which has been put up in south London. Compared with the recent run of Labour posters it is light years ahead in its impact and design. We congratulate everyone who was concerned with the production of the poster and hope that copies of it will soon be going up on billboards all over the country.

A Scottish agent in Glasgow watched with dismay at the poster being covered over a day or two before the Scottish referendum, and it was not seen during the general election campaign. There was also a difference between the groups over how extensively Mr Callaghan should be featured in the advertising strategy:[2] the creative group wanted him to figure prominently on posters and publicity, but the Campaign Committee wanted a less leader-centred campaign.

[2] As the strategy document stated: 'It is our belief that the P.M. should be the major figure in the campaign.'

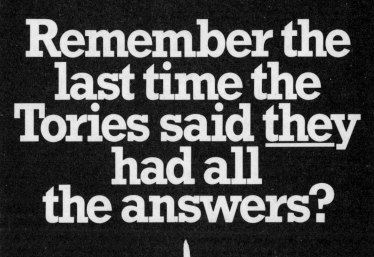

Remember the last time the Tories said they had all the answers?

Keep Britain Labour.

Published by the Labour Party, Transport House,
Smith Square, London SW1P 3JA.

The poster was the work of John O'Driscoll, Caroline Bard, and Tim Delaney

Transport House had its own publicity group, which included two MPs with extensive broadcasting experience, Austin Mitchell and Phillip Whitehead. Previously meetings between this and the independent group had not been successful, and at the beginning of the campaign it was still not clear which one would prepare the party broadcasts. Mr Booth-Clibborn's group pointed to the evidence collected by the BBC Audience Research Department the previous summer which showed that the Conservative broadcasts had been better presented and more successful in converting voters than Labour's. In a lengthy memorandum, entitled 'Eight Good Reasons for making our Party Political Broadcasts more professional', they even suggested that Labour would have done better to have had no broadcasts at all. Eventually, Ron Hayward invited the two groups to meet in his office on April 5. By now an impatient Mr Callaghan expressed a preference for the independent group to proceed. 'They are to be used', he told Mr Hayward. At a traumatic meeting the two sides failed to agree and the independent group went ahead, with little support from Transport House.

The creative team's original strategy document, drawn up for an October 1978 election, reflected the more favourable political background. It heavily emphasised the government's record in lowering inflation and handling the unions, and exploited memories of the conditions which Labour inherited in February 1974 (see, for example, the candle poster on p. 135). Now, however, the party's private polls indicated no obvious basis of strength for the Labour party. The loss of support was more marked among women than men, among working class than middle class voters, and among the young and the old than among the middle-aged. But in spite of the polls, Labour strategists still believed that, because voters were known to be volatile, the campaign could prove decisive. They could also look back to 1970 and February 1974 when the party trailing in the opinion polls at the outset of the campaign closed the gap by election day. Mr Booth-Clibborn's new strategy document, written in mid-March, concluded: 'Therefore we should opt for a longer than normal campaign.'

In looking for issues to regain the support of traditional Labour voters who had strayed in the previous few months, the party's creative team suggested concentrating on issues which appealed to the economic interests of working-class voters and on which Labour had a traditional credibility. Mr Booth-Clibborn identified these 'credible' areas as:

Welfare — pensions, family allowance, health services.
Jobs — creating and saving jobs, decent unemployment benefits.
Interests of public sector — public expenditure, staffing levels, comparative wage levels.
Economic planning and control — incomes policy, price and rent controls.

Labour speeches and publicity, it was recommended, should emphasise pensions, family allowances and the comparability of wages in the public and private sectors. These three issues would be combined into a programme of *FAIRNESS TO ALL*. Surveys showed that the most common unprompted reason offered for voting Labour was that 'Labour looks after the workers' or 'the less well off'. However, it was understood that this would be combined, as Jim Callaghan insisted, with an aggressive questioning of the Conservatives.

To win the support of the undecided, the party had to focus on the three issues of most importance to these voters; these were identified as strikes, jobs and prices. It was generally agreed that Mr Callaghan was the party's greatest asset, and that Mrs Thatcher was a liability to her party. There was therefore an eagerness to hold television debates between the party leaders for they would be likely to reach the target working class voters. Mr Callaghan planned a long campaign — so that the 'argument' would be fully developed. There would be constant repetition of a few themes — jobs, prices and industrial relations. Television would be the priority medium and the major effort of the campaign should come in the last week.

The delayed election suited the Conservatives on policy as well as on electoral grounds. In late 1978 there had been open differences within the leadership on pay policy. By the spring, however, events had given strong support to Mrs Thatcher's claims about the unworkability of pay policy in the long run, and the strikes had united the party behind the proposed trade union reforms. The outcome of the devolution referendums had heartened Conservatives, particularly in Wales where they were the only party to speak clearly for the majority.

The Conservatives had to tread carefully. They had to attack union power without suggesting a renewal of confrontation. They wanted to promise to reduce public expenditure without increasing long-term unemployment or appearing to lack compassion, and to restore free collective bargaining without it degenerating into a free-for-all. They knew who their targets were. Inevitably they were not dissimilar from Labour's, but there was a special emphasis upon first-time voters, C_2 housewives, 1974 Liberals, and people purchasing their own homes. The party would stick to four broad themes; freedom under the law, incentives, Labour's failures, and the threat of economic decline. The message would be: 'time for a change'.

Gordon Reece, the party's Director of Publicity, had an important role in presenting the party's message. The private polls had long shown that many voters thought the Conservatives lacked both compassion and sympathetic leaders. Mr Reece had a number of 'hunches' about what moved the voter and how to set about winning elections.

First, he took 1974 Conservatives largely for granted — five years of Labour government should be sufficient stimulus to keep them in the fold. But how could one add to that base? The target voters were 'soft' or detachable Labour and Liberal supporters. The way to appeal to these people was through television, and to do so in a relatively non-political context. Mr Reece's target voters were more likely to be exposed to ITV than the BBC, to read the *Sun* and *Mirror*, and to vote less on issues than impressions. His approach was: 'Make them think Conservatives are good for you.' Finally, 'pacing' was important; the campaign was, in his own words, 'the final sprint or the last fence in a race'.

The contract for advertising and sound and television broadcasting was awarded to the Saatchi & Saatchi agency in March 1978. The party was looking for an agency that was creative and had resources large enough to take care of all Conservative advertising and broadcasts. The agency was founded by Charles and Maurice Saatchi and Tim Bell in 1970. By 1978 it had grown to the fourth largest advertising agency with business in excess of £40 million. On the day of Saatchi & Saatchi's appointment as advertising agent for the Conservatives, Mr Booth-Clibborn wrote to Mr Callaghan:

Significantly, in appointing Saatchi & Saatchi, the Conservative Party have moved away from the more traditional, staid advertising agencies they have used in the past, and chosen an agency which has a reputation for being aggressive, publicity conscious, energetic and creative. Their work may even be considered controversial.

The strategy brief, prepared by Tim Bell, stressed the concepts of freedom, choice and minimum interference. The firm commissioned depth interviews with small groups of target voters: with these 'four' groups they hoped to gain more understanding of the main concerns of voters. They found that the two main parties' favourable images were in two very different areas. The Conservatives were heavily favoured as the best party to deal with issues affecting people, while Labour was preferred on issues affecting the state. They also found a difference between popular perceptions of the parties' performances on unemployment and prices and the actual facts, few voters appreciated that the Labour Government's record in these areas was worse than that of the previous Conservative administration. The overall theme of the agency's publicity was to make people aware of the government's poor record on productivity, unemployment and prosperity. 'Make them dissatisfied with the government', was how one executive explained his goal.

The firm was skilful in its use of visual gimmicks and sophisticated cinematic techniques in the television broadcasts in a way that seems to have been particularly effective with younger voters. Saatchi also mounted a large poster campaign in the summer of 1978, at a cost of £195,000, directed mainly at women in Labour households, semi-skilled workers and first-time voters. The issues emphasised were jobs, prices, and law and order. The poster used simple slogans: *Educashun isn't working; Britain isn't getting any better; Labour still isn't working; 1984 – What 5 more years?;* and, *Cheer up. They can't last for ever.* Saatchi and Saatchi had 1100 poster sites in summer 1978, and 1400 sites in April 1979 (for constituency campaigning). In January and February 1979 Conservatives held back their funds, anticipating that an election would be delayed until the autumn. But when the leaders and advisers realised the implica-

tions of a Scottish devolution referendum not giving a decisive
'Yes', they increased their efforts again. The press advertising
was concentrated in the popular papers, particularly the *Daily
Mirror* and the *Sun* — 'the only audience that matters,' according
to Mr Reece. The 'Labour Isn't Working' poster was challenged
by Labour on the grounds that the people displayed in the dole
queue were employees of the agency. The charge only gave the
advertisements much more publicity — 'Worth £2 million to us,'
said one official. In fact the queue was composed of Hendon
Young Conservatives. The poster and broadcasting campaign
had been designed to contain the anticipated swing back to the
government during the summer. Some Conservatives claim that
it succeeded so well that it may have forced Mr Callaghan not to
have a dissolution in the autumn. 'We didn't do any harm,'
noted Tim Bell.

The Conservative party had a problem in packaging the leader,
just as they had with Mr Heath. But Mrs Thatcher was much
more willing to adapt herself than was her predecessor. Mr Reece
particularly encouraged her to be filmed doing every-day tasks
like shopping and household work. Each time she appeared on
television he commissioned a poll to assess audience reactions.
He also did his best to arrange that television interviewers would
not be aggressive, because that tended to increase Mrs Thatcher's
own aggressiveness in return. He encouraged appearances in
relatively non-political programmes such as the *Jimmy Young
Show* and *Nationwide*. This single-minded approach to providing
material for the television news gave rise to sharp criticisms
about 'the selling' or 'packaging' of Mrs Thatcher.[3] In fact the
Saatchis hardly met her and only Tim Bell was in regular contact.
The agency's main service to Mrs Thatcher was to provide the
background settings for the press conferences and 1978 party
conference, and to prepare the party political broadcasts. Tim
Bell and his colleagues also made suggestions about her choice
of words and style. They were forthright in asking politicians,
'What is it you are trying to say?'

Conservative strategists hoped to profit from the memories
of the previous winter and the mood of 'time for a new beginning', as the manifesto expressed it. If they were to avoid
exciting or polarising the electorate, they had not so much to

[3] Adam Raphael, 'The Selling of Maggie,' *Observer*, (April 22, 1979).

promise radical departures as remind voters of 'the bloody awful time they'd been having,' as one insider put it. 'What we've got to say is "Do you want more of this?" ' said another. There was some debate in the inner councils about whether the party should pursue a 'hard' or 'soft' campaign. In 1978, the party's publicity was thought to have erred on the former side. There was some feeling that the party now had to adopt a 'peace-time' strategy, employ a more serious broadcasting format, be less 'jokey', and get across that it was a caring party.

In both main parties though more so in the Conservative party there was a marked professionalism about communications. The party leaders were aware of the importance of concentrating on two or three themes, expressing themselves in a few words, making sure they were the correct words, and then repeating them. In both camps there were references to 'buzz-words', 'one-liners' and 'nine word sentences'. The Conservative operation was backed by more resources; they were able to outspend Labour on the broadcasts by two-to-one and had much more money for advertisements and private polls. Their lines of communications between Saatchi and the party were clearer than those of Mr Booth-Clibborn's group with Labour. The Conservatives turned to an agency which supplied all their publicity requirements, whereas Labour relied on a team of professionals who volunteered their services. Although Mr Booth-Clibborn was in daily personal contact with Mr Callaghan, he had difficulties with the Transport House machine. Tim Bell, by contrast, may have seen less of Mrs Thatcher in the campaign but his close liaison with Lord Thorneycroft, Mr Reece and the party's pollsters smoothed his task.

The Conservatives entered the campaign with the largest lead ever reported for any party in the opinion polls at this stage of an election. But more cautious Conservatives dismissed the findings as 'ludicrous', and preferred to think of a more modest, though still clear, underlying lead. Few were prepared to wager that they would have a majority larger than 30 to 50. More important was the need not to panic when the lead narrowed as might be expected during the campaign.

Advisers were aware of the problem involved in presenting Mrs Thatcher. The *Economist* stated on March 31, 1979, 'the issue is Thatcher'. She was firmly identified with the more controversial proposals for trade union reform and the reduction of government intervention in the economy. She was relatively inexperienced and not popular, so Mr Callaghan had an incentive to emphasise the election as a choice of leaders. The party's message should be carried in the television broadcasts, and she would make only a few sorties out of London. At the same time, because Mr Callaghan was a bland figure, Mrs Thatcher should emphasise her different policies, so that she came across as a sharply defined leader.

The day after the government's defeat in parliament, Liberal hopes received a considerable fillip with the spectacular victory of David Alton in the Labour seat of Liverpool Edge Hill. The run of by-election disappointments was reversed and the 32% swing was the largest in any postwar by-election. The result was also important in encouraging last-minute Liberal candidates to come forward. The Liberal party went into the campaign knowing that it had improved its position in the course of each recent general election. It also had a bigger base to appeal to; over 25% of the voters had supported the Liberals at one or other of the 1974 elections. It would also rely upon Liberal spokesmen, who were good on television, getting exceptional exposure. Mr Steel's electoral strategy grew out of his political aims. He believed in coalitions and hoped for a Liberal 'wedge' which would hold the balance in the new parliament. The success of this strategy depended only partly on the number of Liberal MPs; it also required that no party should have a clear majority. In contrast to 1974 there was no talk about forming a Liberal government.

A party needs 330 seats if it is to feel secure against by-election losses in a five-year parliament. Labour required only 11 more seats than it had gained in October 1974; the Conservatives required 53, a figure which would involve a bigger national swing than had been achieved in any post-war election.

The election would be decided in 80 or so key marginals. Since 1950, an average of only 49 seats had changed hands between the parties. Before the war landslides had been more frequent and a larger number of seats had switched. The new element in 1979 was that the results of the 1974 elections opened the possibility of tactical voting. Not only were more parties involved but the party line-up varied in different parts of the United Kingdom. Labour's seats were at risk from a collapse of the Liberal vote in England and, less probably, from an upsurge of the Nationalists in Scotland. Labour could hold or even increase its vote and still not win. In the 25 seats Labour held by a margin under 4%, the Liberals had had on average 13% of the vote. Quite a small Liberal defection could give all those constituencies to the Conservatives. In Scotland, any collapse of the Nationalists stood to benefit the Conservatives who were the main challengers in 8 of the 11 SNP seats. But the major battleground was in England where, in order to deny Mrs Thatcher victory, Labour had to claw back lost support, above all in the 50 or so marginal seats that the Conservatives would win on a 4% swing. The task looked almost impossible, but Mr Callaghan and his followers took it on with surprising zest.

9 Manifestos and Issues

Manifestos are part of the ritual of British general elections. A party manifesto is a multi-purpose document, addressed to different audiences and often designed for conflicting purposes. It is expected to contain something for every significant sub-group, such as consumers, pensioners and immigrants. It must also respect the views of the party faithful and provide commitments for them to wield against ministers, or for ministers to wield against civil servants. Over the years, manifestos have become both longer and more specific. A recent survey by S. E. Finer showed that between 1945 and 1974 Conservative manifestos doubled in length and Labour's trebled. But in 1979 the Conservative manifesto halved its October 1974 wordage while Labour doubled theirs; between October 1974 and May 1979, the Conservatives cut their manifesto promises from 87 to 57 while Labour increased theirs from 72 to 77.[1]

Parties take their manifestos seriously and regard them as authoritative statements of party policy. If the party wins it claims to have a mandate for all of its proposals. In fact few people read the entire manifesto and many disagree with particular promises, even while voting for the party. Most people vote for a party because of its image or its record in office. A party's mandate reflects its voters' support for the broad direction of policy and not their approval for every specific item.

Writing a manifesto is partly an exercise in party management, reflecting the balance of power in a party as well as a set of calculations about how to win the favour of the electorate. In 1979 the political debates and manoeuvres leading to the emergence of the Labour and Conservative manifestos were almost as important in resolving, however temporarily, intra-party tensions over the kind of parties they were, as in laying down policy guidelines for the future. Mr Callaghan's dominance in his own party contrasted with the extent to which Mrs

[1] S. Finer, 'Manifesto Moonshine' *New Society*, (May 13, 1975).

144

Thatcher heeded the views of the colleagues who did not share her own views on some issues; it may be that the Conservative programme consolidated a more durable consensus.

Many observers anticipated a bitter battle over the Labour party manifesto. Mr Callaghan obviously wanted few commitments, least of all those which the left-wing dominated NEC would try and foist upon him. He knew that in 1974 Labour's vote had reached its lowest post-war total and the party had to appeal to non-Labour voters and regain former supporters. He was also aware of the surveys which showed that many of the policies favoured by the Conference and the National Executive Committee were far out of line with views of the ordinary Labour voter.

But in the 1970s Transport House had developed the habit of making policy. The mood of the NEC had already been seen in December and January when, against the opposition of Mr Callaghan and most of the PLP, it insisted upon having exclusive control of the party's Euro-manifesto. Tony Benn was an active chairman of the Home Policy Committee and he and his supporters pushed further state ownership, more public expenditure, and reflation, policies which were at variance with those being pursued by the government.

A distinctive politics has developed since the mid-1960s in the drafting of Labour manifestos. What usually emerges is a compromise between the parliamentary leadership and the National Executive spokesmen. Mr Benn spent much of 1978 and early 1979 in pushing for a meeting of the two sides. His fear was that once the election was under way then the party would be presented with a *fait accompli* by No. 10, and a too moderate manifesto. The left looked back to January 1974 when an agreed campaign document became the party manifesto for the February election. They also hoped that by pushing many radical proposals they would not depart empty handed; Mr Callaghan, it was assumed, could not say no to everything. But the Prime Minister prevaricated. He reasoned that the closer the election deadline, the stronger his position would be. He managed the summoning of the manifesto committee and he could effectively veto items which he did not like.

The Labour party's organisational structure and ideals guarantee a ready flow of ideas for policy. Reformers could turn to *Labour's Programme 1976*, decisions of the annual conferences, reports of several policy groups and the ministerial-NEC working parties. There was also the document, *Into the '80s*, the product of the TUC/Labour Party Liaison Committee. Finally, there were those 1974 manifesto commitments which had not yet been carried out.

Working parties between ministers and NEC members continued to exchange drafts on policies (see pp. 000). On crucial areas of industrial policy, prices, energy, and the economy no agreement was reached between the groups. The hope of the NEC was that the drafts from the NEC/Cabinet Working Group would become a draft campaign which, in turn, would form the basis for the manifesto. It envisaged the final manifesto being discussed at a number of joint NEC/Cabinet meetings. A concession to which the left could point was the agreement at the Home Policy Committee on July 27, 1978 that the next party manifesto should have a detailed programme of action for a future Labour government.[2]

The first attempt to stake out the ground was the publication of a 62-page document, *Keep Britain Labour* by the Research Department, the details of which were leaked to the Communist *Morning Star* on December 8, 1978 (the left alleged that the right had deliberately leaked it to discredit them). This drew together the various drafts of the Working Groups. Its inclusion of proposals for a wealth tax, the abolition of the House of Lords, compulsory planning agreements with the hundred largest companies, discretionary powers to freeze prices, and greater public expenditure were all likely to be unacceptable to Mr Callaghan; they advertised how far apart the NEC was from the Cabinet. There was a quick reply from some trade union leaders, such as Roy Grantham of APEX (who was upset over the proposed nationalisation of banks and insurance firms), Bill Sirs of the steelworkers, and Sid Weighell of the railwaymen. These trade union leaders based themselves on the 1978 document *Into the '80s*. In addition the Manifesto Group of Labour MPs published *Priorities for Labour*, a centre-right document. This rejected import controls, compulsory planning agreements and

---

[2] 'The Manifesto should be seen primarily as a programme of action, clear and unambiguous, for the next Government; *and this consideration should determine the length and nature of the Manifesto* . . . Wherever helpful, a cross-reference should be made to *Labour's Programme 1976*, so that our policy commitments can be as clear as possible.'

suggestions of a massive reflation of the economy. It called, instead, for support for the mixed economy and a permanent incomes policy which would pay attention to the need for differentials and incentives.

On December 20 members of the NEC and the Cabinet met to work through the NEC draft. The group became in effect a manifesto drafting committee.[3] Between January and March 1979 the group met almost weekly; issues on which the two sides could not agree would be referred to the final Cabinet-NEC meeting. On March 28 the NEC agreed to hold a special meeting before the Cabinet-NEC session, should the government be defeated that afternoon. The meeting was arranged for April 2, with a full NEC-Cabinet meeting on April 6.

On March 29, however, the party's General Secretary reacted to the existence of a No. 10 draft, prepared by two of Mr. Callaghan's staff, David Lipsey and Tom McNally. It was widely known that there was such a draft: Tom McNally had written one twelve months earlier and Mr Callaghan talked openly about it. However virtually no member of the PLP had seen it. Some left-wingers feared that the emphasis on producing a brief manifesto quickly would result in it being less specific than they hoped. Geoff Bish, the Secretary of the party's Research Department, produced his own NEC version, which ran to 12,000 words. He wanted to ensure that those drawing up the manifesto would have this draft before them as well as the Downing Street version. In contrast to the No. 10 draft, this included many of the agreements already reached in the NEC/Cabinet group.

A Drafting Committee was appointed and met in the early evening at Downing Street on April 2.[4] There were three key stages in the defeat of the left at this manifesto meeting. The No. 10 draft was circulated to members of the Committee shortly before the beginning of the meeting and time was set

---

[3] The committee included for the cabinet side Messrs Foot, Healey, Mason and Shore and Mrs Williams, as well as ministers responsible for specific subjects under discussion. (A Conservative manifesto drafter, learning of the protracted complexities of the party, commented amazedly on how much more cumbrous and slow it seemed than the processes of his own cautious party).

[4] The Drafting Committee consisted of Messrs Callaghan, Foot, Shore and Benn for the government, and Messrs Allaun, Heffer, Tuck and Mrs Jeger for the NEC. Mr Hayward and the chairmen of the various NEC committees also attended.

aside for members to read it. But the committee started out
with the NEC draft. As the arguments proceeded, however, they
gradually moved to the less specific draft from No. 10. Compared
with the NEC draft, this included only proposals which had
already been agreed between the NEC and the government; it
therefore omitted the more contentious policies. (The NEC draft
placed the non-agreed sections in parentheses.) In effect the
choice of draft document to work on was important in settling
the terms of the argument. It was difficult for NEC members or
left-wingers to make insertions at this stage, given the general
agreement to shorten the draft document. If they wished to
include items from the NEC document they had to move
additions. Proposals for insertions usually collected the support
of only one or two members. The bias was reinforced by Mr
Callaghan's interpretation of Clause 5 of the Party Constitution.
Mr Callaghan correctly observed that, according to this clause,
the manifesto had to be agreed between the NEC and the
parliamentary leadership. He interpreted this to mean that if he
did not agree with a proposal then it could not be included.
And that, of course, was the political reality though no leader
had been so blunt in the past. A party leader can hardly be
challenged once an election is under way. His authority is at its
height.

The second stage was the abandonment of the NEC's formal
decision to have a manifesto which would include several explicit
proposals. Instead the drafters implicitly concurred with Mr
Callaghan's wish for, in his words, 'a manifesto that is short,
punchy and sexy'. Charming and bullying by turns, he got his
way. He frequently appealed to the NEC representatives for
trust. Instead of filling the manifesto with proposals, the NEC
should approach ministers after the election to agree what should
be done. At one stage he said, 'Don't tell me that if it's not in
the manifesto I won't do it. You have to trust us to do the things
that you want us to do without putting it in the manifesto.'
Surprisingly, NEC members refused to push even for policies
which had already been agreed with particular ministers.

Finally, there was the pressure of time. The meeting went on
until 3.30 in the morning and there was general impatience to
conclude the discussions. According to one participant the
mood at the end was, 'Let it go. If Jim doesn't want it he won't
have it.' There were bitter arguments over policies for the House

of Lords and industry; originally these sections were bracketed
to indicate that the drafting committee had not reached agreement. Mr Callaghan twice threatened to resign if the manifesto
proposed the abolition of the House of Lords. The drafting
committee met again on April 4, and made a few minor amendments. The fear of carrying on the argument at yet another
meeting led the participants to give up the struggle. Only three
major issues were left in parentheses: statutory powers for
planning agreements, the House of Lords, and the nationalisation
of the construction industry. A clean draft was prepared by
Geoff Bish and David Lipsey for the Prime Minister. The revised
draft was presented to the full NEC-Cabinet meeting on April 6
at 10 a.m. Most members saw the final version for the first time;
those who had not been on the original drafting committee had
no idea of what items had been omitted or changed. In spite of
all the planning over the previous two years, the manifesto was
rushed through in the circumstances which the NEC had hoped
to avoid.

Labour manifestos, more than most such documents, hardly
make attractive reading for the policy analyst. They reflect the
circumstances of their birth. Members of the drafting committee
have different assessments about how an election can be won.
They also work against a pressing deadline. Ministers, educated
by office, usually argue for vague or cautious phrases, while the
activists usually demand precise wording and explicit policy
commitments.

The general desire to reach agreement was exploited by Mr
Callaghan in his handling of the drafting committee. If he did
not want to consider a proposal then he made clear that he
would not accept it, and that usually ended discussion. At one
point an angry Mr Heffer reminded Mr Callaghan that he was
neither God nor the Labour party. Signs of compromise and
disagreements were reflected in the final version, but Mr Callaghan
had won his key battles. For example, there was no promised
abolition of the House of Lords, but only a promise to abolish
its delaying powers. There were no compulsory planning powers,
but only the possibility of back-up powers. Instead of the
abandonment of nuclear weapons, there was a promise to hold a
debate before any decision was taken. There was no threat to
nationalise one of the big four banks. There was a tough section
on relations with the Common Market and a threat to impose

import ceilings. Even here, however, the tone was much less anti-European than the party's manifesto for the June 7 direct elections.

What was surprising was how easily the left had collapsed. Tony Benn did not provide the expected lead for a more radical manifesto. Even on the increase in child benefits, which was official party policy, and on which the government side was prepared to make concessions, neither Lena Jeger nor Eric Heffer spoke up for the NEC line. NEC representatives were more individualistic, pushing their own particular proposals rather than presenting a common line. A disconsolate Geoff Bish complained after the drafting committee, 'We've lost, we've lost.' Another commented angrily, 'That's five years of policy-making down the drain.' Left-wingers were bitter about what had happened, but while the campaign lasted they suppressed their feelings. The No. 10 team might argue that very little Conference-approved policy had in fact been jettisoned. But some of the omissions, on the House of Lords, industry and the economy, had figured prominently in the party's programme.

No doubt Mr Callaghan was pleased by the outcome. Few could be surprised by his conservative leanings. But he was also happy to fight on a non-controversial Labour manifesto. He wanted above all to focus attention on what he regarded as the dangers of the Conservative programme. The *Economist* considered the final document 'as moderate as any on which the Labour party has campaigned during its 79 years existence'. Other sections of the press, however, did not agree. The *Daily Telegraph*, for example, regarded the proposals as 'a step to 1984'.

A certain mythology was to develop about the production of the manifesto. At the party Conference in October 1979 delegates voted to give the NEC a greater role in formulating future manifestos so that the party leadership would be more accountable to the grass-roots, and unable to impose a *de facto* veto. But the document was hardly a 'right-wing manifesto' foisted on the party. As we show below, there were several proposals for an expansion of the state role in industry and the economy, and for redistribution of wealth. The manifesto contained many of the policies agreed between the government, the TUC and the NEC. Some points raised in the Committee were policies favoured by Mr Benn's Home Policy Committee

"If you must have a Conservative Prime Minister, I'm your man."

Sunday Mirror, April 8, 1979

and had never been before Conference (for example the animal welfare proposals and the nationalisation of power plant manufacturing). As for the House of Lords, Mr Callaghan still carried memories of the abortive attempt at reform in the 1966 Parliament. His own government had just fallen after another fruitless attempt at constitutional reform, which had consumed a vast amount of parliamentary time. He was not keen, in his own words, to offer 'another gift to the backbench barrackroom lawyers'. And the drafting stage is an exercise in compromise. Here the NEC had failed 'to do its homework', as one of its members admitted. Both ministers and members of the NEC lost cherished schemes because of the constraints of space. But the NEC failed to guide its drafting delegates on what it regarded as priorities. Not every policy interest can be represented on the drafting committee, so some briefing is required. The committee's draft on social security was regarded as weak by the full Cabinet-NEC group and the ministers concerned, Stan Orme and David Ennals were able to insert stronger proposals.

The manifesto, *The Labour Way is the Better Way*, was unveiled on Friday evening, April 6.[5] It celebrated Labour's record in controlling inflation, improving living standards and boosting welfare benefits during the previous four years. Its key proposal was to aim to cut the inflation rate to 5% by 1982. This would be achieved by giving the Price Commission greater powers to investigate and roll back prices, by talks with both sides of industry to reach agreement on economic policy, including what could be afforded for wages, and by a 'radical reform' of the Common Market's agricultural policy.

Labour promised to boost employment by an industrial and investment strategy which would achieve a 3% annual rate of growth. These would be greater powers for a National Enterprise Board, which would be armed 'with the necessary back-up statutory powers' to make agreements with major firms. The Girobank would be strengthened to enable it to compete with the clearing banks. Imports would be allowed to enter 'only within acceptable limits'. There was also a promise that within

---

[5] The full texts of the manifestos are available in *The Times House of Commons 1979*, and in the *Guardian* and the *Daily Telegraph* for the day after their publication (Labour, April 7; Conservative, April 12; and Liberal, April 11). For one view of the writing of the Labour manifesto see the chapter by G. Bish in K. Coates ed. *What Went Wrong?* (London, 1979), also reported in *Labour Weekly*, (August 31, 1979).

the life-time of the next parliament no one would be unemployed for more than 12 months without receiving the offer of a job or retraining. A Labour government would increase pensions in October 1979 to £35 for a married couple, and £22 for a single person. At the same time child benefit would go up to £4.50. A wealth tax would be imposed on those possessing more than £150,000. On housing, Labour also promised a substantial programme of building. There would be more rights for council tenants; council house sales would be permitted, except in areas of housing need; and the first-time buyer would be helped.

The manifesto promised a major extension of industrial democracy, reaffirmed a commitment to Scottish devolution, and promised talks with all concerned to improve the existing Scotland Act. On the House of Lords, the key compromise passage read, 'We propose, therefore, in the next Parliament to abolish the delaying power and the legislative veto of the House of Lords.'

The manifesto contained a tough section on the Common Market. Labour would oppose any move to make the Community a federation, and was not prepared to enter a monetary union. It promised that if reforms of the agricultural policy were not quickly implemented, 'we shall protect our interests' if necessary by vetoing further increases in food prices.

Many of the major policy battles of the Conservative manifesto – except on incomes and trade unions – had effectively been decided in 1976 and 1977 with the publication, respectively, of *The Right Approach* and *The Right Approach to the Economy* (see p. 78). Both policy documents were endorsed by Mrs Thatcher and established the common ground within the party. The former was fully discussed in shadow cabinet and endorsed by Mrs Thatcher. She was more reserved about the economic policy document; the shadow cabinet was only consulted on it. The preparation of the manifesto, looking to an autumn 1978 election, helped the shadow cabinet to reach agreement.

Mrs Thatcher, though herself inclined to fly off at tangents, agreed that the contents of these documents constituted official party policy. The most sensitive area clearly concerned anti-inflation policy. The earlier divergence of opinion within the shadow cabinet was reflected in *The Right Approach to the Economy*. Although it warned against the imposition of a 'target' in pay bargaining, the document continued:

> Yet in framing its monetary and other policies the government must come to some conclusions about the likely scope for pay increases if excess public expenditure or large-scale unemployment are to be avoided; and this estimate cannot be concealed from the representatives of the employers and the unions whom it is consulting.

The vague formula papered over the cracks but it proved to be useful in settling the outbreak of party infighting in November 1978 (see p. 119). During 1979 the collapse of the government's income policy and the industrial disturbances helped 'a spontaneous convergence' around the themes proposed by Mrs Thatcher. The 1979 manifesto bore more of her imprint than the 1978 one.

The manifesto for an autumn 1978 election had been drafted by Chris Patten and Adam Ridley, and edited by Angus Maude, during the summer. There was little disagreement with the leader's preference for a manifesto which took 'the high ground' and presented the party's style and philosophy rather than a shopping list of proposals. Preparations followed the usual lines. Reports were prepared by the Research Department and presented to the Steering Committee, and then to senior spokesmen for detailed discussion. The draft manifesto then went to the full shadow cabinet, and the galley proofs to the Advisory Committee on Policy. The shadow cabinet spent several half-day sessions going through draft policy statements during the summer. There were important broad discussions on industrial relations, pay policy and devolution, and some heated exchanges on Scottish policy and domestic rates. Mrs Thatcher, though keenly interested in the questions on the economy and trade unions, usually presented a less clear line than Mr Heath had done in similar discussions in the 1960s.

The 1979 manifesto had an interesting history. Events had ruled out hopes of preserving intact the autumn version. In February 1979, Chris Patten and Adam Ridley were joined by a new Research Department recruit, Dermot Gleason (till recently a member of Christopher Tugendhat's *cabinet* in the Common Market Commission). They prepared two draft manifestos. One was a chapter-by-chapter précis of the 1978 manifesto. The other was a 5,000 word draft based on five themes. The Steering Committee considered the two drafts, preferred the thematic one, and Angus Maude edited the final version. (Contrary to some reports, Sir Ian Gilmour, an experienced manifesto-writer, was not an editor; he agreed to write a separate message for Mrs Thatcher, entitled *Time for a Change*.) A number of items disappeared and there was a more qualified tone in many areas. The only significant addition to the 1978 document was the section dealing with trade union power. The events of the winter made a tougher line acceptable. The proposals on picketing and taxation of strikers' benefits were new and placed at the forefront of the manifesto.

Mrs Thatcher's brief foreword introduced the manifesto as a 'broad framework' for national recovery. The general election was presented as perhaps the 'last chance' to restore the balance in society, which had been tilted in favour of the state at the expense of the individual. The manifesto claimed that in the past politicians had tried to do too much, and neglected priorities. It promised that a new Conservative government would concentrate on priorities and would work *'with the grain* of human nature'.

A Conservative manifesto is drawn from diverse sources; from party traditions, the leader's own preferences, previous policy commitments, reactions to events and the policy stances of other parties, and political circumstances of the time. The variability of these influences is reflected in the contents of the programmes. In 1970 the emphasis had been on incentives and the virtues of the free market economy. This was combined with a technocratic stress on structural reform of trade unions and central government, and on entry to the Common Market. In February 1974 the manifesto was coloured by the industrial crisis and inflation, and pressed for a statutory incomes policy. For the following October, however, the emphasis had shifted to national unity and a housing package. In 1979, Mrs Thatcher's party returned to many of the values and themes expressed in the 1970 manifesto.

Shadow ministers were aware of the constraints of finance and of parliamentary time, and limited their manifesto proposals accordingly. In 1977 and 1979 the shadow Treasury team conducted bilateral negotiations with each shadow minister with a view to holding down expenditure. The goal was to establish a five-year programme of public expenditure for future Conservative governments. Mrs Thatcher herself was determined to avoid anything resembling a shopping list. She frequently reminded colleagues of mistakes made by Hugh Gaitskell — in her view 'the best leader Labour ever had' — when he had swamped himself with detailed policies in 1959. The manifesto preparations could be divided into three categories. First, there were the absolute commitments: these included cuts in tax and public expenditure, increased spending on law and order and defence, and no reduction in expenditure on health. Second, there were those reforms which would be enacted when the state of the economy allowed. Finally, there were policy briefings or 'reviews' which would be filled in at a later stage.

The Conservative Manifesto, 1979 listed its proposals under five main headings. These were:

1. The control of inflation and trade union power.
2. The restoration of incentives.
3. Upholding parliament and the rule of law.
4. Supporting family life by a more efficient provision of welfare services.
5. Strengthening defence.

The main proposals for controlling inflation included a strict control of the money supply and a reduction of both the government's borrowing requirement and the state's share of the national income. Cuts in public expenditure were promised in almost every area. The activities of the NEB would be limited and if help was given to ailing firms it would have to be 'in the national interest and be temporary and tapered'.

A Conservative government would also try to sell back shares in the recently nationalised aerospace, shipbuilding and National Freight operations. On trade unions, the party proposed three changes 'which must be made at once'. First, it would amend the law to limit the right of secondary picketing. Second, it would provide compensation for workers who lost their jobs as a result of closed shops, and also allow a right of appeal to the courts against exclusion or expulsion from any union. Finally, there would be public money to finance postal ballots, and unions would be required to contribute towards support of strikers (unions would 'bear their fair share of supporting those of their members who are on strike').

On pay, a new Conservative government would leave wage bargaining in the private sector to the companies and the workers concerned. It added that 'no one should or can protect them from the results of the agreements they make'. In the public sector, pay settlements would be governed by what each sector could afford. But there was no question of 'subsidising excessive pay deals'. On taxation the party would cut the top rate of tax to the European average (60%) and also the bottom rate of tax so as to take the low-paid out of the tax net; there would also be a switch from direct to indirect taxation.

The party had several proposals for strengthening 'family life'. These included the sale of council houses and provision of a tenants' charter; a revival of rented housing; improved standards in education and the repeal of the 1976 Education Act which compelled local authorities to reorganise secondary education along comprehensive lines; provision of a parents' charter, and the provision of assisted places at independent schools. There was no pledge to reduce or peg the interest rate on mortgages. Instead it was suggested that the party's plans for cutting government spending and borrowing would help to reduce interest rates.

On law and order the party promised to implement in full the recommendations of the Edmund-Davies Committee on police pay. There would be changes in sentencing policy and a free vote in Parliament on capital punishment. A new Nationality Act, to decide who could settle in Britain, was promised, and the entry of Commonwealth immigrants would be regulated by a register for dependents and a quota. The document proposed an increase in expenditure on defence, and promised to work with, not against, Britain's Common Market partners to achieve reforms in the Community's Agricultural Policy, as well as on its Budget and its Fisheries Policy. It would devalue the green pound to a point near to parity with the rest of the Community. On the constitution the document merely proposed discussion on a bill of rights, devolution and referendums.

The decision to produce a brief manifesto, with its consequent omissions and succinctness, created some misunderstandings which were eagerly exploited by Labour spokesmen. The

Guardian, for example, mistook the reduction to one sentence of the passage on incomes policy from *The Right Approach* for a fundamental change of economic policy from 1976. But some changes were of major substance.

The final passage on the constitution was markedly less reformist in tone than that in *The Right Approach*. Lord Hailsham's pressure for constitutional change had abated. The section on devolution had clearly been overtaken by the recent referendums. Earlier references to devolution and 'the establishment of a directly elected Scottish assembly' were now replaced by proposals to discuss the future of government in Scotland. In contrast to the 1974 manifesto, there was no commitment to a Speaker's Conference on electoral reform, and no proposal to limit interest rates for house purchase to 9½% or abolish domestic rates (though these last omissions were made reluctantly). The promises to introduce tax credits and to abolish domestic rates also disappeared. The shadow cabinet had clearly decided that cuts in direct taxation were the first priority. There were also changes in nuances in the sections on agriculture and on worker participation (where Ian Gilmour and Jim Prior failed to move their colleagues).

Preparations for the Liberal manifesto had been well advanced for a 1978 election. The Standing Committee had responsibility for drafting the substantive policy statements of the manifesto, leaving Mr Steel to write the introduction. Insofar as there was any liaison between the two it was provided by a small group chaired by William Wallace, an ex-candidate, who with Peter Knowles, the party Research Director did much of the drafting. The main task of the Standing Committee was to weld the various policies from the different policy panels into a coherent package after consultation with the parliamentary party and various policy groups. By March 1978, the party had decided to campaign on four main themes: political reform, industrial and economic reform, tax reform and ecological issues. A manifesto was ready for the printers in September. Some Liberals professed to see the last theme as the biggest potential vote catcher. The only serious controversy was over John Pardoe's economic proposals. A minority objected to the regressive consequences of a shift to more indirect taxation, while other activists thought that his commitment to a statutory incomes policy offended traditional Liberal principles.

In his preface to *The Real Fight is for Britain* David Steel indicted 'a failed political system' and called for an end to confrontation. He demanded electoral reform as the essential instrument for achieving a more cooperative style of politics and a government based upon a broad majority of the electorate.

The body of the manifesto also identified political and electoral reform as the first step to achieving other social and economic changes. A Freedom of Information Bill, providing public access to all official information except for a few sensitive categories, was promised. There would also be a new second chamber to replace the House of Lords, devolution for the English regions as well as Scotland and Wales, and a Bill of Rights, based upon existing British obligations under the European Convention. The section on tax reform promised a switch from direct to indirect taxes, with income tax rates ranging from 20 to 50%. A tax credit scheme would replace the 'bewildering array of means tests' and personal allowances and welfare benefits. A wealth tax would be imposed and profit-sharing and employee share ownership encouraged. Domestic rates would be abolished and eventually regional governments would be allowed to raise their own money. On the economy there would be a permanent statutory prices and incomes policy, and the synchronisation of annual pay settlements. There would be no further nationalisation or denationalisation. Finally, on ecology, there were proposals for a recycling of resources and conservation of energy.

The Liberal manifesto received a cautious welcome from the press. The *Guardian* welcomed its freedom from vested interests and agreed with its proposals for the reform of political institutions. But it noted that the politics of economic growth sat uneasily with the commitment to protect the environment. The *Economist* complimented the Liberals for having once again produced strikingly the best party manifesto.

In Scotland, Labour's manifesto was hurriedly written after the party obtained the text of the Transport House manifesto. In contrast to its preparations for a completely Scottish-generated Assembly manifesto, the election document was mainly a word-for-word copy of the London manifesto. The important devolution section used the same bland wording, omitting the

term 'legislative' and the phrase 'in the forefront of our programme'. The Conservative Scottish manifesto included a whole
battery of tougher measures on crime which the Scottish shadow
team had pressed for and which were not included in the
London manifesto. But apart from this the manifesto was thin
on specifically Scottish proposals.

The Scottish Nationalists had already published a comprehensive programme, *Return to Nationhood* in September 1978. It
was aptly described by its subtitle — 'a summary of the ideology
of Scotland's right to independence, the guiding principles of
the SNP and an outline of its programme for self-government'.
It included proposals from the 25 policy committees which sat
during the parliament, draft articles for a Scottish constitution,
and excerpts from the Declaration of Arbroath which had been
sent to the Pope in 1320. In a supplement for the election, the
party called for a stronger Scottish voice at Westminster, a
greater role for the Scottish Development Agency, and a larger
proportion of North Sea oil 'to be invested in Scotland'. It
promised that, with a majority of Scottish seats in parliament, it
would seek 'an orderly transfer of power from Westminster to
Scotland, and formulate a new constitution'.

The minor parties also presented manifestos. The Communist
party's *People before Profit* blamed large profits and the lack of
accountability by big business and multi-national corporations
for the economic problems. It called for a large measure of
reflation, including greater public expenditure, more welfare
benefits, a shorter working week, large cuts in defence expenditure and withdrawal from the EEC. The National Front's *It's
Our Country, Let's Win it Back* also made proposals to withdraw
Britain from the EEC and curb the influence of multi-national
corporations. It proposed that all coloured immigrants and their
offspring should be placed on a register and required, eventually,
to leave the country.

The most distinctive set of proposals came from the Ecology
party's *The Real Alternative*. This document forecast unprecedented social and economic upheavals, and called for a break
with the traditional politics of economic growth and the pursuit
of material values. Instead, it suggested that the emphasis should
be based on the conservation of resources, a stable economy
and decentralisation of decision-making.

The rhetoric of manifestos contains important clues to the

values of the political parties and the targets of their proposals. Labour's document referred frequently to the importance of 'care and compassion', 'fairness', and was clearly aimed at 'working people' and 'our people as a whole'. These statements were coupled with a sturdy nationalism in the sections on the Common Market and energy, where it was asserted that Britain needed a free hand to protect her 'vital national interests'. The Conservative manifesto employed a different vocabulary of 'balance', 'incentives', 'freedom', 'personal responsibility' and 'change'. Labour was dismissed as divisive and unable to 'speak for the nation as a whole'. The emphasis in the Conservative manifesto was on creating the conditions in which the economy would grow and on working 'with the grain of human nature'.

There were, however, many points of continuity between the two main manifestos. Mr Callaghan's introduction, for example, emphasised national unity to such an extent that he appeared to be stealing many of the lines of *One Nation* Conservatives. He promised more freedom for the individual and the neighbourhood, taking power 'away from the bureaucrats of town hall . . . and Whitehall' and providing greater choice in the running of schools and in housing. On specific issues it was possible to point to broad similarities in spite of differences in detail. Both parties promised to reduce the burden of income tax and switch to taxes on spending, and agreed on strict control of the money supply. There was a common agreement to holding further talks on devolution, helping the first-time house purchaser, permitting the sale of council houses, and providing a charter for tenants. Finally, both parties promised to take a tough stand over the reform of the Common Market's agricultural policy.

But there was a choice. The Conservatives proposed a lesser role for the state in industry, and aimed to create a climate of opinion that encouraged profits and enterprise in the private sector. Labour, through its reliance on the Price Commission, the Industry Act, the National Enterprise Board and planning agreements, was clearly more interventionist. And, despite proposals for greater spending on defence and the police, Conservatives were obviously bent on making tax-cuts and reducing total public expenditure. Their manifesto identified the areas to be pruned – subsidies to industry, direct labour schemes, waste, bureaucracy and the costly administration of the tax and social security systems.

Manifestos are not iron corsets. They do not cover every eventuality, least of all what may happen in the few weeks of the election campaign. Parties always defend themselves against contingencies by saying that their documents lay down broad outlines. All party leaders were aware of the importance of economic constraints and their inability to foresee future changes. Yet they did not succeed in keeping themselves entirely free from further commitments in the heat of the campaign. The Conservatives, under pressure, agreed to accept whatever comparability awards the Clegg Commission might give to public sector workers. There were statements that the tax rate might be cut to 30% under the Conservatives, and spokesmen provided reassurance about the continuation of regional aid in areas of high unemployment. Labour was stung by the tax issue and Mr Healey promised to raise the tax thresholds to take 1 million people out of the tax net. Mr Callaghan, contrary to the agreed line of the Campaign Committee, expressed his willingness at a later press conference to shift from direct to indirect taxation, if this was the wish of the electorate. Proposals for extending the powers of the Price Commission were announced during the campaign; investigations of a firm would be allowed even when no increase had been proposed and examinations could cover whole industrial sectors.

The surveys of reactions to the manifestos left no doubt of the striking popularity of the Conservative's proposals, and the extent to which they had got across to voters. The Conservative private polls found that whereas 61% knew of the Conservative manifesto the day after publication, less than half were aware of Labour's document. Public and private polls found that almost all of their proposals were approved, even by a majority of Labour voters. As Table 1 shows there was overwhelming approval — and even among Labour sympathisers — of the proposals for trade union reforms (on picketing, the closed shop and cutting benefits to strikers' families), law and order and the sale of council houses. Only the party's proposed sale of some state-owned companies failed to attract majority Labour support.

Some newspapers published a synoptic précis of the rival manifestos. Probably few of their readers struggled through to construct a balance sheet, relating the promises to their own personal preferences. But the policies in the manifestos were

Table 1. *Which Party has the Best Policies?*

(April 1979)

		Con %	Lab %	Lib %	Don't know/none %
Inflation/Prices	Con voters	89	2	0	9
	Lab voters	4	84	1	11
	Lib voters	17	36	26	22
	TU members	38	48	4	9
Taxation	Con voters	94	1	1	4
	Lab voters	16	63	1	21
	Lib voters	33	21	29	18
	TU members	51	33	7	15
Industrial Relations/Strikes	Con voters	75	8	1	16
	Lab voters	6	80	2	13
	Lib voters	20	36	18	26
	TU members	28	52	4	16
Unemployment	Con voters	83	3	*	14
	Lab voters	7	73	*	20
	Lib voters	18	36	17	29
	TU members	37	42	2	19
Common Market	Con voters	67	6	1	25
	Lab voters	8	55	2	35
	Lib voters	21	19	25	36
	TU members	33	34	4	29
Law and Order	Con voters	92	1	0	7
	Lab voters	24	47	1	28
	Lib voters	44	6	19	31
	TU members	58	22	3	17

Source: MORI. *New Statesman* (18 May, 1979).

echoed in candidates' election addresses and formed the basis of much of the party argument during the campaign. There was very little in the Labour manifesto that drew heavy fire – or that won many votes. It was the Conservatives whose promises dominated the campaign.

10 The Choices of the Campaign

It was a snap election but not a short one. Five weeks elapsed between the defeat of the government and polling day, in contrast to the three weeks of the February 1974 contest. It was headlined as a bitter election between the most right-wing of Conservative parties and the most left-wing of Labour parties. In practice, however, it was good humoured and with fewer personal attacks than any post-war election.

Every election campaign has its distinctive character, and each is described by the press as boring. For journalists, the personalities are already familiar and the arguments well-explored. Only if new events stir the public and evoke fresh reactions from the politicians does an election 'come alive' for the media. The 1979 election was, in fact, more free from extraneous events and sensations than any contest since the war.

It was the first general election to be fought in April for more than a century. The Easter break affected tactics, but the weather was good for the time of year. Rainfall was below average and there were no freak storms or cold spells. No one could complain that natural hazards hampered their operations.

The election had one special feature; it took place on the same day as the local council elections over most of England and Wales. Such simultaneity would have been ruled out by Home Office officials as impossible had they not happened to have spent the last few months working out the technical feasibility of holding elections on June 7 both for Westminster and for Europe. They had found that the administrative difficulties (such as the provision of enough ballot boxes) were not insuperable. One consequence of the situation was that some local activists concentrated on council rather than parliamentary politics. The press coverage focused to an overwhelming extent on the national campaign.

Another factor influencing the style of events lay in the security arrangements. On Friday, March 30, Airey Neave, Mrs Thatcher's close ally, and shadow spokesman on Northern Ireland, was killed by a bomb attached to his car as he drove out of the House of Commons car park. No one knew whether this Irish terrorist action was the beginning of a full-scale campaign against British politicians. The police took extreme precautions and surrounded the main party leaders with screens of detectives. They called conferences for candidates and agents and insisted that the itineraries of the leading figures should be kept secret until the last moment, and that their meetings should normally be by ticket only. As the election advanced without incident the alertness of politicians gradually relaxed. But, to the dismay of many of them, the police kept up very thorough safeguards; as one No. 10 aide complained, 'They know that trouble is not likely but, since they want to be quite sure that no one is killed on their patch, they ruin our meetings by their security screens.'

Certainly the election was distinguished by the absence of reports of rotten eggs or other missiles being thrown at the party leaders. As far as they were concerned, it was a notably tranquil affair, although Mr Callaghan was pursued by an organised group of Socialist Unity hecklers demanding 'Troops out of Northern Ireland'.

There were two reasons why the election lasted five weeks instead of the normal statutory minimum of 20 days. A dissolution at the end of March meant that Easter came in the middle of the campaign and, under the Representation of the People Act, the five days around Easter (including two Bank Holidays) are *dies non* for the purposes of the electoral calendar. Parliament was therefore dissolved 26 days before polling day, instead of the usual 20. A second, more political, reason for the election taking place as late as May 3 was that Mr Callaghan had for some time been convinced of the tactical advantage of a long campaign. Labour politicians assumed that the best hope of winning lay in discrediting Margaret Thatcher. It was believed that in the course of a protracted campaign either her health or her voice would break, or she would be lured into one or more of the impulsive indiscretions of which she had shown herself capable. 'MAGGIE'S NERVE IS THE TARGET' was how an *Observer* headline described Labour tactics on April 1. By

| Table 1. Campaign Chronology | | Mr Callaghan's | Mrs Thatcher's | Election |
Date	Events	main speech	main speech	broadcast
Wed 28	Defeat in Commons			
Thu 29	Edge Hill by-election Announcement of May 3 poll			Lab
Fri 30	Neave assassination			
Sat 31				
Sun 1	No TV debate			
Mon 2				Con
Tue 3	Budget			
Wed 4				
Thu 5			Candidates' rally	
Fri 6	Lab manifesto			
Sat 7	Dissolution			
Sun 8				
Mon 9		Glasgow	–	
Tue 10	Lib manifesto	Stockport	–	
Wed 11	Con manifesto	Ilford	Finchley	
Thu 12		Cinderford	–	
Fri 13		Cardiff	–	
Sat 14		Southampton	–	
Sun 15	EASTER	–	–	
Mon 16	Con open campaign	Leicester	Cardiff	
Tue 17		Birmingham	Gravesend	Lab
Wed 18		Hemel Hempstead	Nottingham	Lib
Thu 19		Cardiff	Birmingham	Con
Fri 20		Liverpool	–	Lab
Sat 21		Edinburgh	–	–
Sun 22		–	–	–
Mon 23	Nominations close Southall riot	Wandsworth	Darlington	Con
Tue 24		Coventry	–	Lab
Wed 25		Redditch	Edinburgh	Con
Thu 26		Manchester	Aberdeen	Lib
Fri 27		Cardiff	London	Con
Sat 28		–	–	Lab
Sun 29		–	Wembley	Lib
Mon 30		Chatham	–	Con
Tue 1		Ealing	Bolton	Lab
Wed 2		Cardiff	Finchley	–
Thu 3	Polling day	–	–	–

April 22 it was 'THE SEARCH FOR THE TORY BANANA
SKIN'.

However the Conservatives to some extent nullified Labour's
strategy by refusing to start their campaign until Easter Monday,
April 16, thus confining themselves to two-and-a-half weeks of

publicised electioneering. The Conservatives knew that they were starting well ahead, and so their strategy was to win by not making mistakes. Labour recognised that they were well behind; aggression was essential. At the end of the first week one Conservative strategist boasted, 'Lovely — Callaghan's been punching thin air, while we've been resting.' The Conservatives felt that their only real enemy was complacency. On April 9 Lord Thorneycroft gave a predictable warning to his followers:

I must tell you that victory in this election will only come to the Conservatives through much hard work . . . Do not be misled by the varying fortunes which you see depicted in the opinion polls. Do not despair if the gap narrows as it very probably will. Do not be complacent if our lead looks large. Concentrate everything you've got on winning the only poll that counts on May 3.

Certainly, at the opening of the campaign everyone accepted that the Conservatives were favourites to win. The polls had put them 20% ahead in February, and at the end of March the reported lead varied between 9% and 13%. The bookmakers were quoting the Conservatives as 4 to 1 on favourites. The *Financial Times* share index had risen to 538 and the stock market had patently made discount for a Conservative victory.

Mr Callaghan announced the election formally in a ministerial broadcast on Thursday, March 29. It was not a simple statement naming the day, but a partisan argument for voting Labour. Mrs Thatcher naturallly exercised her right of reply although, because of Airey Neave's death, she postponed the broadcast from the next day until Monday, April 2. She stressed the point that was the Conservatives winning card:

We have just had a devastating winter of industrial strife — perhaps the worst in living memory, certainly the worst in mine. We saw the sick refused admission to hospital. We saw people unable to bury their dead. We saw children virtually locked out of their schools. We saw the country virtually at the mercy of secondary pickets and strike committees and we saw a government apparently helpless to do anything about it . . . Mr Callaghan tried to frighten you with a picture of the Conservatives 'tearing everything up by the roots'. But

we are the party of tradition. Paying your way is not tearing
things up by the roots. Paying your way is good husbandry,
paying your way is planning for the future . . . I think we all
know in our hearts it is time for a change.

One of the few sensations of the campaign was the refusal of
Mrs Thatcher to take part in a televised programme with Mr
Callaghan and Mr Steel. On March 30 *Weekend World* wrote to
propose the meeting — the idea had been floated from Downing
St some time earlier — and the Labour and Liberal parties
quickly made known their acceptance. Since 1964 it had been
normal for the opposition to challenge the government to a
confrontation of leaders and for it to be rebuffed. In the summer
of 1978 Mr Callaghan had decided that he would not take part
in a television debate Now, however, the tables were turned. For
the first time the opposition was in the lead and Mrs Thatcher's
advisers, who had been contemplating what to do since the
autumn, decided that any such encounter should be shunned.
She herself was quite willing to accept, but Lord Thorneycroft,
Willie Whitelaw and Gordon Reece were quite firm in their
advice. It was not so much that they were frightened of Mr
Callaghan defeating Mrs Thatcher forensically. They saw the
confrontation as something which would dominate the whole
election. All the news stories would be about the preparations
for the meeting and the detailed arrangements: and the outcome,
which was perhaps a toss-up, would be seen as deciding the
election. As one of them said 'We wanted the election to be
about the winter, not about a TV programme.' It would also be
very exhausting and distracting to the leader personally. The
Conservatives had another fear. Any rise in Liberal support
would almost certainly hurt them more than Labour. The
prospect of David Steel being interviewed alone by Brian Walden,
and calling 'a plague on both your houses', was a prospect
which did not appeal to Conservative strategists. Moreover, as
one of them put it 'It was a two-way loser. If she had won the
argument, which we thought she would, a lot of people wouldn't
have liked that in a woman and if she lost, she'd have been seen
as no good either. The difficulty was how to decline without
seeming to run away.' One other consideration was that it would
set a precedent that might be embarrassing next time.
Labour was obviously disappointed. Their great advantage in

the election was that Mr Callaghan was more popular than Mrs Thatcher. (As the election advanced this advantage increased. Malcolm Rutherford noted in the *Financial Times* at the end of the campaign, 'If this was a Presidential election there would be no doubt about the outcome'). But Mrs Thatcher wrote to *Weekend World* on April 3:

We should continue with the traditional broadcasting arrangements of presenting the whole policy of a party to the nation . . . Personally I believe that issues and policies decide elections not personalities. We should stick to that approach. We are not electing a President. We are choosing a government.

From then until Easter Mrs Thatcher kept a relatively low profile. She addressed Conservative candidates on April 5. She outlined major points of Conservative policy and said, 'Pray God we don't have another hung parliament.' She asserted that the Conservatives would make only one main promise during the campaign: to cut the rate of income tax at all levels. 'It is paramount in our strategy. It is sustainable but it limits other promises.'

Parliament still had to finish its business. On Tuesday, April 3, Denis Healey presented an interim Budget. It was a muted affair and had been drawn up after consultation with Sir Geoffrey Howe, the shadow chancellor. It was agreed that it was improper for a government which had been defeated to put forward new proposals, and throughout the campaign Mr Healey was careful not to set out what his budget would have contained if he had had a free hand. He pointed to the strict conventions and replied to questioners 'If I answered that, I'd be drummed out of the Brownies.' He described his position in presenting the Budget as like a man turning up to play the leading role in an opera and finding that he was only asked to hold the scenery steady.

In the days after the Budget, parliament quickly got through all the necessary routines, while the parties were busy behind the scenes completing their manifestos and their campaign arrangements. By Friday, April 7, it was plain that Mr Callaghan had outflanked the NEC and the left wing of his party over the manifesto and *The Labour Way is the Better Way* was accordingly

launched . (see p. 152). At the first of Labour's daily press
conferences on Monday, April 9, Mr Callaghan spoke of the five
policies in the manifesto that would strengthen national unity:
the best pension increase ever for widows and retired people;
the abolition of TV licence fees for pensioners; tax cuts for
young people and average-paid workers; easier home ownership;
and tougher powers for the Price Commission.

The Conservative leader waited till April 16 to make her
opening speech. At Cardiff she appealed to the moderate Labour
supporters, the 'soft' target voters in her private polls. She
compared the present Labour party unfavourably with the party
of Roy Jenkins and Hugh Gaitskell. She dismissed Mr Callaghan's
message as 'carry on as we are', and argued that this could only
lead to decline. 'We must have change. We can go on as we have
been going and continue down. Or, two weeks on Thursday, we
can stop and say with a decisive act of will "enough".' In one of
her most inspirational passages she concluded: 'I am a conviction
politician. The Old Testament prophets did not say "Brothers I
want a consensus." They said: "This is my faith. This is what I
passionately believe. If you believe it too then come with me".'

The daily routine of the campaign centred around the party
press conferences as it had done in every election since 1959.
However on this occasion the impact was reduced by the fact
that the Conservative and Labour parties chose the same time —
9.30 a.m. — to meet the media on opposite sides of Smith Square.
In all previous campaigns three-quarters of an hour had elapsed
between one conference and the other, so that the journalists
could attend both, often carrying the argument from one to the
other. In October 1974 Harold Wilson, trusting to his own
dexterity, had been willing to go second — although he subsequently complained that the press allowed the Conservatives
to set the theme for the day. On this occasion both parties
wanted to start earlier so that their leaders could get away on
their travels around the country. Both were determined to take
the first slot. The Conservatives later said that they had been
willing to alternate with Labour on successive days, but they
made this offer only when they were confident that it would be
rejected. Since the Conservatives wanted a quiet campaign and
the Labour party stood to benefit from some confrontation, it
seems plain that Labour had been out-manoeuvred. A noisier
campaign might have irritated the public and benefited the

Liberals, but any Liberal advance was likely to be more at the Conservatives' expense than the Labour party's.

The Liberals held their press conference at the National Liberal Club at about 10.30 a.m. Although they chartered a bus to bring the journalists from Smith Square three-quarters of a mile away, they sometimes failed to attract many passengers. However the messages from the Liberal press conference got almost equal treatment with those from Smith Square. The television cameras did not focus on the thin audience of journalists but on the speaker, usually David Steel, against his own silhouette on the bright orange backdrop.

Indeed all three press conferences were set up for television. The leader was neatly placed in front of an appropriate party slogan and opened with a message which offered the television bulletins the one- to two-minute item which they needed for the lunchtime news. The working press complained of the dominance of the television cameras, but it must be said that the journalists did little to turn the press conferences into interesting contributions to the debate. Questions did not always flow very freely, and there was little cooperative follow-up by others when one questioner received an evasive answer. At times it seemed that some correspondents were reluctant to offer copy to their opponents by asking the pointed questions which they were ready to use in their reflective articles.

The style of the conferences differed. Mrs Thatcher, who presided at 10 of her party's 15 London conferences, tended to make a short statement and then to lay herself open to questions. Although she was always flanked by three or four Shadow Cabinet Ministers, very few were directed at them. Mrs Thatcher had to respond to wide ranging and rather random enquiries. On the Labour side Mr Callaghan (present 14 times out of 18) usually brought three colleagues with him, and they all made prepared statements of much greater length, leaving relatively little time for questions. When they did give answers, it often seemed that they were trying to be unquotable so that the basic message of their initial prepared remarks necessarily dominated any report of the proceedings. Mr Callaghan was particularly careful not to be drawn off his chosen ground. On occasion too, Labour managed to catch the cameramen with a blackboard demonstration. Shirley Williams gave a compelling, school-mistress's exposition of what the Conservatives would have to do to the education system, if they were to save £150 million from the school budget. Joel Barnett used a chart to show the cuts in services which the Conservatives' tax proposals would have to involve.

Some observers commented on the extent to which this election went further than its predecessors in being conducted as a media event rather than an argument. Mrs Thatcher in particular spared no trouble to help the photographers. She was shown waving her shopping basket, or swinging a broom in one factory and tasting tea in another or, in the most extreme and most satirised case, cuddling a new-born calf, which in fact she held for 13 minutes till every cameraman was satisfied. A visit to an old people's home in Paddington was dominated by media equipment: the room contained six Japanese television crews. As the election went on, objection was taken to this packaging. An informed article by Adam Raphael, 'The Selling of Maggie', appeared in the *Observer* on April 22, and reporters more and more often made snide remarks about the pseudo-events devised for their benefit, and about Saatchi and Saatchi.

On the Labour side Jim Callaghan professed reluctance to involve himself in synthetic events. He explained his distaste for the demands of the media: 'It's not my style. If I do [what they want], I'll sound as phoney as she does.' He also remarked 'The voters don't want to see you cuddling a calf. They want to be sure you're not selling them a pig in a poke.' He often spoke sharply to the press as they crowded around him during his walkabouts. But his aides saw to it that he was photographed talking to apprentices in a railway workshop and to old people in a home for the retired; he was also shown attending Easter services with his grandchildren.

David Steel, travelling with his somewhat unreliable 'battle bus', managed to get himself photographed sympathetically in good settings. But he was accused of manipulating outdoor encounters into narrow streets so that he always seemed to be in a thronging crowd.

No strikes interrupted the output of newspapers or the presentation of television bulletins, except for the dispute which had kept *The Times* and the *Sunday Times* off the streets since November. The absence of *The Times* may have affected the whole campaign, since its coverage and its use of verbatim quotes had always been particularly extensive, providing copy and questions for the rest of the media. However the election was also subdued because of the absence of major events in the outside world to which the politicians could react. There were few strikes under way at the time. A dispute at British Leyland fizzled out quickly. But a rumbling quarrel with the civil service unions and a teachers' dispute towards the end of the campaign may have reminded the public of the potential for industrial trouble. They also contained echoes of the winters' disruptions.

The situation in Rhodesia, where the illegal regime was conducting its election in mid-April, was always a potential embarrassment, and the Conservatives were particularly worried about it. They encouraged their official observers not to return to the country until just after polling day. Jim Callaghan seized a headline on April 23 by dispatching Cledwyn Hughes, the retiring chairman of the PLP, to survey the scene in Southern Africa. Although the Shah of Iran had fallen in February, little was heard of the oil crisis that was soon to follow, with its far-reaching implications for the world's economy.

Despite the impending European elections, virtually no news from the Common Market or its members impinged on British consciousness during the election. Although occasionally it was suggested that the EEC was becoming a central issue, the truth was that, as one headline put it, 'SILKIN MOPS UP EEC OPTIONS'. All parties thought the Common Agricultural Policy should be revised and the U.K. contribution to the budget reduced. Labour could be attacked for its grudging way of dealing with Europe, but there were no votes to be gained by a strong pro-European stance. An early and powerful speech by Peter Shore drew a careful reply by Francis Pym, but the exchange was not followed up.

In another way, too, the election was uneventful. Ever since the impact of the trade figures published just before polling day in 1970, parties have worried about routine statistics emerging to upset their campaign arguments. In April 1979 none of the statistics were particularly devastating. The government could take comfort in the retail price index, published on April 12, which kept the rate of inflation just below the magic 10 %; while the unemployment figures on April 19 showed a reassuring fall. A strike of civil servants prevented the publication of the trade figures (which, it later proved, would have been more disturbing).

The Labour party's arrangements for the campaign, even more explicitly than in the days of Harold Wilson, centred upon the party leader and his entourage. There was a daily Campaign Committee meeting, but it was seldom attended by the heavy-weights of the party unless they were to be at that day's press conference. Mr Callaghan's team took pains to keep in touch with Transport House and to coordinate activities with the departments there. But the essential shaping of the campaign was in the hands of Mr Callaghan and those around him. He had at his side Derek Gladwin who took charge of a team based at No. 10 Downing Street, which included David Lipsey and Roger Carroll as speech-writers. When Mr Callaghan travelled he was accompanied by detectives and secretaries from No. 10 to look after him in his role of Prime Minister, and by Derek Gladwin, as well as by Audrey Callaghan and their son, Michael Callaghan, a Ford executive. Back in Downing Street, Bernard Donoughue and Gavin Davis were a source of ideas, and Tom McCaffrey, the prime-ministerial press secretary, although inhibited by his role as a civil servant, offered a familiar presence.

But Mr Callaghan, while relying for speech writing and strategic suggestions on these close colleagues, also needed media support if he was to influence the party's public image. Edward Booth-Clibborn and Tim Delaney played a dominant role in preparing the party political broadcasts and advertisements for Labour, sometimes to the displeasure of those officially charged with such duties in Transport House.

The daily routine began with a breakfast meeting at No. 10 of the essential members of the team. Derek Gladwin accompanied the Prime Minister to the Campaign Committee which met at Transport House at 8.30 a.m., and which already had briefing material from the Research Department's scouring of the day's press and, usually, from Robert Worcester of MORI, the party's pollster. After the 9.30 a.m. press conference there would be a further short meeting with various people discussing matters informally with Mr Callaghan before he set off on his travels. These were usually devised for him to be back in Downing Street by 10 or 11 p.m. for a final brief chat with his team. Unlike his predecessor, he tried to be in bed by midnight.

It was not just because the Conservatives were in opposition that there was a much closer integration between the party headquarters and the leader's entourage. Mrs Thatcher had great faith in Lord Thorneycroft, who was very much in command of 32 Smith Square. There everything went more or less smoothly along lines laid out in a 'war book' devised by a General Election Committee under Alan Howarth.

The Conservative routine began very early with a pre-briefing meeting under Adam Ridley, acting head of the Research Department, with his staff and also with John Hanvey of ORC. Mr Ridley then went over to Central Office to take a leading part in the 8.15 a.m. press conference briefing, which was attended by Mrs Thatcher and the shadow ministers who were to share the platform. Lord Thorneycroft and a few officials from research and publicity departments, as well as some of Mrs Thatcher's staff and secretaries. Tim Bell of Saatchi and Saatchi was also present. After the press conference there was a little-used opportunity for a small informal gathering with Mrs Thatcher before she and Mr Thatcher set off on their travels, and the Chairman held his routine 10.30 morning meeting attended by department heads. As in previous elections there was a working lunch at St Stephen's Club attended by any senior officials available. 'It was a bit of a muddle. But somehow Peter Thorneycroft got us through the agenda though it was usually all scrambled together under item 1.' At 9 p.m. the Chairman had an evening meeting with department heads – 'often the best meeting of the day'. It was envisaged that Lord Thorneycroft might have to foregather with Mrs Thatcher late in the evening after her return from speaking, but although this happened once or twice there does not seem to have been any crisis which made this necessary.

Lord Thorneycroft, unlike previous Chairmen, remained in Central Office throughout the campaign, in undisputed charge of affairs and with his assistant, Alan Howarth, making many decisions. He steadied his colleagues when there were demands for a drastic response to Labour's unexpected tactics, or when the later opinion polls were momentarily alarming. He had Angus Maude, the Deputy Chairman, with him each morning. Lady Young, the other Deputy Chairman, travelled with Mrs Thatcher throughout, and provided constant liaison with headquarters. David Wolfson, one of Mrs Thatcher's two principal staff members, also travelled with her, while the other, Richard Ryder, stayed in London. Roger Boaden organised her travels. One of her two parliamentary private secretaries was also to have been with her but, because John Stanley was unwell, while Adam Butler had a marginal seat, this was not possible for much of the time. Among other key figures at the centre of the Conservative Campaign were Humphrey Atkins, the Chief Whip, (who kept a political oversight on the broadcasting arrangements), Alistair McAlpine, the Treasurer, Tony Garner, the Chief Organisation Officer, Adam Ridley, and the indefatigable Gordon Reece in charge of publicity.

In an election there is always a great deal of bustle at headquarters, some of it essential and some of it to very little avail. There are also great opportunities for internal wrangling and for backbiting from those whose suggestions are ignored or who are excluded from the inner councils. But it does seem that in 1979 the Conservative machine operated exceptionally smoothly and without rancour at least until the final week. How far its efforts were rewarded is discussed on in Chapter 16.

The Liberal campaign was as leader-centred as the others. David Steel was very much in personal charge of his own tour but left many other matters to his organisers at Liberal headquarters in the National Liberal Club. Lord Evans of Claughton was in command there, aided by Hugh Jones, the Director General, and Geoff Tordoff, the chairman of the executive, who also acted as press officer. Archie Kirkwood was the headquarters link with David Steel. Richard Holme had a key role as trusted London confidante of the leader, and there were one or two other unofficial 'ideas men' who helped to draft press statements and to suggest strategic initiatives. The arrangements were very informal but reasonably efficient, with quick consultations before and after the press conference, and a thoroughgoing review of strategy each weekend.

David Steel addressed 11 out of the 17 press conferences in London. He visited 50 constituencies, making news wherever he was travelling with his well-publicised battle bus; but he kept in close touch with Lord Evans.

An election offers an interesting test of the appeal of individual politicians. The parties put those who they think will draw most sympathetic attention into the firing line. The media focus their coverage on those whom they find most newsworthy. In this election, as later chapters on the press and on broadcasting will show, there was even greater emphasis on the leaders than before. In many ways the battle was presented as Jim Callaghan versus Margaret Thatcher, with David Steel fighting a separate campaign. But on the Labour side Mr Callaghan gave most prominence to Shirley Williams (underlining the contrast between her personality and Mrs Thatcher's) and Denis Healey (recognisable as authoritative on financial matters). Roy Hattersley, Peter Shore and John Silkin were given some opportunities at press conferences. Such major figures as Michael Foot and Tony Benn were less publicized; this was not because they were inactive – each indeed attended one press conference and made many speeches – but because it was recognised that they were not found so sympathetic by the voters at large.

The national press, for all its partisanship, did not manage to trip up Mr Foot or Mr Benn in any serious way, although Michael Foot was teased by Mr Whitelaw for saying in an April 28 broadcast 'Who are they going to shoot?' in relation to an imposed policy of trade union reform. Tony Benn drew headlines on April 9 for saying, 'A vote for Labour in this election will be a vote against the Common Market as it now operates.' To which Mr Callaghan replied the next day:

> I don't endorse Mr Benn. He does not endorse me. We each make our own speeches. We are not a lot of automatons in the Labour party. I am not here to comment on other people's speeches . . . We are all working towards the same end. We are going to put an end to the agricultural policy in its current form.

It could not be said that any leading Labour figure committed a conspicuous gaffe during the election, except perhaps for Sir Harold Wilson. On April 27 Gordon Greig, in the *Daily Mail*, under the heading – 'EXCLUSIVE – the most intriguing – and perhaps indiscreet – interview of the campaign', reported Sir Harold as saying that Lady Wilson might vote Conservative because Mrs Thatcher was a woman. Sir Harold quickly issued a qualification. Although he made several speeches he was hardly felt to have been an asset to the Labour campaign.

Mrs Thatcher dominated the Conservative efforts. The party was notably lacking in outstanding platform orators or television personalities. Apart from Mrs Thatcher, Ted Heath drew most attention, almost all of it sympathetic. He was one of the few people in the election to talk about foreign policy, and it was widely suggested that he was trying to make his peace with Mrs Thatcher and win from her the Foreign Secretaryship; he made vigorous, if self-righteous, speeches across the country. Willie Whitelaw, Sir Geoffrey Howe and Jim Prior all received some publicity – but much less than their eminence in the party might have suggested. Sir Keith Joseph was almost as conspicuous by his absence from the reporting of the Conservative campaign as Tony Benn was on the Labour side. His most-noticed contribution was on May 1 when he argued that Britain was:

> in danger of total economic decline . . . growth has been virtually eliminated by a combination of union-enforced Luddism and over-manning, punitive taxation, excessive state borrowing and spending, excessive legislation and bureaucracy and excessive state interference, control and ownership.

The Liberal party had plenty of newsworthy characters among its MPs and some of them, notably Alan Beith and David Penhaligon, got special opportunities as spokesmen for the party on television – a great advantage to members fighting marginal seats. John Pardoe was exceptionally prominent partly because he was more willing to leave his constituency to appear on the media but something was also seen of Cyril Smith. Less was heard from the two former leaders. Jo Grimond on the whole stayed in Scotland. Jeremy Thorpe, under the cloud of his indictment, was cold-shouldered; there was a lot of publicity about his North Devon campaign and headlines about the postponement of his trial from April 30 to May 7 to allow him to fight the campaign.[1] The propriety of his standing while under this cloud excited some discussion, and so did the injunction which he secured on April 26 against the distribution by Auberon Waugh, his 'dog-lover' opponent, of a supposedly libellous election address.

One outsider who had attracted major headlines in the previous three elections drew less attention this time. Nonethe-

---

[1] On June 22 he and his co-defendants were acquitted on all charges after a 6-week trial.

less on April 29 Enoch Powell was widely reported when (while advising voters in Northern Ireland to support the Unionists) he told voters in Britain to support Labour as the most anti-Market of the parties.

Another group of names got well-orchestrated headlines as they advocated Conservative votes. Six former Labour ministers in turn told electors to support the Conservatives. Reg Prentice was, of course, a Conservative candidate. But Lord Robens, Sir Richard Marsh, Lord Chalfont, Lord George-Brown and Lord Wilson of Langside each explained why he had turned against his past. There was also publicity for an appeal from a less titled group of converts to the Conservatives, ranging from Kingsley Amis to Max Beloff.

Another party 'desertion' made headlines. When nominations closed at noon on Monday, April 23, Christopher Bailey, the Liberal candidate against Mr Callaghan in Cardiff South-East, an industrialist who had fought a notable battle against shipyard nationalisation, deliberately failed to place his papers in time and then advised the local Liberals to vote Conservative. If they were all to do so, Mr Callaghan would lose his seat. Mr Bailey was promptly expelled from the Liberal party, but there was no evidence that, except in consuming time at headquarters, his ploy had much impact.

In all, 2,576 candidates were nominated, 324 more than the previous record in October 1974. In addition to full slates from Conservative and Labour (except in the Speaker's seat and Northern Ireland) and an unexpected 576 from the Liberals, there were 303 from the National Front. The Workers' Revolutionary Party with 60, and a new force, the Ecology Party, with 53, also put enough standard-bearers into the field to qualify for the election broadcast awarded to any group with 50 candidates. The Communist Party, with 38, fell below the margin.

The Ecology Party got a sparse but not unsympathetic press, and their existence may have damped down the impact of the green power appeal that David Steel attempted to identify with the Liberals, in particular his stress of the need for safeguards if nuclear fuels were to be exploited. As the campaign advanced little was seen in the London press about the special campaigns of the SNP fighting every seat in Scotland, and Plaid Cymru fighting every seat in Wales. There were a few reports from

Ulster about confusions in the orange and green camps as 64 candidates strove for 12 seats.

The one subsidiary party which did draw attention throughout the campaign was the National Front. This was achieved less by its own activities than by the efforts of the Anti-Nazi League to disrupt its meetings. A massive show of police force avoided serious trouble in Leicester on April 21. In Southall on Monday, April 23, there occurred a disastrous confrontation between the police and the forces opposed to the National Front (which was holding a small meeting with few supporters in the Town Hall). In the course of the riot more than 300 people were arrested, and later in the day one protester, Blair Peach, was killed in confused circumstances. There were accusations of police over-reaction and suggestions that the incident would bring immigration, and law and order to the fore in the election. But there was no serious trouble at National Front rallies in Plymouth on April 24, in Newham on April 25, or in Bradford on April 30. In fact, as with the Airey Neave killing, all parties joined ranks to condemn violence and no one could be accused of exploiting the episode. If it had any effect, it may well have been in making immigrants even more solid in support for the Labour party — as the lesser evil.

Throughout the early stages of the campaign there were occasional stories about troubles over the nomination or adoption of particular Labour candidates (see p. 280—3). One in particular made headline news. In Newham North-East on April 10, James Dickens, the Labour nominee who had replaced Reg Prentice, resigned his candidature on the ground that the local committee only approved his election address by 18 votes to 14. There were suggestions that even Mr Dickens, a left-winger, was not far enough left for this notorious party. Activists were allegedly pushing him out to make room for Nick Bradley, the 'Young Socialist' representative on the NEC. However, the National Executive intervened, and in the next few days a new selection took place; a well-known anti-marketeer candidate, Ron Leighton, was chosen to succeed Mr Dickens. The whole episode provided a text for the Conservative speakers and for the press to elaborate the theme of the extremist takeover of the Labour party. This was also developed in respect of a few conspicuously left-wing candidates notably in Croydon Central, Hornsey, Bristol North-West and Dundee West. An unimportant

Labour faction, the Social Democratic Alliance, provided further publicity by denouncing the Marxists in the party. And at the national level the idea that Jim Callaghan was only there on sufferance from the left wing, and was a stalking-horse for a takeover by Tony Benn and the Marxists was extensively developed by politicians and by cartoonists. Mr Prentice argued that the left was 'using Mr Callaghan as a front man for their facade of respectability' and that Mr. Gaitskell's successors had just 'trimmed and trimmed and trimmed again'. As Mrs Thatcher said in Edinburgh on April 25:

> Whatever name they choose to operate under these left-wingers have the same aim. It is to destroy our present society with the hope that their brand of extremism would clamber to power over the wreckage. They want to build a state in which the freedom of the individual is utterly destroyed. Every action, including his choice of job, home and school is determined by bureaucracy.

She pointed out that the Prime Minister had complained of the infiltration of the Labour party by those who misused the name socialist, but that Labour's National Executive had responded by appointing an avowed Trotskyist as its youth officer. She observed that at election time all this was kept under wraps; there was no mention of Socialist heroes such as Keir Hardie and Nye Bevan; Tony Benn was being kept off the bandstand until the concert was over.

Apart from giving prominence to Shirley Williams, Labour did little to respond to these attacks, or to stress the dominance of moderates in the PLP and still more in the Cabinet. They did not even make as much capital as expected of the supposed lurch to the right in Margaret Thatcher's Conservative party.

Trade unions played some part in the election, both as a positive force and as a target. The Trade Union Committee for a Labour Victory (see p. 57) was busy during the election in raising funds for the party, in launching an independent £100,000 press advertising campaign and in encouraging trade union organisers to take leave to work in marginal seats.

There were varied reports about the effectiveness of this committee. Some of the trade unionists who went to the constituencies did not prove very helpful, and some would have

Daily Express, April 18, 1979

done the work anyway. The publicity for the Trade Union Committee for Labour Victory, and the press conferences held by its leaders, may have been counterproductive, since the polls indicated that the Labour party's tie with the trade unions was very much a mixed blessing for them as far as the electors were concerned. While the reported union interventions in the campaign may have rallied the support of some faithful trade unionists, they may have alienated more people in the middle of the road. The most notable saying of the election was perhaps that of Sid Weighell, the General Secretary of the Railwaymen, who, echoing an earlier speech, said on April 10 that if the Conservatives wanted a wages free-for-all — which he did not — then, 'I don't see how we can talk to Mrs Thatcher . . . I will say to the lads, come on, get your snouts in the trough.' Tom Jackson of the postmen, one of the most moderate of trade union leaders, spelled out on April 23 the spectre of confrontation which Margaret Thatcher seemed to be raising: 'The alternative to Labour is the most extremist, most reactionary government since the war.' And Len Murray, the General Secretary of the TUC, spoke bluntly on April 26, advising Margaret Thatcher not to seek trouble in the way that she and the Conservatives seemed to be doing, and to 'cool it'. However on April 24 the Scottish TUC had failed to agree on a resolution supporting the Concordat on which the Labour party based its claim to have got over the union troubles of the winter. On May 1, David Basnett, as Chairman of the TUC, said that he would cooperate with a Conservative government, but challenged the Conservatives to respond: 'Will Margaret Thatcher accept?' The Tory form of cooperation was:

the same as their concept of consultation in industry. They will tell us what they have decided. The Tory policy towards trade unions consists of a long list of criticisms and complaints of the kind that can be heard any day in the directors' dining rooms in the city and the more opulent taverns and restaurants of the Home Counties: criticisms and complaints that are founded in ignorance and prejudice and peevish, ill-informed gossip.'

However Jim Callaghan thought it desirable to dissociate himself from the unions to some degree. On April 16 he said:

Strikes should be a last resort and not a first resort. New rules
are set out to protect individuals in the matter of the closed
shop. The Concordat recommends that there would be
arbitration on disputes instead of strikes, and a call for more
secret ballots; it recommends limiting the powers of picketing
... The kind of legislation the Conservative party is now
talking about would solve nothing, would make matters
worse.'

In general Mr Callaghan did not strike an inspirational note.
Reporters accompanying him commented that his tone was
'elegiac', 'half-hearted', 'fastidious', and 'dignified'. He was
serious and avoided any personal criticism of Mrs Thatcher. A
light-hearted attack on Mr Heath on April 30 was dramatised by
the press. The Prime Minister commented sadly at his next press
conference on the difficulty of being cheerful and spontaneous.
The schedule originally designed by Transport House was relaxed.
His visits and his speeches were oriented to the marginal constituencies where he would look in at party committee rooms and
the occasional shopping centre. Instead of addressing two meetings a night he confined himself to one. His speeches were
generally concerned with the dangers of change. He was determined to dent the credibility of the Conservative party. In the
first week he concentrated on unemployment and the threat to
jobs which would come from the implementation of public
spending cuts. He calculated that a grand total of 1.2 million
jobs were at risk if the Conservatives were returned. In each
marginal constituency he had a reference to the number of local
jobs threatened.

    In the second and third weeks his speeches concentrated on
prices and taxes. The Labour party knew that it could not
compete with the Conservatives on tax reductions. Instead Mr
Callaghan spelt out the consequences for prices and public
services which would follow the tax cuts and public expenditure
cuts. At the end of the campaign Mr Callaghan tried to strike a
more positive note by drawing attention to the new Concordat
with the trade unions. Without any such agreement, he stated,
there would be the free-for-all that occurred the previous winter.
The trade unions had given him a pledge and 'I shall expect the
trade unions to live up to this agreement.' Protests from Moss
Evans about criticisms of trade union conduct over the previous

winter may have led Mr Callaghan to moderate his approach more than he had intended. But there was a general recognition among those around the Prime Minister that the party lacked credibility. One said: 'Last October we could have been the government that conquered inflation and worked with the trade unions. We can't do that now.'

Mr Callaghan, perhaps sensing that the tide was running against him, was defensive about public spending, although in one speech he commented: 'Public expenditure, yes — let's defend it. Let's be proud of it. It's providing industries and jobs.'

The election was notable for some of the issues that were not discussed. Foreign affairs were hardly referred to in any of the reported speeches, except those of Mr Heath. Defence drew little comment, although there were some cynical remarks about the large increase in forces' pay which was announced on April 18, and Mrs Thatcher on April 19 stressed that the Conservatives had two priorities, the cut in taxation and the restoration of Britain's defence strength.

The problems of energy were singularly neglected, in view of the developing crisis, but Labour spokesmen did refer to the possible selling-off of Britain's North Sea oil assets to the multi-national oil companies. As Mr Callaghan said in Glasgow on April 19: 'The difference between Labour and the Conservatives is that they believe the oil belongs to the multi-national companies but we believe it belongs to the people.'

Immigration was hardly debated, although Mrs Thatcher in television and radio interviews stressed her sense of the importance of the problem, and defended her use of the word 'swamped' in relation to the feelings of some of the indigenous population. This brought on her a sharp riposte from David Steel. 'I had hoped we might get through this campaign without making the colour of people's skins an issue at the hustings. Can she not imagine how the word "swamped" must sound and feel to an unemployed black teenager?' However even the clash at Southall, with its large Indian population, failed to bring immigration to the forefront.

Capital punishment was another issue which had considerable potential yet attracted only a few headlines and a few phone-in questions. Mrs Thatcher said on the *Jimmy Young Show* 'This is not a question of votes. It is a question of my deep belief. I think the vast majority of people in this country would like to

see the death penalty restored.' The Conservatives probably did
manage to get across the idea that capital punishment was more
likely to be restored under them, although they only promised a
free vote.[2] Law and order was a theme often touched on by
Conservative speakers, but it never became a headline issue.

Northern Ireland was perhaps the subject most notable for
its absence from the electoral discussion. The murder of Airey
Neave and the noisy if scattered activities of the 'Troops Out'
hecklers might have been expected to make more headlines. But
when, on April 19, Mr O'Neill, the Speaker of the U.S. House of
Representatives, said in Dublin that Britain was treating Ulster
'like a political football', the essential bipartisanship of the
British approach to Ulster was made plain in a curt and unanimous refutation of his position from all the party spokesmen.
The persistent 'Troops Out' shouting during Mr Callaghan's
speeches, and the pauses for the removal of the interrupters did
at times put him off his stride, and may have prevented his
message from getting across — but it also provoked him to one
of the most effective platform performances of the campaign, as
on April 24 he replied to a heckler with a moving reference to
those just murdered by the IRA.

There were accidental flurries that made headlines. On April
18 the press drew attention to an obscure article by Sir Robert
Mark, the recently retired Commissioner of Metropolitan Police.
He wrote:

Not only do the unions enjoy a high degree of immunity
from the law; in any critical situation in which the law does
not support them the Government of the day — their partner
or their puppet, according to your view — declares its
intention to change the law in their favour.
This is not unlike the way in which the National Socialist
German Workers' Party achieved unrestricted control of the
German State between 1930 and 1938.

Mr Whitelaw joined Mr Callaghan and trade-union leaders in
repudiating such language from the police.

---

[2] On July 19, 1979, in the promised debate, the House of Commons 243 MPs voted
for the restoration of capital punishment and 362 against (with 228 Conservatives for
and 94 against).

On April 20 observations by Lord Denning at a degree ceremony in Canada were cabled back to Britain. The Master of the Rolls' remark that unions were now 'almost above the law' provoked a small storm. Michael Foot observed 'Lord Denning must learn that it is Parliament which makes the laws in this democratic country and the business of judges is to administer the law and not to intervene at election time.'

On April 30 Denis Healey boasted that Sir Michael Clapham, a recent president of the CBI, had refused to let his firm, Imperial Metal Industries, contribute to the Conservative party because Labour had done more for industry. Sir Michael wrote to the Chancellor to say that his remarks had been taken out of context: 'It is not my view that Labour has done more for British industry unless you mean more for its decline.'

The most notable feature of the election, as the days went by, was the subtle reversal in role between government and opposition. Normally elections are fought by a government defending its record and an opposition attacking. On this occasion the thrust of the argument was an attack by the government on the opposition's proposals. At the very beginning of the campaign, prompted by a strategy memorandum from Bernard Donoughue, Jim Callaghan challenged the Conservatives with three questions: How many jobs would be lost by Conservative policies? Where was the money coming from to pay for their tax cuts? How were they going to keep prices down? The Conservatives deliberately refrained from direct replies. But it was plain that Labour was on the offensive. The Conservatives grew furious as television coverage of successive Labour press conferences showed Cabinet ministers challenging the Conservatives in detail on their policy. Labour began to hope that they were going to carry out in reverse the Conservative campaign strategy of 1959, with its central question 'Where's the money coming from?' In mid-campaign there were plenty of Conservatives who, when asked privately what troubled them most on the doorstep, cited first the personality of Mrs Thatcher and second the taxation question, 'How were the Conservatives going to pay for their promised tax cuts?' By April 26 Ian Aitken could write in the *Guardian*:

Conservative tacticians believe that Mr Callaghan has, almost single handedly, achieved a major success in undermining the credibility of Mrs Thatcher's sweeping promises of substantial and immediate tax cuts.

People believed that the Conservatives would bring taxes down: the party's polls indicated that there was a response to the theme of Sir Geoffrey Howe 'Every Labour government puts taxes up. Every Conservative government gets taxes down.' But there was worry about where the money was coming from. Commentators recalled Hugh Gaitskell's tactical error in 1959, when he promised that Labour could meet all its expenditure without any increase in taxation.

The form of the Labour assault seems to have caught the Conservatives off guard. They wanted a low-key campaign and they were not spending much effort on criticising Labour's record. Labour's attacks on their promises were necessarily hypothetical. Shirley Williams' blackboard demonstration of what would have to be cut from the education system if its budget was reduced by £150 million was only one example. Denis Healey observed that finding specific policies in the Conservative manifesto was 'like looking for a black cat in a dark coal cellar'. Jim Callaghan's reiterated questions on prices, taxes and jobs could not be answered specifically. Taxation, too, provided a major theme for Denis Healey and Joel Barnett, who suggested that the income tax pledge would involve the doubling of Value Added Tax.[3] The Conservatives could counter by asking Denis Healey how much he planned to increase VAT if he was returned to power.

The switch to indirect taxes would hit old people most. Pensions also caused the Conservatives substantial worry. Yet the Conservatives were reluctant to be trapped into a cast-iron pledge to link pensions to the retail price index, or to average industrial earnings, whichever was the highest, as the Labour government had promised. The polls indicated considerable anxiety among old people about how their pensions would fare under the Conservatives.

Another Labour challenge concerned public sector pay. On April 13 Mr Callaghan asked if the Conservatives would accept the findings of the Clegg Commission on comparability for

---

[3] In the first Conservative Budget on June 12, VAT was in fact increased from 8% to a standard 15%.

public sector workers. The Conservatives hesitated to give a blank cheque but said that they would honour any clear commitments they inherited. Labour unquestionably scored some points on prices. Everyone accepted that prices were due to rise. Labour argued that the Conservatives' VAT increases would be heavy and would in particular hurt the lower paid. On April 19 Roy Hattersley, the Prices Secretary, promised an increase in the powers of the Price Commission, even beyond the phrases of the Labour manifesto, and on April 26 the Price Commission clamped down on an increase in the cost of a loaf. Sally Oppenheim, the Conservative prices spokeswoman, was conspicuously outpointed in television debates with Roy Hattersley. On April 26 she got herself seriously entangled by misquoting EEC figures on the price impact of devaluing the green pound, and thereafter efforts were made to keep her off the air.

On employment Labour had the advantage of a fall in the jobless figures for March announced on April 19. Labour could challenge the Conservatives repeatedly about what would happen if they cut regional subsidies. Unemployment in Merseyside, Wales and Scotland offered spectres for Labour spokesmen to use with what a Conservative described as 'a skilfully specious precision'.

On industrial peace the Conservatives could exploit the 'winter of discontent'. There were many who followed less eloquently in Lord Hailsham's footsteps:

After complimenting us on our excellent phrases, [Mr Callaghan] said that what [Conservatives] really stood for was a purely materialistic view of the world, the law of the jungle, and the weakest going to the wall. With its usual slavish imitation of their master's voice, the *Mirror* said 'Women and children last', and Mr. Healey in his usual robust language said 'Devil take the hindmost'.

Do they really think we have forgotten last winter? We have seen the gravediggers refusing to bury the dead. We have seen the refuse accumulating in the streets. We have seen the schools shut in the face of children because the caretaker has walked off with the key. And now we see the teachers making them do without their lunches. We have seen cancer patients having to postpone their operations because hospital laundry is not done, floors not swept, or meals not cooked . . . I could go on indefinitely. These are facts. What is theirs but the law of the jungle? What is it due to but a selfish and materialistic view of the world? What is this but the weakest and the most vulnerable, the old and the sick and the poor going to the wall? What is this but women and children last and the devil take the hindmost? You would think Mr. Callaghan and Mr. Healey had been in Opposition for the last five years instead of orchestrating this shambles of industrial confrontation by the Trade Union laws they have been passing. And that estimable man Mr. Len Murray is saying 'cool it'. How I wish he had said this to some of his friends this winter.

Labour replied with memories of the confrontation of 1974 and pointed to poll evidence that, despite the winter, the public still thought Labour was likelier to preserve industrial peace. If Mrs Thatcher's pay policy were to be followed, said Peter Shore, 'We could expect public sector strikes . . . to become a regular annual event. Every year we would have the rubbish piled up in the streets. Every year we would have a disrupted health service.' Denis Healey could stress the Concordat to an USDAW conference on April 29. 'We had a damaging setback last winter . . . Too many negotiators fell for the seductive arguments which Mrs Thatcher was using to attack common sense in pay negotiations.' The Concordat, he argued, had restored the relationship between the government and the TUC which had been the foundation of the government's success in the last five years in reducing inflation and unemployment. On May 1 David Basnett spoke for the trade unionists: 'We expect, once a Labour government is elected, to deliver the assurances that are in the Concordat.'

Housing was another important issue. The Conservatives paraded their promise of selling council houses at half price, and canvassers' reports showed it was popular, particularly in some large council estates, especially in the Midlands and in New Towns. On the other hand Labour could make heavy play with the Conservatives' hostility to council tenants. 1½ million copies were printed of a leaflet reproducing an indiscreet letter to the occupant of a council house in the name of Matthew Parris, Mrs Thatcher's correspondence secretary, who wrote:

I hope you will not think me too blunt if I say that it may
well be that your council accommodation is unsatisfactory
but considering the fact that you have been unable to buy
your own accommodation, you are lucky to have been given
something that the rest of us are paying for out of taxes.

One other Labour challenge that received considerable
publicity was that the Conservatives would indulge in 'the sale
of the century' disposing of British Airways and North Sea oil
to private investors.

All these challenges put the Conservatives on the defensive,
and there was great pressure from the constituencies (as well as
some within the central councils of the party) for an alteration
of tone and for a stronger counter-offensive to be launched.
Lord Thorneycroft resisted these firmly, recognising that the
public did not like the spectacle of politicians slanging each
other. As one senior Conservative put it 'We know we're ahead:
we've just got to play out time.' But the Conservatives did of
course respond to what they saw as Labour's 'smears and
scares'. On April 17 Sir Ian Gilmour described a suggestion by
Frank Allaun that Conservative policies could cause a third
world war as 'the smear to end all smears'. Even the usually
emollient Mr Whitelaw observed that the Prime Minister's tactics
were 'not an edifying spectacle for someone trying to put
himself forward as "a statesmanlike leader".' There was particular
resentment at the use of the warm and moderate Shirley Williams
to put forward what Conservatives saw as some of Labour's
worst slanders. The Conservatives wanted Mrs Thatcher to be
positive and not to answer the other side. The trouble was that
when other spokesmen delivered ripostes to particular charges
they often failed to get reported. Partisan material was fed to
the newspapers. The most extreme example was provided by
the *Daily Mail* which, on April 26, covered its front page with a
story 'LABOUR'S DIRTY DOZEN'. The 12 'lies' about what a
Conservative government would do if elected had been supplied
by the Conservative Research Department and were subsequently
made the subject of exact quotation in a Central Office handout.[4]

---

[4] The 'lies' were often rather blurred statements — but Labour could claim that at
least five of the 'lies' had been shown, during the summer of 1979, to have had substantial foundation.

As always the campaign was heavily influenced by the opinion polls. The Conservative lead ebbed slowly down from an average of 11% to an average of 5%. Mr Callaghan's personal popularity advantage over Mrs Thatcher increased. Labour did not however seem to be advancing fast enough to have a chance of victory until, on Saturday April 28, a MORI poll reported that the Conservative lead was down to 3%. Gallup on Sunday failed to confirm this (though its field-work was conducted prior to MORI) but on Tuesday morning the *Daily Mail* caused a major sensation with its NOP poll showing Labour 0.7% ahead. If this was indeed the latest trend, the Labour advance during the campaign had achieved enough momentum for them to snatch victory against all expectations.

For the greater part of the campaign Conservative confidence was assured but there was unease in Central Office a week before polling day. Concern in the constituencies about the party's stand on pensions and on prices was reinforced by evidence from the private polls. Lord Thorneycroft asked Mrs Thatcher, then in Scotland, to adopt a 'softer' line on the economy. Some strategists thought that an appearance by Mr Heath, flanking the leader, at the press conference, would help recapture the initiative. The suggestion was conveyed to Lady Young at Manchester Airport on April 26. Mrs Thatcher and her entourage dismissed the request as a collective failure of nerve in Smith Square and relations were tense for a time. She was determined to run things in her own way.

The first word of the MORI poll of April 28, the false rumours of what Gallup would say on April 29, and, even more, of the news of the NOP poll of May 1 produced moments of sharp queasiness among the Conservative high command. On May 2 Peter Jenkins wrote in the *Guardian* 'It would no longer be amazing to see Mr Callaghan win by a whisker.' There was a widespread feeling that the Conservative campaign had lost momentum, that the tax appeal had been blunted and that on prices and jobs Labour had defended itself well; private polls in both parties showed that there was no longer much to choose between the parties on these issues.

However none of the later polls confirmed the slide. The betting odds moved little, and at the end were still at 4 to 1 on the Conservatives (the main bookmakers took almost £2m. on the election). The Stock Exchange wobbled only slightly, the

"BECAUSE ITS THERE!"

Daily Telegraph, April 19, 1979

F.T. Industrial index dipping from 538 on March 28 to 524 on April 4 and then rising to 553 by May 3. Private polls were showing that people claimed to want a new approach, a new start. And that is what the Conservatives could offer. Inside the Labour camp there was never complete defeatism, but never very much hope.

Yet by the Monday before polling day Mr Callaghan probably knew that he would lose the election. Mrs Thatcher had not cracked up (though for a brief moment on April 27 her voice and even her temper seemed to be in danger). Mr Callaghan was the more tired of the leaders, and seemed tetchy when he handled questions in the Granada 500 programme on April 30. But at the end his concern appeared to be to lose with dignity. His comments became even softer; as one aide complained, 'We're not allowed even marginal pot shots.'

The strongest trend in the polls was late in appearing. During the campaign, the Liberals advanced from 6% to 14%, but it was only in the last week that this upsurge became apparent. It was a source of great encouragement to David Steel, who had manfully been saying that the polls belied reports from the constituencies, particularly from those where the Liberals were strong. The Liberal advance worried the Conservatives, whose private polls showed that as many as a sixth of Conservative (and of Labour) voters thought it would be a good thing if the Liberals held the balance of power, and that as many as a third thought they should be 'given a chance'.

David Steel had earlier used Punch and Judy puppets to mock Conservative and Labour squabbles, and suggested that the big parties were offering a choice between beefburgers and fishburgers. He argued that a Liberal vote was an insurance policy against their follies. He predicted a minimum of twenty Liberal seats and a House with no clear majority. David Steel's final broadcast on Sunday, April 30, with its appeal for a 'People's Parliament' was generally judged one of the most powerful heard in an election.

Mr Callaghan ignored the Liberals and claimed that because the Conservatives were moving so far to the right under Mrs Thatcher, Labour had now been given the prospect of occupying the centre ground. But David Steel observed 'In fact I am feeling rather lonely on the centre ground': the Conservatives had departed from it and the loony lefties in the Labour party were preventing Mr Callaghan from occupying it.

In the later stages of the campaign David Steel discussed what should be done if no party secured a clear majority. Mr Callaghan agreed that there would have to be inter-party discussions but Mrs Thatcher was less forthcoming: she indicated that she would try to go ahead with a minority government: 'The experiences of the last two or three years have been utterly abhorrent. It reduced the whole standard of public life and parliamentary democracy to a series of wheels and deals.'

The final thrust of the campaign came with an advertising blitz. The Conservatives, who spent nationally almost £500,000 on press advertising during the campaign, took major space over the last five days in the popular dailies, addressed to their target audience. The Labour party advertised on a wider but less intensive basis, spending over £175,000 in the national and £60,000 in the provincial press, most of it on double-page spreads in the last week. The Trade Union Campaign for a Labour Victory spent £79,000 largely advertising in regional papers. The Liberals decided at the last minute on a single round of national press advertising at a cost of £25,000. On the final Sunday the Conservatives held a very successful rally for Tory trade unionists at Wembley. Various entertainment stars appeared and a crowd of 2,000 was there to hear Mrs Thatcher give a clarion call. Idealism not polemic dominated her final broadcast on Monday, April 30; her closing words were:

> Somewhere ahead lies greatness for our country again. This I know in my heart. Look at Britain today and you may think that an impossible dream. But there is another Britain which may not make the daily news, but which each one of us knows. It is a Britain of thoughtful people, tantalisingly slow to act, yet marvellously determined when they do. It is *their* voice which steadies each generation . . . Its message is quiet but insistent. It says this: Let us make this a country safe to work in. Let us make this a country safe to walk in. Let us make it a country safe to grow up in. Let us make it a country safe to grow old in. And it says, above all, may this land of ours, which we love so much, find dignity and greatness and peace again.

Jim Callaghan did not raise the tempo of the campaign in the final days. He was equable and statesmanlike in his remarks at his final London press conference on Tuesday, May 1. And in his final broadcast that evening he tried delicately to stress the difference between his qualifications and Mrs Thatcher's, observing what a help it had been to him as Prime Minister to have been Chancellor, Home Secretary and Foreign Secretary on his way there. But he ended in much the same tone as Mrs Thatcher:

> Let me in conclusion before you vote sum up my attitude to the Eighties. We have got great opportunities if we work together. North Sea oil has given us a wonderful chance. We must use its resources the revenues to modernise our own industry to create more wealth. We have still got to end poverty. Build homes. Care for the sick and the needy, and privilege to be ended. And Britain's influence to be used to strengthen world peace and give a strong lead on international matters. Now it is achieving these aims that will be the true expression of Britain's greatness. That is what the Labour Party stands for. It is why I joined it many years ago, and so

it is on that basis — the basis of what we have done so far, the basis of what we set out to do — in the next five years that I am asking for your continued support for this Government. And I ask for your vote for Labour on Thursday of this week. The Labour Way is the Better Way. Goodnight.

Polling day passed off without mishap. The weather was fair. The only appreciable rain was reported from Scotland and the West Country. The count, too, produced fewer problems than expected. Scottish and London constituencies, where there were no local votes to be separated, reported earlier than the rest, and at 11.34 p.m. Glasgow Central, the seat with the smallest of all electorates, won the race to be first, by a full half-hour, from Cheltenham.

After the first few results it was plain that Mrs Thatcher had won — but without a landslide. The Liberal vote had dropped but they were holding on to most of their seats — and the Scottish Nationalists were faring disastrously.

In all, 74 seats changed hands. The Conservatives gained 51 seats from Labour but forfeited four of their by-election gains, and in a sensational result lost their Scottish spokesman, Teddy

How the Tories plan to put prices up.

To pay for their tax cuts the Tories would put up VAT.

The Price Commission was created to hold down prices. The Tories would abolish it.

The Tory policies on Common Market food prices would mean dearer butter, cheese, sugar, bacon, bread and beef.

The Tories would reduce the school meal subsidy. That'll mean an estimated increase of 10p a meal.

The Tories housing policy would put up rents by £2 or more.

That's the Tory plan on prices.

How Labour plans to keep prices down.

The Price Commission will be given powers to reduce prices, not just hold them.

Labour will freeze Common Market food prices.

Labour will not charge you to visit your doctor or stay in hospital.

Labour will continue help to keep rents and school meal prices down.

Labour have an agreement with the unions to cut price rises by half within three years.

That's Labour's plan on prices.

The Labour way is the better way.

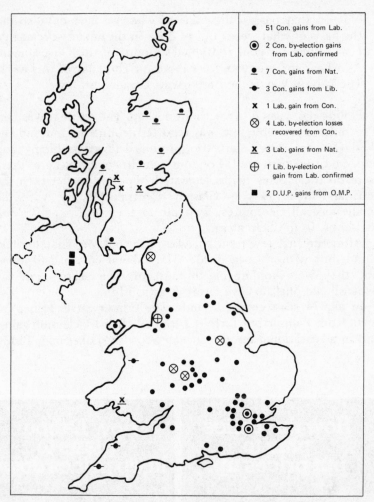

Diagram 1. Seats Changing Hands 1974—9.

Taylor to Labour at Cathcart. Labour also recovered the three seats lost by desertions. The Liberals lost three of their most senior members, Jeremy Thorpe, John Pardoe and Emlyn Hooson, but their remaining 11 MPs were returned. Nine of the 11 Scots Nationalists were defeated and so was Gwynfor Evans, the Plaid Cymru leader. Mr Paisley's Democratic Unionists won two Belfast seats from the Official Unionists. Shirley Williams was the most notable of the Labour casualties, but she was joined by 8 junior ministers and some well known members of the *Tribune* Group, including Arthur Latham, Tom Litterick, Ron Thomas and Hugh Jenkins.

The swing — 5.1% — was the biggest since the war. It was markedly greater in the South and Midlands and in Wales than in the North or in Scotland. Anglesey and Montgomery returned Conservatives for the first time in their history, and around East London, and near car factories, the movement to the Conservatives was exceptionally big. Except for East London, it was well below average in constituencies with large immigrant populations (notably in Leicester and Bradford) and in development areas.

The outcome was accepted tranquilly enough. At 2.30 on Friday afternoon Mr Callaghan drove to Buckingham Palace to resign. He was followed an hour later by Mrs Thatcher, who kissed hands with the Queen as the first woman Prime Minister of the United Kingdom.

11 Balanced Broadcasting

by Michael Pilsworth[1]

From the first limited television coverage of a general election in 1959 the broadcasters have cautiously but steadily chipped away at the defences of the parties, introducing innovations such as interviews with front-bench politicians in the studios, phone-ins and televised confrontations between voters and party leaders. The news and current affairs teams increasingly took the initiative in selecting issues, a tendency (labelled 'producerism' by some) which reached its apogee in February 1974. There was obvious public dissatisfaction over the heavy coverage of that election, and the broadcasters' efforts in October 1974 were on a smaller scale. But the approach was also more passive, and focused on the routine reporting of events rather than on the analysis or discussion of issues. Whilst this promoted a more relaxed atmosphere between broadcasters and politicians, there was a widely-held view after the election that some re-thinking would have to be done before the next one.[2] A major enquiry into election broadcasting was commissioned by all three main parties and both broadcasting organisations. The report of this enquiry[3] recommended a new format for party broadcasting that would encompass both advocacy and scrutiny within the same format; news coverage of the campaign should be based more on news values than the

[1] The author is deeply grateful to Peter Hardiman Scott, John Gau and Tony Crabbe of the BBC; David Glencross and Mallory Wober of the IBA; Don Horobin and Derek Murray of ITN; Brian Walden of LWT; the BBC Audience Research Department; Doreen Stainforth (Labour Party); Gordon Reece and John Lindsay (Conservative Central Office); Ann Dawson (Liberal Party); Bernard Tate and Ann Sloman (BBC Radio); and Daffyd Williams (Plaid), all of whom gave me interviews and supplied material. I have drawn extensively on criticisms of early drafts by Jay Blumler, Michael Gurevitch, Martin Harrison and Hugo Young.
[2] See M. Harrison's chapter in *The British General Election in October 1974*;
[3] See J. Blumler *et al.*, *The Challenge of Election Broadcasting*, (Leeds, 1978).

balance stopwatch, with more time allocated to 'news analysis'; and election programming should be cut to reduce the dangers of overkill. Initially, at least, all those involved appeared to welcome the recommendations in principle.

But just how different a picture of an election campaign was the audience offered in May 1979? The period was notable for the increasing sensitivity of broadcasters to political opinion (the Annan Report, the allocation of the fourth channel, the renewal of the commercial television franchises, and the continuing inadequacy of the BBC's licence fee arrangements were contributing factors); it is not surprising therefore that few significant changes were introduced; in fact the blueprint for the coverage of the October 1974 election was taken off the shelf and used again in 1979.

In anticipation of an autumn election, both the BBC and the ITV general election working parties met in June 1978, and decided to do much the same as in the previous election. In the ten months that intervened between these decisions and the start of the 1979 campaign neither the BBC nor the ITV companies changed their plans. In the past the broadcasters had always encountered difficulties in attempting to persuade politicians to debate with each other and to meet the public. However, they had few such problems during this election. The main difficulties arose in persuading the leaders to do half-hour interviews. BBC Television, for example, did not carry any interviews with the main party leaders until the final evening of the campaign.

The possibility of a televised confrontation between Mr Callaghan and Mrs Thatcher had first been raised in June 1978, when the BBC had invited the leaders to consider taking part in a studio debate. At that time Mrs Thatcher was said to be interested whilst Mr Callaghan was opposed. However, by September the proposal seemed to have been quietly laid to rest. Just before the election campaign began it was disinterred by London Weekend Television's *Weekend World*, with some encouragement from Downing Street, and invitations were sent out to the party leaders.

In a deft piece of political gamesmanship, Mr Callaghan immediately accepted and the decision was leaked to the sympathetic Terence Lancaster of the *Daily Mirror*, and run as a page one lead on April 2 under the banner headline 'FACE TO

FACE – NOW IT'S UP TO MAGGIE'. The *Sun* followed the next morning with a banner headline 'TAKE HIM ON MAGGIE!' (see p. 168). Despite the fact that Mrs Thatcher was keen to accept the invitation, her publicity adviser Gordon Reece was strongly against such an 'uncontrolled' television appearance. He eventually won the day and she turned it down, arguing that 'issues and policies decide elections, not personalities'

What was in effect a four-week campaign, punctuated by a somewhat unnatural break for the Easter weekend, started with the launching of the Labour manifesto on April 6. The broadcasters were diffident in their response, as they had planned to 'play down' the election campaign until after Easter Monday; the intention was to cover election news on merit by the *Tonight* programme on BBC until then. In the event, however, *Tonight* was metamorphosed into *Campaign '79* on April 10, a week sooner than planned. Similarly, although ITN did not introduce its ten-minute extension to *News at Ten* until April 17, it still devoted between fifteen and twenty minutes of its thirty minutes to the campaign during the previous week.

Few external events intruded into a generally restrained and quiet campaign. With no fresh news stories to enliven the daily round of morning press conferences, midday walkabouts and evening speeches, the length of the campaign soon began to take its toll of originality and interest. The political correspondents of the broadcasting organisations began to complain that the parties were 'saying much the same thing again' after only one week of campaigning. Ironically, current affairs producers complained bitterly afterwards that it had been a 'newsman's campaign', with the main party leaders reluctant to be drawn into serious interviews until the last moment, and with the emphasis throughout being on 'two-minute picture sessions'.

It was a much more 'presidential' campaign than had been the case in October 1974, when Mr Heath and Mr Wilson had each received 51% of the coverage devoted to their parties. In May 1979 Mr Callaghan received an average of 63% of the time devoted to his party in the news, whilst Mrs Thatcher received 59% and David Steel as much as 73% (see table 1). The increased attention given to the leaders was largely a result of the parties' own campaign strategies; the broadcasters knew before the campaign began that Labour would be 'pushing' Jim Callaghan and Denis Healey as their avuncular spokesmen, and that the

"HIYA BEAUTIFUL! HOWD'YA LIKE TO GET INTO SHOWBUSINESS?"

Daily Telegraph April 1, 1979

Tories were planning to minimise Margaret Thatcher's speaking engagements whilst maximising her appearances in 'telegenic' locations at times best suited to catch the early-evening news programmes. Central Office staff even drew up maps which indicated how long it took for news film to reach process laboratories and studios from various parts of the country.

There was the usual crop of cancelled and postponed programmes (twelve in all) with both the BBC and IBA companies taking great pains to avoid infringing the Representation of the People Act. Transport House officials complained to the IBA about a showing of the 20-year-old satirical film about industrial relations, *I'm All Right Jack*. The IBA persuaded London Weekend Television to cancel the film, due to be broadcast in the London area on Easter Sunday. Despite all of this sensitivity on the party of the broadcasters, audience research carried out by the IBA[4] immediately after the campaign showed that 73% of the audience believed that television comedy should be 'free to carry on in the normal way' during election campaigns.

News programmes

From the start of the campaign the lunchtime television news programmes were extended by five mintues in order to cover the morning press conferences. In October 1974, Labour's press conferences had followed the Conservatives, and Labour strategists felt that they had been on the defensive; they were eager to 'bat first' this time. In the event the two press conferences began simultaneously, contributing, it was argued, to the somewhat desultory daily reporting. Some attempts were made to overcome these problems. Broadcast journalists attempted to listen to one press conference on their headphones while sitting in on the other, hoping that a Labour remark could be turned into a question for the Conservatives or vice versa. This worked only occasionally and was much disapproved of by the parties. ITN tried to cope with this problem by judicious editing; in the first week of the campaign they linked film of Labour challenges with what appeared to be Conservative replies. This brought a sharp complaint from Conservative Central Office.

The BBC lunchtime news contained a daily five-minute

[4] M. Wober, *The May 1979 General Election: Viewers' Attitudes to Television Coverage*, (London, June 1979), p. 14.

package, usually as the first item, presented by its Gallery
Correspondent, Christopher Jones. His forte is the treatment of
politics as theatre, and he brought an acerbic wit to bear on the
daily press conferences to good effect in terms of entertainment,
though interpretation and analysis may have suffered. ITN on
the other hand, used longer extracts from the morning conferences introduced by their regular news reader, Peter Sissons.
These first television bulletins of the day had to rely on the
morning press conferences for their material, although Mrs
Thatcher's campaign managers sometimes managed to schedule
'walkabouts' early enough (around nine o'clock in the morning
in one case in Leicester) to be in time for the lunchtime television news.

The party's primary target, however, was the early evening
news, which had an audience of 7.4 m. Mrs Thatcher's publicity
adviser, Gordon Reece, had devised a campaign media strategy
more than a year earlier. His aim was to present Mrs Thatcher
as a person who could relate to ordinary people, and he worked
at 'softening' her image. He thought that votes could be won
from women in Labour households, from social class C2 in
general, from skilled workers and from young first-time voters.
These voters were concentrated in the audiences for the early
evening news, *Nationwide*, *Newsbeat* on Radio One, the *Jimmy
Young Show* on Radio Two, and regional television programmes,
less in the audiences for the serious current affairs programmes
and main evening news programmes.

An experienced television director, Mr Reece knew that news
editors needed pictures, particularly for the early evening news.
He had devised over the eighteen-month period before the
election the 'controlled walkabout', a form of activity which
created maximum visual interest.

In the context of the increased security measures following
Airey Neave's assassination this strategy paid handsome dividends. A 'controlled walkabout' involved a planned secret visit
to a factory, a farm or an old people's home, where the party
leader could converse informally with a few people, and, using
an appropriate 'prop', produce several photogenic scenes full of
visual interest and with some entertainment value. The viewers
were shown Mrs Thatcher tasting tea at a tea repository in
Newcastle, having her heart-beat tested electronically at a factory
in Milton Keynes, sewing ladies' garments in a workshop in

Leicester, and holding a new-born calf in a field at Eye. Such scenes proved to be irresistible to the news editors, though the reporters accompanying Mrs Thatcher showed signs of dis-affection as the campaign continued to produce such scenes with relentless regularity. Indeed, reporters from both the BBC and ITN increasingly referred to such scenes as 'media events' and longer camera shots filled the television screen with pictures of jostling photographers. Even Mr Callaghan's advisers were caught up in the enthusiasm for such walkabouts, and towards the end of the campaign the Labour leader was persuaded into a disastrous outing to a supermarket. The television coverage of the 'event' was of hapless and protesting shoppers being crushed by camera-men and journalists. However, most of the time Mr Callaghan was less willing to tailor his campaign to the requirements of the cameramen. As Michael Sullivan, the BBC reporter who 'accompanied' the Labour leader, wrote ruefully after the election in the *Listener* (May 3) 'Jim's style was to treat his tour as a private affair between himself and the electorate, making no concession to the television-age razamatazz adopted by the publicity men at Conservative Central Office.' Whereas journalists accompanying Mrs Thatcher were offered seats on the campaign tour for £600 per head, the reporters covering Mr Callaghan's campaign had trouble keeping the prime-ministerial Rover in sight. Whereas Mrs Thatcher paid meticulous atten-tion to the requirements of the television newsmen and was often heard to ask 'Are you running sound?' or 'Would you like to do another take?' the newsmen covering the Callaghan campaign were brusquely pushed aside by security men. Inter-estingly, in party terms, this was almost a complete reversal of the situation that obtained during the 1970 general election campaign, when Mr Wilson had engaged in constant walkabouts and Mr Heath had stuck doggedly to speeches on the issues. (See *The British General Election of 1970*, p. 207).

Much the greater part of the daily campaign coverage appeared in the evening news programmes. The BBC *Nine O'Clock News* (audience 7.9 m) had changed a great deal since the October 1974 election, with the inclusion of long (in television news terms) reports on issues, placed approximately mid-way through the programme. These reports established a tradition of specia-list coverage that came to be known as 'news analysis'. The general election campaign coverage was treated in a similar

fashion, with the BBC's Political Editor, David Holmes, introducing a ten-minute package into a nightly news programme,
lengthened by five minutes from April 9.

The independent television network relied on a lengthened
News at Ten for all of its national coverage of the campaign,
having no nightly networked current affairs programme. ITN,
like the BBC, also departed somewhat from straightforward
news treatment, with special reports on Scotland and four
other regions that made extensive and excellent use of the VT30
visual display computer in order to illustrate voting patterns
and key marginals. ITN also carried out an analysis of the five
main issues of the election, as defined by their own survey of
voters carried out by ORC. Their Political Correspondent,
Glyn Mathias, looked at the ways in which the three main
parties' manifestos dealt with inflation, the trade unions,
unemployment, law and order, and income tax. With between
fifteen and twenty seconds allocated to each party's manifesto
in each of these special reports, the treatment was, inevitably,
cursory. Television is notoriously bad at dealing with abstract
concepts such as inflation, and ITN's attempt to provide visual
interest through the use of cartoons was half-hearted and poorly
executed. Both the BBC and ITN broadcast a series of constituency reports after nominations had closed on April 23. The
most extensive coverage was devoted to Jeremy Thorpe's
constituency of North Devon, but here, even more than elsewhere, the reporting was constrained by the legal requirement
to cover the campaigns of every candidate (there were nine of
them); often however this was reduced to a formality, with
fringe candidates being shown in a mere flash. The Conservative
in North Devon did complain of getting only 40 seconds coverage
to Mr Thorpe's 150 seconds. *News at Ten* featured short interviews with the main party leaders on April 20 and April 27 and
on May 2. Mrs Thatcher was interviewed throughout by the
courteous, but dogged, Julian Haviland. The persistence of
ITN's David Rose in questioning Jim Callaghan on May 2 led to
a major row of the campaign. Mr Callaghan broke off the interview at one point, and left the studio because of questioning
about the government's record on industrial relations:

> *Rose:* Industrial relations and picketing. What about the
> TUC putting its house in order?

Callaghan: The media's always trying to find what's wrong with something . . . Let's try and make it work.

Rose: What if the unions can't control their own militants? So there are no circumstances where you would legislate?

Callaghan: I didn't say anything of that sort at all. I'm not going to take the interview any further. Look here. We've been having five minutes on industrial relations. You said you would do prices. I'm just not going to do this . . . that programme is not to go. This interview with you is only doing industrial relations. I'm not doing the interview with you on that basis. I'm not going to do it. Don't argue with me. I'm not going to do it.

The Prime Minister was later persuaded to return and a second interview was recorded for that night's *News at Ten*. The first interview *was* shown, however, to 15 million viewers in the United States by NBC—TV who had access by contract to all ITN material, and reported in full in the *Daily Telegraph*. ITN had not foreseen such an occurrence, and subsequently had to apologise for failing to ensure that the videotape was not released anywhere. This incident showed very clearly both the deference of ITN and the means by which party politicians can effectively censor news material that does not accord with their requirements.

BBC's Radio 4's main daily news bulletins all contained a two- or three-minute package on the election campaign; well over half the time was given to recorded statements from the three party leaders. But on the Conservative side Mr Heath also received appreciable coverage as Table 1 shows.

The news outlets were scrupulously fair in the allocation of time to the three main parties, as Table 2 shows, although the Liberals were down by one sixth from October 1974. The ratio of coverage was almost exactly 5-5-3, as had been agreed for the party election broadcasts. The SNP, the NF and Plaid Cymru all complained about the treatment of their manifestos in the news bulletins, arguing that their views had been distorted, or that too little time had been devoted to them. The broadcasters were on the whole resistant to such arguments, though the BBC did accept one SNP complaint.

Table 3 shows that both television news services devoted most of their campaign coverage to film of the leaders' tours,

Table 1.   Politicians Quoted in News Bulletins

Number of times quoted, with percentage share of their party's coverage in brackets. Total number of politicians appearing: 85

	BBC-1	ITN	Radio 4
Labour:			
Callaghan	39 (60)	44 (67)	53 (62)
Williams	8 (9)	8 (5)	7 (7)
Hattersley	8 (4)	8 (2)	7 (5)
Healey	5 (3)	8 (8)	9 (6)
Shore	3 (3)	7 (4)	3 (4)
Wilson	2 (1)	4 (2)	4 (3)
Benn	3 (2)	4 (<1)	3 (1)
Silkin	2 (2)	4 (2)	2 (1)
Varley	3 (2)	3 (3)	2 (3)
Barnett	3 (3)	2 (<1)	1 (3)
Foot	3 (<1)	1 (<1)	3 (<1)
15 others	20 (10)	17 (5)	10 (5)
Conservative:			
Thatcher	40 (63)	45 (61)	46 (52)
Heath	4 (3)	12 (6)	11 (16)
Prior	9 (6)	12 (7)	4 (2)
Whitelaw	5 (4)	10 (4)	5 (4)
Howe	3 (2)	4 (3)	9 (9)
Heseltine	4 (2)	4 (4)	4 (2)
Joseph	3 (3)	6 (2)	3 (2)
Prentice	3 (3)	4 (2)	1 (1)
Pym	2 (1)	1 (1)	3 (1)
Hailsham	1 (4)	3 (3)	— —
16 others	18 (9)	25 (7)	17 (11)
Liberals:			
Steel	38 (69)	42 (80)	43 (69)
Pardoe	8 (13)	9 (8)	6 (19)
Beith	2 (3)	2 (2)	3 (4)
Alton	2 (2)	3 (3)	2 (3)
Thorpe	4 (7)	2 (3)	— —
6 others	10 (5)	8 (3)	4 (5)
Others:			
Wolfe (SNP)	2 (19)	5 (29)	3 (34)
Tyndall (NF)	4 (20)	3 (13)	3 (15)
Evans (Plaid)	3 (19)	3 (22)	1 (33)
Molyneux (OUP)	— —	2 (3)	2 (9)
19 others	19 (42)	13 (33)	3 (9)

Table 2.   Party Shares of Election News Coverage

	% Con	% Lab	% Lib	% Other
BBC-1	34.8 (35)	34.7 (35)	21.9 (26)	8.5 (5)
ITN	36.6 (34)	37.4 (38)	20.6 (25)	5.3 (3)
Radio 4	39.0 (35)	39.5 (37)	18.1 (20)	3.4 (8)

(October 1974 figures in brackets)

the first time that this had happened since television coverage of elections began. Radio news, far less reliant on the 'media events', hardly spent any time on the leaders' tours.

Both channels were agreed that the main issues were prices, law and order, the unions, taxes and jobs. One or more of these tended to be adopted as the 'theme of the day' each day, with news editors selecting those parts of statements or speeches which related to the selected issue.

The Southall riot on April 23 (see p. 180) encouraged coverage of the law and order issue, and the announcement of a Labour initiative on Rhodesia (the sending of Cledwyn Hughes to Southern Africa) brought some coverage in the third week. ITN were very quick to report NUR leader Sid Weighell's reference to his men 'putting their snouts in the trough' (April 10). This was one of the first uses of Electronic News Gathering equipment (ENG) in a British general election campaign.[5] The newspapers only picked up this story two days afterwards.

Opinion polls received brief but regular coverage in all news outlets throught the campaign, particularly in the final week, as the Tory lead seemed to be cut back. ITN broadcast a special report of the methods employed by the pollsters, and regularly referred to the results of its own poll which had sought voters' views on how broadcasting should cover the election (respondents preferred phone-ins, debates and comparisons of the

[5] ENG equipment is a lightweight video camera used in combination with either portable videotape recording facilities or with a small transmitter that can send pictures directly to the newsroom, or even onto the airwaves. Mr Richard Francis, the BBC's Director of News and Current Affairs, has predicted that election coverage will be revolutionised with the full introduction of ENG over the next few years (*The Times*, July 18, 1978).

Table 3. Prominence of Principal Themes in Election News
(in rank order)

	All	BBC-1	ITN	Radio 4	April 9–15	April 16–22	April 23–29	April 29 – May 2
Leaders' Tours	1	1	1	16	2	1	1	1
Prices/Inflation	2	2	2	3	1	2	6	4
Law & Order	3	3	3	4	—	5	2[a]	—
Unions/Industrial Relations	4	4	4	2	3	4	3	3
Taxes	5	7	7	1	4	10	5	5
Jobs/unemployment	6	5	5	6	7	3	8	8=
Cost of Tory tax cuts	7	10	9	5	6	8	10	6
Industry & New Tech.	8	6	8	11	—	—	4	—
Ills of Socialism	9	11	6	12	5	11	11	9
Northern Ireland	10	9	10	13	—	6[b]	—	—
Education & Teachers' strikes	11	8	11	13=	—	—	7	7
EEC	12	14	16	7	10	7	—	—
Coalition	13	13	12	9	8	12	12	8=
Polls	14	12	17	8	11	—	9[c]	2
Rhodesia	15	15	14=	10	—	—	—	—
Housing	16	16	13	15	9	9	—	—
Devolution	17	17	14=	17	9	—	—	—

[a] Southall Riot
[b] Tip O'Neill's statement on Ulster
[c] Callaghan's announcement on Cledwyn Hughes' mission.

policies of the parties, in that order) and which issues were perceived to be the most important.

Although Mr Callaghan was heckled on every appearance by groups protesting about the presence of troops in Northern Ireland, the broadcasters tended to play down such events, and they did not form a major part of the campaign coverage. Where shots of heckling were shown they usually depicted the Prime Minister reacting forcefully, and Transport House was pleased with the way that such interventions had been handled.

The Liberal leader used a photogenic orange executive coach to travel around the country's motorway network. Broadcast journalists gleefully reported the various mishaps that befell the coach: it broke down in the middle of its first showing to the press and on several subsequent occasions. Even the first report from North Devon on Mr Thorpe's campaign focussed on the Liberals' 'continuing transport problems', after his car had broken down.

Did the broadcasters, then, improve their television news coverage of the campaign, following their rather lacklustre performance in October 1974? Some attempts were made. One example was the switch to a 'news analysis' approach by the BBC *Nine o'Clock News*, with the BBC's Political Editor, David Holmes, manfully trying to stitch together the reports of the day's events into a meaningful whole. ITN also tried to be more analytical, with its survey of voters and its special 'issue reports'. However, more analysis would have required basic structural and procedural changes. The rigid demands of the balance stopwatch remained, as did the restrictive (and self-imposed) rules on the coverage of press conferences (the broadcasters agreed in 1964 not to show live broadcasts, and to screen only platform material and shots of their own reporters). The tendency of editors to allow themselves to leave the initiative to the party media specialists was perhaps even more marked than in October 1974. Correspondents, confined in many cases to the editing suites at Television Centre or ITN House, were once again content to patrol the videotape monitors in the search for topical two-minute 'jewels', gaffes, jokes, losses of temper and interesting pictures, sometimes frustrating the best efforts of campaign reporters in the field in the process. Thus the best intentions of the broadcasters were thwarted, or at best diminished, by their unwillingness to consider genuine

structural innovation in their news coverage of election campaigns.

Current affairs broadcasting.
The current affairs coverage of the election campaign followed
the pattern established in October 1974, although there were
four notable exceptions, all from the BBC. The BBC's main television coverage was assigned to *Campaign '79*. Chaired by David
Dimbleby, and drawing on the talents of Robin Day and Bob
McKenzie, the magazine format established for this type of
programme over the years dealt with the daily reporting of the
campaign. However, the programme was unable to get the party
leaders to agree to full scale interviews with Robin Day until the
last programme before the poll, which was shown at an earlier
time in the evening. Although *Campaign '79* did attempt to
analyse the issues, the treatment was somewhat superficial, and
it tended to fall back on the familiar two-way and three-way
studio confrontations between party spokesmen. Since it was
broadcast only 40 minutes after the main evening news, repetition was inevitable. The audience for *Campaign '79* was lower
on average than for *Campaign Report* in October 1974.

BBC1's *Nationwide* programme was considered to be far
more important by the parties, and attracted much larger
audiences than did *Campaign '79*.[6] *Nationwide* carried a series
of profiles of key marginals and regions, and also looked at the
lighter side of the election campaign. Bernard Clark viewed
the progress of the campaign in one constituency, Gravesend,
and there was an excellent film about the financing of the main
political parties.

There were the usual three *Nationwide* 'On the Spot' programmes in which leaders of the main parties answered questions from viewers and from Robert McKenzie. *Nationwide*
introduced one innovation with its 'Nationwide Debates'.
Chaired by Robin Day, the debates were lively and illuminating, and the invited audiences of party supporters enthusias-
tically cheered their protagonists. On the Bristol programme

[6] *Campaign '79* averaged a 1.7m audience; its equivalent in October 1974 averaged
2.1m. The 1979 audience for *Nationwide* 'On the Spot' was David Steel (April 11)
11.1m.; Margaret Thatcher (April 20) 6.6m.; Jim Callaghan (April 27) 7.2m.; *Nationwide* 'Debates': (April 17) 4.9m.; (April 24) 4.7m.; (May 1) 6.1m.

Eric Varley, John Nott and David Penhaligon answered questions on jobs and industrial relations; the Manchester programme on the economy involved Denis Healey, Geoffrey Howe and John Pardoe; and the Birmingham programme on the future of Britain, Michael Foot, Michael Heseltine and Jo Grimond. These programmes captured something of the hurly burly of a political meeting, which plainly pleased both the politicians and the studio audience.

Another innovation was introduced by the weekly BBC current affairs programme *Panorama*. Traditionally it has looked at issues in depth, but in this campaign it offered its time to the two main parties as an 'Election Access' programme.[7] Francis Pym, the Conservative spokesman on Foreign Affairs, introduced the Conservative manifesto in the first programme, and was then subjected to a tough cross-examination first by the chairman, Robin Day, and then by two Labour MPs. Mr Pym was allowed two minutes at the end of the programme to sum up. Central Office, somewhat dismayed by the manner of Francis Pym's mauling at the hands of Joe Ashton and Bryan Gould, decided to adopt the same tactics when it was the Conservatives' turn to question Denis Healey on the Labour manifesto the following week. Two Tory MPs, Lynda Chalker and Leon Brittan, laid into Mr Healey with gusto, Mr Brittan asking him at one point whether he had once believed in Communism. 'I once believed in Santa Claus,' retorted the combative Healey. This form of party advocacy and scrutiny tended to degenerate into a knockabout at times. Discussion of the issues had been virtually exhausted by the time of the *Panorama* programme in the third and fourth weeks of the campaign. If Mr Pym's performance significantly lowered his standing, Mr Healey lived up to his robust reputation. The two major parties liked the format, however, though the Liberals and the minor parties were understandably upset that they were not allowed equal access to put their case.

The main parties also approved another BBC innovation in

[7] A term coined by J. Blumler, M. Gurevitch and J. Ives in their *Challenge of Election Broadcasting*, (Leeds), pp. 48–53. The two *Panorama* programmes followed on much the same lines as those suggested by Blumler *et al*. The Liberal Party was not allocated a slot in this series, though John Pardoe was allowed to present a similar item in a *Campaign '79* programme in the first week of the campaign – but to a much smaller audience.

election coverage, *Hustings*. This new programme was broadcast after the late news on BBC2. It consisted simply of edited versions of evening speeches, providing an opportunity to make full use of the outside broadcast facilities already installed for news coverage. It also allowed individual speeches to be run at much greater length than was possible either in the news or current affairs formats. Although they had some worries over political balance in the first few days, the parties soon appreciated that it was not possible to adhere strictly to the statutory ratios on a daily basis in such a programme. BBC2's only other election coverage was in *The Money Programme*, which looked at unemployment and public expenditure on April 18 and April 25.

Before the 1979 general election BBC television had always tried to avoid politics at weekends, but in 1979 two new programmes were launched on the last two Sundays of the campaign. *Campaign Diary*, in mid-afternoon on BBC1 was introduced by Fred Emery of *The Times* and Bob McKenzie. It was no doubt useful for viewers who had somehow contrived to miss the week's campaign coverage on television. Its sister programme, *Campaign Review*, was broadcast in mid-evening on BBC2 and was also introduced by Bob McKenzie. This provided an opportunity for political journalists Andrew Alexander (*Daily Mail*), David Wood (*The Times*) and Ian Aitken (*Guardian*) to discuss the style of the campaign. The newspaper journalists, much the most forthright critics of the election campaign, were extended a degree of licence denied to broadcast journalists, and they used it to good effect.

Both broadcasters and parties were in agreement that the four innovations in the BBC's broadcast coverage provided more effective, interesting and informative programmes than the traditional style of BBC election coverage, offered in *Campaign '79*. In many respects *Campaign '79* was eclipsed by *Nationwide* and by the main evening news and, since it followed the news so closely, it was often forced to retread a well-worn path through the day's events.

Independent Television's network coverage by the weekly current affairs programmes followed exactly the same pattern as in the October 1974 election, with Thames Television's *TV Eye* (formerly *This Week*) carrying half-hour face-to-face interviews with the three party leaders, and London Weekend Television's *Weekend World* analysing the issues. The Granada team produced their *Granada 500* format, with the three main party leaders facing an audience of 500 voters from the key marginal constituency of Bolton East.

Thames faced a predictable problem with their *TV Eye* interview series; it was well known that Conservative Central Office did not approve of their interviewer, Llew Gardner and Mrs Thatcher refused to appear on the programme. After urgent consultation with the IBA and Conservative Central Office, it was agreed that Denis Tuohy, who had recently left BBC's *Tonight*, would interview Mrs Thatcher in place of Mr Gardner. It is doubtful whether any advantage could be said to have been gained by the Conservatives in this manoeuvre: when an interviewer is publicly blackballed, the substitute is forced to show his mettle. Denis Tuohy proved to be a determined interviewer of Mrs Thatcher, and the resourceful David Steel was able to make political capital out of the affair when caught unawares by an awkward question from Llew Gardner on proportional representation:

> *Gardner:* . . . Let's take proportional representation. Ah, when you took me on a round tour of Europe a minute ago, you conveniently left out Italy . . .
>
> *Steel:* Yes
>
> *Gardner:* . . . which is not a shining example of ah — I would have thought [Steel tries to interrupt.]
> . . . may I finish the question, Mr Steel — of stable government. And surely, in addition, one result of proportional representation is that you open a Parliamentary door to minorities such as the Communists and the National Front.
>
> *Steel:* I was going to be able to answer your question before you'd finished . . .
>
> *Gardner:* Well, I, I didn't doubt it for a minute.
>
> *Steel:* . . . I, I — (PAUSE) I, I now see why Mrs Thatcher doesn't let you interview her.
>
> (LAUGHS)

Weekend World actually devoted four programmes to the general election, beginning earlier than most current affairs coverage on April 1 with a study of voting patterns and electoral trends and with an analysis of marginal seats. A survey of 100 key marginals was maintained throughout the campaign, and the results were reported in successive programmes. Further programmes dealt with the unions, taxes and the economy in a considered and thoughtful manner, blending filmed material, expert opinions and studio discussions with party spokesmen. Perhaps the most informative television programmes on the election, they attracted only relatively small audiences (Apr. 1, 1.3 m.; Apr. 8, 1.8 m.; Apr. 22, 1.5 m.; Apr. 29, 1.8 m.). The Granada current affairs programme *World in Action* avoided the election until the Monday before polling day, when *Granada 500* was given an hour of peak viewing-time in order to show the three main party leaders responding to questions from a representative sample of 500 voters from Bolton East. Both Mrs Thatcher and Mr Callaghan were occasionally cutting in their treatment of questioners. Whereas the Prime Minister was somewhat hectoring, and commited the surprising error of bullying a nurse, Mrs Thatcher struck a populist note on the issues of capital punishment and immigration. The audience responded warmly, and an opinion poll showed that she scored over Mr Callaghan (see p. 000).

The ITV companies were active in covering their own regions in their local programmes. Granada produced eight nightly discussions with its panel of 500 Bolton East voters asking questions of a series of experts. Yorkshire Television mounted seven live mid-day outside broadcasts from locations as diverse as a fish-and-chip shop and a brewery, whilst ATV put on outside broadcasts as part of specially-extended editions of the regional programme, *ATV Today* at 6 p.m. on April 20 and April 27. The first, from the Triplex Safety Glass Factory canteen at King's Norton was on pay and prices, with Roy Hattersley enjoying an in-built policy advantage over Sally Oppenheim and Emlyn Hooson. The second came from Bentinck Colliery Miners' Welfare Club in Kirkby-in-Ashfield, where Eric Varley, Kenneth Clarke and Richard Wainwright answered questions from the audience. Lively and well-produced, these regional broadcasts did much to counter the general tendency towards low-key coverage in the nationally-networked programmes. All fourteen ITV companies in the UK (Channel TV did not cover the general election) produced discussion programmes with party spokesmen and carried constituency reports from their own regions. Notable among the smaller companies' efforts were those of Anglia Television, which not only broadcast regular 'Election Specials' in its local news programme, but also produced three studio discussion programmes under the title *Campaign Challenge*. Representatives of local interest groups put questions to party spokesmen in these late-night programmes.

BBC radio divided its coverage between Radio 4, the main news and current affairs channel, and Radio 2's *Jimmy Young Show*, a music and chat show with an audience of 2.1 m. This was BBC radio's biggest audience-puller for election coverage, and for the first time ever during an election campaign all three party leaders appeared on the programme.

Election Call (Radio 4, daily at 9.05 a.m., audience 800,000) was presented, as ever, by the ubiquitous Robin Day, with party leaders and spokesmen answering questions put by listeners over the telephone. This programme proved once again that phone-ins are more illuminating and interesting than most other forms of election coverage, and their place in the British electoral scene is by now firmly established. However the practice of the main parties, who sometimes tried to 'pack' the phone-in customers, especially on local radio, can present problems.

The day's main speeches were edited and run at some length in *Election Platform* each weekday at 11.30 p.m. (audience 100,000). *The World Tonight* and *Today* were extended by ten minutes, with a special hour-long edition of the *World Tonight* on each Friday of the campaign. *Any Questions?* (400,000), *Money Box* (200,000) and *Analysis* (100,000) were devoted to the election during the campaign, whilst on Saturday mornings Anthony King assessed the parties' campaign strategies in *Destination Downing Street* (200,000).

Local radio contributed to election coverage to a greater extent than ever before, if only because eleven new commercial radio stations had gone on the air since October 1974. The larger local radio stations in areas such as Manchester, Liverpool, Birmingham and London decided to give wider coverage to the general election than to the local elections taking place at the same time. Stations in rural areas with few parliamentary constituencies tended to concentrate on the local elections, but a few stations, such as Pennine Radio in Bradford, set up special general election units. Most stations broadcast constituency reports and phone-in programmes, with the larger metropolitan outlets also producing current affairs and discussion programmes. The parties, particularly at the local level, thought local radio very important, and they invested a good deal of effort in securing appearances by their spokesmen and candidates. The Liberal party was particularly successful in this, a strategy that was well suited to their 'grass roots' approach in selected constituencies.

Local radio was dogged throughout with problems over the Representation of the People Act rules on balance. One station, Radio 210 in Reading, encountering a problem in every one of its six constituencies. In several cases candidates could not even be traced. Panel discussions were ruled out in most areas because of the refusal of some candidates to appear on the same platform as others. This hit the smaller stations particularly severely as they had fewer constituencies to fall back on in case of difficulties. They complained vociferously to the IBA and officials admitted after the election that the law needed to be looked at again in the light of these developments.

Radio was not alone in having problems with the Representation of the People Act. On Thursday, April 26, Jim Marshall, the Labour candidate for Leicester South, had applied to the High Court for an injunction to prevent BBC *Midlands Today* showing a film of him 'going about his business' in a constituency report, on the ground that the filmed report would also include footage of the National Front candidate. The following day the BBC successfully appealed against the injunction before Lord Denning sitting with Lord Justices Waller and Cumming-Bruce. Section 9 of the Representation of the People Act states that if one candidate 'takes part in' a broadcast report on a constituency, then either all the candidates must take part, or they must sign a waiver giving their agreement for the others to take part without them. Lord Denning ruled that 'to be shown in' a programme does not necessarily mean that one has 'taken part'. 'Taking part', then, was interpreted as 'active participation' and, because no candidate was interviewed, the film did not contravene the terms of the Act. Mr Marshall's counsel was refused leave to appeal to the House of Lords. On then learning that the BBC proposed to transmit the programme that evening (April 27) Marshall's counsel immediately sought a further injunction to prevent the programme item from being transmitted until the following Monday, to allow him an opportunity to appeal to the Lords. Lord Denning and his colleagues rejected this plea, and the BBC transmitted the item later the same day, as planned.

ITN faced somewhat similar problems when the SNP applied for an interdict to ban all ITV's news and current affairs programmes on the election that did not give equal time and treatment to the SNP. This legal action was based on the SNP complaint that, when nationally networked programmes such as *News at Ten* were shown in Scotland, the SNP did not have the right to equal time. In the event, on April 18, Lord Robertson (in the Scottish Court of Session in Edinburgh) refused to grant the interdict, on the grounds that it would have forced the cancellation of all networked news and current affairs output on ITV, and would have made the IBA abandon its statutory duties.

Long in advance of the election, producers began planning for what all are agreed the broadcast media do best: the reporting of the results. Both ITN and BBC attached great importance to these 'telethons' which tested the endurance of broadcasters and audience alike as they rambled on into the small hours and over much of the following day. ITN's programme, *The Nation Decides*, had an immediate forecast of the result based on the largest election-day poll ever carried out in Britain, with a sample of 15,000. Alastair Burnet, back with ITN after two elections with the BBC, presented his sixth election results programme, and Peter Snow operated the impressive VT30 computerised display system. Though ITN was quicker than the BBC to report some of the early results, and achieved a slightly smoother production quality, the audience showed once again that it naturally turns to the BBC for coverage of great national occasions. The BBC's election night programme, *Decision '79*, presented by David Dimbleby, had an average audience of 5 m., whereas ITN's programme attracted only 3.5 m., according to ITV figures. BBC Audience Research reported that at 11 p.m. the BBC had 11.4 m. watchers to ITN's 4.7 m. However, whereas the BBC results programme had an ITV appreciation index of 78, the AI for ITN's *The Nation Decides* was 81. As the results came in during the second day, ITV claimed 2½ m. viewers to the BBC's 2 m.

BBC Radio 2's *Jimmy Young Show* ran an election results service for the first time, broadcasting a mix of music, interviews and results throughout the night and into the following afternoon.

The coverage of the results on both radio and television was demonstrably the fastest ever, with many more results broadcast live. The technical prowess displayed in the results programmes formed an ironic epitaph to the generally restricted and fragmentary reporting of the campaign and of the issues.

Party broadcasting

The broad agreement between the broadcasters and the main parties over party access to broadcasting was hammered out at a meeting of the Committee on Party Political Broadcasting[8] on Tuesday, July 18, 1978. The broadcasters wanted to allocate time on a percentage basis of one broadcast for every 10% of the vote (as had been the practice in Scotland and Wales) rather than on the basis of one broadcast for every two million votes. This arrangement would have given the two main parties four broadcasts each, and the Liberals two broadcasts. However, the parties would not accept this, and a ratio of 5-5-3 was eventually agreed. In turn, the broadcasters were not willing to accede to Conservative requests for splitting up the allocation of time into shorter segments, allowing for broadcasts of two minutes in length. Such short broadcasts would, it was argued, approach the format of advertisements, raising problems for the IBA, and changing the nature of election broadcasting.

The Labour and Conservative parties were each allocated five television broadcasts of ten minutes each, the Liberals three. Each of these was transmitted simultaneously on all channels at 9 p.m., except the final Liberal party broadcast, which was transmitted at 7.15 p.m. on the final Sunday of the campaign, owing to the fact that the Liberals had finally succeeded in persuading the Committee that they had been discriminated against in the past by having their last election broadcast restricted to the Saturday, five days before polling day; this was the first election in which party election broadcasting had been allowed on a Sunday. The SNP was allocated three ten-minute television broadcasts in Scotland; and Plaid Cymru one ten-minute television broadcast in Wales.

The Labour and Conservative parties were each allocated four ten-minute broadcasts on Radio 4 at 8.50 a.m. (Liberals received

---

[8] This is a secretive body with no official status, established in 1947; see G. Wyndham-Goldie's *Facing the Nation* (London, 1977), for a full description and for a copy of the Aide-Memoire setting out its terms of reference.

three), three of five minutes duration on Radio 2 at 6.40 p.m. (Liberals had two) with the SNP receiving three ten-minute radio broadcasts in Scotland, and Plaid Cymru having one broadcast of ten minutes in Wales.

The three main parties were again given the facility of regional opt-outs in Scotland and Wales in order to balance the amount of time given to the SNP and Plaid Cymru. The Ecology party, the National Front and the Workers' Revolutionary party each qualified for one five-minute broadcast on television and radio by nominating more than the required minimum of 50 candidates.

Although advertising experts had been involved in helping the parties to produce their party election broadcasts in previous general elections, this was the first election in which they were involved in a major way. Conservative Central Office decided in April 1978 to allocate the responsibility for all of their advertising and broadcasting to Saatchi and Saatchi, an agency renowned for its creative approach to advertising. Whilst the overall policy was decided by Central Office, Saatchi and Saatchi had the task of proposing a campaign strategy and of converting the party's policies into arresting phrases, visual ideas and even key words which had been tested with groups of voters in the major target groups (C2 women, skilled workers and first time voters), identified in systematic and regular surveys. Thus 'inflation' became 'prices', 'unemployment' became 'jobs', and statements of policy were made as simple as possible. 'It's time for a change' and 'Look how much they've taken from my pay packet' were key phrases that had been derived from research work with the target groups.

The campaign strategy was devised by Tim Bell, Chairman of Saatchi and Saatchi, to promote dissatisfaction with the Labour government's record and to make abstract concepts such as choice, freedom, and reduced state interference politically seductive. The election campaign was the culmination of 14 months work by Saatchi and Saatchi, and the first two election broadcasts followed very closely the themes and methods of presentation established over the previous year. The first broadcast, a satirical film showing runners at an athletics track (the British pair literally weighed down by taxation and inflation imposed by Labour managers) met with a highly critical response from the Conservative party in the country. Though

Gordon Reece defended the broadcast on the ground that it was aimed only at the target floating voters, some Central Office staff felt that satirical 'peacetime' techniques were inappropriate during a campaign. There was also some criticism in the party over the extensive reliance in the election broadcasts on two 'unknown faces', those of the Tory Chief Whip, Humphrey Atkins and the Party Chairman, Lord Thorneycroft. Both had been selected by Saatchi and Saatchi, Mr Atkins because he was thought to be a good television performer, and Lord Thorneycroft because he was thought to have 'style', another feature of the Conservative image which Saatchi and Saatchi had successfully promoted in the run-up to the campaign (they had devoted an entire party political broadcast to a speech by Harold Macmillan to the Young Conservative's Annual Conference). Both were also members of the planning group that met with Saatchi and Saatchi in order to design the broadcasts.

The first four Conservative broadcasts were shot on 35 mm. film and were highly polished productions. The final broadcast, the most straightforward, was videotaped and featured only Margaret Thatcher talking straight to camera. The final bill for the five broadcasts was in the region of £100,000.

Whilst the Labour leadership was quick to accuse the Tories of selling their policies like soap powder and of using paid actors in their 'commercials', the Prime Minister had in fact drawn on the help of a group of sympathetic advertising men (see p. 00).

CONSERVATIVE TELEVISION BROADCASTS

I. *Apr 19.* Film of runners running around athletics track. Voice-over: Welcome to the International Prosperity Race run over five years. British runners under Labour management weighed down by taxation, unemployment, inflation; intercut with graphics and voice-over giving facts: inflation under Labour worst since Great Plague, dole queue from London to Inverness. British runners left behind by Japanese, French and German teams. Film of bottles on conveyor belt: production low under Labour. Cut back to race: British runners collapse, crowd calls for change of management: Conservatives step in, take off all weights, intercut with graphics and facts: take-home pay higher under Tory governments since war, Tories cut taxes. Heseltine: We'll provide incentives. Tories have created a million jobs since war. Twice as much inflation under Labour. Tories will reduce government interference. British runners go into the lead. Thatcher: We have sense of humour (needed lately) but also gift for invention, initiative, hard work, wasted under Labour. Need incentive, increase production, reduce prices. Don't just hope for a better life, vote for one.

II. *Apr 23*. Opening shots of winter of discontent: rubbish in streets, super-markets empty, graves undug, hospitals picketed, airports closed, intercut with graphics and voice-over: 'Crisis, what crisis?' Cut to Atkins: Labour policies make workers bitter. Skilled workers, firemen, nurses suffering. Cut to shot of couple in dock. Guilty of wanting better schooling for children, wanting to buy home, making profit. Sentenced to nationalisa-tion. Pensioner, skilled worker and housewife also plead guilty to crimes under Labour. Voice-over: Labour taxes ambition, enthusiasm and achievement, the very things that create wealth. Cut to Atkins: Tories better for working men. Labour can't get production moving (film of bottles on conveyor belt). Cut to film of Frenchman, Italian and German being paid more than British worker at cashier's window. Atkins: higher production equals higher wages. Labour good intentions, but Tories create more wealth.

III. *Apr 25*. Lord Thorneycroft in wing chair. No light relief tonight: we'll present facts. Presenter: wages dependent on production. Voice-over: Britain manufacturing less today than five years ago. British wages lowest in EEC apart from Eire. Inflation worst of any industrial country since Labour came to power, unemployment record bad under Labour, tax greater, public spending falling. Would Tories do better? Official govern-ment records show Tories better on production, wages, inflation, employ-ment, tax and public spending. The key is production. Thorneycroft: why gaze in crystal ball when you can read the book: more goods produced under Conservatives, more cash to go round, more caring.

IV. *Apr 27*. Atkins in panelled office: What would you do if in next govern-ment? How get production moving? Howe: production is key. Need incentive. Need to reduce taxes. What would you do? Lynda Chalker: inflation results from government spending; would you reduce it? Gerry Vaughan: social services a tricky problem; would you spend on them or on nationalisation? Howe: should we tax what we earn or what we spend? Heseltine: would you let people buy their own house? All above are Tory policies. Thatcher: All around country people say cut taxes to give incentives, but worried over VAT rise. But many things not subject to VAT — children's shoes, pensioner's fuel etc. You have choice, and incentive to work overtime.

V. *Apr 30*. Thatcher in office, head and shoulders, voice quiet and low. Moment of decision after tumult and shouting. Decision crucial, problems grave. Many cherished things disappearing: money that keeps its value, real jobs that last, paying our way in the world, feeling safe in the streets, especially if you're a woman, chance for those from modest background like mine to get on. Need change for better now. We are not naturally socialist country. Prosperity leads to caring society. Unions have enough rights, not enough duties. Need strong defences against Soviets. Never had woman PM before, but what matters are your convictions. My vision: greatness lies ahead, I know this in my heart. Voice of reason calls for balance, for a land where all may grow, safe to work in, walk in, grow up in, grow old in. May this land of ours, which we love so much, find dignity and greatness and peace again.

The broadcasts were prepared by this group in the face of considerable opposition from broadcast specialists at Transport House, who had not been informed until the last moment that they would not be preparing the broadcasts themselves. Partly as a result of this conflict of interests and the consequent confusion, the first Labour election broadcast was prepared in only five days and the production quality suffered accordingly. There were some complaints that the Labour broadcasts had used subliminal techniques because some symbols appeared momentarily on the screen after the appearance of Mr Callaghan; in fact they were chinagraph pencil editing marks — in the rush to finish the broadcast a 'slash' print had to be used. However, the sober style of the Labour broadcasts with their deliberate emphasis on statesmanship and 'authority' contrasted sharply with the rather gimmicky style of the first two Conservative ones, and the audience appreciation figures for the Labour broadcasts (which cost only £50,000) were markedly higher than those for the Conservatives.[9] The parties' private polls on the broadcasts were at times dismaying. The Conservatives were worried that they did not do better and that the Liberals did so well. Labour was astonished to find that, out of line with the trend, Lord Thorneycroft's broadcast was the highest rated.

The Prime Minister was reluctant to use the advertising film makers for his last election broadcast from Downing Street, partly because of the bad experience of the first Labour PEB, but also, perhaps, in order to mend fences with Transport House. In the event London Weekend Television supplied an outside broadcast unit and the final broadcast was recorded at No. 10 on May 1.

The Liberal party sought advice from supporters with advertising experience, notably Adrian Slade, and enlisted the help of a professional film maker, Justin Cartwright. But their approach was traditional and relied much more extensively on studio

---

[9] IBA Research Department data shows that audience appreciation indices for the PEBs were as follows:

	May 1979	October 1974
Labour	50	47
Conservative	45	45
Liberals	49	54

LABOUR TELEVISION BROADCASTS

I. *Apr 17.* Graphics illustrating Tory promises collapsing. Long-shot of Callaghan in No. 10 Downing St, slowly zooming in to close-up. Tories offering more promises of the kind that caused the mess in 1970–4. This election about the future: dangers are passing; inflation reduced; balance of payments in credit; jobs protected; families helped. Britain back on road to economic recovery despite rough winter. Labour has team of experienced ministers. Photographs of Healey, Silkin, Williams, Orme and Owen with voice-overs on their achievements. Healey in book-lined study in 11 Downing St: unemployment cut, taxes cut. Graphics illustrating facts. Shirley Williams: Tory tax cuts will be paid for by you. Three questions for Tories: will they scrap Price Commission, introduce NHS charges, scrap job schemes? Callaghan on the Concordat with the TUC: the Labour way is the better way.

II. *Apr 20.* Shirley Williams in study intercut with graphics and voice-overs: Tory ideas in 1970–4 brought the country to its knees. Labour will co-operate with unions. Summary of Concordat: union reform; annual economic summit; Public Pay Commission. Tories will cut income tax but raise VAT. Green pound will be devalued and subsidies removed. Are you prepared to pay for these measures? Economy healthier under Labour. Still no answer from Tories on three questions: what would be effects of higher VAT, public spending cuts and would there be another million unemployed? Labour offers change without chaos.

III. *Apr 24.* Graphics and voice-over describing Labour job-creation and job-saving measures. David Owen to camera on Labour's record on unemployment: a million jobs saved over five years. Vox pop interviews of people who had found jobs through Labour's programmes: if you need a job, the Tories won't help you.
Owen: Tories out of step – France, Germany and America create and save jobs. Helene Hayman to camera on the benefits of the European Airbus deal. Cut to Owen looking forward to 1980s, must invest oil money wisely. Labour way on jobs is responsible and sensible.

IV. *Apr 28.* Shot of large fruitcake: the money Britain earns. At the moment we all get a slice. How would Tories slice it up? Healey, to camera: Tories will put up VAT, rents and school meals. Visual of slice of cake being taken away and given to better off. Vox pop housewives in Liverpool: 'Disgusting', 'Disgraceful'. Cut to Ann Taylor: Tories will destroy Price Commission and prices will go through the roof. Cake further reduced. Tory policy on Common Market will lead to food price rises. Cake disappearing. Vox pop woman in Liverpool: 'We won't be able to afford the goods we really need.' Cut to Bryan Gould on jobs followed by cake-slicing and vox pop. Cut to Healey: wages free-for-all will hit worse-off. Cake disappears. Vox pop woman: 'We'd emigrate if the Tories got in.' Cut to Ann Taylor: Labour would share out cake (now miraculously re-assembled) differently: prices held down, food subsidised. Healey: Labour will cut taxes for low paid, help children, pensioners, first-time home buyers and with union cooperation reduce inflation.

V. *May 1.* Long establishing shot of Callaghan at desk in Downing Street, straight into medium long-shot. PM is alone: the buck stops here. Greatest help that I had, experience as Chancellor of Exchequer, Home Secretary and Foreign Secretary in long political life. Experience of the greatest value. PM trustee of whole nation. Some worries over Tory manifesto: pulling out aid for industry, Green Pound policy will send food prices up. Free-for-all is too big a gamble. Difficult weather ahead; making progress; mothers, families, pensioners better off. Industrial relations improved by agreements with unions. Winter of discontent caused by free-for-all. We must use oil revenues to create more wealth. Labour way is better way.

production facilities provided, as always, by the BBC, with a limited amount of film edited into the first two broadcasts. The final broadcast was a masterpiece of political broadcasting, with a relaxed David Steel apparently sitting in his living room at home in Ettrick Bridge with his son, Rory, playing at his feet. In fact it was recorded in great haste using a stage-set in a BBC studio, though few viewers could have known.

The SNP used the Glasgow studios of the BBC for its three Scotland-only television broadcasts. Opening to the strains of Sibelius, the first broadcast involved George Reid, Margaret Bain, Gordon Wilson and Tom McAlpine, showing how the

LIBERAL PARTY TELEVISION BROADCASTS

I. *Apr 18.* Opening shots of David Alton winning Edge Hill by-election. Presenter: tremendous victory. Grimond: Labour and Tories have abandoned liberal values and ideals. Alton: no such thing as safe seats, Edge Hill proved that. Steel: Who is to speak up for small people ignored by big battalions? Need to end class-based politics. Big parties can't solve our problems. Ordinary people miss out. Asking now for substantial wedge of Liberals in next parliament to strengthen the politics of the centre.

II. *Apr 26.* Vox pop interviews with nurses, black lady, men in street: big parties not for our interests. Alan Watson in park: We will bang the heads together of the other two sides; need united nation. Businessman in Rolls Royce car: frustrations in industry; I'm going to vote Liberal. Stephen Ross, Westminster in background; two-party system has failed. Cyril Smith, head and shoulders: Everybody sick and tired of confrontation. Liberals serve people not parties. Need unity. Need your votes.

III. *Apr 29.* Steel as if at home, son Rory playing at feet: polls show increase in Liberal support. Country in decline, failure as a nation. I've travelled widely in last few weeks, met many people; they are fed up with main parties, don't believe promises. Victory for Tory or Labour a defeat for Britain. Liberal vote not wasted vote.

English parties had broken pledges over a Scottish assembly, unemployment and land. The second broadcast used presenters and attacked the Westminster system. A university lecturer, Isobel Lindsay, claimed that Westminster was out of touch with the Scottish people. In the third broadcast, the SNP argued for an oil-fund and a Scottish Assembly.

Plaid Cymru's single television broadcast, seen only in Wales, concentrated on Labour's poor record on unemployment. A Merthyr Tydfil councillor, Emrys Roberts, showed Labour's failings in specific industries (steel, for example) and specific areas (Cardiff, Ebbw Vale). These failings were contrasted with the successes of the three Plaid Cymru MPs over water costs in Wales, the Welsh Development Agency agreement and the slate quarrymen's dust disease compensation act. Plaid Cymru's General Secretary Daffyd Williams complained vociferously to the BBC and the IBA throughout the campaign, arguing that the restriction of their election broadcast to Welsh transmitters alone effectively cut their Welsh audience by 35%,[10] and that the amount of network coverage of Plaid's campaign was lower than the elections of either February or October 1974.

The three English minor parties (the National Front, the Workers' Revolutionary party and the Ecology party) shared the basic format used by parties that cannot afford the cost of film. The spokesmen were shown in a studio setting in head-and-shoulders shots. Jonathan Porrit, Chairman of the Ecology party, delivered a well-reasoned and refreshingly simple message for the 'green vote'. John Tyndall, Chairman of the National Front, made an appeal to dormant nationalism against the backdrop of an enormous Union Jack. Corin Redgrave, Chairman of the WRP, spoke quietly and with professional ease on the need to combat the armed police and the state apparatus.

Broadcast at peak times, the main party television broadcasts managed to attract reasonably large audiences,[11] but they were

[10] In key areas such as Cardiff viewers prefer to tune in to BBC West's transmitters. Plaid had no complaints about BBC Wales' or HTV's coverage.

[11] BBC Audience Research figures:

All channels	May 1979	Average Audience size (millions)		
		Oct 1974	Feb 1974	June 1970
Con (5)	12.2	10.00	10.9	10.1
Lab (5)	10.2	9.9	10.5	10.3
Lib (3)	8.8	10.2	10.2	9.4

regarded with some disdain by the viewers. The IBA Audience Appreciation Index data (see p. 225) supported those IBA officials and politicians, such as William Whitelaw, who argued that the traditional format of party election broadcasting on television would have to be changed before the next general election. There was also a degree of concern at the IBA over the increasing reliance on 'media events'.

Brian Walden, the presenter of London Weekend Television's *Weekend World*, was the only senior broadcaster publicly to reflect the concern expressed privately by senior IBA officials. Speaking at a meeting of the Royal Television Society at the Dorchester Hotel on May 14, Mr Walden accused broadcasters of having abrogated their responsibilities in their coverage of the election. They had contented themselves with accepting the messages that the parties had wanted to put across, and had failed to serve the public. Brian Walden's great fear was that the American system of 'selling' political figures through judicious management of the pictures made available to television teams had been imported and applied during the British general election in 1979.

Although the advertising experts and publicity managers did not have things all their own way, there was clear evidence that the campaign was the most presidential ever and that the personalities of the two main party leaders were seen by the broadcasters to be as important as their policies.

Towards the end of the campaign broadcasting policy-makers were musing on the implications of the increasing sophistication of the party managers. Brian Walden went so far as to propose the blackballing of 'media events', by refusing to cover those events that would not have occurred had the cameras not been there. But the parties would undoubtedly view such a proposal with some concern.

Both parties and broadcasters were guilty of extreme caution and conservatism in their approaches to change in broadcast coverage of the election campaign. The parties fell back on the familiar and manifestly unsatisfactory ten-minute access slots; these were regarded with scorn, and in many cases outright hostility, by voters (the IBA received more complaints from the public over the Party Election Broadcasts than ever before). The broadcasters for their part failed to introduce significant structural changes in their news coverage. They thereby handed the initiative to the parties to convey their own images and perceptions virtually untrammelled by normal journalistic news values.

Is this likely to change? Some developments are inevitable. The pressure to alter the RPA, the introduction of electronic news-gathering equipment, together with opening of the fourth television channel in 1982, and the renewal of the television companies' franchises in the same year are likely to produce some changes in the coverage of the next general election. Whether the underlying assumptions of election broadcasting will be any different is another matter.

12 Fleet Street

by Michael Bilton and Sheldon Himelfarb[1]

The role of the press can change from election to election, sometimes because the structure and ownership of the press has changed, and sometimes because events call forth a different response. In 1979 the partisanship of the popular dailies was cruder than usual, while the quality papers did not have *The Times* to counter-balance, to borrow from or to criticise. The nature of the argument and the style of the campaign gave journalists little to get their teeth into — yet the parties were attacked for reducing the contest to a 'media event'.

The four main alterations in the formal structure of Fleet Street since 1974 were, first, the Beaverbrook family's sale of Express Newspapers to Trafalgar House Investments under Victor Matthews; second, the launch by Express Newspapers of the Manchester-based *Daily Star*, in an attempt to steal the bottom of the market from the *Daily Mirror* and the *Sun*; third, the takeover by an American oil company, Atlantic Richfield, of the *Observer;* and, fourth and most important, the disappearance, albeit temporary, of *The Times* and the *Sunday Times* (see Table 1).

In 1978 the *Sun* and the *Daily Mail* had been the only two national newspapers to increase their circulation from the 1974 level. By the time the election campaign began, all four of the more established tabloids were experiencing falls in circulation; estimates put the new *Daily Star* circulation at nearly a million (see Table 1).

Because of the absence of *The Times*, the quality dailies experienced a very different market shift. On November 30, 1978, after a long series of clashes between management and unions, Times Newspapers suspended publication of two of Britain's most influential newspapers, *The Times* and the

---

[1] The authors are indebted to Deirdre Saunder for her help in preparing the tables.

Table 1. National Dailies

Name of paper Proprietors Editor Preferred result on on May 3	Circulation[1] (Oct 1974 in brackets) ('000)	Readership[2] (Oct 1974 in brackets) ('000)	% of its readers in social class: 3 (Oct 1974 in brackets)			
			AB	C1	C2	DE

Daily Mirror
  Reed International
  (A. Jarratt—Chairman)
  Ed. M. Molloy
  Lab victory
	3,783
	(4,256)
		11,603
		(13,506)
			6
			(5)
				17
				(19)
					41
					(42)
						35
						(35)

Daily Express
  Trafalgar House Ltd.
  (V. Matthews)
  Ed. D. Jameson
  Con victory
	2,458
	(3,255)
		6,807
		(9,222)
			18
			(15)
				27
				(28)
					32
					(31)
						24
						(27)

Sun
  News International Ltd.
  (Rupert Murdoch)
  Ed. L. Lamb
  Con victory
	3,942
	(3,152)
		12,371
		(11,368)
			6
			(4)
				16
				(18)
					42
					(43)
						35
						(35)

Daily Mail
  Associated Newspapers
    Group Ltd.
  (Ld Rothermere)
  Ed. D. English
  Con victory
	1,973
	(1,762)
		5,423
		(5,098)
			21
			(16)
				30
				(31)
					29
					(29)
						21
						(25)

Daily Star
  Trafalgar House Ltd.
  (V. Matthews)
  Ed. M. Grimsditch
  neutral
	N/A	N/A				

Daily Telegraph
  Daily Telegraph Ltd.
  (Ld. Hartwell)
  Ed. W. Deedes
  Con victory
	1,358
	(1,421)
		3,306
		(3,648)
			51
			(42)
				29
				(35)
					13
					(14)
						8
						(10)

Guardian
  The Guardian and Man-
    chester Evening News
    Ltd.
  (Scott Trust)
  Ed. P. Preston
  Lab victory
	275
	(346)
		865
		(1,069)
			54
			(40)
				30
				(36)
					10
					(16)
						6
						(8)

Financial Times
  Pearson Longman Ltd.
  (Ld. Cowdray)
	181
	(194)
		731
		(917)
			54
			(53)
				27
				(29)
					13
					(12)
						6
						(5)

[1] Average of ABC Figures Jan—Dec 1978.
[2] Joint Industry Committee for National Readership Surveys, Jan—Dec 1978.
[3] JICNAR's definition classifies estimated population aged 15 and over as follows:
AB — 16%, C1 — 22%, C2 — 33%, DE — 29%.
Note: these figures may not = 100% for each paper due to fractional differences.

Sunday Times. The dispute centred around the implementation
of new technology, a problem which has periodically plagued
Fleet Street.[2] Closure of *The Times* saw an upsurge in circulation
for the *Financial Times*, the *Guardian* and the *Daily Telegraph*.
Following a period of decline, they rose markedly to just above
the 1974 level. The *Guardian* benefited most in circulation,
increasing by about 19% while the circulation of the *Daily
Telegraph* climbed by 6% and the *Financial Times* by 8%.
Similarly the absence of the *Sunday Times* produced large gains
in circulation and advertising revenue for both the *Observer* and
Sunday Telegraph.

A long drawn-out election campaign brought with it acute
difficulties in terms of coverage for the press, including the
awkward problems caused by the two major parties holding
their morning press conferences simultaneously. After four
weeks of the hustings the event, which had previously been
hailed by commentators as 'the most important election since
1945', had turned into 'the biggest yawn of the year' in the
words of the *Daily Express* on April 26. The *Sunday Mirror,
Daily Telegraph* and *News of the World* also thought the electorate had become bored.

The press had to compete against the immediacy offered by
television and radio with their news and current affairs programmes, radio phone-ins, and their disc jockey interviews with
election personalities. Few had doubts that the campaign was
dominated by James Callaghan and Margaret Thatcher, but in
the opinion of the press they appeared to be performing solely
for television. As in 1974, newspaper journalists following the
campaign trail found themselves pushed into the background
while special arrangements were made to accommodate the
television cameras. On the morning after the vote the *Guardian*
declared that British general elections were now an armchair
affair. 'Camera stunts and careful timing of election events to
make the early evening news, appearances on mass-appeal
programmes and filmed coverage of the hustings which has
come with the development of TV journalism, have all brought
the election into the living room' (May 4). The press was faced
with the problem of how to make the election appear fresh to a

[2] For an analysis of the dispute see S. Jenkins, 'The Vanishing of *The Times,' Encounter*,
(August, 1979).

Table 2. Profile of Press Content

Name of Paper		Daily Mirror	Daily Express	Sun	Daily Mail	Daily Star	Daily Telegraph	Guardian	Financial Times
Mean number of pages, April 9 to May 3 (Oct 1974 election in brackets)		32 (31)	42 (21)	31 (30)	46 (38)	30	35 (29)	27 (28)	43
Lead stories on elections April 9 to May 3 (Oct 1974 election in brackets)	No.	12/21 (5/18)	14/21 (15/18)	12/21 (12/18)	14/21 (13/18)	3/21	15/21 (11/14)	15/21 (15/18)	13/20
	%	57 (28)	67 (83)	57 (67)	67 (72)	14	71 (79)	71 (83)	65
Leading articles on election April 9 to May 3 (Oct 1974 election in brackets)[1]	No.	13/15 (11)	20/35 (18)	25/31 (14)	22/34 (19)	15/29	31/51 (20)	25/45 (21)	15/36
	%	87	57	81	65	52	61	56	42

Circulation ('000)[2] Jan–Mar 1979 (1978 Circulation in brackets)	3,623 (3,783)	2,447 (2,458)	3,855 (3,942)	1,963 (1,973)	880[6] N/A	1,441 (1,358)	327 (275)	195 (181)
Difference (after *Times* stoppage)	−160	−11	325	−10		+83	+52	+14
Readership ('000)[3] Jan–Mar 1979 (1978 readership in brackets)	11,846 (11,603)	6,657 (6,807)	11,846 (12,371)	5,249 (5,423)	N/A	3,617 (3,306)	1,308 (865)	795 (731)
Difference	−257	−150	−525	−174		+311	+443	+64

[1] Percentage of leading articles for Feb. 1974 is not available.
[2] Average of ABC Circulation figures (Jan 1978 – Mar 1979) since publication of *The Times* ceased Oct 1978.
[3] Circulation (Table 1) minus (Table 2).
[4] JICNAR's National Readership Survey (Jan – Mar 1979).
[5] Readership (Table 1) minus (Table 2), therefore change is an average.
[6] Figures available for the month of April only.

readership which already had the issues and personalities
entering their homes by television and radio.

Politicians had some control over both these media; if a
television company or radio station wanted an interview, or to
film a particular event, it would be timed to suit politicians'
wishes. The effect of the 'electronic election' was to diminish
the traditional newspaper scope for innovation and investigation.
A wry comment on the difficulties Fleet Street faced in competing with television and radio came from David Dimbleby, the
television presenter: 'Of course the best questions to politicians
in this campaign have come from the electors themselves on the
radio phone-in programmes.' The national press was left to
report what the politicians had been saying on television and
radio.

The *Daily Express* mounted a massive front page attack on
the 'television election' — 'NOW SWITCH OFF THESE TV
BORES' (April 26): 'The masterminds who control our television
diet are turning this critically important election into the biggest
yawn of the year . . . night after night the nation's living rooms
are invaded by politicians endlessly contradicting each other —
and frequently themselves as well.' The *Sun* — 'FADE THEM
OUT' (April 19) — felt that televised election coverage was at
saturation point. 'If there is one proposal which would earn the
gratitude of viewers of all political persuasions it is the promise
that these bland, boring (party political) broadcasts will be
faded out.'

Five weeks elapsed between the defeat of the government
and polling day, so that the campaign proper did not really get
under way until after Easter. Much of the pre-holiday election
coverage had a phoney-war air about it. This was in part due to
the assassination of Airey Neave on March 30, the day after the
date of the election was announced. As the killing dominated
the news pages for days afterwards, two major questions
emerged: would Neave's murder make the return of the death
penalty a major election issue? and, as the *Daily Mail* asked on
March 31, would 'the threat of terrorism on the hustings
seriously disrupt the forthcoming General Election campaign'?

The *Daily Mail* and *Daily Telegraph* warned that in addition
to the IRA there were dark and sinister forces at work in Britain
who were determined to undermine democracy. The *Daily
Telegraph* editorial went a stage further, and managed to link

the kind of intimidation intended by Neave's assassination with the threat of trade union power. 'How could it happen' stories appeared the following Sunday, including a major feature by George Gardiner, MP. His *Sunday Express* article was headed: 'There's only one thing to be done about these IRA thugs — I'D PUT THEM UP AGAINST A WALL AND SHOOT THEM' (April 1).

For a short time the death penalty monopolised the editorial columns. The *Daily Telegraph* — 'TORIES TO BACK VOTE ON HANGING' (April 2) — predicted that the forthcoming Conservative manifesto would commit the Party to a free vote on the return of the death penalty. A similar article carried in the *Daily Express* the same day claimed: 'Mrs Thatcher is now determined to seek the restoration of the death penalty for terrorist killers.' There was also rare agreement between the two biggest mass-circulation dailies, the *Daily Mirror* and the *Sun*, against a return to hanging. Otherwise the two tabloids stood on opposite sides of the political fence throughout the election, the *Sun* supporting Margaret Thatcher (though it proclaimed at the start and end of the campaign 'The *Sun* is NOT a Tory newspaper') while the *Daily Mirror* threw its full editorial weight behind the Labour party. But on the question of the re-introduction of the death penalty, they were completely united. The *Daily Mirror* argued that, while the inevitable demand for a return of hanging was understandable, it was nevertheless wrong. Martyrdom of executed IRA terrorists would only aid their cause. A similar argument was adopted by the *Sun*: 'To restore hanging — even for terrorists alone — would not only be wrong but ineffective.'

Partisan support by the four major tabloids, the *Daily Express, Daily Mail, Sun* and *Daily Mirror*, was quite clearly defined in their coverage of the campaign. Each displayed their partisanship by giving positive support to their favourite, while treating the opposing campaign in a pejorative fashion, or ignoring it. The *Guardian* noted sadly that 'explicit and cynical polemics . . . have taken over the news pages. No issue has been spared manipulation.' However, this accurate assessment of the subjective style of both reporting and presentation of news by the tabloids during the election failed to refer to the constraints under which the popular press operates.

During an election, although they might prefer to follow a

partisan line, newspapers have to continue Fleet Street's traditional rivalry for circulation (which accounts for 60% of their income) and for advertising revenue. In elections, as at other times, the methods of news presentation are directly correlated with commercial considerations, while bias reflects proprietorial influence. During the course of the general election the two become fused together.

The tabloids sought to influence their readers' voting intentions by confirming the prejudices of those who agreed with them and by evoking sympathy from 'don't knows' or sceptics. In this respect the way in which the election news was presented was of paramount importance. The layout of a tabloid is designed not only to entertain and inform, but also to imprint clear images on the mind of the reader. The tabloids were able to retain the allegiance of those readers who were either hostile to politics generally, or held views contrary to those of the paper because they presented political news and commentary, and treated it as entertainment. Even so, for the most part it was scarcely disguised propaganda.

Particularly on the front pages, tabloid headline writers were able to make skilful use of small-type straplines which lead on to bold banner headlines. When juxtaposed carefully with reverse type (white lettering on a black background) key election points could be made clearly. The written text merely served to reinforce the 'images' the headline writers wished to suggest to the reader, so much so that the medium of the headline was often more useful in propaganda terms than the accompanying article. Many headlines seemed designed to remain fixed in the reader's consciousness, in a subliminal fashion, while the written text had almost a secondary function of filling in the space between the headline and the bottom of the page.

In their treatment of the election and in their search for new readers the popular dailies were forced to show greater skill and flair than ever before because of an increasingly competitive market. For example the *Daily Mirror*, in order to outshine its main rivals, tried to treat the election with greater seriousness. On April 22 it made a virtue of ceasing to publish its pin-ups, preferring instead 'to present facts about election issues'.

The following day the *Daily Star* told its readers that its girls would be staying put: 'Since we are not in any party's pocket we shall continue to leave out the boring propaganda and give

the facts. And the *Star* lovelies will get all the room they deserve.'
This statement seemed to sum up the *Daily Star's* almost
dismissive attitude towards the election; its editorials reflected
general scepticism about electioneering, politics and politicians,
and while its election coverage was fair, it was also minimal and
uninspiring. As the chart on p. 243 shows, the *Daily Star* gave the
main lead to the election far less than any other paper. It
steadfastly refused to promote any one party's cause over
another, and commercial reasons were thought to lie behind the
decision not to follow the *Daily Express* in supporting the
Conservatives. It was argued that the *Daily Star's* target readers
were unlikely to be Tory sympathisers. The paper rejected the
slanging match that the rest of Fleet Street was having over the
election. Proclaiming its objectivity, the *Daily Star* noted: 'This
newspaper believes in fair play and fair comment. It has no
blind allegiance to anyone. There is no monopoly of virtue — or
vice — in either of the two main parties.' A week later, on April
25, its editorial reduced the election to the following equation:

The Tories are good at making money. Labour is good at
spending it for the good of the largest number of people. So,
if you favour means first you should vote Tory, if you favour
ends then vote Labour. There's no alternative. An amalgama-
tion of both might be ideal but a coalition is out of the
question. It's your choice.

Its sister publication, the *Daily Express*, had no inhibitions
about telling its readers which way they should vote. Throughout
the campaign, like the *Daily Mail* and the *Sun*, the *Daily Express*
was committed to Mrs Thatcher and the Conservatives. All three
carefully paced the volume of their coverage and comment,
building up to a crescendo of enthusiastic support for the Tories
and the vision of a new Britain which, they assured their readers,
Mrs Thatcher was offering.

The most striking illustration of tabloid partisanship could be
found in their coverage of the party manifestos, the tone of
which ran completely against Labour, and appeared to confirm
the traditional complaints from the party's managers that they
never get a fair hearing from the Tory Press. The pro-Conservative
bias in Fleet Street was taken up by the *Daily Mirror*, which
reprinted the masthead of each national newspaper, and beneath

it a comment about that paper's political stance. The article was headlined: 'BRITAIN'S PAPER TORIES' (April 17). It described the *Daily Mail* as 'Fleet Street's dirty tricks specialist; known in the trade as the Tory Party's house magazine.' The *Daily Star* was said to be 'so desperate for circulation that it might support whichever party it thinks will be the most popular.'

The *Sun* relegated the Labour manifesto to an inside page. Its preference for the less serious and more lurid aspects of life was evidenced by its front page headlines: 'SEX PRISONER LOCKED IN PACKING CASE', while its rivals concentrated on Labour's election platform. This sordid sensation was only bettered by another front page headline in the *Sun* 'VICAR'S WIFE RUNS OFF WITH LORRY DRIVER' (April 9) on the day the rest of Fleet Street thought the election had already got under way. The *Sun's* account of Labour's manifesto, 'LABOUR PLEDGES ON PERKS', was trivial in the extreme, and deemed its most newsworthy aspect to be a commitment by the Labour Party to cut down the honours system and 'jobs for the boys'.

The *Daily Mirror* was supportive: 'JIM DOES IT HIS WAY' (April 7), and noted that the Prime Minister had out-manoeuvered Labour's left wing in drawing up the manifesto. While other papers presented this in a negative context the *Daily Mirror* wrote:

> Premier Jim Callaghan last night unwrapped Labour's General Election manifesto — and scored a major personal victory . . . OUT went nationalisation of banking and insurance. OUT went abolition of the House of Lords. OUT went public ownership of the drugs industry. OUT went any suggestion that Britain would leave the Common Market. Now the Prime Minister ('You know, I think we're going to win') will fight the election on HIS terms with HIS policies.

The other papers had a very different tone: ' . . . an unhappy compromise between Left and Right Wings on the Labour Manifesto. It is hard to resist the conclusion that the aim of it is not so much to provide a constructive theme for the nation, as to provide a formula which will hold the Labour Party together in a difficult election campaign.' (*Daily Express*). 'The invitation clearly offered by this Labour prospectus is "Steady as she goes" under the same old skipper. But precisely where have we been going these past five years? Nowhere.' (*Daily Mail*).

This 'more of the same' theme ran through most of the editorials, 'JIM'S BIG CON' . . . 'Don't be fooled by the Labour Party's cosy General Election manifesto. It is window dressing — designed by the Prime Minister to con the electorate. It simply prescribes the same remedies for Britain's sickness that have already failed to provide a cure.' (*Sun*).

Whereas the pro-Conservative papers emphasised the 'no change' aspects of Labour's platform, the *Daily Mirror* offered a similar description of the Conservative manifesto. Its analysis appeared on an inside page headlined: 'YESTERDAY'S MENU', a take-off of Labour's 1970 slogan for the Tory front bench. 'The new Thatcher policies look like the old Heath ones, up-dated, restyled and blue-rinsed. Where they're the same, they're no better, and where they're different they're worse.' Throughout the election the *Daily Mirror's* leading articles were slick and punchy, bearing the hall-mark of the paper's leader-writer, Joe Haines, one-time speech writer for Harold Wilson. The paper's style was reminiscent of the *Daily Mirror's* aggressive campaigning on behalf of the Labour Party in the 1940s and 1950s.

Front-page coverage of a speech by Mrs Thatcher took priority over news about the Conservative manifesto in the *Daily Mail*: 'MY PLEDGE TO BRITAIN — BY MAGGIE' (April 12). 'Margaret Thatcher last night struck to the heart of the issue that may decide whether she wins the General Election, the end of union tyranny and union abuse of power.' The paper's editorial said the Tory manifesto and the party's leader had challenged Britain to dare to hope and work for better days. 'She holds aloft the beacon of optimism. To read the Tory manifesto is to feel the spirits rise.'

The *Daily Express* gave the Conservatives extensive coverage on inside pages: 'CUT, CUT AND CUT AGAIN — MAGGIE'S SCALPEL WILL SLASH STATE SPENDING, RED TAPE, CRIME AND UNION POWER' (April 12). On another page 'MAGGIE: HOW I'LL CHANGE BRITAIN' headlined a long interview with Mrs Thatcher by George Gale. The *Daily Express* editorial proclaimed that, in contrast to Labour, the Tory manifesto 'offers the country a new and more hopeful approach. And we need it.'

The *Sun* — 'I BELIEVE!' (April 12) — bubbled over with enthusiasm: 'Tory leader Margaret Thatcher yesterday declared her faith in a better, brighter, booming Britain. She set the

Table 3. *Subjects of Lead Stories During the Election 9 April – 3 May*

Date	Guardian	Daily Telegraph	Daily Express	Daily Mail	Daily Star	Daily Mirror	Sun	Financial Times
APR –9	Benn and Lab Manifesto	Callaghan launches campaign	SDA letter to Callaghan	Con criticism	(Kidnap plot)	Con denationalisation plans	Wife of vicar runs off with vanman	Election strategies
10	Callaghan press conference	(Immigration men's strike)	(Strike threats)	Callaghan on TV	('Monopoly' crime)	Callaghan statement	(Triangle of death)	(Woolworth take over)
11	Thatcher election pledges	(Leyland strike talks)	Communists and Labs	(Uganda invaded by Tanzania)	(Strike leader probed)	(Northern Ireland)	Weighell statement	(Leyland talks)
12	Newham candidate resigns	Thatcher pledges	Newham candidate resigns	Thatcher attacks unions	Uganda	(Murder)	Thatcher launches manifesto	Con manifesto
14	(US expels SA diplomats)	(Raid on Nkomo's home)	(Raid on Nkomo's home)	(Mountain climbing tragedy)	(The skiver father)	(After-sex pill)	(Strike threat)	NEB take-over
16	(Yugoslav earthquake)	(Yugoslav earthquake)	(The impossible baby)	(Yugoslav earthquake)	(Murder squad copped)	(Yugoslav earthquake)	(Weather article)	No paper
17	Thatcher speech	(Teachers' pay protest)	Thatcher speech	(Rail crash)	(Murder)	Thatcher speech	(Rail crash)	Thatcher speech
18	Services pay rise	(Times shutdown)	Party politicals attacked	(Times shutdown)	(Spy story)	(Lovers jailed)	Services pay rise	(Times shutdown)
19	Earnings up 14.9%	Thatcher on economy	(Lee Marvin's mistress)	Mark attacks government	(Birth pill)	Callaghan on jobs	(Lee Marvin's mistress)	Prices and election

Date								
20	(IRA attack in Ulster)	Thatcher on defence	(Northern Ireland)	Thatcher on police	(Northern Ireland)	(Northern Ireland)	Opinion poll	Taxes and election
21	Callaghan on taxation	Thatcher on immigration	Denning on unions	Denning on unions	(Dustbin Kid)	(Sex; education)	(Pregnant — then sacked)	Taxes and election
23	(Palestinian terrorist raid)	Con strategy	(Rolling Stones)	Union leaders' campaign	Anglo-American relations	Leading article	Opinion poll	Opinion poll
24	Southall riot	Southall riot	Southall riot	Southall riot	(Love-tangle vicar)	Southall riot	Southall riot	Labour on taxes
25	Southall riot	Southall riot	Opinion poll	Southall riot	Southall riot	Southall riot	Southall riot	Southall riot
26	Election tactics	Southall riot	Thatcher speech	Labour platform	(Olympics in Britain?)	(Mother/son reunion)	Opinion polls	Callaghan and unions
27	(Human rights decision)	Tories and Unions	(Murder)	Wilson on Thatcher	(Murder)	The women voters	(Murder)	(US petrol shortage)
28	Opinion polls	Labour anger at Wilson	Opinion poll	(Queen's Road accident)	Opinion poll	Opinion poll	Leading article: vote—Tory	Thatcher on unions
30	(Times overseas edition)	Thatcher on unions	(Times overseas edition)	(Times overseas edition)	(Queen's Road accident)	Anti-Thatcher leader	(Murder)	(Times overseas edition)
MAY 1	Extremist threat	Labour's scare campaign	Callaghan speech	NOP poll-Lab lead	(Murder)	(Murder)	Poll shows Lab lead	Callaghan speech
2	Thatcher speech	Thatcher speech	Vote for Thatcher	Vote for Thatcher	(Fugitive Brothers)	Anti-Thatcher article	(Murder)	(Texaco rations petrol)
3	Polls predict Con win	Polls show Con lead	Polls show Con lead	Polls show Con lead	Polls show Con lead	Vote Labour	Polls show Con lead	Polls show Con lead

Date	News of The World	Sunday Express	Sunday Mirror	Sunday People	Observer	Sunday Observer
APR 8	Poll story	Cons and Council homes	(Police bribery scandal)	(Booze-up ban)	Cons and Council homes	Con Manifesto
15	(Beware of the Bishop)	Newham candidacy	(Weather)	(Northern Ireland)	(Uganda)	MPs pay visit
22	Politician's sex scandal	Election strategy	(Actress has cancer)	(Actor's heart attack)	Opinion poll	Opinion poll
29	Opinion poll	Heath attacks Callaghan	(The Royal Family)	(Stigmata miracle)	Opinion poll	Opinion poll

election alight as she promised the Tories would slash taxes, curb union power, combat crime and reform schools.' At the top of its front page the paper carried a smaller headline which quoted Mrs Thatcher: 'THIS COULD BE OUR LAST CHANCE TO BUILD A BETTER BRITAIN'; it had a doom-laded ring, which was repeated in various forms throughout the campaign.

Perhaps because of the absence of *The Times* (which did however manage to produce one international edition, printed in Germany and sold only in Europe, on April 30) the quality dailies, the *Daily Telegraph*, the *Guardian* and the *Financial Times*, were more objective in their reporting and comment about the election than in previous campaigns. Each took its responsibilities seriously, and gave the widest possible coverage to manifestos, speeches, personalities and constituency reports.

The *Daily Telegraph*, not unexpectedly, gave its support and encouragement to the Conservatives early on; its lead stories were generally geared to positive accounts of the Tory campaign and how it was progressing. Its reports of the activities of Labour, Liberal and minority parties were both detailed and plentiful. This approach led Mr Callaghan to praise the *Daily Telegraph* publicly for its campaign coverage. Each day the paper produced a double page 'Election Special' which reported on the campaign in three or four marginal constituencies, covered key speeches of all parties in depth, and included an 'Election Sketchbook' column, a light-hearted look at some of the more unusual aspects of the campaign. Frank Johnson offered a witty account of Mrs Thatcher's visit to a chocolate factory in the Midlands: 'TORY WHIRL AMONG THE SOFT CENTRES' (April 20).

The 'heavies' gave extensive coverage to the manifestos of all the major parties, but only the *Financial Times* reprinted each of them in full. On the day Mrs Thatcher launched the Conservative campaign, the *Daily Telegraph* ran six pictures of her in various poses at the morning press conference. Its lead headline: 'TORIES PLEDGE UNION CURBS' (April 12) reflected the paper's continued interest in the subject of union power. While it saw this as 'the single most important issue', it also gave wide coverage in the initial stages of the election to the Conservatives' tax proposals, another area of vital interest to its readers: 'TAX CUTS PLEDGE BY THATCHER' (April 3), and 'TORIES MAKE INCOME TAX KEY ISSUE' (April 6). However, this issue tended to fade into the background in the *Daily Telegraph* when Labour began challenging the Conservatives' pledge and asked where the money to fund the cuts in income tax would come from.

Both the *Daily Telegraph* and the *Guardian* noted that the election was 'odd' in that the major parties had reversed their traditional roles. The Conservatives now offered radical policies, a position usually reserved for the Labour Party, which in this campaign stood on a platform that seemed to eschew change and prefer the *status quo*. The *Daily Telegraph* described Mr Callaghan as 'A Tory in everything except essentials.' The *Guardian* was equally definitive in its description of this role reversal: 'The party of change and reform has become the party of benevolent immobilism. The party of resistance to change has sought to become the party of (at least rhetorical) revolution. Only the Liberals from one election to the next have proved tolerably consistent . . . '

Despite this perceived consistency, however, the Liberals were regarded by the Press as less central in terms of the eventual outcome. This was primarily due to the party's lower standing in the opinion polls, while a secondary factor was the cloud left hanging over Jeremy Thorpe. Objective assessment of Liberal policies was overshadowed by the former Liberal leader's impending trial. Almost all of Fleet Street gave coverage to Mr Thorpe's attempt to delay the start of his trial: 'JEREMY WINS TIME. (*Daily Express*, April 4), and his successful request for a High Court order preventing *The Spectator* from publishing an article, which it was argued might prejudice his trial. The North Devon constituency was well-trodden by both the British and international news media, conscious of Jeremy Thorpe's vulnerability. Most papers noted that it was the only constituency held by the Liberals which the Party Leader, David Steel, would not be visiting. The Liberals received additional negative coverage when their candidate against Mr Callaghan in Cardiff South-east, Christopher Bailey, managed at the last moment to evade nomination and urged Liberal voters to unseat him by voting Conservative. Mr Bailey's subsequent expulsion from the party also captured the headlines.

As a result of a special survey of Liberal-held seats the *Sun* foreshadowed 'DISASTER LOOMS FOR LIBS' (April 26), although the *Daily Telegraph* disagreed and predicted the party would do better than expected. On polling day the *Daily Express* warned 'A LIBERAL VOTE IS A WASTED VOTE' and the *Daily Mail* urged Liberals to vote for Mrs Thatcher. The party received its most hostile treatment from the *Sun* with such comments as 'Anyone who votes Liberal next Thursday is nuts.' While admitting that some Liberal policies were sound and that some Liberals 'are sensible chaps', the *Sun* argued that to vote Liberal 'could help bring in a majority Labour Government dominated by the wreckers and crackpots of the extreme Left'. The paper's advice was 'If you cannot bring yourself to vote Tory tomorrow, stay at home.'

Throughout the election the Labour party received trenchant criticism from most of the dailies over the role of its left wing. In this context repeated prominence was given to three dramatic events; the defection of several former Labour ministers to the Tories; the resignation of the Labour candidate at Newham North-East; and the publication of a list of alleged left-wing Labour politicians by the Social Democratic Alliance. The *Sun* ran a series of articles by Lord George-Brown, Sir Richard Marsh, Lord Chalfont and Reg Prentice on why they had switched from Labour to Conservative. Accounts of the defections were repeated in other papers together with stories about Newham. The *Daily Express* interpretation of events was typical: 'FORCED OUT BY THE REDS' . . . 'NOT EXTREME ENOUGH! TROTS OUST LEFT-WINGER IN NEW BLOW FOR JIM'. The previous day the *Express* had alluded to the fact that the Labour Party and the Communists were running for election 'on almost identical manifestos' — 'THE RED FACE OF LABOUR'. The *Sun's* anti-Left stance was evidenced by a centre-page feature 'HOW MANY REDS IN LABOUR'S BED? — POWER OF THE WILD MEN WILL GROW IF UNCLE JIM IS ELECTED AGAIN' (April 24).

For its defence the Labour Party had to rely on the support it received from the Mirror Group, whose papers accused the Conservatives of trying to frighten the voters with the bogey of extremists taking over from Labour moderates. The *Sunday Mirror* illustrated the group's position in a scathing editorial on April 22: 'Have you noticed a rather unpleasant smell in the air, like being next to a badly-run pig farm? Don't worry. It's just the Tories with their usual silly election muckraking.' However, during the campaign the paper did give space to the alternative view by continuing to publish articles by its regular columnist, Woodrow Wyatt, an ex-Labour MP now close to Mrs Thatcher, whose views were very contrary to those of the *Sunday Mirror*.

The *Financial Times*, which followed the City in its support for the Conservatives, reported the debate in a more restrained manner, in the context of trade union militancy rather than a left–right dichotomy inside the Labour party: 'CALLAGHAN ATTACKS CONSERVATIVES OVER UNION CO-OPERATION' (April 26). The *Guardian* noted that the Conservative politicians projected the issue of extremism into the centre of the campaign just before polling day: 'TORIES PLAY THE RED CARD' (May 1).

The election was unusual for the number of scare stories it produced. Conservatives claimed that Labour was using scare-tactics in a bid to discredit the Tory programme, and the words 'smear' or 'scare' repeatedly appeared in headlines and stories. George Gardiner warned in the *Sunday Express* on April 8 that Labour's 'secret election weapon' would be to 'create fear and then trade on it'. The Tory strategy for dealing with Labour attacks on Conservative policies appeared to have been formulated early in the campaign. But by the end of the election almost every Labour Party criticism of Tory policy seemed to be dismissed as a smear by Conservative politicians. A good example of how the pro-Conservative papers co-operated in neutralising Labour's attacks on Conservative policy and in mounting the subsequent counter-attack of 'smear', came with the *Daily Mail's* front page of April 25 'LABOUR'S DIRTY DOZEN – 12 big lies they hope will save them'. (see p. 191).

The heavy concentration of press coverage on the more colourful and superficial aspects of electioneering, such as muckraking and personality contests, had a tendency to blur the substantive issues in the campaign. For most papers the important topic tended to be the ones the politicians were talking about at that particular moment. The quality dailies did ponder various issues at length in editorials; taxation, inflation and union power were some of the main themes of the election.

Immigration only became an issue when it was mentioned by Mrs Thatcher on a radio phone-in: 'MAGGIE STICKS TO HER GUNS IN NEW RACE ROW' (*Sun*, April 18). The following day the *Daily Star* urged the politicians to stop 'pussyfooting around' and end all, not just coloured, immigration. A later

"Surely, sir, you won't leave us to risk going into Mrs Thatcher's Chamber of Horrors?"

Daily Express, May 2, 1979

pledge on immigration made by Mrs Thatcher on television was translated in the *Daily Telegraph's* main story as 'TORIES TAKE STERN LINE ON MIGRANTS' (April 21). Race was unexpectedly thrust into the news columns a few days later by the violence in Southall (see p. 180). It was an example of an event which was moulded to fit the particular position a paper was taking. Thus the *Daily Mail* was able to treat the riot as an example of extremism and the breakdown of law and order, both of which had been among the paper's prominent themes. The story faded away, however, after two days headlines.

Extraneous news events, both inside and outside Britain, attracted a good deal of space (see Table 3). The Rhodesian election, the military defeat of President Amin in Uganda, and the disaster at a nuclear power station in the United States all provided front-page news and an alternative to reports of the hustings. Nearer home, the comments of the American congressman, Tip O'Neill, on a visit to Ireland, provoked momentary fury.

Occasionally statements made by some prominent personalities outside the political spectrum received widespread attention because they could be linked to election issues. Lord Denning's reference in Canada to British trade unions being almost immune from the law, provoked the *Daily Express* headline the next day (April 21) 'DENNING RAPS UNION POWER'. When the former police commissioner, Sir Robert Mark, wrote in an obscure trade journal that the relationship between the trade unions and the Labour Government was 'not unlike the way the Nazi Party seized power' the *Daily Mail* hailed it as 'MARK'S BROADSIDE AT LABOUR' (April 19). In an editorial the paper recognised that the former police chief had 'overstated his case', but it did not diminish the weight which the *Daily Mail* gave to his comments. It believed that Sir Robert had 'done a public service by intervening with his own contribution, however provocative, to an issue which should be at the heart of the General Election'. It demonstrated that what might be 'good copy' at other times could become 'sensational news' during the course of an election when newspapers search for an 'exclusive' or a new angle on an old theme.

Another example of this was a comment by a trade union leader, which backfired; Sid Weighell, of the National Union of Railwaymen, had said that if Mrs Thatcher won the election he would tell his members to join the pay queue outside No. 10 and to 'Get your snouts in the trough.' It was a provocative phrase which, in the middle of an election, offered a natural headline. Paul Johnson (*Daily Mail*) and Peter Jenkins (*Guardian*) both commented in their columns that the Conservatives' advertising agency, Saatchi and Saatchi, could not have provided a better slogan for the Tory's cause. The (pro-Conservative) *Sun* described Mr Weighell as 'Silly Sid', and the (pro-Labour) *Sunday Mirror* later redubbed him 'Sensible Sid'.

The role of women generally, and of one woman in particular, became a popular topic on the news and feature pages. The unique opportunity for a woman to become Britain's Prime Minister provided a natural angle with which to link Mrs Thatcher to a large section of the electorate whose decision on polling day would be crucial. Newspapers which supported the Conservative cause were able to assist the party by explaining to women just how 'vital' they would be in deciding the final outcome of the election, and by portraying Mrs Thatcher as someone with whom ordinary housewives could identify. On her campaign trail she was pictured almost every day in a casual pose shopping, talking to housewives in the street or across a garden fence, or having tea with workers in a factory, chatting about ordinary things that ordinary working women do discuss — teabags and the price of bread — or meeting 'the home-buying Parker family'.

The *Sun* took pains to explain that undecided women voters could swing the election one way or the other, and emphasised the housewife's concern for rising prices, an issue which could be laid squarely at Labour's door. 'WHY A WOMAN'S PLACE IS IN No. 10' headlined the *Sun* (April 21) which, like the other pop-dailies, prominently displayed Mrs Thatcher's comments on a television phone-in programme: 'I know what it's like running a house and running a career. I know what it's like to live within a budget and I know what it's like having to cope.'

On-the-road reports about the campaigns of the three party leaders and senior politicians like Denis Healey and Edward Heath were featured prominently. Most papers carried descriptions of what it was like to travel around the country aboard the Liberal leader's 'Battle Bus'. Dr David Owen was unfavourably depicted in the *Sun* as 'DR. SMUG', and in a report from the Foreign Secretary's Plymouth constituency, the paper asked, 'CAN

LABOUR'S POMPOUS PIN-UP SAVE HIS SEAT?' The phrases used by the press to portray the two central figures in the election were less severe than this, though occasionally slightly caustic. Although the *Daily Telegraph* did carry one complete article devoted solely to Mrs Thatcher's hairstyle (where she had it done, how it was cut, what kind of rollers she used, etc. etc.), descriptions of the party leaders were generally respectful in tone even when the partisan support was clearly revealed. There was some evidence of a desire by papers to redress the 'Iron Maiden' and 'Milk snatcher' labels which had previously been used to describe the Conservative leader. The *Daily Telegraph* emphasised her boldness and positiveness, and described her campaign as 'a carefully arranged exercise which left little to chance'. She presented her case with 'dignity, moderation and statesmanlike force'. The *Observer*, on the other hand, felt that her manner at the Press conferences was 'a bit headmistressy'. By 'sticking to her guns' over immigration, the *Sun* said she presented an image of toughness. The *Daily Mail*, which frequently boasted that it had been the first paper to back Mrs Thatcher's bid for the Conservative leadership, viewed her admiringly. It quoted an American observer saying: 'She's the best meeter-of-the-people I've come across.' The *Daily Mirror* was unimpressed: 'The cosmetic creation' was its description; and the *Sunday Mirror* said that Mrs Thatcher was being sold like toothpaste. The *Observer* approach was more analytical, with an excellent study of the Conservative image makers, 'THE SELLING OF MAGGIE' (April 22).

By continually pleading 'MORE FACTS, MAGGIE' the *Daily Mirror* attempted to portray Mrs Thatcher and the Conservative advertising campaign as being less than honest. The *Daily Express* sought to convey a similar type of image of 'hiding the truth' about Labour's left wing. The description of Mr Callaghan as avuncular continued during the course of the campaign, and several headlines referred to him as 'Uncle Jim'. The *Daily Mail* likened his campaign to an endearing old traction engine in one article, but noted in another, somewhat contradicting itself, that the improvement by Labour in the polls was due to Mr Callaghan's 'brilliant showmanship'. The *Observer* called him 'Square Deal Jim', and on April 29 endorsed him as their choice to continue as Prime Minister. His no-gimmick campaign was said to be a mixture of shrewd strategy and his own seriousness. For the

Sunday Telegraph Mr Callaghan was 'the most accomplished purveyor of comfortable conservatism our politics have seen in many a long year'. But it was Mrs Thatcher who caught the newspapers' eye. Of the 57 photographs of politicians appearing on Fleet St. front pages between April 19 and May 3, 24 were of Mrs Thatcher and 9 of the Prime Minister.

Several academics contributed to Fleet Street's analysis of the election campaign. Anthony King wrote each week during the campaign on The *Observer's* eccentric opinion poll findings; Hugh Berrington contributed to the *Sunday Telegraph* and Richard Rose to the *Daily Telegraph*. The *Observer*, on April 29, carried Samuel Beer's 'Election Notebook', which gave an American academic's perspective on the hustings. The politicians were given space in the editorial pages to state their case: both Mrs Thatcher and Mr Callaghan wrote (or had written for them) features for the *Sun, Daily Express, Daily Star* and *News of the World*, on 'Why you should vote for me.' Denis Healey (who also explained his proposed wealth tax in *Money Mail*) and Jim Prior contributed to the *Sun*, while Sir Geoffrey Howe and Jo Grimond wrote pieces for the *Daily Telegraph*, which also provided room for 'A view from the Left' by Tom Litterick, a member of Labour's *Tribune* Group.

Special surveys among different sections of the electorate provided a means whereby papers were able to inject some originality into the campaign coverage. The *News of the World* examined the voting intentions of first-time voters: 'YOUNG BRITAIN SWINGS OVER TO THE TORIES' (April 8); the *Daily Express* gathered together a group of 'ordinary women to answer ten vital questions' about the election. It deemed women the 'vital' factor — the 'ones who must be wooed and won'. Another of its surveys revealed that coloured voters would play a 'vital' role in 20 key marginals. The *Daily Star's* survey of drinkers in a pub bar revealed intense boredom with the election, but each day it interviewed entertainment personalities for its 'Starvote' column. The *Daily Mirror* rivalled this with an 'Election '79 Showbiz special' which polled 3 votes for the Liberals, 6 for the Conservatives and 13 for Labour.

A notable feature of the campaign was the extensive coverage given to opinion polls. The *Observer* consistently devoted a major part of its front page to an account of the divergent RSL poll, but it also summarised what other polls had disclosed earlier in the week. The dailies were similarly consistent in their coverage of the opinion polls and, while giving priority to those which they had commissioned, exploited other findings which they felt were newsworthy. The net effect was the almost daily appearance of poll stories throughout the campaign.

Criticism of the polls appeared nearly as regularly as the surveys themselves. One *Guardian* reader suggested in a letter that the next Parliament should consider prohibiting the publication of opinion polls during an election campaign. This prompted a rebuttal from the directors of two polls, Robert Worcester of MORI and Norman Webb of Gallup.

The gross divergence between RSL and the other polls served to encourage general criticism of polls. Although the criticism of RSL was chiefly directed at the survey itself, it was impossible to ignore the negative implications which such unreliable results had for polls in general. The *Observer* responded to the criticism by acknowledging the possibility of an element of error in their sampling method which may have led to a pro-Tory bias. But they also believed that they deserved credit for having published their results nonetheless.

The survey which attracted the most attention was the startling findings of the NOP poll in the *Daily Mail* a few days before the election took place. For the first time it showed Labour in the lead — although the margin was only 0.7%. The headline in the *Sun* was indicative of the response which the poll precipitated: 'TORIES IN POLL SHOCK' (May 1). The result of this poll seemed to generate a new interest in what the polls were saying, and many pro-Conservative papers felt it necessary to try and discredit the results. At the same time, most papers were predicting a close-run end to the campaign.

However, on May 3, the day of 'the only poll which counted', the *Sun* showed Mrs Thatcher ahead by 6%; the *Daily Express* put her in the lead by 5.6%; but the *Daily Telegraph* had a much narrower lead of only 2%. The *Daily Mail*, which two days earlier, had splashed 'LABOUR IN THE LEAD', across its front page was unapologetic. On polling day it ran an even bigger headline: 'POLLS GIVE MAGGIE THE LEAD'. In its main story the paper explained the apparent inconsistency of their previous poll findings: 'The Tory lead had probably bottomed out at the beginning of this week and this tendency may have been exaggerated by sampling variations in the NOP poll.'

The paper which made the least use of polls was the *Daily
Mirror*. One explanation for its reluctance to publish poll stories,
although they were an important ingredient in other papers'
election coverage, was that the result of the surveys consistently
favoured the Conservatives. This would seem to indicate just
how important they were as a propaganda device. The *Daily
Mirror's* editorial on April 10 pointed out the inconsistencies in
the poll results in order to discredit them. It summarised its
criticism succinctly and indirectly: ' . . . and that leaves ORC,
NOP, RSL, MORI, GALLUP and the rest in only one place. UP
THE POLL.'

The way in which poll findings were reported was another
illustration of partisanship on the news pages. For example, a
poll story in the *Daily Express* of a 7% Conservative lead was
reported in the *Daily Mirror* as a Labour advance, with stress on
the percentage by which the Tory lead had diminisheed. At
other times emphasis was placed on the surveys which measured
the popularity of Mr Callaghan and Mrs Thatcher, since these
consistently gave the Labour leader the advantage. Such polls
conveyed the strong impression that Mr Callaghan's personality
was largely responsible for keeping Labour in the contest.

The pro-Tory papers published the results faithfully, recognising on occasion that the election might not be going the way
they hoped. When NOP showed a cut in Mrs Thatcher's lead,
the *Daily Mail* reported it as: NOW IT'S 6% TORY LEAD'
(April 6). Most papers warned their readers not to take a
Conservative victory for granted, and suggested that the Tories
were going to have to fight to win.

Poll fever was by no means exclusive to Fleet Street. The
New Statesman carried the findings of MORI surveys which the
Sunday Times was unable to publish. Invariably the provincial
press reiterated those poll results which aroused public attention
at a national level. They also made use of special regional polls
in order to gauge local opinion. Among the most prominent of
these was the System Three poll — oracle of the *Glasgow Herald*
— which provided a measure of the Scottish mood in competition
with an ORC poll in the *Scotsman*.

Few firm conclusions can be drawn from an examination of
the role that provincial newspapers played in the general election.
The wide range of readership and differing styles of news
coverage inherently produces a quality of election reporting

whose diversity is as great as that between the tabloids and the quality dailies at a national level. During the election the provincial press provided a synthesis of national issues with the local reader in mind.

Headlines like 'NOTHING NEW AS CAMPAIGN SAGS' (*Eastern Daily Press*, April 27) reflected the generally subdued nature of much of the campaign. 'SHOCK POLL FOR TORIES' (*Liverpool Daily Post*, April 28) echoed local interest in the outcome. Issues of national prominence had their local implications stressed. The *Yorkshire Post's* treatment of the racial violence which occasionally flared up during the campaign offered a good example.

The weekly status of magazines such as the *Economist, Spectator* and *New Statesman* enabled them to be more analytic. The manner in which they covered certain topics reflected their differing ownership and priorities. The *Economist* looked at a wide range of election themes, but isolated taxation as the major issue. The *New Statesman* gave a long analysis to economic policy and the class structure of the electorate, as well as an examination of Fleet Street's role in the campaign. The *Spectator's* approach was more personalised. Profiles of political celebrities outweighed the issues, and on April 28 it featured three names associated (or formerly associated) with the Conservatives: 'Mrs Thatcher's Passion Play'; 'Powell among the Irish', and 'Heath's separate election'. While the *Economist* maintained relative objectivity in its presentation of news, both the *Spectator* and the *New Statesman* were clearly partisan. At the onset of the election the *Spectator* declared 'The bribery and political (not personal) corruption which has marked the end of his (Callaghan's) ministry is typical of his methods. Indeed the Government will be remembered for one long series of bribes.' The partisanship of the *New Statesman* equally manifested itself: 'We understand the importance of thwarting the plans which the Tories have for us all . . . ' 'You think Labour isn't working? You haven't seen anything yet.'

The climax of a long and drawn out campaign brought with it an intensification of partisan support, particularly in the tabloids. Front pages were given over to editorials and bold headlines urging readers which way to vote. The pro-Conservative papers stressed that it was time for a change, and asked readers to give Mrs Thatcher a chance.

Daily Mail: 'THE WOMAN WHO CAN SAVE BRITAIN'.

Sun: 'VOTE TORY THIS TIME – IT'S THE ONLY WAY TO STOP THE ROT'.

Daily Express: 'DON'T FORGET LAST WINTER – Give the girl a chance to make Britain great again'.

Daily Mirror: 'FORWARD WITH THE PEOPLE – Vote LABOUR Today'.

The Times international edition, finally published in Germany, headlined its election leader: 'THE CHOICE FOR THE COUNTRY' (April 30), and came down on the side of the change which Mrs Thatcher and the Conservatives offered. The Communist *Morning Star* summed up its view in a two word banner headline – the boldest seen anywhere in Fleet Street throughout the campaign: 'STOP THATCHER'. For their main front page stories the remaining dailies concentrated on the predictions of the polls, and saved their election hopes for inside leader pages; 'ODDS ON MAGGIE' (*Daily Star*, May 3); 'POLLS POINT TO A MODEST TORY VICTORY' (the *Guardian*, May 3); 'TORY HOPE OF 30 MAJORITY' (*Daily Telegraph*, May 3); 'OPINION POLLS GIVE TORIES THE EDGE' (*Financial Times*, May 3).

Party leadership overshadowed party policy as the fundamental election issue upon which the press focussed during the course of the campaign. In retrospect this seems to have been a feature of the 1970s where the expanding influence of television has encouraged the packaging of 'images' for the presentation to the voting public. The implications which this has had for the press were obvious in 1979: the coverage of the campaign appeared as a by-product of carefully planned news management by both parties, but particularly by the Conservative Party.

Spontaneous news events were at a premium in this election, since Labour and the Tories employed similar strategies aimed at creating or maintaining a particular image of their individual leader. In this sense tactical forward planning worked; positive reporting of the Labour campaign largely centred around Mr Callaghan. On the negative side the industrial disputes of the previous winter and the moderate/left division inside the party provided natural targets for press criticism.

For the Conservatives, the projection of the correct image for Mrs Thatcher was a major priority, and in this respect her

Wednesday, 2 May 1979

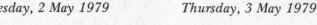

Thursday, 3 May 1979

Thursday, 3 May 1979

Thursday, 3 May 1979

progress along the campaign trail was carefully planned by party
professionals and well-reported by Fleet Street. The impression
given was that everything had been worked out in detail to
avoid slip-ups while ensuring favourable coverage of Mrs
Thatcher's speeches and visits throughout the country. As a
strategy it paid off; there was little hostile criticism, except in
the *Daily Mirror*.

The campaign itself lacked excitement, and that was reflected
in the press coverage. The main news items, based on public
appearances by the party leaders, the 'Red' scare and Conservative
pledges to cut taxes, were all familiar themes. Throughout the
1970s the findings of opinion polls have become a device for
the Press to inject an element of surprise and spontaneity into
the conflict: 'CALLAGHAN LEADS THATCHER'; 'TORIES
IN FRONT'; 'LABOUR NARROWS THE GAP'. The 1979
election was no different, despite the fact that, with one notable
exception, the polls consistently indicated a Conservative victory
on the cards.

The strongest impression of Fleet Street's role during the
campaign was the extent of bias among the popular dailies. The
uncommitted voter could not have relied for informed election
coverage upon any one of the tabloids – rather he needed to
have turned to the quality dailies for a balanced judgment.

The popular press is now completely tabloid; it has a combined circulation of more than 12 million and a readership in
excess of 36 million (see Table 1). Thus it is an ideal vehicle for
propaganda. The Conservatives spent large sums throughout the
campaign on full page advertisements in the tabloids, sometimes
taking two or three pages in the same edition. Labour concentrated its more limited resources in the last ten days – but in
the same newspapers as the Conservatives. Little is known about
what effect such advertising or editorial bias has on the voting
behaviour of newspaper readers during an election. The results
of one survey published during the course of the campaign
raised some doubts about the ability of newspaper readers to
perceive bias in the press. The *New Statesman* (April 27)
produced the findings of a MORI poll commissioned by the

Sunday Times in which respondents were asked about the bias of the newspapers they read.

Table 4.   Perceptions of Newspaper Partisanship

Readers of:	Con	Lab	Unbiased	Don't know
D. Express	44	5	33	19
D. Mail	45	9	34	12
Sun	28	9	41	22
D. Mirror	24	19	38	18

Respondents in the MORI panel were asked whether newspaper coverage they had seen was biased towards Conservatives or Labour, or whether it had been unbiased. Rather surprisingly, the staunchly pro-Labour *Daily Mirror* was seen by more people as being biased in favour of the Conservatives, while only 28% thought of the *Sun* as a pro-Tory paper. At the very least the results of this survey suggest that this is an area which calls for much greater research, not to determine whether the British press is biased, but to analyse whether that bias has an influence on the outcome of elections.

13 Opinion Polls

In a general election the press sponsors public opinion polls which are concerned with predicting the result; the parties sponsor private opinion polls which are concerned with analysing reactions to the campaign. Selling newspapers and winning elections are two different operations. There were occasional headlines on the relative standing of Mr Callaghan and Mrs Thatcher, and there was some analysis of how voters were responding to issues. But in 1979 the Fleet Street reports of survey findings were still largely concentrated on the question of which party would win.

There were, in fact, more nationwide poll reports than in any previous election. This was not because there were more polling organisations involved, but because the campaign period was longer than any since the early 1950s (when Gallup had the field almost to itself). It was interesting that once again almost every national newspaper thought it worthwhile to carry its own poll. Criticisms of the polls in the last three general elections failed to discourage continued sponsorship. The exceptions were the *Daily Mirror*, which had always shunned polls, and the *Guardian* which, apart from 1966, had never commissioned them – though it had always reported fully on the polls of others.

In 1970 four public polls out of five wrongly predicted a Labour victory, and even the fifth underestimated the Conservatives lead. In February 1974 every public poll indicated a Conservative victory and, though the margins were small and the Conservatives were in fact a shade ahead in the final tally, each understated the Labour vote. In October 1974 eight published polls correctly predicted a Labour victory, but exaggerated the margin: the result was 'right' but the percentage error was on average greater than in the two previous elections when the 'wrong' winner had been picked.

In the years that followed there was much speculation why, after twenty years of relative success, the polls had gone astray in their predictions. The voters might be becoming more capricious in their behaviour; or more disingenuous in their answers to interviewers. The polls themselves might be having an effect on the election, developing a self-falsifying quality by inducing voters to act differently once they were presented with evidence of a coming landslide or a coming deadlock. Certainly the pollsters' conscientious self-examination, and the enquiries of the Market Research Society revealed no simple explanations for error.

But after 1974 the pollsters did at least have the 1975 Referendum on the EEC to cite as evidence that they could predict the outcome of an unfamiliar vote on a relatively low turnout. All the four published forecasts overestimated the 'Yes' proportion but two, Gallup and Marplan, were within 1% of the correct answer (although the other two, Harris and ORC, had 5 % to 6% errors which would have been disastrous in a close general election).

The newspaper polling business sees shifting allegiances. Gallup had an enviable record of secure tenure and regular publication in the *Telegraph* since 1960. National Opinion Polls (NOP) continued to be published by the *Daily Mail* — though much less regularly. The *Evening Standard* had dropped Opinion Reasearch Centre (ORC) and began to use Market & Opinion Research International (MORI) occasionally. The *Daily Express* abandoned Louis Harris and in 1977 entered into a regular contract with MORI, which also did surveys for Thames Television and Granada Television and for the unpublished *Sunday Times*. The *Sun*, as in the past, sponsored Marplan polls from time to time. The *Observer* turned to Research Services Ltd., a new version of an old company, but one without recent experience of regular political polling. Thus the associated firms of Louis Harris and ORC, which had such a leading role among the published polls in the early 1970s, disappeared from the Fleet Street scene while MORI, owned by the American Robert Worcester, largely took their place. ORC was still in evidence, polling for Independent Television News and, north of the Border, for the *Scotsman*, as well as doing private work for the Conservatives to match MORI's private work for Labour. System Three continued to do Scottish polls for the *Glasgow Herald*, and MORI conducted two polls for the *Scottish Daily Express*.

From 1974 onwards public opinion had been as unstable as

in the 1960s. After the victory of October 1974 Labour had sunk to a 20% deficit by early 1977 (when the Stechford and Ashfield by-elections were lost on record swings) only to draw level with the Conservatives by June 1978 (see p. 29). But the usual upsurge in government popularily during the summer recess did not occur in 1978, and polls played some part in dissuading Mr Callaghan from an October election (see p. 44). None the less Labour regained a small lead in November before collapsing again to a 20% deficit in the hard times of February 1979. The party entered the election about 11% behind. Only in September 1951 had the opposition gone into a campaign with a double-figure lead in the established opinion polls.

Apart from RSL in the *Observer*, the polls broadly agreed on a trend, as Table 1 shows. The Conservative lead dropped from about 11% to about 5%, and then rose again slightly in the last few days. The Liberal vote rose from about 8% to almost 14%. But the movement was not a simple one from Conservative to Liberal; the Conservatives were losing both to Labour and Liberal, while Labour's gains from the Conservatives were offset by losses to the Liberals.

During the campaign, references to the polls were affected by the deviant findings of RSL. In the four Sundays of April Conservative leads of 21%, 16%, 20%, and 11½% were reported. Sophisticated observers soon recognised that something must be wrong with surveys so far out of line with the established polls. As Bob Worcester wrote in his private reports to the Labour party on April 8 'Ignore it. It looks like a rogue poll.' Less bluntly, the Conservative Research Department noted on April 16, 'RSL have little experience of political polling and [their] results . . . should be treated with considerable caution.' However, few editiors were ruthless enough to cut the RSL findings from the 'poll of polls' averages which they published to summarize the state of public opinion, although the inclusion of the RSL figures raised the Conservative lead by up to 3%. On April 26, RSL asked the directors of the rival polls to foregather (in the offices of ORC) to discuss what RSL was doing wrong: those attending the meeting were satisfied with the good intentions of the firm but failed to find an answer, unless it was that the inter-viewers guidance about selecting respondents, based on com-mercial experience, led to an under-representation of Labour voters.

Table 1. Campaign Polls

Fieldwork	Date, place of publication	Poll	Con %	Lab %	Lib %	Nat./Oth %	Con % Lead	Sample Size*
28 Mar–2 Apr	5 Apr *Telegraph*	Gallup	49	38½	9	3½	10½	970
29 Mar	29 Mar *Thames*	MORI	51	42	5	2	9	1,075
1–2 Apr	4 Apr *Express*	MORI	51	38	10	1	13	1,041
2–3 Apr	6 Apr *Mail*	NOP	48	42	8	2	6	1,036
3–4 Apr	8 Apr *Observer*	Research Serv.	54½	33½	9	3	21	1,188
6–9 Apr	12 Apr *Telegraph*	Gallup	50	40	8	2	10	1,855
8–9 Apr	11 Apr *Express*	MORI	49	39	10	2	10	1,054
10–11 Apr	15 Apr *Observer*	Research Serv.	53	37	8	2	16	1,181
13–14 Apr	17 Apr *Mail*	NOP	48	42	8	2	6	1,076
14–18 Apr	22 Apr *Sun Tel*	Gallup	47½	42	9	1½	5½	1,977
17 Apr	19 Apr *Express*	MORI	50	38	10	2	12	1,032
17–18 Apr	22 Apr *Observer*	Research Serv.	54	34	9½	2½	20	1,199
17–18 Apr	20 Apr *Sun*	Marplan	51	41	6	1	10	1,189
18–19 Apr	23 Apr *Sun*	Marplan	49¾	39¾	9	2	10	1,264
19–21 Apr	25 Apr *Telegraph*	Gallup	46½	41½	10	2	5	2,036
21–23 Apr	25 Apr *Express*	MORI	46	40	11	3	6	1,099
23–25 Apr	29 Apr *Sun Tel*	Gallup	48	40	10½	1½	8	2,144
24–25 Apr	29 Apr *Observer*	Research Serv.	49½	38	10	2½	11½	1,185
25 Apr	27 Apr *Sun*	Marplan	48	40	10	2	8	1,247
26 Apr	28 Apr *Express*	MORI	44	41	12	2	3	1,051
29–30 Apr	1 May *Mail*	NOP	42.4	43.1	12.2	2.3	−0.7	1,080
Final Predictions								
29 Apr–1 May	3 May *Express*	MORI	44.4	38.8	13.5	3.3	5.6	947
1 May	3 May *Sun*	Marplan	45	38.5	13.5	3	6.5	1,973
1–2 May	3 May *Mail*	NOP	46	39	12.5	2.5	7	1,069
1–2 May	3 May *Telegraph*	Gallup	43	41	13.5	2.5	2	2,348
2 May	3 May *Eve Stand*	MORI	45	37	15	3	8	1,089
	Actual Result		44.9	37.7	14.1	3.3	7.2	

* All polls but the MORI 29 April – 1 May poll used quota samples; the latter was a reinterview of a random sample. Almost all polls mentioning the proportion of 'don't knows' excluded them from their percentages, and that practice is followed in this table. But the *Sun/*

The polls offer clear evidence that the Liberal campaign was making headway during the last two weeks. As for Labour, the position is less clear. The recovery was from the exceptional abyss of February. The return to old loyalties was universally expected, and some notable incompetence during the campaign would have been needed to prevent it. Yet perhaps Labour can take some credit for the extent of their revival during April. In answer to the question 'Who would make the better Prime Minister?', Gallup found that Mr Callaghan led Mrs Thatcher by 39% to 33% on April 12, but this increased to 44% to 25% by the end of the campaign. Gallup also found that the Conservative advantage over Labour as the party best able to handle the country's most urgent problem declined over the same period in percentage terms from 43–31 to 39–35½. MORI, in a poll for the unpublished *Sunday Times*, found the judgment of a panel of 900 voters moved substantially in Labour's direction between April 4–6 and April 24–26. In answer to a question about which party was winning the argument, there were net movements to Labour of 9% on taxes; of 3% on prices; of 9% on strikes; and of 9% on jobs.

The final predictions of the polls usually contained some cautious hedging, about the behaviour of the 'don't knows', about the possibilities of last minute switches, and about the difficulty of relating votes to seats. In fact, as is shown on p. 425ff, the Conservative lead of 7.2% secured them a majority in seats 22 less than past precedent might have suggested.

Table 2.   Error in Final Forecasts (%)

	Con	Lab	Lib	Error on Con Lead	Average error for 3 parties
MORI/*Express*	−0.5	+1.1	−0.6	−1.6	0.7
Marplan/*Sun*	+0.1	+0.8	−0.6	−0.7	0.5
Gallup/*Telegraph*	−1.9	+3.3	−0.6	−5.2	1.9
NOP/*Mail*	+1.1	+1.3	−1.6	−0.2	1.3
MORI/*E. Standard*	+0.1	−0.7	+0.9	+0.8	0.6
Average error	0.8	1.4	0.9	1.7	1.0
Actual result (G.B.)	44.9	37.7	14.1	7.2	−

As Table 2 shows the actual performance in prediction was as good as in any year since the 1950s. But an awkward question remained. Did the very factors which perhaps gave a self-falsifying quality to the polls in their disasters of 1970 and 1974 save them in 1979? There were three polls in the last week which changed the atmosphere of the election. On the Saturday, MORI showed the Conservative lead down from 7% to 3%. On the Tuesday, NOP actually put Labour 1% ahead, a finding much publicised in the broadcast news bulletin. On election day itself, Gallup showed the parties 2% apart. These widely reported findings helped to suggest a cliff-hanger. On election day, Gallup found that 81% of their sample expected a close result. If a modicum of Labour voters had been influenced by land-slide forecasts in 1970 and in October 1974 to switch against the party, then suggestions that 1979 might after all produce a close result could be expected to steady the more fickle of Conservative supporters who, while not wanting a Conservative landslide, wanted the return of Labour still less. The evidence is not conclusive. It is plain that a larger than ever section of the public was correctly aware of the tenor of the poll predictions (66% according to a Conservative private poll on April 8), and that a lot of partisans favoured a hung parliament; but proof on the motives for the switching or non-switching of votes is lacking.

In Scotland there was a lively polling rivalry. ORC in the *Scotsman*, System Three in the *Glasgow Herald*, and MORI in the *Scottish Daily Express* reported the trends. They had fared well in the Referendum on the Scotland Act on March 1. Now they were all agreed in recording advances by both Labour and Conservatives at the expense of the SNP, but they differed on who was gaining most.[1] However, as Table 3 shows, their final forecasts were all within a reasonable margin, granted the size of sample.

Virtually all the polling in this election was by quota samples. The virtues of this method (under which it is left to the inter-viewer to select the respondents, according to a due quota by age, sex and class) are speed and economy. Mathematical purists

---

[1] The SNP on April 26 claimed that a straw poll of their own, with 900 interviews, weighted towards their strongest areas in the North and the West, found 26% support for them, 35% for Labour and 23% for the Conservatives.

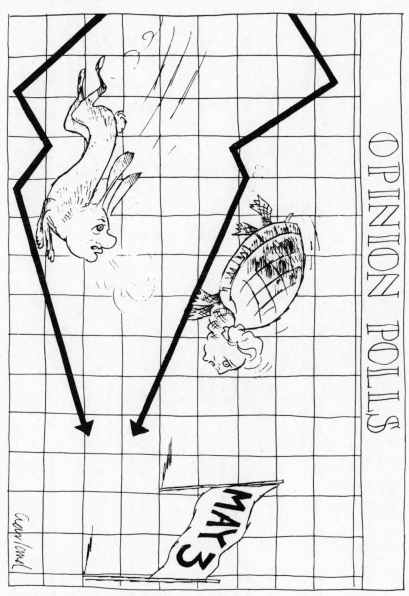

OPINION POLLS

MAY 3

Table 3.   Scottish Campaign Polls

Fieldwork	Date, place of publication	Poll	Con %	Lab %	Lib %	Nat %	Lab Lead %	Sample type, size *
26 Mar–2 Apr	4 Apr Glasgow H.	System Three	29	45	6	19	16	1,003
29 Mar–2 Apr	5 Apr Sc. D. Express	MORI	34	46	4	15	12	1,000
10–12 Apr	17 Apr Glasgow H.	System Three	27	49	6	17	22	1,079
20–23 Apr	25 Apr Scotsman	ORC	33	42	9	16	9	1,015
23–25 Apr	30 Apr Daily Mail	NOP	33	44	6	16	11	806
Final Predictions								
27–29 Apr	30 Apr Scotsman	ORC	34	42	8	15	8	1,016
28–29 Apr	1 May Glasgow H.	System Three	30	41	11	17	11	1,091
31 Apr–1 May	3 May Sc. D. Express	MORI	30	44	6	18	14	1,025
	Actual Result		31.4	41.5	9.0	17.3	10.1	
	Average Error		1.8	1.2	2.0	1.1	2.3	

* All these surveys used quota samples.

prefer the random method, with respondents selected from the electoral register, but this may require repeated callbacks to find the chosen voter, entailing substantial cost and delay. Pollsters felt under particular pressure of time in this election because of the deterioration of the postal services and of express despatches by rail. Delays in distributing and returning the questionnaires put a premium on interviewer speed. But, although this has not caused trouble in the past, quota samples always leave an anxiety lest those who are readily accessible for interview prove for some special reason different from those whose life-style makes them less likely to fall within the pollsters' net.

The only substantial poll to use random sampling throughout was the panel study conducted by Marplan for London Weekend Television: by reinterviewing the same respondents they ensured that the chances of sampling were not responsible for the trends apparent in the three successive surveys. The final MORI polls for the *Daily Express* also used reinterviews to check for the last minute swings, but, like the MORI *Sunday Times* panel study, they started with a quota sample.

One interesting development during the campaign was the use of telephone surveys by Marplan. Telephone surveys are speedy and cheap, but because Britain has only 60% saturation of telephone ownership, heavily biased towards the better-off, such an approach needs far more delicacy in use than in the U.S.A. or Australia where there is 90% telephone saturation. More will undoubtedly be heard of political telephone surveys in Britain. But the *Sunday Times* surveys did illustrate one hazard of panel surveys: 92% of the panel claimed after the election to have voted, and there could be little doubt that the mere experience of regular reinterviews had stimulated interest and turnout.

All the polls were cautious in allowing their statements about percentage party support to be translated into forecasts of seats in the House. Memories were still strong of February 1974, when the party with the most votes did not secure the most seats.

Polls may be used to influence opinion, although established polling companies would frown on the practice. A novel factor in 1979 was a plan to play majority views back to the public as a method of influencing public opinion, by showing people

that they do in fact constitute a majority. T. F. Thompson, once
political editor of the *Daily Mail*, and for ten years at the head
of ORC, raised funds from industry to carry out a series of polls
in marginal constituencies as the election approached. Not
surprisingly these showed that, on the issue of further nationalisation, the majority of Labour voters were not nearly as left-
wing as official Labour policy. These polls were quite widely
reported in the local press. On April 11 the *Daily Mirror* reported
that Mr Thompson was seeking funds from industry for a further
survey on trade union power, with the implication that it was
an exercise in union bashing. In a letter to the *Guardian* on
April 17 Mr Thompson explained that his polls had nothing to
do with ORC, and were not in any way sponsored by the
Conservative party. In the light of the *Daily Mirror* article and
of protests from both trade unions and the Conservative party,
the sponsoring committee of industrialists, under Lord Plowden,
decided to delay publication of the trade union survey until
after the election.

The BBC, following a disaster in October 1974 and some
unsuccessful experiments in by-elections, decided not to employ
the post-polls — interviews outside the polling stations with
those who had voted — which had been important in their
election night reporting in 1974. But the BBC did commission
an interesting last-minute survey from Gallup for use in explaining
the result (see p. 333—4). ITN despite a 4% error in the Scottish
referendum, again commissioned ORC to conduct a polling day
survey: at 10 p.m. they deduced from their findings in marginal
seats that the Conservatives would beat Labour by 349 to 257
(339 to 269 was the final result).

There were special polls: of teachers for the unpublished
Times Educational Supplement (NOP); of young mothers for
the *News of the World* (Marplan); of new voters for the *Sun*
(Marplan); and of marginal seats for the *Daily Telegraph* (Gallup)
and the *Daily Mail* (NOP). There were also polls in individual
seats conducted for various media sources — in five Welsh
constituencies for the *Western Mail* (Research & Marketing Ltd.)
and in four for the BBC (Abacus); in three Midlands constituencies for the *Birmingham Mail* (Marplan); in Bolton East for
Granada (MORI); and in Ilford South for Thames TV (MORI).
The error in the predictions was, as always, far higher on average
than for national polls — most were taken far earlier and the

samples were smaller. One (the BBC poll in Brecon & Radnor) managed to be 29% out in its estimate of the majority; however all but one of the others picked the right winner, if often by too large a margin (the wrong call, Bolton East, was a close-run affair).

Marplan conducted a London-wide poll for Capital Radio which, two weeks before the vote, suggested a 10% swing to the Conservatives. Marplan also did a special poll for the *Sun*, published on April 26, in the constituencies held by Liberal MPs and, on the overall average, concluded that only five of them were likely to hold on to their seats — a finding which caused considerable stir in the Liberal camp, and which, given the late rise in Liberal support, may well have been right at the time.

Polling is expensive. A quota sample of 1,200 will cost a newspaper from £3,000 to £6,000. The total outlay of the *Daily Express* on polls (including the *Scottish Daily Express*) between March 28 and May 3 was a little over £20,000 and the *Observer* spent £24,000 on the RSL polls. The Conservative party's annual expenditure on polls in 1975–8 was nearer £50,000. During the campaign, polls must have cost the Conservatives well over £60,000 and Labour £25,000.

Both parties continued to employ the same private pollsters, but the relationships and indeed the strategies were different from 1974. Part of the change flowed from the change in the pollsters' own positions. MORI now had regular public outlets and, reading Robert Worcester's polls in the *Express* and *Evening Standard*, the Labour party no longer regarded itself as the exclusive recipient of his skills. ORC (and Louis Harris) had lost their principal press outlets, and the Conservatives could feel more possessive about their findings. John Hanvey had succeeded the more ebullient Humphrey Taylor as managing director, and the link with the higher echelons was less intimate.

Neither pollster was at the very centre of the day-to-day tactics of the campaign. Although Mr Worcester made presentations to the daily Campaign Committee, he rarely stayed for the discussions. He was deliberately excluded from the White Drawing Room meetings on strategy in No 10 Downing Street, and had little contact with the party's media group. Mr Hanvey was a less forceful exponent of his material than his predecessor, Humphrey Taylor. He was involved in the early morning briefing and he attended the daily lunches at St Stephen's and some other meetings, but he relied heavily on two-page summaries of his findings to get his messages across.

Since the 1960s both main parties have used private polls to chart the main issues of the campaign. But however modest the cost of the parties' polls, they have their critics, who are more numerous in the Labour party. Pressed for funds, the outlay on Mr Worcester's polls represented an opportunity cost; more might be spent on, for example, the hard-pressed Research Department or the National Agency Service. Ron Hayward was certainly worried about costs. Mr Worcester received no indication that his budget would be expanded until the campaign was under way.

But a pollster for the Labour party faces an additional hazard. His findings inevitably become a weapon in the bitter left versus right disputes in the NEC and the Campaign Committee. The findings about the public hostility to the unions and to the personalities and policies associated with the left wing aroused bitter antagonism. Norman Atkinson, the party Treasurer, expressed an extreme view when he claimed that his constituency management committee was as reliable a barometer of public opinion as the private polls and much cheaper.[2]

Robert Worcester's company, MORI, had conducted polls for Labour since 1970. In the first year or two after 1974 the Labour party, for financial and other reasons, conducted no polls although Mr Wilson privately funded some MORI research during the 1975 Referendum. This was presented to the ministerial steering group, then headed by Mr Callaghan, the Foreign Secretary. Apart from a few-by-election studies, the Labour party only resumed polling on a substantial scale in 1978, after the NEC had voted £50,000 for such work on February 20 by 11 to 7 (Tony Benn was in the minority but another member of the left, Eric Heffer, supported the move as a 'reluctant convert'). A committee of sympathetic academics gave independent advice on Mr Worcester's polling strategy, and in April Ivor Crewe of Essex University made a presentation of his British Election Study findings to the Campaign Committee. A large scale study in Scotland was one of the first fruits of MORI's contract. It

---

[2] On October 3, 1979 Norman Atkinson told the Labour Party Conference that in 1978 and 1979 £87,000 had been spent on opinion polls, 'A service which I personally consistently opposed.'

showed that devolution was a low priority among Scottish electors, but the impact of its findings was diminished by the fact
that the Labour victories in Garscadden and Hamilton occurred
while the survey was being processed. A more influential study
of marginal seats was also initiated. It was a panel study with
something under 1,000 respondents in 71 seats. They were
interviewed first in April 1978, then in August, and then again
in January 1979.

The first survey was particularly gloomy, suggesting that
Labour was faring even worse in marginal seats than in the
country as a whole. Some of the findings were leaked to the
press in July. As someone complained, 'There seems to be a
direct conduit from the Campaign Committee to the *Guardian*.'
These marginal results may well have had an influence on Mr
Callaghan during his August meditations on whether to call an
autumn election. The August survey was also depressing but,
contrary to rumour, Mr Callaghan did not have access to the
findings at the time of his final decision in early September. The
surveys carried bad news not only on voting intentions but on
attitudes to issues. On the problems to which voters gave most
priority – unemployment, law and order, and inflation –
Labour trailed the Conservatives. The only comfort was that
Mr Callaghan was seen as a better Prime Minister than Mrs
Thatcher would be.

When the election came, MORI was authorised to produce
regular private polls, though on a more limited scale than hither-
to. Between April 7 and April 30 there were 10 'quickie' polls
in contrast to 17 during the shorter campaign of October 1974.
A quota sample of 720 electors, 10 from each of 72 marginal
seats were asked a dozen or so questions. The results were
phoned in by 6.30 and a report was prepared by Bob Worcester.
If there was anything startling he would phone Mr Callaghan
and Mr Hayward that night. He would send the figures together
with a photocopied handwritten report to No 10 Downing
Street for the 7.30 breakfast meeting. He presented his findings
to the heads of departments meeting and the 8.30 a.m. Campaign
Committee. He appended to his survey reports a summary of
the main findings of his own and his rivals' public polls.

The story his polls had to tell was of an advance on all fronts
– but one that was too slow to make up for the initial deficit.
Even at the end of the campaign, the Conservatives were seen as

having the better policies on all the main issues except the handling of strikes and the health service. On taxes and on law and order Labour was over 30% behind. Labour had lost ground among young housewives in the C2 group. The most consoling findings were that Labour was seen as having the better leaders, that Labour's party political broadcasts were more appreciated and that the Conservatives were slightly more blamed for making the election a slanging match, and for making promises which the country could not afford. The MORI polls showed areas in which Labour policies were popular but not understood by the public, for example on free T.V. licences for pensioners, and the pledges to offer the unemployed a job or retraining. They also suggested a greater emphasis on the Common Market and the health service.

On April 26, he wrote: 'The party must, in the last few days, give Labour supporters a belief that the election does matter — and that the Labour Party is a party of compassion and one that keeps its promises.' His final report on April 30 contained what he termed 'better news': 'The public now thinks that prices would go up faster under the Tories, as would strikes *and* unemployment. They still believe, however, that the average person's take-home pay would be higher under the Conservatives.'

Reading through the reports, however, it is hard to see what important action points could have flowed from them in this rather sluggish campaign. The issues that mattered to the electorate did not change very much, and the findings did not conflict with what the public opinion polls were saying. In Labour circles there was some unfair criticism of Mr Worcester because he was now so deeply involved in newspaper polling. But his balanced reports of the private polls and his syntheses of the public polls did offer a monitoring of the situation which some at least of those at the centre of the campaign greatly appreciated. There is no doubt that Mr Worcester's greater visibility in the mass media created tensions. In particular a television appearance just after Mr Callaghan's September 7 announcement that there would be no election was taken, quite incorrectly, as a claim that MORI's advice had been decisive (see above p. 40). A sharp message was sent, 'Curtail your public role or stop polling for us.' And in the campaign a senior official sourly commented, 'he's less use to us now that he's gone public.'

He would like to have provided much more comprehensive

coverage as he had done in 1974, with more issue polls, with more check on elections broadcasts including the Liberals, and with quickie polls each day.[3] He would also have liked to play a more prominent part in the campaign, with close contact with Transport House, the academic advisory committee, the NEC and the Campaign Committee.

The Conservatives spent more on polls than Labour; they were more consistent in sponsoring them and more sophisticated in making use of them, particularly in the years before the election. During the general retrenchment of 1975 they scarcely reduced their polling budget even though, largely for technical reasons, they gave up their long-term panel studies conducted by BMRB. But they tried inventive new approaches on public reactions to new issues and policy stands and to ways of communicating them. Mrs Thatcher displayed less obvious interest in polls than Mr Heath, but the people she appointed to key positions appreciated them. Lord Thorneycroft at Central Office and Angus Maude at the Research Department wanted an independent check on the public mood.

In 1976 and 1977 John Hanvey was asked to make presentations at Central Office to senior ministers and party officials once or twice a year. ORC conducted polls in a number of by-elections. It also did studies on reactions to particular issues. There were no polls explicitly on personalities; adverse findings could cause trouble. Taped interviews and group discussion however did yield reactions which may have influenced those who were advising Mrs Thatcher on how she should present herself. Some of the achievements of the private polls in this period were, as so often, negative ones. Politicians were warned off issues which had no public resonance, and any lurch to the right may have been tempered by ORC's findings. But there were also some positive contributions. The sale of council houses, first promoted in the 1967 GLC elections and then taken up as national policy, was based on an ORC suggestion. Polls also contributed to the elevation of the tax issue to its unprecedented prominence in the Conservative programme — and indeed to the whole way in which the economic argument

[3] As his official post-election memorandum complained: 'In this campaign MORI was unable to fulfil its function of tracking and analysing British public opinion for the Labour Party as the campaign progressed to the degree that was possible during the two 1974 campaigns.'

was presented. Above all, the pinpointing of target voters, the skilled working class and especially the women, was firmly based on research. The ruthless concentration of advertising in the *Sun* and the *Daily Mirror*, and the choice of themes in political broadcasts, stemmed directly from poll evidence about the background and the interests of the most switchable voters.

The findings of the ORC polls were much more widely disseminated through the party hierarchy than under the old regime (but there were notably few leaks) and relations with the Conservatives were helped by the fact that ORC was now doing no nationwide newspaper polling.

During the election the Conservatives, like Labour, abandoned the daily polls of 1974. Their major effort went into four 'state of Battle' surveys (based on voters in England and Wales), ready on each Monday from April 3, and on five 'quickie' surveys each mid-week (a sixth was added on April 28). They also conducted a survey after each party election broadcast (except the last two Liberal ones). These were supplemented in an important way by special surveys of Liberals in two types of English constituencies (strong Liberal seats and Conservative-Labour marginals) and of the situation in three types of Scottish seats. Up to 50 copies of the findings were quickly circulated with a brief commentary on the key points by Keith Britto of the Research Department, who worked full-time on the polls, in conjunction with John Hanvey and Charlotte Tatton-Brown of ORC. A regular report on the findings of the published polls was also produced.

The polls were rather longer and more wide-ranging than the Labour ones, and on the whole their readers must have found them highly encouraging, including the overwhelming majority (65% to 25%) recorded on April 23 for 'a completely new approach'. On the other hand, Conservatives, though priding themselves on their forbearance under Labour's 'scares and smears' (see p. 191), must have been dismayed to find as many people blaming the Conservatives as Labour for engaging in 'slanging'. A two-to-one majority thought that a Conservative government would mean more trouble with the unions, and the same proportion thought that old age pensioners would fare better under Labour. But the really worrying finding in polls, although they indicated no major trend as the campaign advanced, was the continued evidence of the Liberals' potential.

By April 15, 47% of the electorate, including well over one third of Conservative and Labour supporters, agreed with the statement 'It's about time we gave the Liberals a chance.' The polls did give early warning that the Conservatives were not doing well among pensioners and led to specific efforts to reassure them.

Politicians are, as a rule, more inclined to heed polls when their import justifies the current strategy. The polls provide only one sort of evidence, and it has to be set against reports from the constituencies, and the leaderships' own sense of the electoral mood. Mr Hanvey's findings gave encouragement to campaign advisers who resisted pressure for a bold counter-attack on Labour. 'He gave us ammunition to defend the present position', said one. His critics took a 'so what?' stance towards some of the findings. They were not clear about the consequences of the research for policy and presentation, and would have welcomed some political advice.

The Liberals could afford no private polls. It is interesting to speculate on how much of a handicap this was. Some of the information that private polls supply is available, without cost, from the public polls. Some findings, though interesting, cannot be used as a basis for action by even the most sensitive of party leaders and party machines (and in the height of an election few could be so described). When little is stirring the electorate, the great value of up-to-date private polls is that they can justify the leadership in staying firmly on course, unpanicked by its excitable supporters. As someone commented, 'We couldn't sit and wait for the public polls. We needed instant evidence that we didn't have to worry. The polls had a very stabilising effect.' On the rare occasions when there is a change in mood or the emergence of a new issue in mid-campaign a daily poll can give some measure of scale to a phenomenon that would not in any case go unnoticed. In 1979 the situation did not arise.

14 Selecting Candidates

The composition of parliament changes slowly. On average 47 incumbents have been defeated in each post-war general election, and 55 have retired voluntarily; a further 10 have died or retired each year during the life of parliaments. Of the 635 members elected in October 1974, 469 were returned in May 1979. The remaining 166 places were filled by 26 MPs returned in by-elections (including 4 ex-MPs), 11 more ex-MPs making a comeback, and 129 complete newcomers. These figures are fairly close to the pattern of the past.

But an MP's security of tenure was much more discussed during the 1974—9 parliament than ever before. A few publicised efforts by constituency parties to get rid of their member, together with left-wing efforts to subject every Labour MP to a re-selection process, led to the supposition that customs were changing.

There was much speculation, but little solid evidence, on whether the composition of the parties was, in fact, altering either socially or politically. Much was made of the jump in strength of the *Tribune* group, which rose from 47 in 1973 to 79 in 1975. Of the 60 Labour MPs who first entered the Commons in February or October 1974, 32 joined the *Tribune* group, and it was suggested that the parliamentary party was undergoing a violent lurch to the left. In fact the *Tribune* group was somewhat diluted by this new influx; a number of middle-of-the-road members joined for diplomatic reasons: 'It's fire insurance against the left-wing critics in the constituency,' said one. The group became a more diverse and perhaps less effective political force.[1] Many of its new recruits held marginal seats and 13 were defeated in 1979. Any movement to the left after 1974 can best be measured by those chosen to replace sitting members. 25 of the 1974 Labour MPs left the House or the party during the parliament, and 35 more did not stand again in

[1] See C. Hitchens, 'The Tribune Group goes missing' *New Statesman*, (July 21, 1978).

1979. It is not easy to classify politically those who withdrew or those who were chosen to succeed them. However, our enquiries suggest that in 10 of the 60 cases the replacement was clearly to the left of the departing MP, and in 4 cases clearly to the right. In most of the remaining instances any move was probably leftwards, but seldom very significant in degree. Against this drift must be set the substantial counter-movement that took place as the experience of office edged MPs' opinions in a rightward direction. If Labour had won exactly the same 319 seats in 1974 that it won in October 1974 the PLP would on balance certainly have been no more left-wing than five years earlier. But since left-wingers were somewhat concentrated in marginal seats, it was clear that the PLP of 1979, with only 269 members returned, was more to the right than that of 1974.

On the Conservative side, the political classification of members is even more difficult. But there is no evidence that the replacements chosen in 1974—9, or the winners of marginal seats, were different in political complexion from the MPs elected in 1974. It was noted that among the first 25 replacements chosen in 1975 and 1976 no fewer than four were eldest sons of peers (as against only two among the 277 sitting MPs) and three more were younger sons. Was the party turning back to the aristocracy? If so, most of the gentlemen involved were clearly on the left of the party. The party had no success in getting working-class candidates selected for winnable seats, and little in recruiting people from senior posts in industry. An effort by the CBI to encourage firms to follow the example of ICI and to release executives so that they could seek candidacies without losing their jobs bore no obvious fruit.[2]

Conservative selection processes did not change, although in Sevenoaks the selection conference took place before a mass meeting of 700. One of the first acts of Lord Thorneycroft as Chairman in 1975 was to countermand the current pruning of the official lists of candidates: but very little of the dead wood which might have been eliminated was in fact short-listed or selected. Those involved in selections claimed that there was no

---

[2] See D. Butler and M. Pinto-Duschinsky, 'The Conservative Elite 1918—78' in Z. Layton-Henry, *Conservative Party Politics*, (London, 1980); and C. Mellors, *The British MP*, (Farnborough, 1978). See also the CBI working party report, *Helping MPs into Parliament*, (London, 1978).

significant change in the type of candidate coming forward and figures that follow reveal no strong trends.

In all parties clashes between members and constituency parties have been a familiar phenomenon and every parliament has seen one or two enforced retirements of MPs.[3] But the great majority of the rows have involved personal matters — drink, divorce, or neglect of constituency duties. The 1974—9 parliament saw more disputes that, outwardly at least, were political in character. It is therefore worth enumerating the cases in which sitting MPs were openly challenged.

In Hammersmith North, the local Labour party decided to choose a new candidate to replace Frank Tomney, a 69-year-old right-winger and pro-European who had sat since 1950. Personal points were made, but the main objection to him was plainly political. Mr Tomney protested, but the NEC decided that all the proper procedures had been followed. Mr Tomney's troubles excited much less sympathy than those of Reg Prentice, a Cabinet minister, whose Newham North-East party moved against him shortly after the European Referendum. It could later be argued that his local party had perceived his floor-crossing propensity, but at the time it seemed as though he was being punished by left-wing zealots merely for being a loyal member of the Labour cabinet.

Over the next two years, there was a protracted battle between the right- and left-wing factions in Newham. Two young Oxford law students helped to organise the 'loyalists' and they took the left wing, led by Andy Bevan, the Trotskyite youth officer at Transport House, to court several times. After initial victories they failed in an attempt to enjoin the National Executive for acting *ultra vires* in suspending the local officers. The whole affair was damaging to Labour; it offered evidence of how a party might be taken over by infiltrators; it also showed how the rules of procedure could be twisted — and what hazards were involved when party members turned to the courts to remedy malfeasances. (The cost of the final action were estimated at £20,000.)[4] And, of course, Mr Prentice let down his defenders,

---

[3] See D. Butler, 'The Renomination of MPs', *Parliamentary Affairs*, (Spring 1978).
[4] See P. McCormick, *Enemies of Democracy*, (London, 1979) for one description of the affair. See also Lord Denning's Judgment, *The Times*, (February 8, 1978).

locally and nationally, when in October 1977 he resigned the Whip and then the following October began to seek a Conservative nomination.

Even that was not the end of the Newham affair. James Dickens, a Tribunite ex-MP, was selected as candidate, but when on April 13, 1979 his supporters voted only by 18 to 14 to endorse his election address he resigned his candidacy. Purely personal considerations may have come into his decision, but it gave the papers some more opportunity to make insinuations about a Trotskyite takeover. However, despite their suggestions, Nick Bradley, the Young Socialist leader, was not chosen. The NEC hastily put forward the names of three candidates with leftish reputations but of considerable standing, and on April 17 the local party chose Ron Leighton, a leading anti-Market campaigner.

One other MP was denied renomination. On May 20, 1977 the Edge Hill party in Liverpool followed the proper procedure and voted by 37 to 3 to reject Sir Arthur Irvine, who had annoyed some by his moderate views but more, perhaps, by seeming neglect of the constituency which he had represented for 30 years. His son threatened to stand as an Independent, but when Sir Arthur died, the challenge was left to the Liberals who, in the March 1979 by-election, overwhelmingly defeated the Labour candidate.

Two other re-selection sagas drew headlines for Labour. In Hayes and Harlington a left-wing group endeavoured over two years to repudiate Neville Sandelson as their MP. He was a pro-European party loyalist and no-one had accused him of neglecting his constituency: he was being attacked for supporting government policy. The local party never quite met the procedural requirements for getting rid of an MP, and even though on April 1, 1979 they voted against him by 31 to 25, the NEC endorsed his candidature.

An even more publicised case concerned a *Tribune* MP. But in this case it was personal conduct more than political position which seems to have lain at the centre of the dispute. On September 27, 1977, the Northampton North party voted by 23 to 18 to replace Maureen Colquhoun, who had been much publicized in the popular press for her lesbian sympathies, for her apparently pro-Powell remarks on immigration and for trivial incidents such as a brush with a parking attendant. She described the battle as 'left against left'.[5] The NEC decided that due procedures had not been followed and, despite further moves, she was still the candidate for her marginal seat when the election came; she was defeated on a slightly larger than average swing.

Other Labour MPs felt under some threat. Challenges to the sitting members were publicly reported in the cases of Eddie Lyons (Bradford West) and Harold Lever (Manchester Central). One or two older members — for instance Ernest Perry in Battersea South — may have decided to retire rather than fight on. But none of the Labour MPs under 60 who did not stand again seem to have been under serious pressure.[6]

Thus, despite the furore about the left takeover and the new insecurity of MPs, only Frank Tomney, out of the 319 Labour members elected in 1974, clearly could and would have stood as a Labour candidate in 1979, but for his local party. In each of the three cases where renomination was refused, there were personal as well as political grudges; two of the MPs were nearly 70 and the third was on the point of switching to the Conservatives. However, the troubles of these members may have affected the conduct of others; a few trimmed to the left and more took extra steps to build up their local parties and to be visible in their constituencies.

The NEC also had to arbitrate in other selection disputes: Kettering, where the indefatigable Robert Maxwell among others sought nomination against a local steelworkers' leader; Stockport South, where the Prime Minister's political secretary, Tom McNally, found that the defeated faction would not accept his nomination; and Dundee West, where the ex-Communist Jimmy Reid was nominated, although he had been only eight months in the party instead of the normally required two years.

The Conservatives had their troubles, too, though in only one

---

[5] See M. Colquhoun, 'The Northampton Story', *New Statesman*, (October 21, 1977).
[6] Ill-health was the reason for the withdrawal of Ken Lomas, 56 (Huddersfield West) and Colin Jackson, 57 (Brighouse and Spenborough). John Lee, 52, (Birmingham Handsworth) a left-winger, wanted to return to the bar. Colin Phipps, 44 (Dudley West) gave up to seek — unsuccessfully — a nomination to the European Parliament, and Paul Rose, 42 (Manchester, Blackley) repudiated parliamentary life on February 22, 1979, with a blast at its frustrations, 'banging one's head against a brick wall', he claimed.

case was there a publicised attempt to oust a sitting MP. Nicholas Scott, who had succeeded to the Chelsea seat in October 1974, was challenged by a right-wing element led by the constituency chairman. But on September 27, 1977, by a vote of 69 to 21, he was re-endorsed. Burnaby Drayson, 66, member for Skipton since 1945, did not stand again after criticism of his renomination in 1974; and Robert Cooke, 49, withdrew after twenty-two years in Bristol West, when moves were under way to repudiate him.[7]

There were however a few publicised rows over Conservative prospective candidates whose conduct or qualities displeased some in their local parties; switches were made in, for example, Huddersfield East, Halifax and Grimsby. Mr William Walker, who ultimately won Perth and East Perthshire for the Conservatives, on April 2, 1978 survived by 367 to 226 a vote of the Constituency Association on whether he should continue as candidate.

In the election two ex-MPs stood against their old local party. Eddie Milne continued his battle with the Blyth CLP, running candidates successfully for the local council and fighting lawsuits, while James Sillars fought South Ayrshire for his own Scottish Labour Party. Both polled strongly, although they were defeated. They had the distinction of being the only candidates outside the established parties to save their deposits.

On the Conservative side Tom Iremonger, the former MP who had been discarded after his 1974 defeat, stood in the Ilford North by-election and was not deterred by the 2% that he received from standing again; in 1979 he only secured 0.9% of the vote.

Reg Prentice, after four or five setbacks, was chosen as Conservative candidate for Daventry. No other MP since the war had crossed the floor and found a safe seat on the other side without interrupting his parliamentary service.

The quality of MPs does not necessarily emerge from an enumeration of their social characteristics. Yet it still seems useful to continue in the pattern set by earlier Nuffield studies to record the most obviously quantifiable facts about the

---

[7] All the other withdrawals of MPs under 60 seem to have been entirely voluntary and for personal reasons: Daniel Awdry, 55 (Chippenham); Richard Wood, 58 (Bridlington); James Scott-Hopkins, 57 (West Derbyshire) and John Cockcroft, 45 (Nantwich).

candidates. The evidence about age and past candidacies is clear cut enough, and so is that about educational background, though it is impossible to say how much candidates profited by their opportunities, and there are a few candidates who suppress or exaggerate their record. Occupation presents more difficulties; candidates have often passed through many jobs, and in many cases one can only guess which was the 'first or formative occupation' that we try to record here.

There were 2,576 candidates, 324 more than the previous record in October 1974. The increase was due mainly to the National Front (303), the Workers' Revolutionary party (60) and the Ecologists (53). Since none of these got more than 7½% of the vote and only 32 exceeded 2%, their main impact was to lengthen the ballot paper and to make balanced local television coverage more difficult.

Women candidates, though slightly more numerous, were less successful than before. The Conservatives put up 32 (8 successful) and Labour 52 (11 successful). The two SNP women MPs were defeated. The new House contained only 19 women, the lowest figure since 1935 (though there were only 19 in 1951 too). Jewish representation fell compared to 1974, the Conservative increase from 9 to 11 failing to offset the Labour decrease from 35 to 21.

No major trends appear in age. For Conservatives the median ages were the same as in 1974. But since the younger men who had won marginal seats in 1974 were being defeated in 1979

Table 1.   Age of Candidates

Age on 1 Jan 79	Conservative Elected	Defeated	Labour Elected	Defeated	Liberal Elected	Defeated
21—29	6	50	—	36	1	92
30—39	68	123	48	170	3	209
40—49	129	76	72	102	1	157
50—59	95	29	99	40	3	90
60—69	38	5	40	4	2	17
70—79	3	—	10	2	—	—
	339	283	269	354	13	565
Median Age						
1979	47	34	51	37	47	40
1974	47	34	49	34	45	37

it is not surprising that the average age of Labour MPs rose from 49 to 51, although it is more notable that their defeated candidates were also older. There were almost twice as many septuagenarians as in October 1974 (10 Labour and 3 Conservatives as against 6 and 1). Julius Silverman (Lab) and Frederick Burden (Con), born in 1905, were the oldest MPs. Stephen Dorrell (Con, born 1952) replaced David Alton (Lib, born 1951) as the youngest MP; the youngest Labour MP was John Home Robertson (born 1948). In Hackney North, Ernie Roberts who at 67 succeeded the veteran David Weitzman, the last MP to be born in the nineteenth century, was the oldest Labour candidate to enter parliament since 1945 at least. But he was probably not the oldest new member; John McQuade won North Belfast for the Democratic Unionists at the reputed age of 68.

John Parker, the new Father of the House, was the only pre-war MP left in the House, and there were only 10 other Labour survivors from the 1945 triumph. On the Conservative side, Ronald Bell had had a brief taste of the wartime parliament and three others had sat since 1945.[8]

[8] The survivors from the 1940s were
Labour
   J. Parker, 72, 1935–
   J. Callaghan, 65, 1945–
   A. Lewis, 61, 1945–
   J. Silverman, 73, 1945–
   G. Thomas, 69, 1945–
   F. Willey, 68, 1945–
   Sir H. Wilson, 62, 1945–
   A. Bottomley, 71, 1945–59, 1962–
   M. Foot, 65, 1945–55, 1960–
   I. Mikardo, 72, 1945–59, 1964–
   A. Palmer, 66, 1945–50, 1952–9, 1964–
   D. Jay, 71, 1946–
   R. Mellish, 65, 1946–
   Sir T. Williams, 63, 1949–59, 1961–

Conservative
   R. Bell, 64, May–June 1945, 1950–
   H. Fraser, 60, 1945–
   Sir J. Langford-Holt, 62, 1945–
   Sir D. Walker-Smith, 68, 1945–
   T. Galbraith, 61, 1948–
   F. Harris, 63, 1948–
In addition to the five Labour names in this list five other Labour septuagenarians were elected R. Edwards, 72; J. Johnson, 70; D. Jones, 70; A. Roberts, 70; and E. Wainwright, 70. F. Burden, 73; Sir D. Kaberry, 71; and Sir S. McAdden, 71 were elected for the Conservatives.

Table 2.   Parliamentary Experience of MPs

First entered parliament	Con	Lab	Lib
1945	4	12	—
1946—51	17	11	1
1952—9	50	20	—
1960—9	59	94	3
1970—4	127	82	6
1975—9	82	50	1
	339	269	11

Table 3.   Education of Candidates

	Conservative		Labour		Liberal	
	Elected	Defeated	Elected	Defeated	Elected	Defeated
Elementary only	—	—	13	3	—	1
Elementary +	—	—	25	6	—	1
Secondary only	28	32	40	58	3	79
Secondary +	10	52	44	60	1	119
Secondary & University	55	61	100	178	1	208
Public School only	68	58	2	9	2	45
Public School & University	178	80	45	40	4	112
Total	339	283	269	354	11	565
Oxford	90	32	37	38	2	58
Cambridge	77	27	18	24	1	58
Other University	63	82	99	141	2	205
All universities	230 (68%)	141 (57%)	153 (57%)	203 (57%)	5 (55%)	321 (57%)
Eton	51	9	1	1	1	3
Harrow	8	3	—	—	—	2
Winchester	7	2	2	—	—	1
Other	180	120	43	44	5	82
All public school	246 (73%)	135 (48%)	46 (17%)	45 (13%)	6 (55%)	88 (16%)

* Information was inadequate on 51 Liberal candidates. In this table they have been imputed backgrounds proportionate to the other 514.

Table 4. Occupation of Candidates

| | Conservative | | Labour | | Liberal | |
	Elected	Defeated	Elected	Defeated	Elected	Defeated
Professions:						
Barrister	51	25	15	11	1	21
Solicitor	19	31	10	21	—	29
Doctor/Dentist	3	6	5	2	—	7
Architect/Surveyor	4	5	—	2	1	7
Civil/Chartered Engineer	8	9	3	9	1	11
Chartered Sec./Accountant	12	25	4	11	1	17
Civil Servant/Local Govt.	14	7	16	22	—	18
Armed Services	20	7	—	4	—	3
Teachers:						
University	5	3	15	16	1	16
Adult	2	4	5	32	—	42
School	11	20	36	51	2	104
Other Consultants	2	2	2	4	—	13
Scientific Research	3	3	6	9	—	11
Total	154 (45%)	147 (52%)	117 (43%)	195 (55%)	7 (64%)	299 (56%)
Business:						
Company Director	16	12	—	1	—	21
Company Executive	43	34	12	11	—	21
Commerce/Insurance	37	24	1	4	—	24
Management/Clerical	2	—	7	10	1	40
General Business	17	18	2	8	—	28
Total	115 (34%)	88 (31%)	22 (5%)	34 (10%)	1 (9%)	134 (25%)
Miscellaneous White Collar	4	7	5	38	—	31
Politician/Pol. Organiser	8	3	13	17	—	2
Publisher/Journalist	31	12	13	28	2	27
Farmer	22	9	—	2	1	11
Housewife	2	7	1	2	—	4
Student	—	1	—	1	—	4
Local Administration	—	1	4	—	—	—
Total	67 (20%)	40 (14%)	36 (13%)	88 (25%)	3 (27%)	79 (21%)
Railway Clerk	—	—	1	—	—	1
Miner	—	—	21	4	—	—
Skilled Worker	2	5	40	24	—	20
Semi/Unskilled Worker	1	3	21	10	—	4
Total	3 (1%)	8 (3%)	95 (35%)	38 (10%)	0 (—)	25 (5%)
Grand Total	339	283	269	354	11	537*

* No information available on 28 candidates.

Educationally the parliamentary parties in 1979 were much the same as four years earlier. The proportion of university educated candidates was almost constant in both parties. The proportion from public schools went down, but 73% of Conservative MPs had that advantage — and 15% had been to Eton.

The same continuity is evident in occupations. The professions and business provide two-thirds of all MPs. For once the proportion of working class Labour MPs did not fall.

Indeed, for the first time since 1935 virtually half of Labour MPs were union sponsored. The number of union-sponsored candidates rose from 141 to 165 and, despite the net loss of 50 Labour seats, union-sponsored MPs rose from 129 to 133. Sponsored MPs tend to have safe seats and are less at risk. Only 15 sponsored MPs were defeated. The main reasons for the

Table 5.   Sponsored Candidates

	Total	Elected
Transport and General Workers' Union	28	20
Amalgamated Union of Engineering Workers	24	21
National Union of Mineworkers	18	16
General and Municipal Workers' Union	14	14
Association of Scientific, Technical and Managerial Staffs	12	8
National Union of Public Employees	8	7
Association of Professional, Executive, Clerical and Computer Staff	6	5
National Union of Railwaymen	13	12
Union of Shop, Distributive and Allied Workers	6	5
Transport Salaried Staffs Association	3	3
Union of Post Office Workers	2	2
Union of Construction, Allied Trades & Technicians	4	2
Electrical, Electronic & Telecommunications & Plumbing Trades Union	4	4
11 other Unions (none with more than 2 candidates)	13	8
Confederation of Health Service Employees	6	3
Post Office Engineering Union	4	3
Total union-sponsored	165	133
Co-operative Party	25	17
All sponsored candidates	190	150

increase were that 6 more small unions provided sponsored candidates and that the Railwaymen decided to use more of their political levy in this way. The number of NUR candidates increased from 6 to 13, and 12 of them were successful. This was due mainly to the recruitment of sitting MPs, mostly without direct experience in the union. Tam Dalyell and Phillip Whitehead, previously unsponsored, accepted NUR support, together with three former Transport and General sponsored MPs, Messrs O'Halloran, Cook and Anderson. They illustrate the fact that a significant proportion of union-sponsored MPs are by no means working-class in background. At least one-fifth were university educated and still more were recruited to union parliamentary panels without any previous grass-roots experience in the union.

A great deal of effort is expended in the selection of candidates, yet in the end it is an arbitrary process with judgments being made on the basis of a brief speech and the answers to a few questions. Constituency committees are autonomous and show their varying prejudices, so that a moderately diverse body of MPs is the result. Yet neither main party managed to present a 'balanced ticket' in the American sense: it is not only ethnic minorities which go unrepresented; large categories of occupation, most notably housewives, were awarded very few spokesmen. Above all the working-class Conservatives, who provide the party with half its votes, are still not to be seen on the benches of the House of Commons.

15 Local Electioneering

In an election with a couple of thousand candidates, a quarter of a million party workers and forty million electors, spread over 635 constituencies, any summary of the diverse activities conducted in pursuit of votes must be unsatisfactory. Press reports and candidates' letters, together with interviews at many levels, do however offer some picture of the main campaigning operations and their variants. But how effective they were in getting people to the poll, let alone in persuading them to change their minds, is a question that cannot be precisely answered.

If elections are won by local efforts, a lot must depend on the long haul, on the preparations and the image-making over the months and years before. The 1979 election, although it came suddenly, had long been anticipated; certainly by the autumn of 1978 everyone should have been ready — but, of course, they were not. One Conservative observed justly that the non-election of October left his party more deflated than its opponents because Conservatives had marched further up the hill with their preparations and therefore had further to march down. A well-publicised reason for Mr Callaghan's delay — though hardly the central one — was the poor state of Labour organisation in key marginals. But the winter probably did little to remedy the deficiencies. There was plenty to keep the parties occupied. In Scotland and Wales there were the preparations for the March 1 referendums. Everywhere there were the problems of getting ready for the June 7 Euro-elections, setting up Euro-constituency organisations and selecting candidates. One Conservative Area Agent said 'Thank God for Europe. It keeps our troops busy.' But the understaffed Labour party could ill afford the diversion from the ordinary routines of improving preparations in marginal Westminster seats.

Conservative candidates were aware that they were going to the country at an extremely favourable time. In spite of claims to the contrary, it seems clear that opinion polls were important in affecting the morale and expectations of party workers and candidates. Yet a number of Labour candidates remained in good heart because they were so well-received in their established centres of support. There was little of the apathy and even resentment against the Labour government that candidates had experienced in the 1970 election. Some on the Labour side claimed to sense an improvement in the penultimate week of the election and then a falling away in the final days. Many candidates reported that they had thought to the end that Labour might still win, or at least deny the other side a majority. The main complaint among Conservative activists was the lack of a more visible or aggressive campaign at the centre. In particular there was a feeling that the party leadership should fight back vigorously against Labour smears. Liberal candidates entered the campaign on the crest of a wave — David Alton's striking capture of Edge Hill showed what could be done when dedicated local activity was combined with negligence by the other parties. The Nationalists in Scotland and Wales sadly sensed that the tide in favour of their case was at its lowest point since 1974.

Since 1970 candidates have had freedom to put six words of political description after their name. Usually they simply proclaim their party: 'Labour' or 'The Liberal Candidate' or 'Official Conservative Party Candidate'; but a few do take the chance of self-advertisement of themselves or their views. Julian Amery was 'Privy Counsellor, Author, Conservative'. The victor in Liverpool Garston was 'Conservative candidate, River Mersey Pilot'. A few candidates drew attention to the fact that they were 'Queen's Counsel, Conservative' or 'Labour former member', and a handful of Liberals nailed their colours to the mast as 'Liberal and Radical' or 'Liberal and Electoral Reform'. The MP for Leominster was 'Conservative who stands for the future', while an Eastbourne candidate was 'Labour Need not Greed'. The less successful of the Nottingham brothers who stood against each other as Independents in Brigg was perhaps the most eloquent of all the slogan-seeking candidates: 'Disillusioned Labour. Tory? No thank you.'

Local electioneering follows an established ritual of canvassing, distributing leaflets and addressing public meetings. Candidates aim to be as visible as possible, appearing at clubs, factories, and shopping centres, and touring the constituency with a loudhailer. There is no strong evidence to show that effective local organisa-

tion decides many results. Local electioneering has been overtaken by the nationalisation of the campaign and the growth of
the mass media. Moreover, most seats are so safe that it is difficult for even the most highly efficient organisation to produce
an upset. In the marginals a good organisation and campaign can
clearly score over a lack-lustre opposition. The fact remains,
however, that candidates continue to push themselves because
they are expected to do so; they have to do something to justify
their selection as candidates, and they can never shrug off the
possibility that their activities might prove decisive on polling
day.

Candidates sought to find new ways of attracting the attention of the voters — but with little success. There were Saturday
motorcades, placarded walkabouts through the crowds, phone-in
hours, and recorded messages on a well-advertised phone number.
Tony Benn was much photographed in a home-made palanquin
strapped to the roof of his car for his loud-speaker forays
through South-East Bristol.

In Table 1 we show the Gallup findings on the extent of local
activities. The extent of the activity is rather similar to that of
the previous election.

In the candidates' retrospective observations on the campaign,
there was a certain pathos. They had spent four or five desperately busy weeks making hasty, and usually unsatisfactory,
contact with a great number of people, but only really getting
to know the leading few among the small army of party volunteers working for their election. But the candidates had no way

Table 1   Election Activities

	% 1979	(Oct 1974)
Read election addresses delivered to home	50	(43)
Heard local candidates at indoor meeting	3	(6)
Heard local candidates at outdoor meeting	3	(3)
Canvassed for candidate	2	(2)
Did other work for candidate	4	(3)
Put up party poster in window	10	(11)

Source: Gallup poll

of knowing what the frenetic activity accomplished. They usually had addressed under a thousand of their constituents at meetings and twice that number, at most, on doorsteps and in walkabouts; and they could have no reason to suppose that they had changed the votes of more than a handful.

Candidates have to keep in touch with the national campaign, for they are constituency representatives of the national party. Most candidates claim to have ignored the findings of opinion polls and the reports on television, and to have relied more on communications from headquarters and reading the press and leaders' speeches. There is a paradox about modern election campaigns. Most voters get their information from the television, whereas the candidates are far too busy most evenings to watch any television at all. One Labour member in a Northern seat wrote:

It's an odd feeling fighting the General Election. You are pounding the streets looking for people and they are all sitting at home watching on the telly and imbibing prejudice from the newspapers. It is almost as if you are distracting them from the election campaign. I quickly came to the conclusion that it was more important to exude goodwill and enthusiasm than actually to argue about such unimportant things as issues. You were really putting a face to the party label. All this absorbed so much time that I saw very little of the national campaign. But the electors were watching.

Another candidate wrote in a similar vein:

A candidate's mood is so mercurial that he is the worst possible guide to opinion in the constituency. One minute you are up, the next cast down. The real problem is to keep smiling and hide the wild fluctuations in your own moods and opinions. This is mainly produced by exhaustion. A candidate is like a cushion who bears the impress of the last person who sat on him — or the mark of the last door that slammed in his face.

The divergence in individual constituency results, even when we allow for regional variation, shows the importance of local factors in certain cases (see p. 410–4). Some Labour candidates, either sensing the national tide was running against them, or because it was their own particular style, campaigned on the basis of their local reputations. Reports suggest that Bruce George in Walsall South, Greville Janner in Leicester West, and Ken Weetch in Ipswich did this. The Ipswich result is particularly interesting because there was a 1.4% swing to Labour when the rest of Suffolk was moving markedly the other way. Ken Weetch was one of only two Labour candidates to have two full-time agents (one worked exclusively on the postal vote), and he also seems to have been widely recognised as a personally energetic, but politically moderate, MP (see p. 413)

Canvassing is supposed to be the staple of electioneering – record where your own supporters are and then on polling day make sure that any laggards have voted. The aim is to achieve a mark on the register rather than win converts. Ben Pimlott, the Labour candidate for Cleveland and an academic student of elections, justified canvassing on the grounds that it provided a minimal physical contact between the candidate (or his party) and the electorate. He wrote to us:

> People are generally pleased to be asked and even hold it against you if nobody calls. I also believe that a voting 'promise' has some importance. If a slight wavering traditional Labour voter told the canvasser that he would probably *vote* for the party, that helps to make up his mind.

A great deal of canvassing is still done, but the amount is much below past standards. In 1970 29% told NOP that someone had canvassed them; in 1979 it was only 15% according to MORI. It is harder to recruit canvassers and, on the whole, in a television watching world, they receive a less sympathetic response on the doorstep. Canvass returns are certainly as misleading as ever – experienced Labour agents testified that there was no falling off of support, and they were puzzled, since they knew from the polls that they were losing the election. Yet part of the value of canvassing lies in its educative effect on candidates. Many Labour MPs admitted to being startled by the vehemence with which, even in strong Labour territory, dole-scroungers and union leaders were attacked, as well as by the popularity of council house sales. There was a lingering resentment at the dislocation caused by the strikes of the previous winter, and this feeling was visited on some Labour candidates. Conservatives were made aware of scepticism about Mrs Thatcher personally, and about her tax proposals.

Inevitably many Labour candidates had to spend their time covering up for organisational shortcomings. Some found themselves dealing with printers, arranging and encouraging canvassing parties, phoning Transport House about simple organisational matters, and transporting people and election literature. As one of them noted 'A candidate is one of the very few people who is free all day throughout the campaign.'

Some of the public (10%) told the Gallup poll that they displayed window bills for their party, the same proportion as in 1970. The figure would excite scepticism among those who campaigned in the election and those who observed it. Over most of the country it was notably invisible occasion: one might count 20 window bills in a day's drive of 200 miles. And, except around party committee rooms, posters were almost equally inconspicuous. In a few city centres and station approaches and in some close fought constituencies, there were big hoardings – mostly with the Saatchi poster 'Labour *still* isn't working' remained up from the spring campaign. Conservative headquarters spent almost £250,000 on posters during the campaign. Transport House spent £112,000. A few constituencies devised their own displays – usually a single hand-painted copy. There were, of course, a lot more double crown (30" x 20") posters shouting with the traditional simplicity: 'Vote for Bloggs', 'Bloggs for Labour', 'Bloggs for Blankshire', or 'Bloggs Again'. But it can hardly be said that display advertising on the billboards or in the local press was what made people aware of the election, or eager to rush to the polls in support of their old loyalties.

The decline of the public meeting continued. Most candidates drew quite a throng of loyal supporters to their adoption meetings, at which a large portion of the election expenses was often raised (though few could match John Pardoe, who drew £9,000 from the pockets of North Cornwall Liberals). In rural areas Conservatives usually had the organisation to manage three or four village meetings a night, though faced with arranging halls, publicity and chairmen, their opponents often contented themselves with informal loudspeaker stops and walkabouts. In towns some candidates did without meetings altogether, and others drew humiliatingly small audiences even for front-bench speakers. The proportion of voters claiming to have heard candidates at public meetings further declined from 1974 to only 3%. Even well-established MPs were having to cancel meetings when no one turned up. The ticket-only meetings for Mr Callaghan and Mrs Thatcher secured full halls. But even the Chancellor of the Exchequer had on one or two occasions to be content with a few dozen listeners, though he faced several hundred in some marginals. Kevin McNamara, the Labour member for Hull Central, defended the holding of public meetings, in spite of the voters' apathy, on the grounds that the candidate should expose himself in a public forum to the questioning of voters.

In the 1979 election the exceptional security arrangements that followed Airey Neave's death combined with the long-term decline in public meetings to produce an exceptionally orderly election. There were no stories of eggs being thrown, or anything beyond the good-humoured jostling of shopping crowds as far as the vast bulk of politicians were concerned. Almost the only heckling caught by the television cameras was the concerted pursuit of Mr Callaghan on the Northern Ireland issue. The one real unpleasantness of the election surrounded the National Front: it had the greatest difficulty in holding meetings without disruption by the Anti-Nazi League and other groups. In Plymouth their meetings were neatly frustrated by their opponents' filling every seat in the hall long in advance – but in other cases there were ugly confrontations and a huge display of police strength was used to preserve order. A march in Leicester on April 21 led to arrests, and in Southall on April 23 there was the tragic collision between, on the one side, demonstrators from the Anti-Nazi League and youths from the local Indian community, and on the other, the police – the handful of National Front supporters were hardly involved. 300 arrests were made, and near the end of the encounter, one man, Blair Peach, died, possibly at the hands of the police.

MPs boasted of their constituency services – of grievances redressed and benefits achieved, (see p. 413 for an assessment of their impact). Local issues did matter in particular places – examples were offered: a nuclear plant in Norfolk and in North Wales, the completion of the bridge across the Humber and the acceleration of specific by-passes. In rural areas bus services and farming problems could intrude just as fishing limits and EEC policy did in coastal constituencies. But it must strike anyone who sits through local press reports how overwhelmingly the candidates concentrated on national themes. Regional and constituency issues got very little mention, and some candidates commented on how at meeting after meeting not a single question strayed beyond the central issues of prices and productivity, unions, and law and order.

Many local papers during the campaign contained more news of the district and metropolitan contests than of those for Westminster. Headlines such as 'Split in Conservative party'; 'Candidate charges Waste', 'Chance for Independents' or 'Labour gains likely' referred to local feuds. In some cases general election and local candidates cooperated constructively, sharing out territory and making helpful references to each other in their addresses, but sometimes each ploughed his own furrow. For many party activists, local politics is more important than the Westminster dimension.

Election addresses are the most widely read items of partisan propaganda. Roughly two-thirds of the candidates of both main parties agreed that the election would turn on the Labour government's record, but a study of their contents offers additional evidence of how far it was the Conservatives who defined the issues in the campaign. While candidates echoed the manifestos and national party leaders to a considerable degree, a random sample of their addresses in England and Wales reveals differing emphases in different constituencies; the addresses were of course drafted at a very early stage in the campaign.

Labour candidates touched less on the issues of taxes, crime and trade union reform, which Conservatives emphasised. Among Conservative candidates 88% promised tax cuts but only 44% of Labour candidates touched on the issue; they usually observed that the cuts were just for the rich, and stressed the offsetting loss of public services and the VAT increases which would result (points which only 36% and 14% of Conservatives mentioned). Law and order was a favourite Conservative topic: 87% issued tough calls for action in an area where 66% of Labour candidates were silent; most Labour allusions to it argued that only social reform could reduce crime. Labour candidates generally ignored the specifics of Conservative proposals for trade union reform and relied on a vague call for union co-operation. When Conser-

Table 2. Election Addresses (England and Wales)

	Conservative			Labour			Liberal
	All N=107	Elected N=63	Defeated N=44	All N=105	Elected N=43	Defeated N=62	All N=45
Nature of Election							
Save Freedom, etc.	33%	37%	30%	—	—	—	—
Oppose Tory Racialism	—	—	—	28%	19%	34%	2%
'Curse on Both your Houses'	—	—	—	—	—	—	92%
General Labour performance	67%	63%	70%	72%	81%	66%	—
Lib role in stabilisation	—	—	—	—	—	—	6%
General							
Own party moderate	1%	2%	—	3%	5%	2%	36%
Con slogans 'We'll All Win, Don't Just Hope'	9%	10%	9%	—	—	—	—
Lab slogan 'The Better Way'	—	—	—	18%	26%	13%	—
Lib slogan 'The Real Fight'	—	—	—	—	—	—	24%
Libs no vested interests/national unity	—	—	—	—	—	—	51%
Break 2-party system	—	—	—	—	—	—	64%
Invitation to tactical vote	6%	8%	—	2%	—	3%	18%
Libs could form government	—	—	—	—	—	—	4%
Libs could hold balance of power	—	—	—	—	—	—	33%
Lib-Lab pact/Libs support Lab	17%	21%	11%	—	—	—	51%
Labour left/Extremism	34%	38%	27%	—	—	—	33%
Tory right/Extremism	—	—	—	6%	10%	3%	24%
Electoral Reform	1%	2%	—	3%	2%	3%	76%
Lords Reform	4%	5%	2%	6%	7%	5%	9%
Bill of Rights/Written Constitution	3%	2%	—	3%	5%	—	42%
Devolution/Federalism	5%	6%	2%	3%	5%	2%	24%
Regional issues	5%	5%	5%	4%	2%	5%	—

Mention of Ulster	1%	2%	—	6%	5%	6%	13%
British decline	12%	21%	12%	3%	2%	3%	24%
Local issues	37%	46%	25%	46%	47%	45%	29%
Constituency service	41%	59%	16%	47%	79%	24%	11%
Personal background	72%	63%	84%	82%	84%	81%	82%
Message from wife	8%	13%	2%	5%	12%	—	—
Colour printing	97%	100%	93%	89%	93%	85%	58%
Leaders							
Thatcher	28%	33%	20%	13%	9%	16%	20%
Callaghan	8%	8%	9%	23%	26%	21%	6%
Steel	—	—	—	—	—	—	31%
Economic Issues							
Inflation	83%	79%	77%	82%	84%	81%	64%
Incomes Policy	9%	11%	7%	23%	26%	21%	51%
Price Controls/Food subsidies	—	—	—	46%	44%	47%	18%
Taxes/tax cuts	88%	94%	80%	44%	35%	52%	67%
Spending Cuts	35%	44%	25%	42%	42%	46%	11%
Shift to indirect tax	14%	22%	2%	15%	16%	15%	69%
Trade Union Reform	71%	76%	64%	5%	5%	8%	31%
Winter of 78/79	31%	33%	27%	8%	12%	5%	18%
Winter of 73/74	—	—	—	47%	48%	45%	6%
Union co-op/Avoid confrontation	—	—	—	65%	63%	66%	37%
Unemployment/Jobs	86%	77%	84%	85%	91%	81%	49%
Shorter work week	—	—	—	16%	19%	15%	9%
Micro-electronics/tech change	—	—	—	25%	21%	24%	6%
Industrial policy/Lame duck aid	6%	3%	9%	53%	49%	60%	13%
Mention nationalisation	30%	35%	23%	8%	9%	6%	36%
Mention 'socialism'	50%	55%	43%	18%	19%	18%	31%
Attack capitalsim	—	—	—	8%	9%	6%	—

	Conservative			Labour			Liberal
	All N = 107	Elected N = 63	Defeated N = 44	All N = 105	Elected N = 43	Defeated N = 62	All N = 45
De-nationalisation	6%	8%	4%	1%	–	2%	2%
Free business/encourage enterprise	60%	63%	55%	15%	19%	13%	9%
Wealth tax/redistribution	3%	2%	4%	27%	23%	29%	4%
Industrial democracy/'partnership'	1%	2%	–	3%	2%	3%	71%
Minimum wage/Income	1%	2%	–	10%	7%	11%	53%
Small business	38%	40%	36%	9%	2%	13%	58%
Agriculture	23%	37%	4%	12%	16%	10%	16%
Environment	2%	3%	–	28%	15%	35%	56%
Transport	2%	3%	2%	7%	5%	8%	33%
Energy–general	1%	–	2%	5%	5%	8%	5%
North Sea Oil	21%	24%	18%	47%	42%	50%	18%
Social Issues							
Housing –general	21%	21%	20%	35%	37%	34%	42%
Council house sales	54%	51%	59%	15%	28%	6%	20%
Aids to homebuyers/mortgages	36%	33%	39%	46%	33%	55%	16%
Rents/rates	5%	2%	9%	57%	53%	60%	18%
Pensions-general	34%	37%	23%	82%	91%	76%	33%
Free TV licences	12%	17%	4%	20%	26%	16%	–
End earnings rule	18%	17%	18%	1%	–	4%	2%
Social welfare general	18%	17%	18%	25%	14%	34%	6%
NHS–general	41%	46%	34%	70%	65%	74%	24%
Pay beds	–	–	–	25%	23%	19%	–
Aid to disabled	12%	14%	9%	44%	56%	35%	16%

Education general	11%	16%	4%	66%	63%	68%	37%
Comprehensives/selection	21%	22%	20%	27%	16%	34%	6%
Standards	49%	35%	68%	4%	—	6%	9%
Parental choice/charter	33%	32%	34%	5%	2%	6%	16%
Law & order—general	87%	86%	87%	34%	33%	35%	27%
Death Penalty	35%	54%	36%	—	—	—	4%
Immigration	25%	19%	34%	4%	5%	3%	2%
Race Relations	14%	5%	23%	27%	28%	26%	27%
Women's Rights/Pay	—	—	—	37%	40%	35%	18%
Abortion	3%	2%	5%	3%		3%	4%
Youth—general	1%	2%	—	15%	21%	11%	11%
Grants to 5/6 formers	—	—	—	18%	19%	18%	18%
Cheaper transport 14/16	—	—	—	4%	5%	3%	—
Child benefits	—	—	—	50%	56%	45%	4%
Europe							
Pro	13%	22%	2%	2%	5%	—	16%
Anti/Threaten Withdrawal	1%	—	2%	29%	28%	37%	—
CAP/Green £	16%	25%	2%	60%	67%	55%	24%
British contribution	3%	5%	—	25%	23%	26%	2%
Foreign affairs—mention	23%	39%	—	14%	14%	15%	16%
Rhodesia/Southern Africa	7%	13%	—	7%	7%	6%	4%
Defence/Soviet threat	57%	71%	36%	17%	5%	26%	13%

vatives pointed to price increases (83%) and the recent 'winter of discontent' (31%), Labour addresses admitted some failures, but 44% invoked the spectre of what had happened five years earlier in the winter of 1973–4.

Candidates of both parties mentioned unemployment with almost equal frequency (85% Labour, 86% Conservative). Labour candidates stressed their party's record and proposals in the social field – education (66%), pensions (82%), health (70%), women's rights (37%), child benefits (50%) and provisions for tenants (57%), as well as Labour's industrial policy (53%), and its forward-looking emphasis on preparation for technological change (25%). Conservatives made little reference to their party's promised cuts in industrial subsidies, though many argued that a return to prosperity through the encouragement of enterprise (60%) and of small business (38%) would reduce joblessness and permit increased social spending; 54% also gave prominence to council house sales, a subject on which 85% of Labour candidates were silent and the rest were critical. A scattering of candidates in both parties discussed animal welfare,[1] perhaps in response to the vigorous lobbyists in that field.

While virtually all Labour addresses ignored the immigration issue, one quarter of the Tory candidates repeated Mrs Thatcher's call for a reduction in numbers. Only 14% of Conservatives (compared to 27% of Labour candidates) referred to race relations; one managed to commend immigration restrictions as a favour to Asian girls who 'have been distressed by being forced into arranged marriages contrary to the customs they have observed here'. Very few candidates made pro-EEC remarks but Labour candidates (at 29%) were almost alone in expressing explicitly anti-Market views; 60% of Labour candidates attacked the Common Agricultural Policy, and many slated the Tories as 'soft on the Common Market'.

The issues not stressed by the two main parties were as revealing as those which were: future pay policy, the centrepiece

---

[1] Mr Auberon Waugh, standing as a 'Dog Lover' in North Devon, got into trouble with his election address. He was standing to protest against Jeremy Thorpe's renomination while under indictment for conspiracy to murder. The only death in the case was that of Norman Scott's dog Rinka, and Waugh issued his call, 'Rinka lives. Woof Woof. Vote Waugh to give *all* dogs the right to life, liberty, and the pursuit of happiness.' The Court of Appeal, unamused, banned the address's publication on April 26, and required the withdrawal from sale of an issue of the *Spectator* containing it, on the grounds that it could prejudice the trial of Mr Thorpe.

of the 1974 elections, was mentioned by just 9% of Conservatives, and only 23% of Labour candidates (usually with elliptical references such as 'a new system of pay bargaining'). Institutional reforms were hardly touched on, and few candidates discussed the record of Britain's long-term decline under both parties. Foreign affairs also received short shrift, and so did the simmering situation in Northern Ireland.

Liberal candidates mirrored their leader's presentation of their party as the moderate but distinct alternative to the bipartisan extremism of Labour and Tory. In one guise or another 92% touched on the theme of 'a plague on both your houses'. Owning up more openly (and self-interestedly) to Britain's long-run decline than either major party, many called on voters to 'break with the past'. They stressed institutional reforms as the means to achieve this, including a Bill of Rights (42%), devolution and decentralisation (24%), and, especially, proportional representation (76%). (At Bath, Christopher Mayhew's address dealt with that issue alone.) On social and economic issues, the main focus of the class-based parties, the Liberals' emphasis was more blurred, touching upon social welfare far less than Labour, and going lighter on traditional Conservative issues as well. Their discussions of economic policy stressed industrial partnership (71%) and union co-operation (31%), though the latter lay uneasily alongside calls for statutory pay policy (51%). Although their party was explicitly pro-European, only 16% of Liberal candidates said so, barely more than among the Conservatives. The Lib-Lab pact was mentioned by 51% of Liberals.

Liberal incumbents, a colourful and individualistic lot, stressed their records of constituency service and their personal appeal. For instance, the voluble Cyril Smith told his constituents, 'There are very few MPs, if any, who in such a short space of time, have become so well known nationally. It is truly a wonderful record of achievement.'

Conservative candidates sometimes went a good deal further than their party's leading spokesmen in their attacks on extremism and the Labour left. One Conservative charged Labour as 'committed to the most extreme left wing programme ever adopted by a political party in Britain', and more than one third presented the voters' choice as between freedom and socialism; 64% of Conservative candidates attacked nationalisation or socialism, while a mere 24% of Labour candidates mentioned either (and very few went as far as Michael Foot's promise of 'a good socialist future for Ebbw Vale, Tredegar and Rhymney'). A few Conservatives also claimed Labour wanted to end all immigration restrictions.

Labour had its excesses, too. One class warrior painted the election as a contest of 'the business millionaires against the working millions'; another proclaimed, 'A Thatcher government would double the dole queues'; while a third warned, 'Our opponents intend to double the expenditure on defence.' Liberal bombast included one candidate's claim, 'What have Russia, Poland, China, Hungary, Uganda, Iran, and Cuba all got in common with Britain? For the past 30 years or so they have all had one-party government.'

The addresses themselves were, with scattered exception, printed in the party's colours (though some Labour and more Liberal candidates contented themselves with cheaper black and white addresses). Liberal addresses showed the most variety, while Conservative addresses showed more standardisation in format, and Labour in content (though many of the latter showed identically-posed pictures of a *distrait* Mr Callaghan limply shaking the candidate's hand). All candidates stessed the importance of the election. Incumbents almost uniformly mentioned their records of constituency service, and around 40% of candidates dwelt on local issues; the embarrassing practice of banal messages from the candidate's wife appeared to be in decline.

The most surprising results of the analysis came in the mention of party leaders. Mrs Thatcher, despite her relative unpopularity, was mentioned in Conservative addresses more often than Mr Heath had ever been as leader of the Opposition (28% compared to a range from 11% in Oct. 1974 to 20% in 1970). But she was less frequently a target of Labour candidates than the Conservative leader had been in either 1974 election. (Mr Heath's own address, like his campaign speeches, made no mention of Mrs Thatcher.) Mr Callaghan, though recognised as an asset to his party, appeared in just 23% of its addresses. He was mentioned more than Harold Wilson had been in his last three elections (20% in 1970, 2% in February 1974 and 5% in October 1974) though much less often than in the 47% of addresses which had mentioned Mr Wilson in 1966. Among Liberal candidates 31% mentioned their party's leader, a higher proportion than in either main party, although candidates of the latter ignored him completely.

The losing Conservative candidates placed less emphasis on issues of appeal to the Conservative faithful such as tax cuts, foreign affairs, nationalisation, Labour extremism and agriculture than did the successful ones. They played more on issues appealing to working-class voters, such as unemployment (82% compared with 73%), though there was no clear evidence of ideological differences between the two groups (for example, almost equal percentages called for the death penalty). Labour losers tended to be slightly more explicitly left-wing than winners, and certainly expressed stronger opposition to Conservative policies than the winners, but the differences were not great (for example, nearly identical proportions mentioned nationalism or socialism).

Every election produces some eccentric addresses, and 1979 proved no exception. One Conservative candidate began 'This is a political address. You might be right to throw it away. I might be wrong in posting it to you, but read it – it concerns you.' Another, even more self-effacing, candidate argued 'I can only be better than some of the MPs we already have... You have nothing to lose by giving me a try.' One Labour candidate produced a supplement to his address in five languages, including Turkish and Gujerati; while Denis Howell, by his own account minister for natural disasters, bragged 'on each occasion Denis has been appointed he has wrought the oracle (*sic*) and the crisis has passed upon the instant.'

Pride of place however, must go to Dennis Skinner of Bolsover, whose entire address was written in strained verse, beginning:

The election is here again, nine years since my first try,
How strange that the issues haven't changed by and by,
The Tory leader then was Ted Heath, who promised you less tax
Lower prices, and civil servants to be removed from your backs.

About two million of Britain's 40 million electors are of New Commonwealth origin. Although most are concentrated in safe Labour areas in city centres, there were a number of marginal seats, notably in Bradford and Leicester, and one or two parts of London, where their votes were crucial. In the past the overwhelming bulk had gone to Labour. The Conservatives tried, not very successfully, to tackle the problem: Andrew Rowe, Director of the Community Affairs Group in Central Office, established a West Indian Conservative Committee and fostered existing Indian activities; the Conservatives put forward Asian candidates in two unpromising seats, Greenwich and Glasgow Central. Labour nominated one West Indian in the Cities of London and Westminster, and the Liberals did the same in Nuneaton. All parties issued election literature in Urdu, Gujerati or other dialects (though they often faced difficulties in distributing it to the appropriate households). Very little evidence is available about the impact of all these efforts; but the swing to the Conservatives in places such as Leicester, Bradford and Southall was notably low (see p. 398—9).

In Leicester South a leaflet written in Gujerati was circulated to the immigrant areas in the last days of the campaign. It identified the National Front with the Conservative party, and contained the Labour party agent's name at the bottom of the page. The agent and the candidate issued apologies and retractions.

The Labour party counts on trade-union help during an election. Shop stewards are usually sympathetic, and many branch officials are willing to give some of their time and their facilities, such as a car and a duplicator, to the party. On this occasion, the new organisation, Trade Unions for a Labour Victory, was giving more publicised support for the cause, and union journals listed the regional officials (all GMWU or TGWU officers) who could be contacted to direct volunteer help to the marginals where it was most needed. In some areas, notably the South West there were tributes to what was achieved — but in many other places questions about union help evoked only a cynical laugh. 'The shop stewards can't even muster a token crowd for us at a factory gate meeting when we know there'll be press photographers there.'

There were many complaints about the Post Office. Letters and literature from party headquarters in London were delayed or even lost and Conservative Area Offices made increasing use of the telex. At the constituency level, there were reports of troubles over the use of the free post. Local postmasters (and, it was darkly hinted, local post office union branches) had their own interpretation of the regulations, and could not be relied upon to deliver the election address on the date considered tactically desirable. One candidate who tried to use the free post to deliver a supporting message from his wife had the whole consignment refused on the ground that she was not a candidate.

Local radio stations increased in number in the mid-1970s, and so did their established audience. On the whole the stations, both BBC and commercial, tried to respond to the challenge of the election, and candidates were very ready to accede to the increased demand to take part in interviews, phone-ins and debates. Some party officials described this as the most important single development in electioneering, but the impact was limited because some stations were inhibited by the rules of balance: broadcasts were blocked by the refusal of Labour and other candidates to appear with the National Front. The Leicester case (see p. 219) came too late to ease the situation.

There were more complaints of partisanship in the local press, but for the most part the weeklies and to a lesser extent the evening papers maintained a reasonable balance in their reports of local happenings.

An election is an occasion for pressure groups to try to extract pledges from politicians, and every candidate received letters from pro- and anti-Europeans, pro- and anti-abortionists, animal lovers, road-users, ecologists, ethnic groups, and from every sort of social welfare organisation. Most candidates dismissed the bulk of these approaches as worth no more than a civil answer, but they took more trouble with the ethnic and religious groups where cohesive leadership might actually move a significant block of votes, and there was a chance to get a message through to electors who might otherwise be difficult to reach. Sometimes United Nations Association branches or churches provided a convenient forum for a joint meeting of rival candidates.

The awareness that the election is decided in a limited number of seats obviously affects the parties' allocation of resources. The Labour party recognised 80 marginals — the 21 Labour and the 29 Conservative seats subject to a 2% swing, with special constituencies added following by-elections or because of the challenge of the SNP or the Liberals. The Conservatives, with a greater need to gain seats, designated as 'critical' 97 seats, 62 to be won from Labour, 7 from Liberal and 8 from Scottish Nationalist, as well as 6 by-election gains and 14 other Conservative seats to be defended. Liberals concentrated on the 14 seats they held and 14 other priority 'target seats' as well as a further 17 possibles. It is, however, one thing to put a seat on a list in London and another to transform the situation out in the field. The Labour and Liberal parties did not have the resources to put a professional agent in every marginal — less than half of them had full-timers, but with money, and subsidised literature, and big name speakers, they could do quite a lot to stimulate activity. The regional officials naturally focussed their efforts in this direction; Labour assistant regional organisers were often allocated four or five marginals to take personally under their wing. The Conservatives, better equipped in every way, could usually ensure that there was a competent agent in every critical seat and could, where necessary, give more help in kind. The fact that the swing in these marginals was below average may be testimony to the limited amount that party organisation can ever achieve.

The three main party leaders concentrated their walkabouts in the marginals, but the Labour campaigners in Bosworth may not have felt this helpful when an ill-briefed Prime Minister used the wrong candidate's name throughout his speech.

If parties were perfectly organised and wholly dedicated to getting more MPs into parliament, they would direct all their workers from safe seats to marginals. A great deal of effort does go into planning mutual aid in order to deploy party workers where they can have most impact. But distances are often great, and party workers are reluctant to travel. The paper schemes can come to nothing, as Area Agents wryly admit. There can be successes — a bevy of volunteers will always flock to a by-election and elsewhere regular routines can sometimes be managed. The Conservatives are much better placed. A weekly busload of canvassers from a safe seat in Sussex to Central London, and one from a Cheshire stronghold to a Lancashire marginal were reported; and during the campaign rock-solid Wanstead put a large part of its resources at the disposal of the neighbouring Ilford marginals. But over the country as a whole, such activity amounted to a very small portion of the whole, even for the Conservatives. In April 1979, too, the local elections took their toll: even in the safest Westminster seat some council seats are marginal, and councillors wanted their friends to help them to be re-elected on May 3.

The Liberals found that they suffered from the Lib-Lab pact; it was the commonest explanation offered by those deserting to the Conservatives, although the Thorpe affair does seem to have added to their problems in the constituencies adjacent to North Devon. The Liberal campaigns varied greatly. In some of the seats where a last-minute candidate was put up, spurred by the Edge Hill result, the organisation was virtually non-existent, and only a few hundred pounds were spent putting out an election address to just a small proportion of the electors. In others the effort fully matched that of the major parties in money, in helpers and in activities.

Despite its 303 candidates the National Front was not really very much in evidence, except in the half-dozen cases where its meetings or marches provoked disturbances (see p. 180). But it won more publicity than any other of the small groups, none of whom had the resources to mount anything resembling the traditional constituency campaign. More publicity was drawn by the gimmicks of Commander Boaks fighting three seats under his 'Democratic Monarchist Public Safety White Resident' banner, or Mr Keen personally contesting five constituencies in his 'Campaign for a More Prosperous Britain', than by the dedicated efforts of the WRP, Communist and Socialist Unity groups. The Ecologists, with their novelty value and their sympathetic programme, attracted some national attention, though locally electors often remained unaware of their efforts.

All too often the image of the minor party was of a single independent candidate shyly and clumsily buttonholing passers-by in a shopping centre and desperately pushing out duplicated handbills. Frank Hansford-Miller, the English Nationalist in Mr Thorpe's Devon North seat, attacked the media for ignoring him: 'They know that if I had 15 minutes on television I would sway the whole country. They know that unlike any other present politician I have charisma, brains, sincerity and drive.'

The essential feature of the 1979 campaign in Scotland was the eclipse of the Scottish dimension.[2] Neal Ascherson caught the mood in his *Scotsman* review:

If this is a dreich, colourless election in Scotland, the Scots

[2] The following paragraphs owe much to William Miller, the author of Chapter 6.

made it so. The referendum and its aftermath abruptly withdrew the brightest theme ... For five years, political argument
and planning has been conducted in the Scottish dimension.
Now, suddenly, the dimension is hardly there. The campaign
in Scotland is part of the UK campaign, on smooth worn
issues which the big UK parties present in Bathgate as they
would present them in Blackpool. We had forgotten, perhaps,
how dull British politics are.

After the referendum the parties could find very little to say
about devolution and the issue was not much raised on the
doorstep. The media, which had given devolution saturation
coverage in January and February, switched to British news and
personalities in April as much in the search for novelty as for
their inherent importance. While the Callaghan, Thatcher and
Steel travelling circuses attracted media attention, only the Scottish Conservatives planned their campaign to focus on a limited
number of personalities — Teddy Taylor, George Younger, and
Alex Fletcher — who took the daily press conferences in rota-
tion and presented the radio and TV broadcasts. The SNP
especially had a rooted objection to personality cults. It had
no leader in the sense in which that term is applied to the
other parties and whereas its Chairman, William Wolfe, had
done a helicopter tour in 1974, he was too busy fighting West
Lothian to repeat it in 1979. SNP MPs stuck to their own
constituencies in a desperate struggle to hang on to their seats
against the tide. Since Margo Macdonald was not a candidate,
she could have provided a touring circus, but her popularity
with the media aroused resentment in the party and she was
instructed to stay off television until the election campaign was
over.

The constituencies most likely to change hands were SNP
seats at risk to the Conservatives. Neither party was popular in
Scotland at the time; so both fought sub-national campaigns
appealing to the special interests of the electors in the dozen
SNP/Tory marginals. SNP MPs emphasised their role as good
local members. The Conservatives directed Mrs Thatcher's
Scottish tour through the critical Grampian region — Aberdeenshire, Banff, Moray and Nairn and the Grampians. Conservative
candidates made a public, and partially successful, attempt to
force Mrs Thatcher into a very hard line against the Common

Market's fishing policy, which had aroused great resentment in North-East Scotland.

All the parties in Scotland turned more to professional advertising agencies than in the past, though the results were hardly encouraging. The Scottish Conservatives opted out of three of the five British Conservative election broadcasts. But all three opt-outs were filmed in a Glasgow hotel by Saatchi and Saatchi, instead of relying on BBC Scotland as in the past. Two of the three were typical Saatchi and Saatchi programmes with a Scottish accent. Labour, too, used one professionally filmed opt-out, which was widely criticised for presenting a non-Labour undergraduate as an ordinary Labour working class voter. And the SNP broke with precedent by hiring an advertising agency.

In Wales, as in Scotland, the campaign was much affected by coming in the aftermath of the referendum. Despite the government's advocacy — and that of the Liberals and Plaid Cymru — only 11% of the Welsh electorate had cast 'Yes' votes. The Conservatives, the only party united in opposition to a Welsh assembly, were in excellent heart, and Plaid Cymru were especially downcast. Local issues were more in evidence in Wales than elsewhere: there were arguments over the fourth TV channel and how far it should broadcast exclusively in Welsh; there were also arguments about the closure of works — most notably the threatened steel plant at Shotton; hill-farming, nuclear power, and water resources also diverted attention from the mainstream of the national debate. And constituency polls — including notably erratic ones in Brecon & Radnor and in Cardigan — attracted more publicity in Wales than elsewhere. Wales is a land of safe seats. Besides the four that changed hands, only two or three more were in the remotest jeopardy — and indeed the Conservatives' victories in Anglesey and Montgomery were totally unexpected; none of the party officials had spotted what was happening in rural Wales (see p. 418).

In Ulster the election had its separate sectarian agenda. It was a self-contained campaign, with issues and personalities and parties which were a world apart from Smith Square. Mercifully, the violence which was anticipated in the wake of Airey Neave's assassination did not materialise. The different Unionist groups, already gratified by the provision of extra seats for Ulster for the subsequent Parliament, demanded the return of the Stormont Parliament, suspended since 1972. But clearly no British party would concede this, unless all the parties agreed to power-sharing or a form of rule acceptable to the Catholic minority.

Ulster politics was complex. Since 1974 the Unionist party had fragmented into different loyalist groups. The Official Unionist Party fought 11 seats. The Unionist Party of Northern Ireland (founded by the late Brian Faulkner) had three candidates, the United Ulster Unionist Party had four, and the Revd Ian Paisley's militant Democratic Unionist Party had five. Attempts to arrange a unity pact between the groups to ensure that the 'loyalist' vote would not be split were fruitless. There were doubts whether Enoch Powell, the official Unionist MP for South Down, would retain his 3,900 majority over the SDLP, because of the threatened intervention of Cecil Harvey (UUUP); the threat was removed at the last moment. The pro-Catholic minority also had difficulties. Austin Currie of the SDLP challenged the Westminster abstentionist, Frank Maguire, in Fermanagh and South Tyrone. Only the non-sectarian Alliance Party contested all twelve seats.

Labour organisers were heartened by the dry weather reported throughout most of the country on May 3. They were further encouraged by indications of a high turnout.[3] The Gallup survey reported in Table 3 shows the time at which people claim they had voted.

A MORI survey found that Labour had a slight lead among those voting between 11 a.m. and 6 p.m. But Conservatives had a large lead among those voting before 11 a.m. and, contrary to conventional wisdom, among those who went to the polls after 6 p.m.

The turnout of 76.0% was 3.2% higher than in October 1974, but the increase was attributable to the more recent register.

---

[3] The fears that there would be serious confusions at the polling stations and the count because of simultaneous parliamentary and local voting proved unfounded. But the number of spoilt ballot papers did increase from 37,706 (0.1%) in October 1974 to 117,848 (0.4%) in 1979. The number voting for more than one candidate jumped from 3,492 to 71,663. The Home Office did spend £148,605 on a 30-second television commercial (starring Jimmy Young) explaining the procedure with white (parliamentary) and grey (local) ballot papers. This was shown 8 times nationwide on May 1–2. The Home Office spent £3418 on advertisements in the ethnic minority press and a further £279 on booking time in the Asian cinemas to show explanations of the procedure.

Table 4   Time of voting

Time	1979 %	(1974)
7 — 11.59 a.m.	34	(29)
12 noon — 4.59 p.m.	22	(22)
5 p.m. — 7.59 p.m.	32	(34)
8 — 10 p.m.	11	(12)
Postal votes or 'don't know'	2	(3)

MORI found that of those who did not vote 52% said they would have voted Labour. The reasons given for failing to vote varied. Some were not very interested (16%). Some were not convinced that any of the parties represented their views (14%) or would be able to solve Britain's problems (11%). Others had practical reasons: they were ill, or caring for someone who was ill (16%) or they had recently moved (15%).

The scope for postal voting varies with the length of time since the register was compiled. Only half as many people will have moved in a May election as in an October one. But half the postal votes go to people permanently registered as infirm, or likely to be away on business. In 1979 there were 847,000 names on the postal voters register, and 681,000 actually cast valid votes; a fall of 166,000 compared with 1979. The percentage of ballot papers returned (82%) was the lowest ever. In a few cases the fall may be due to names being left on the register from year to year, but on the whole the decrease in post office efficiency must be held responsible.

There were 42 seats (20 Con, 19 Lab, 1 Lib, and 2 in Ulster) where the postal vote was greater than the majority. Conservatives are undoubtedly better at organising postal voting and middle class people are in any case more likely to both apply and qualify for such votes. In almost every constituency there were more Conservative than Labour postal votes. The only seats where it seems at all likely that the postal vote made the crucial difference are listed in Table 4.

If we assume that the postal vote split two-to-one in favour of the Conservatives (and that none went to minor parties) then they owed six seats to it. On a three-to-one assumption it accounted for eight seats, and on an extreme four-to-one assumption eleven seats. The ITN/ORC survey found that those

Table 4.   Postal votes and Conservative Victories

	Postal vote	Con majority over Lab	Majority as % of postal vote
Preston North	1546	29	2
Paddington	763	106	14
B'ham Northfield	939	204	22
Luton West	1008	246	24
Kingswood	1169	303	26
Nelson & Colne	1613	436	27
Bebington	1413	486	34
Brigg & Scunthorpe	1204	486	40
Lincoln	1173	602	51
Aberdeen South	1447	772	53
The Wrekin	1609	965	59
		Con majority over SNP	
Moray & Nairn	1515	420	28
Banff	1490	799	54
Aberdeenshire E.	1007	558	55
		Dem. U. majority over OU	
Belfast East	485	64	13

in marginal seats who claimed to have voted by post divided in a 5 to 3 ratio in favour of the Conservatives.

The postal votes in the 20 safest Conservative seats averaged 1151, in the 20 most marginal seats 1455, and in the 20 safest Labour seats 545.

The largest postal votes, as always, came from Northern Ireland: Fermanagh & South Tyrone with 6682 (10.7%) once again provided the record and Mid-Ulster, 6,295 (9.6%), was close behind. Londonderry, 3,747 (5.9%), and South Down, 3,222 (5.0%) also exceeded any seat in Britain. Only 25 seats in mainland Britain received as many as 2,000 valid postal votes, the highest being in North Cornwall, 2,823 (5.9%);Carmarthen, 2,603 (5.0%); and Dover, 2,834 (4.6%). Liverpool Scotland-Exchange with 98 (0.5%); Glasgow Central with 104 (0.9%); and Newham

S. with 160 (0.5%) were at the other extreme. The variation in postal votes from a few hundred to over 2,000 in part reflects differing social conditions, but the wide differences between similar and adjacent seats must be a commentary on party organisation. The postal register offers one area where efficient preparation can unquestionably reap a dividend in votes: it is somewhat astonishing to find marginal seats where the parties could not manage to garner even 1,000 votes.

The permitted maximum which candidates could spend had been increased in July 1978 to allow for inflation, and on average they were now allowed £3050 in boroughs and £2725 in counties. In fact although they spent more than in any previous election (£3,557,000 in all) the average per candidate for each party was a lower proportion of the maximum. As Table 5 shows Labour candidates spent £1897 (66% of the maximum), Conservatives £2190 (76%) and Liberals £1013 (35%). In Scotland and Wales, Labour actually outspent the Conservatives. The

Table 5. Candidates' Election Expenses, 1979

	Average £ per candidate					% of permitted maximum (average)				
	Con	Lab	Lib	Other	All	Con	Lab	Lib	Other	All
England	2262	1876	1001	316	1379	78	65	34	12	48
Wales	1915	2080	1103	857	1432	68	74	38	32	52
Scotland	1802	1958	1091	1408	1599	66	72	40	55	60
N. Ireland	–	–	–	1622	1622	–	–	–	46	46
All	2190	1897	1013	612	1394	76	66	35	21	48
All Oct. 74	1275	1163	725	487	963	79	72	72	30	59

The average expenditures per candidate for the other parties were as follows (October 1974 figures are in parentheses): National Front – £227 (£236); Communist – £560 (£403); Scottish National Party – £1737 (£900); Plaid Cymru – £1113 (£733); Ecology Party – £257; Workers' Revolutionary Party – £498.

All figures exclude candidates' personal expenses, which do not count against the legally permitted maximum. If personal expenses exceed £100, the candidate must itemise them when he files his return. Personal expenses averaged £54 per candidate (Conservative and Labour candidates spent higher that this – £79 and £78 on average, respectively). Many candidates declare no personal expenses at all, but others spend several hundreds of pounds (the Conservative candidate for St Albans reported having spent £806 on personal expenses, while the Labour candidate for Whitehaven submitted the figure of £633).

The total reported spending for all candidates was £3,557,000. Of this, the candidates of the three largest parties spent: Conservative £1,362,000; Labour £1,181,000; Liberal £583,000.

£2,874,000 (78%) of candidates' expenditure went on printing.

Leslie Seidle played a major part in the preparation of these figures.

Liberals were at no disadvantage where it mattered most: in their 30 best constituencies they spent 91% of the maximum, while the 13 MPs elected in October 1974 spent 94%. In the 62 most marginal of Conservative/Labour contests (under 5% majorities in October 1974), Conservatives spent 91% of the maximum, and Labour 87%. Money is not essential to success. George Younger spent only £682 defending his safe Conservative seat in Ayr while Ernest Armstrong only spent £666 in his even-safer Labour stronghold of North-West Durham. Jocelyn Cadbury gained Northfield for the Conservatives on £1472 (50% of the maximum) and David Samuel failed by only 618 votes to win Mitcham and Morden on an outlay of £1242.

Looking back on the campaign, candidates recognised that the party's message was essentially carried by the party leaders via the television screens — they only offered a small sideshow. Labour candidates expressed warm appreciation for Mr Callaghan's campaign. But there was a general complaint about the party's general lack of vision and positive policies for the future. Candidates fell back on a defence of the government's record, and warnings about the policies which would be pursued by a future Conservative government. Labour candidates seem to have spent at least as much time talking about Mrs Thatcher as about Mr Callaghan. Many reported that she was important in hardening the loyalty of party activists and usually evoked negative reactions on the doorstep. Few Conservative candidates or organisers suggested that Mrs Thatcher was a plus with the voters.

Labour candidates were unanimous in regarding the result a massive rebuff for their party. Defeat was not softened by its being regarded as inevitable after the events of the winter and the slow rise in living standards over the previous four years. Some candidates still had hopes of Labour winning, or of forcing a hung parliament. They were depressed at the reactions of housewives and skilled voters over council house sales, and the promise of tax cuts. More than a few candidates dismissed the verdict as 'a vote for greed'. The Conservatives welcomed the outcome as a return to the two-party system, although a few noted that the Liberals were still poised to threaten the Conservatives. The general feeling among Conservatives was that it was a vote for change, yet more a vote against Labour than an expression of firm commitment Conservative policies.

16 The Campaign in Retrospect

Post-election analyses are always open to charges of retrospective wisdom. It does not follow, however, that they should be avoided. The fact is that party strategists themselves spend time examining the campaign and wondering how they might have done things better. Politicians also seize on the issues, themes and outcomes of an election as tools in debates about the policies and the leadership of the party. There were protracted post-mortems following Labour's defeats in 1959 and the Conservative losses in 1974. In 1979 Labour continued the process. But the Conservatives' margin of victory was so clear cut that it is not plausible to single out any one event or decision in the campaign that might have made a basic difference to the outcome. To a large extent the parties were playing out the hands that had been dealt to them by the events of the preceding months.

To talk of 'the campaign' conveys an impression of single purpose organisations and of a concentrated activity in which workers, the rank and file, the candidates, and the officials at the centre work together towards agreed goals. In all party headquarters we heard arcane discussion about 'pacing' and 'peaking', and analogies with military campaigns were inescapable.[1] It is misleading, however, to impute business-like rationality, careful planning and well-considered election strategies to the British parties, notwithstanding their claims to the contrary. Election campaigns are characterised by *ad hoc* decisions, accidents, routines and inertia, day-to-day reactions to events, flashes of individual intuition as well as attempts at planning. The party leaderships certainly operated within loose guidelines

[1] For example, several Conservatives compared their strategy to Dien-Pien-Phu; i.e., it was a holding operation. Another compared Heath's speaking tour to the late arrival of Blucher at the battle of Waterloo.

covering timing, their party's strong and weak issues, the allocation of their time, the identification of target voters and the
division of labour between different people. But participants in
election campaigns are often highly individualistic, pursuing
their own concerns and, at the local level, almost all are volunteers. The correlation between the goals of strategists in Smith
Square and what actually happens in the constituencies may be
quite tenuous.

Travelling around the country, and talking to strategists both
in London and the constituencies, we were struck by the extent
to which people went through established routines of canvassing,
addressing meetings, telephoning and posting literature, while
apparently giving little thought to the usefulness of these
activities. Pollsters, publicists, organizers and candidates were
primarily wrapped up in their own worlds. Candidates and
agents were rarely sure whether 'electoral reality' was to be
found in the constituencies or in Smith Square.[2] Growing
awarness of volatility had made campaigners less sure about the
electoral mood. Remarks by strategists in Smith Square give
some flavour of how people approach election campaigns:

'My job? To win the election.'   (Conservative official).
'To sell Margaret Thatcher.'   (Conservative publicist).
'To win the argument.'   (Labour researcher).
'To win the battle for policies for the next Parliament.'
                                                    (Labour policy adviser).
'To sit tight on our lead.'   (Conservative Shadow Minister).
'What the hell can we do? It's up to the Liberals if we're to
    be saved.'   (Labour official).

It was understandable that many observers professed to find
it a boring election. The absence of unexpected or diverting
events, or *gaffes* by major personalities centainly starved them
of headlines. It was difficult to sustain interest in a lengthy
campaign which had so long been anticipated. And both leaders
fought in a deliberately low-key way, though Mr Callaghan's
morale and patience were tested by the persistence of the
'Troops Out' hecklers. Opinion polls found that levels of interest,

---

[2] One Labour minister wrote: 'It's a media election. My mood flutters with the
polls. There is so much wishful thinking and it's so easy to lose all power of judgement.'

determination to vote, and caring about which party won (52% according to Gallup) were all higher than in 1970 or October 1974. The eventual turnout confirmed the voters' interest in the election.

The election was more than ever dominated by the mass media. It was not that the mass media provided more coverage than usual; in fact, as Chapters 10 and 11 showed, they did not. The influence was reflected in the conduct of the campaign.[3] The morning press conferences were timed to provide stories for the mid-day news bulletins, the leaders' afternoon walk-abouts were staged for the benefit of local and national evening news broadcasts, and their major speeches were scheduled to catch the 9 p.m. and 10 p.m. bulletins. Some experienced observers detected an important change in the content of election campaigns, one which was not always welcome. As David Wood commented in the European edition of *The Times* of April 30:

> There has been no leader's election campaign before the war or since that so blatantly exploited modern communications in public relations terms. Words were at a discount. The writing press were the spears in a Shakespearian play who march on and off looking like an army. To adapt McLuhan, the picture was the message and the message was the picture. Perhaps the public relations men were right: if you are ahead in the opinion polls, show business is the answer and you may be as apolitical, anti-verbal, anti-rational as you wish.

Expectations of a bitter election were not borne out. Private polls for the main parties warned of the public dislike of an adversarial style. Mr Callaghan was determined not to make

[3] Increased press advertising combined with inflation to make it the costliest of elections since 1964. The Labour party estimated the cost of their central campaign from March 28 to May 3 at about £1 m (excluding some regional expenditure). The Liberal party say that their campaign, including headquarters expenses, national press publicity and broadcasting as well as David Steel's tours, cost £135,000 (excluding Scotland and some regional expenditure). The Conservatives, whose accounting year ends on March 31, had more difficulty in arriving at a comparable estimate, but it seems that the figure must have been around £1,300,000. For details of Labour campaign finance see the speech of Norman Atkinson, the party Treasurer, to the Labour Party Conference October 3, 1979. For a full discussion of 1979 campaign finance see M. Pinto-Duschinsky's chapter in H. Penniman ed. *Britain at the Polls 1979* (Washington, 1980).

personal attacks on Mrs Thatcher. He rarely mentioned her by name, preferring to refer impersonally to the leader of the Conservative party. His own calculation was not only that women voters would be alienated by personal attacks on a woman, but also that the electorate was in no mood for them. Conservatives concurred with this interpretation of the popular temper. They preferred a quiet campaign; they were firm favourites and they knew the danger of prompting a Liberal upsurge. 'There's a lot of Liberal in all of us', said Lord Thorneycroft, and the party's private poll showed the potential for a Liberal breakthrough.

There were many reports from the constituencies that voters were in a serious frame of mind, and the Conservative private polls showed that they were blamed slightly more than Labour for 'slanging'. Central Office toned down the election broadcasts after the negative reaction to the party's first one (see p. 223).

The public polls showed only a limited change in the two main parties' shares of the vote. But this overall stability masked some shift in voting intentions by individuals. A MORI *Sunday Times* panel found that 24%, or 8 million electors, changed their voting intention at least once, with the movements between the two main parties nearly cancelling each other out. This volatility, however, was on a smaller scale than in the three previous elections: in October 1974 one third of the voters had changed their minds in the campaign. A likely explanation for the greater stability of voting intention was that the campaign had been so long anticipated that more voters had made up their minds.

Though the pollsters measured the prevailing dissatisfaction with the *status quo* and a general desire for a new approach, the situation was actually quite complex. On the most salient issues, proposals for trade union reform and taxation were the only ones on which voters preferred the Conservative position by a decisive margin; there was unease about Mrs Thatcher herself. There was no general support for tax cuts if this involved a reduction in government services (see p. 342). But once a government has had a fair time in office, 'time for a change' is the most compelling of slogans for any opposition party. Mr Callaghan knew this and found it as difficult to overcome as the incumbent Conservatives had done in 1964. Conservative private polls showed that 78% of all voters (including 40% of Labour voters) agreed that it was time for a change. Labour's private polls, though bearing out the desire for change, also found that voters thought the situation regarding jobs, strikes and prices would actually be worse with a change of government. The public believed, however, that the average person's take-home pay would be higher under the Conservatives.

There was uncertainty about how to read this mood in all political parties. There was some resignation in Liberal and Labour quarters in the first two weeks of the campaign, when the opinion polls showed little movement. But all parties eventually found reasons for some cheer. Canvass returns and impressionistic reports suggested that Labour's vote was holding up; there was a good response in their traditionally strong areas in the North, and they hoped that 'don't knows' offered prospects of gains. But, as more detached Labour people knew, they had to improve on the 1974 vote if they were to win the election. Labour strategists had been conditioned by the experience of the February 1974 campaign. Then they had managed to shift the campaign onto the preferred ground of prices and away from the 'who governs?' issue, and they had been rewarded by a late shift in votes. In 1979, however, the salience of issues, according to Mr Worcester's polls, remained disconcertingly static. The surveys showed Labour behind on all the important issues (except on dealing with the trade unions) and it was not clear what, if any, was favourable ground for the party. Even when Labour drew level on prices and jobs, the switch in votes did not follow. Moreover, some of his findings were depressing for party morale. In 1974 Labour had been far ahead on such questions as 'which party is best at keeping its promises?' and 'which party is best for people like yourself?' By the beginning of the election, the Conservatives were well ahead on these questions, though Labour did catch up appreciably as the campaign advanced. Mr Callaghan later spoke at the October 1979 Labour Conference of his shock at a poll report during the campaign that the Tory Party was regarded as having more concern for ordinary people than the Labour party.

Liberals were encouraged by the reports from constituencies and, perhaps implausibly, saw the late rise in the opinion polls as a catching-up with reality. There was much goodwill for the party. Conservative private polls found that a third of Labour and Tory voters favoured giving the Liberals 'a chance'. But one daunting finding for Liberals was that the mood for change appeared to be coupled with a desire for a clear result. A MORI poll found that only 20% of voters thought it would be a good thing if no party got a clear majority. And only 35% of Liberal voters favoured a deadlock, compared with 53% who thought it would be bad for the country.

Conservative strategists never entertained the idea of a Labour win. Their private polls suggested that some ground was being lost among pensioners, who were particularly concerned about higher indirect taxes; they also pointed to a general unease about the party's abillity to co-operate with the unions, and a failure to pin responsibility on Labour for rising prices. In the last weekend some insiders certainly feared that the rise of the Liberal vote might produce a deadlocked parliament. When the MORI poll reported a narrowing of the Conservative lead to 3 points, a worried Mrs Thatcher could find some consolation in the party's polls which actually reported an increase in the Conservative lead. But the private polls and their own soundings failed to present clear signals for any change in strategy. In retrospect Conservatives were pleased that, in spite of negative reactions to the low-key campaign and to their first election broadcast, they stuck to their strategy. They largely ignored Labour questions and accusations. (But had they lost the election, strategists were anticipating a formidable indictment of 'the do-nothing Central Office'.) They had a clear idea of who their target voters were — the first time voters, 1974 Liberals, and C2 housewives — and they made strong gains among the first two.

The campaign was more presidential than ever, as the broadcast coverage showed (see p. 211). The secondary political figures had little impact. Mr Foot and Mr Benn were almost ignored and, in spite of the importance of the economy as an issue, Mr Healey and Sir Geoffrey Howe did not receive extended media coverage. If a message was to get across, it had to be via the party leader. Mrs Thatcher's sex and personality inevitably coloured the leadership issue. Both Conservative and Labour strategists were aware of something called the 'Thatcher factor', although they were not very clear what they meant by it. But the question, 'would she stand the strain of prolonged exposure?' was more a Labour hope than a Conservative fear.

Conservatives were remarkably self-critical about their campaign. The *Economist*, which supported Mrs Thatcher, and thought that the outcome had never been in doubt, commented:

> She has emerged as a leader uncertain under pressure and she
> has yet to demonstrate an ability to inspire great confidence
> or affection among the uncommitted voters, let alone among
> those who voted against her. Her shadow cabinet did not
> come through strongly when pitted against an experienced,
> self-confident Labour cabinet.

Peter Jenkins noted in the *Guardian* on May 2, 'By general
consent Labour has won the campaign even if not quite the
election.' The most frequently heard criticism was that the
Conservative campaign had, under Labour's onslaught, lost
momentum. Though Mrs Thatcher dominated the media coverage
of the Conservative compaign and was the ablest communicator
in the shadow cabinet, she fell steadily behind Mr Callaghan,
according to the polls, as the campaign progressed. She was 7
points behind the Labour leader at the outset of the campaign,
and 19 points behind at the end. At the end of April, Gallup
showed that Mr Callaghan had improved his ratings from 40% to
44%, David Steel from 14% to 22%, while Mrs Thatcher declined
from 33% to 25%. Even among Conservatives only 56% thought
that Mrs Thatcher would make the best Prime Minister compared
to 43% who thought that Mr Callaghan would do a better job.

The difficulties with Mrs Thatcher's image were illustrated
in a MORI poll (*Economist*, April 28) which showed that
her personality as much as her sex seemed to be turning potential
supporters away from the Conservative party. The characteristics
on which Mrs Thatcher generally fell behind Mr Callaghan were
that she was perceived as being less experienced, less in touch
with ordinary people, more extreme and more condescending.
But sex was a factor; voters decisively preferred a man as Prime
Minister, and when offered the choice of Mr Heath as the
Conservative leader the Tory lead shot up from 5% to 18%.
Women divided evenly in their support for Mr Callaghan or Mrs
Thatcher, while men preferred the former by a 2 to 1 majority.

Labour strategists wondered whether Mrs Thatcher would be
'unmuzzled' or carefully restrained in her public utterances.
Some Conservatives appeared to be haunted by memories of the
February 1974 election, when the Conservatives had been
regarded as the more divisive and negative party. They had to

soften the leader's image and avoid any impression of aggressiveness. This had been an important consideration in rejecting the television debate. Mrs Thatcher frequently queried her staff about the 'tone' of her campaign, seeking a judicious blend of the crusader and pragmatist. There was some evidence of progress. She was generally thought to have outscored the other leaders in her appearance in the *Granada 500* programme. A MORI poll on which leader 'came across best' found that 46% mentioned Mrs Thatcher, 33% mentioned Mr Steel, and only 19% Mr Callaghan. When private polls asked which leader had had 'the best campaign', the response was Mr Callaghan 33%, Mrs Thatcher 33% and Mr Steel 29%.

By the final week the adherence to a low-key campaign and the narrowing of the party's lead was taken by some critics to indicate the party's lack of confidence in its policies. The decision to avoid any debate with the Labour party also meant that there was little critical examination of Labour's own manifesto plans and its cost. There were reasonable hypothetical questions to ask about Labour's assumption of a 3% growth-rate or what it would do if the February Concordat with the unions failed, as previous agreements had done.[4] The fear of being engaged in adversarial politics inhibited the party from tackling Labour claims more vigourously.

The frequent claims that spokemen could not provide further details until they were able to 'look at the books' wore thin by the closing stages of the campaign. Conservative strategists claimed that they had never anticipated such a vehement counter-attack by the Labour party. In fact, they had failed to develop an effective strategy for handling the inevitable questions about their public expenditure plans. The omission left Labour free to go ahead with their own costings of the Conservative programme and to exploit fears about the consequences for unemployment, prices and the Welfare State. Once again it appeared that the Conservatives lacked good communicators who could press home their advantage on the tax issue. The economy was the battleground and Sir Geoffrey Howe was not a compelling speaker, certainly not when set against Mr Healey. Mrs Oppenheim was not impressive on prices when pitted against Mr Hattersley, and Francis Pym appeared hapless on a *Panorama*

[4] See 'What if the Concordat Collapses?' *Guardian*, (April 28, 1979).

television interrogation when it turned to Conservative economic policies.

The Labour campaign was effectively Mr Callaghan. He took the major decisions, dominated the daily meetings of the Campaign Committee, and when he declared his lack of interest in a particular idea this effectively killed further discussion. Hopes among party officials that there would be close relations with Transport House were not borne out. There were not the jealousies and tensions that Harold Wilson's association with his personal entourage had created in the past. But Mr Callaghan's main strategy discussions were held with a small group of aides in Downing Street at the end of each day (see p. 174). On day to day tactics and preparation of the first four election broadcasts, Transport House was by-passed. The party machine lacked any figure of Lord Thorneycroft's weight to act as a campaign manager. There was little attempt to orchestrate the speeches of Labour ministers and hardly any contact with senior figures. Mr Callaghan's personal dominance was neatly captured during a television programme when his political adviser, David Lipsey, said, 'It's Jim's campaign'.

There was the maximum exposure of Mr Callaghan – the party's chief asset. The calculation was that the more he was seen, the more wavering voters might focus on the leadership factor. He came over as tough but fair, wanting cooperation between all sections of society, and avoiding risks or confrontation. In an eve-of-poll interview with Robin Day he accepted the validity of a comparison with Stanley Baldwin, the Conservative Prime Minister who had helped to soothe class bitterness in the inter-war years. Yet he was also reluctant to be seen following the highly personal campaign style of Harold Wilson in 1970. Some advisers felt later that he should have fought an even more personal campaign, because he had greater personal strengths than Mr Wilson. However, there was unstinting admiration for Mr Callaghan's campaign among both Transport House officials and Cabinet colleagues. As one of them expressed it midway through the campaign, 'Jim has not put a foot wrong.'

Yet as memories of the campaign receded, so some Labour strategists complained about Mr Callaghan's failure to mount a frontal attack on Mrs Thatcher. Having originally asked his staff for 'broken bottles', he was reluctant to use them. A more vehement campaign would probably have helped the Liberals, as voters, saying 'a plague on both your houses', turned to them, and the Conservatives would have lost from such a development. But the evidence of the private polls was that, whoever did the slanging, both parties were blamed fairly equally.

Labour's target was its traditional Labour voters. The awkward question, however, was that if the party had only gained 39% of the vote in October 1974, why should it do better in 1979? Conservatives, though impressed by the defensive nature of the Labour campaign, thought it only made sense if it was designed to prevent a Conservative victory; a defensive emphasis was no way to make converts. There were tactical discussions in the Labour camp about how to recapture the support of trade union members, first-time voters and young married women in the C2 class. The party's private polls stressed that a key issue was prices. Roy Hattersley, the minister with responsibility for prices, played a prominent role, and during the campaign a freeze was announced on bread prices and the powers of the Price Commission were stiffened.

Labour could also feel that it had effectively blunted the Conservatives' vote-winning issue of tax cuts. The surveys showed the overwhelming popularity of tax cuts. But when the question was one of trading off tax cuts against cuts in government services, the mood changed sharply. The BBC Gallup poll found that, by 70% to 30%, people preferred to maintain the services, even if this meant no tax cuts, rather than the reverse. The Conservative private polls found that 45% said they would be worse off with a change from direct to indirect taxes and only 25% thought they would be better off (see p. 342). On expenditure, Conservative voters were plainly more reluctant to cut defence and education, while Labour voters saw pensions, the health service and housing as more important. But there was a realisation in all the parties that many voters were deciding how to vote, not on the basis of the campaign and its issues, but in response to the memories of the previous winter and the desire for change. As one Labour MP noted, 'We have nullified the Conservatives' tax pledge but not the image of a hearse being turned away from a graveyard in front of a NUPE picket sign.'

There was nevertheless some substance to Labour's claims to have won the campaign. An averaging of the opinion polls during the campaign shows a swing of some 3% from Conservatives to Labour. The *Sunday Times* panel had a net swing of 4%

to Labour. According to the final Gallup poll, Labour's initial lead of 3% on the question of 'which party had the best leaders?' grew to 15% at the end. A Labour deficit of 2½% on 'which party is best for people like yourself?' was transformed to a 2½% lead. The party also whittled away a Conservative lead of 8% on 'which party had the best policies?' and drew level by election day.

Table 1 on p. 328 shows the changes in the electorate's confidence in the parties' handling of five key issues (a) over the long term, from August 1978 to May 1979, and (b) over the campaign period, from 4–6 April to 4–6 May. On most issues Labour improved its standing relative to the Conservatives.

But the Conservatives retained some advantages on key questions. Gallup found that 12% more Conservatives said that they were very interested who won and 11% more thought there was a lot of difference between the parties. There were other indications of greater Conservative commitment. All the polls showed the Conservatives supporting their party's issue positions more loyally than Labour voters. When the BBC poll asked people why they chose their party, 68% of Conservatives said that there was something they *liked* about their party; only 48% of Labour voters offered this positive reason for their vote.

The party may also have gained from opinion poll reports in the fourth week, which showed a narrowing of the Conservative lead. The BBC Gallup poll conducted on election day found that among voters claiming to have heard or read of an opinion poll the great majority of those expecting a Conservative victory thought that it would be a narrow one. In the last two days, the polls found a widening of the lead. Fear of a deadlocked outcome probably spurred enough wavering voters to give the Conservatives a more decisive victory.

The Liberals took some pride in David Steel's campaign. The disaster, widely predicted at the outset, was averted, and the party registered a steady improvement in the opinion polls. David Steel came over as an apostle of reason and moderation, and no party leader improved his opinion poll rating as much as he did. Again, the party showed what could be done with little manpower or money. The press unit, for example, often lacked a typist; only one person dealt with the leader's tours; and the regional organisation was patchy at best. Though the concentration of resources on the most winnable seats made sense, it was difficult for the party to profit from emphasising electoral and constitutional issues, given their low salience. The appeal for a deadlocked parliament, or a people's parliament as Mr Steel preferred to call it, was not easily made attractive to

Table 1. *Changes in Voters' Attitudes towards Major Issues*

Issue and party rated best	Campaign Panel				Change	
	Aug 78	Aug 79	Apr 4–6	May 4–6	Long-Term (a)	Campaign (b)
Industrial relations; strikes						
Con	32		35	39	+7	+4
Labour	41		36	41	0	+5
Con advantage	−9		−1	−2	+7	−1
Prices/inflation						
Con	31		36	44	+13	+8
Labour	40		33	39	−1	+6
Con advantage	−9		+3	+5	+14	+2
Unemployment						
Con	36		37	42	+6	+5
Labour	29		28	36	+7	+8
Con advantage	+7		+9	+6	−1	−3
Law and Order						
Con	42		49	58	+16	+9
Labour	24		19	19	−5	0
Con advantage	+18		+30	+39	+21	+9
Taxation						
Con	NA		48	54	NA	+6
Labour	NA		24	28	NA	+4
Con advantage	NA		24	26	NA	+2
Average Con advantage	+2		+13	+15	+10	+2

Source: Data derived from Market & Opinion Research International, *British Public Opinion: General Election 1979* (London: MORI, Final Report, 1979), pp. 57–88, 77. Table adapted from Richard Rose, 'Towards Normality: Public opinion-polls in the 1979 Election', in Howard Penniman, ed., *Britain at the Polls 1979* (Washington, 1980).

(a) Long term change from August 1978 to May 1979.
(b) Campaign change from 4–6 April to 4–6 May.

voters. And because the main parties did not indulge in slanging, there was less scope for the Liberals to appeal to the moderate centre. Once more a large proportion of voters (36%) told pollsters they would probably have voted Liberal had they thought the party would win many more seats.

It is always difficult to isolate the main theme of an election or to interpret what exactly voters mean when they agree that 'unemployment', 'rising prices' or 'trade unions' are the important issues. Even within the same party, people disagreed on the agenda of the election. Commentators and politicians had their own reasons for billing the election as a time of decisive choice. Party leaders opportunistically pictured the election as a choice between freedom and socialism, or cooperation and confrontation, or fairness and a free-for-all. And of course there was always Mrs Thatcher's personality which tended to polarise people. However, as any analysis of manifestos and strategies clearly shows, both parties were aware of the middle ground, though there was some dispute as to where this was located.

It is possible, however, to discern in the main speeches and manifestos of the parties certain salient themes. Voters were essentially invited to consider what kind of society they wished to see. Spokesmen for the Labour and Conservative parties suggested that certain decisive consequences would follow victory for one or the other side.

In considering the arguement of the campaign, there is a paradox: the opposition behaved like the government while Labour behaved almost as the opposition, with debate centering on what the Conservatives would do if they were returned to office. Mrs Thatcher justified the Conservative platform of cutting income tax, curbing public expenditure and reducing the role of government on three different grounds. First, there was the claim that the government was now doing so much that it was threatening the freedom of the individual. She argued that the levels of direct taxation and public expenditure were out of line with those prevailing generally in 'the free world'. There was, therefore, a 'moral as well as a material case' for cutting direct taxes. Second, there was the emphasis upon greater efficiency and incentives. Rather than answer questions about cuts in public expenditure, or who would 'lose' in the shift from direct to indirect taxation, she stressed that her policies would help create the extra wealth to generate more employment and finance public services. Finally, there was the need for a 'fresh start'. The manifesto promised 'a fundamental change of course', a break with the consensual collectivist politics which had prevailed since 1964 and had coincided with the increasing pace of the country's relative decline.

Conservative leaders have rarely tried to promote reform or win elections on the promise of making radical changes. That was traditionally left to Labour. Some of the claims and counter-claims of the parties have changed in recent years — which is perhaps an index of the extent to which Conservatives have felt on the defensive. In presenting the Conservatives as the party of change, Mrs Thatcher was, in a sense, acting as the 'disturber' or radical that Mr Callaghan portrayed. Mrs Thatcher was forthright in expounding her beliefs. 'Conviction politics' was the phrase applied to the style and substance of her campaign. She was determined to do things her own way; with a week to go to polling day and the outcome apparently in the balance, she rebuffed high-level suggestions to soften her line or to invite Mr Heath to a press conference.

In contrast Labour provided reassurance to those voters who were fearful of radical change. Labour leaders portrayed Conservatives as purveyors of theories which had been tried and failed in 1970 or, alternatively, of ideas which were new and untested. 'A Conservative government was', Mr Callaghan claimed, 'too big a gamble to take'. Of course, Mr Callaghan gave due emphasis to his record in bringing the country through the recession and called for a parliamentary majority so that he could carry on the fight against inflation. But the main theme of the government's campaign was a defence of active central government. (Ironically, Mr Callaghan himself had often warned people against looking to government to solve their problems.)

It was possible to detect in Mr Callaghan's speech echoes of President Franklin Roosevelt's speeches during the New Deal. Mr Callaghan defended the role of the government, firstly, as a protector of the family and the weak, through the provision of welfare services. Secondly, it was the promoter of advanced technology through its assistance to the National Enterprise Board and investment in the micro chip industry. Thirdly, it was the defender of the national interest, as seen in the government's vigorous campaign for reform of the Common Agri-

cultural Policy and Britain's control of North Sea oil. Above all, the government was a protector and creator of jobs, 1.2 million in all according to Mr Callaghan. The choice presented to the electorate was to trade off the direct tax cuts promised by the Conservatives for the social wage provided by the Labour party. Labour ministers' calculations were that only the very well-off would gain from the exchange. Essentially, Mr Callaghan was saying: 'Look at all the things goverment does for you', while Mrs Thatcher was saying: 'Look at the mischief done by big government.'

As the campaign progressed, so the cross-examination of the parties' claims pointed up the main areas of difference and agreement. The choice on May 3 was an incremental, not an absolute, one. As Peregrine Worsthorne commented in the *Sunday Telegraph* on April 29, 'Whatever happens in the election this week it is not going to make all that much difference.' Scoffing at the two parties' portrayal of what their opponents might do with untrammelled power, he continued: 'There will be neither revolution nor counter-revolution', and any change will be measured 'in inches not miles.' Most commentators thought that there was little scope for direct tax cuts, and that subsidies to industry would have to be phased out gradually or else there would be a large and unacceptable increase in unemployment.

If the area of choice was limited, this surely had something to do with how the parties conducted themselves during the campaign. For example, the most articulate spokesmen of radical change in the Conservative and Labour parties were Sir Keith Joseph and Tony Benn. Both, however, were carefully kept off the central stage. The Conservatives provided few specific details about the size of their public expenditure cuts. The public was asked to accept as an act of faith that the tax cuts would change the climate of opinion, liberate the energies of workers and managers. Finally, the remarks of Jim Prior on Merseyside, Margaret Thatcher in the North East and Teddy Taylor in Scotland provided reassurances to voters in these areas that regional aid would be continued.

It is interesting to speculate whether voters were presented with the sort of choice which they would have preferred. Surveys suggested that even Labour voters were disenchanted with the party's emphasis upon state intervention and close ties with the trade unions. There was no evidence of widespread support for Sir Keith Joseph's free market philosophy, and there was a general unease about how the Conservatives would get on with the unions. According to the Conservative private polls 60% of voters thought that a Conservative government would lead to trouble with the unions. Even a quarter of Conservative voters thought that Labour was the best at handling the unions. Peter Jenkins noted in the *Guardian* on April 17 that, whereas the more successful Western European economies combined a liberal economic strategy with collectivist social goals, such a programme was not on offer at the British election: 'We are obliged to choose between Labour's heavy-handed interventionism and the Conservatives' casual laissez-faire attitude.'

Both parties moved carefully on the issue of extremism. The conscious self-restraint of the parties was seen in reactions to the Southall disturbance and to developments in Rhodesia. There were attempts by Labour spokesmen to portray a future Conservative government as 'the most reactionary since the war', and Conservatives tried to invoke the devil-figures of Mr Benn, trade union power and the Trotskyites. But much of this scaremongering was carried by the tabloid press or non-politicians. Mr Callaghan was the more worried of the two leaders on this issue. At the final meetings of the Campaign Committee his patience snapped at the continued taunts by the 'Troops Out' movement at his rallies; he conflated them with Trotskyites and extremists. This was the background to his declaration on the *Jimmy Young Show* that he would retain the leadership of the party for the lifetime of the next parliament. At one stage he shouted to the Campaign Committee 'If we lose this election it will be because of the Trotskyites.'

Some poll evidence indirectly supported Mr Callaghan, though this was not accepted by all of his colleagues on the Committee. For example, trade unions were widely thought to be run by extremists and the trade unions were associated with the Labour party. It is difficult to isolate, or even weigh, the relative influence of extremism upon voting compared to other factors. It is likely that Conservatives on balance gained from the issue. The BBC Gallup poll on election day found that there were three times as many references to extremists in the Labour party as there were to those in Conservative party. The survey also found that, among those voters moving between Conservative and Labour, 20% of defectors from Labour mentioned 'extremism' compared with 14% of defectors from the Conservative party.

There are some differences in the polls' findings on the relative strength of the parties on the issues. The polls agreed that the four main issues were; Unemployment/Jobs, Prices/Inflation, Trade Unions/Industrial Relations, and Taxation. The BBC Gallup poll found that Labour was ahead on the first three issues but decisively behind on Taxation. Other polls, including the two parties' private surveys, gave the Conservatives a narrow lead on unemployment and on prices as well. We may plausibly assume that the parties were pretty level on these two bread-and-butter issues, with the Conservatives ahead on taxes and Labour on the unions. Labour therefore did well on the key issues, so well in fact that it appears difficult to explain the size of its defeat.

But if we look at the issues which concerned vote switchers then we gain an insight into why the Conservatives won. Jobs, prices and law and order are examples of what political scientists call *valence* issues, that is parties and voters are largely agreed on the objectives of more jobs and stable prices. But many voters doubted the capacity of any party to improve the situation. *Position* issues are those on which the parties take different stands, e.g. taxes, trade unions, and de-nationalisation. Here a voter's choice of party is determined by his own preference, his awareness of the difference between the parties, and his perception of which party will further his views. Those who decided to vote Conservative put taxes and law and order first. On both issues the Conservatives were clearly seen to have the best policies (see p. 328). The tax issue was particularly salient to those who claimed to be 1974 Liberals and first-time voters, two groups who shifted sharply to the Conservatives. The last-minute Labour voters, by contrast, put jobs first. According to the *Sunday Times* panel survey, there was a sharp fall in Labour's position on the four main issues in the last week.

An election, however, is not decided only by voters' reactions to specific issues. Participants were aware of a serious mood, a sense of concern, among voters. It seemed to be a compound of lingering resentment against the unions, and hope that the country's relative economic decline would be reversed, as well as a worry about what a new Conservative government might intend. In the event Conservatives were right to think that they would profit from this mixture of dissatisfaction and hope. During the winter, Labour's confident slogan 'Keep Britain Labour and it will keep getting better' had lost its power; new apprehensions conditioned the mood of the country.

17 A Watershed Election ?

On May 4, 1979 Mrs Thatcher, as Britain's first woman Prime Minister, stood on the steps of No. 10 Downing Street. As she entered her new residence she quoted St Francis of Assisi:

> Where there is discord may we bring harmony. Where there is error, may we bring truth. Where there is doubt, may we bring faith. Where there is despair, may we bring hope.

A few minutes earlier Mr Callaghan, wishing her well 'in the great responsibilities which fall to her', had observed 'for a woman to occupy that office is a tremendous moment in the country's history.'

Any change of government excites interest. But in 1979 expectations were particularly heightened. The new Prime Minister's sex, her personal style, and her declared determination to reverse the course of the country's recent history, raised the question of whether the election was a great turning point.

Every election generates its own myths, myths about what the politicians were saying, about what the electorate thought they were saying, and about what the electorate meant by its votes. The Nuffield series of studies had its origin in R. B. McCallum's desire to prevent the 1945 election from being as much misunderstood as the 1918 one had been. So before offering even a tentative verdict on the wider significance of the 1979 election, let us first summarise what can be learnt from the actual votes. The results are analysed in detail in Appendix I; the conclusions set out there by John Curtice and Michael Steed can be summarised:

1. Turnout at 76.2% went up compared with October 1974 — but not compared to February 1974. This was largely due to the differing age of the register. There was a slight trend to higher turnout in English big cities. No party gained significantly from changes in turnout.

2. Of those who went to the polls, 81% supported one of the

two main parties — the joint total was 6% more than in the 1974 elections but 7% less than in any other post-war election.

3. The Liberal share of the vote dropped by 5.3% in England and Wales but rose 3.6% in the Scottish seats where a comparison could be made. The Liberal vote per candidate (14.7%) was higher than at the end of the other two full term Labour governments in 1951 and 1970.

4. The Nationalist vote dropped in Scotland and Wales. Incumbent MPs suffered less than others, even though 10 out of 14 lost their seats.

5. Two ex-MPs polled strongly (Jim Sillars, SLP, 31% in Ayrshire South, Eddie Milne, 29% in Blyth) but no other candidates outside the main parties won more than 8%. The National Front, with 303 candidates, only exceeded 3% in 26 constituencies, and in every comparable case its vote fell compared with 1974.

6. In Northern Ireland, Ian Paisley's Democratic Unionists showed unexpected strength and the two seats gained from the Official Unionists in Belfast heralded Mr Paisley's further advance in the European elections a month later.

7. Swing between Conservative and Labour varied more than before. The main distinction was that it was 4.2% in North Britain — Scotland and in England north of a Humber-Mersey line — and 7.7% in South Britain.

8. In addition, there were exceptionally high or low swings in some clearly identified groups of constituencies:

High	Low
East London and its surrounding areas particularly previously strong National Front areas	Immigrant communities outside London
	University towns
Welsh speaking rural Wales	Fishing towns and east coast ports
Mining areas	Labour-held marginals
Some New Towns and car manufacturing centres	Large cities

9. The low swing in Labour-held marginals seems to have been due mainly to personal votes built up by the Labour MPs who had won these seats in 1974.

10. The Liberals did noticeably well in constituencies which they held or were close to winning in 1974. In most such seats they

limited the scale of the Conservative advance and held the tactical Labour votes won in 1974; in a few they drew additional tactical support from third place Labour candidates.

11. The Conservatives won fewer seats than they might have expected. If the swing of 5.2% (the highest in post-war elections) had been uniform they would have won by 350 seats to 258, not 339 seats to 269. The largest cause of this difference of 22 seats in the majority seems to have been the personal vote which saved the seats of some of the Labour MPs who won seats in 1974.

12. Fewer seats now change hands for each 1% of swing. This, together with the effect of minor party voting, has made hung parliaments more likely.

On May 15, 1979 in her first speech in the Commons as Prime Minister, Mrs Thatcher spoke of the election as a watershed. The Conservatives had won by a majority that brooked no argument. They were 43 ahead of all other parties put together, enough to guarantee a full-length parliament. The electoral uncertainty, which had continued since late 1973, was at an end.

But had Britain really swung to the right? If so, what did this mean beyond support for reduced taxation and, by implication, reduced state expenditure, and a few restrictions on trade unions? There were foreign observers who saw the result as part of the rightward shift manifest in recent West European elections; others pointed to the demand for reduced state expenditure reflected in the Proposition 13 referendum in California. The *Guardian* considered the result to be 'as positive an affirmation of faith as the British have contrived for three decades'. The *Economist* suggested 'the British people have voted for change'. The *New Statesman's* verdict was, 'not a defeat, a disaster'. Political scientists have developed the notion of a critical or realigning election, one which marks a fundamental shift among the voters, and leaves the balance of the political parties permanently altered. In May 1979 commentators wondered, as they had in 1959 after Labour's third successive defeat, if the party was doomed to permanent decline, or even a complete break-up.[1] But another characteristic of a watershed election may be simply that it overturns previously established ideas. During the

---

[1] See David Marquand, 'Inquest on a Movement', *Encounter*, (July, 1979), and Anthony King, 'The people's flag has turned deepest blue'. *Observer*, (May 6, 1979).

1979 campaign both Mrs Thatcher and Mr Callaghan agreed that the Conservatives wished to make a break with the mix of policies which had prevailed since 1964.

In fact, the 1979 election may not prove to be a watershed in either sense. When the Conservatives returned to office in 1951 and 1970 there was similar speculation about a Conservative counter-revolution. The resurrection of the theme in 1979 testifies to the continuities of post-war British politics. The Conservative gain of 7% in its share of the vote was indeed the biggest advance by either of the two main parties in any election since 1945. But the Conservatives' 44% was the lowest percentage support for any post-war government except in 1974 — 56% of votes had gone to candidates in greater or lesser degree opposed to Conservative policies. The Conservative recovery in 1979 supported the analyses of those who held that the party's collapse in 1974 was largely a function of the issues and personalities associated with the February election. Surveys then had showed that many of the defectors from the Conservative party retained a sympathy with its main policies and could be won back. There was, however, little evidence of any growth of permanent underlying loyalty to the party. Even on election day the BBC Gallup survey suggested that Labour still retained a fractional lead on the basic party identification question: 'Leaving aside this election, would you say you *generally* think of yourself as Conservative, Labour, Liberal or what?' The Conservatives actually seemed to be losing ground among the middle class, and whether they could hold on to their new skilled working class and trade union votes would depend very much on how the economy performed. Electoral victory might continue to depend as much on disillusion with Labour as on effective governmental performance by the Conservatives.

The evidence about the public mood also suggests caution about accepting that there had been a breakthrough in terms of ideas. The attitudes manifest on the doorsteps were familiar ones: high levels of direct taxation, trade union power, welfare payments to strikers, and continued nationalisation have been unpopular with a majority of voters ever since the mid-1960s. But, despite this and much else, during 1978 the Labour party was able to draw level with the Conservatives in the opinion polls and was regarded as the best party to handle the issues of prices, jobs, and industrial relations. In November of that year more than one Conservative shadow minister could speak in the blackest tones about his party's prospects. It was only the winter of discontent that blighted Labour's recovery. The Conservatives in two short months moved into a decisive lead on the key issues — prices and trade unions — as well as on voting intentions and ratings of the rival leaders. They managed to hold onto some of those leads up to election day.

The events of 1979 offer a good example of a government losing an election rather than of an opposition winning it. Mr Callaghan interpreted the election outcome as 'a vote against the events of last winter'. But this was surely too simple. The government's overall record, with the worst unemployment for more than 40 years and prices up by over 100%, was not inspiring. The Conservatives were well placed to catch the plum that fell into their laps. But it was the Labour movement that shook it off the tree. It is worth stressing that since 1959 no British government has won re-election at the end of a full term in office. In the country's declining position, the old rule about governments losing elections may apply more forcefully than ever. As one of Mr Callaghan's advisers complained, 'In today's world, it's jolly difficult for a government not to lose.'

General elections are not referendums on particular issues. Voters expressed no more confidence in the Conservatives' ability to do a good job on prices or on jobs than they had expressed towards Labour. The polls showed that voters had a good idea of the policies which a Conservative government would pursue: cuts on direct taxes, increases in VAT, and a reduction in spending on welfare and on industrial subsidies. There was overwhelming support for tax cuts[2], and yet when voters were asked specifically to balance tax cuts against reduced expenditure on health or education or pensions a very different picture emerged. As Table 1 makes plain, a majority expressed a willingness to accept the tax burden involved in maintaining existing social services. Table 1 reflects questioning at the beginning and end of the campaign and, despite a difference in question wording, the answers do not support claims of a swing to the right during the campaign.

[2] Our story ends on May 4. But it is worth noting that when the first Conservative budget on June 12 handsomely fulfilled the promises of direct tax cuts which voters had told the pollsters that they wanted, it proved the most unpopular budget since Gallup started sampling budget reactions.

FASTEN YOUR SEAT BELTS

Cummings

Sunday Express, May 6, 1979

Table 1.   Opinions on Government

People have different views about whether it is more important to reduce taxes or keep up Government spending. Which of these statements comes closest to your own view?

Taxes being cut, even if it means some reduction in Government services such as health, education and welfare.	34%
Things should be left as they are.	25%
Government services such as health, education and welfare should be extended even if it means some increases in taxes.	34%
Don't know.	7%

(Gallup survey March 21–26, 1979).

People have different views about whether it is more important to reduce taxes or keep up government services such as health, education and welfare. How about you? Which of these statements comes closer to your own view?

Cut taxes, even if it means some reduction in government services such as health, education and welfare.	30%
Keep up government services such as health, education and welfare even if it means that taxes cannot be cut.	70%

(BBC Gallup survey May 3, 1979).

Labour candidates knocking on doors were made very well aware that the Conservatives had approval for most of their main election pledges. Mrs Thatcher had asked for a 'last chance' to reverse the country's decline. Many voters were willing to gamble in order to bring about change. Sceptics could point to the similarities between her programme and Mr Heath's in 1970. There was the same commitment to trade union reform (though on a more modest scale), to free collective bargaining, to greater competition, and to a reduced role for government. There was the same inheritance — the problems of a growing

Table 2. How Britain Voted

(%)	Class			Trade Union		Sex		Age				All
	ABC1	C2	DE	Member	Non-member	Men	Women	18–24	25–34	35–54	55+	
% of voters	35	33	32	30	70	51	49	12	21	31	36	100
Con	59	40	34	35	50	45	45	41	43	45	48	45
Lab	22	42	49	50	35	40	36	42	39	35	38	38
Lib	16	15	13	12	15	12	17	12	15	17	12	14
Swing to Con since October '74	−1	11	9	8½	5½	7	4	8½	4½	8½	3	5½
Swing back to Lab in campaign	−½	4	3½	−2	3½	−1	5	3½	2	2	½	2

(*Source:* MORI).

rate of inflation, of intransigent trade unions, and of an increasingly uncompetitive manufacturing sector. Mr Heath had had to abandon some of his key policies before his administration was halfway through. Would Mrs Thatcher do any better? She had said she was prepared to confront the unions, to defend inequality and profits, and to argue that full employment was not the government's responsibility. But she was also a pragmatic person, and among her colleagues and her civil servants, she could face pragmatic arguments from those who did not share her views and who had to take immediate decisions on immediate problems. After a short time in office ideology has always tended to yield to practicality.

In the aftermath Mr Callaghan inevitably was blamed for not calling an election the previous October. He might not have won, but he would surely have done better. The winter of discontent must have been worth more than the 21 seats that gave Mrs Thatcher her clear margin over all other parties. It could be no consolation to Mr Callaghan that influential Cabinet ministers had agreed with him in September, or that Mr Wilson in 1970 and Mr Heath in 1974 had also mistimed their dissolutions. He could also be blamed for obdurately persisting in the 5% policy and for misjudging the mood of union leaders and workers in the new pay round. His success in turning around the nation's and the party's fortunes by 1978 eventually turned sour. Labour's left wing would agree with Mrs Thatcher that social democracy as a means of promoting economic growth had failed yet again — as it had with the Wilson government; what was needed to cope with the crisis of capitalism was an alternative strategy which would break sharply with the policies of previous Labour governments. The sense of disappointment with the Wilson and Callaghan records was shared by right-wing and centrist members. It was the left, however, who were able to claim that their own policies had not yet been tried.

The third successive election in which Labour had gained the support of less than 40% of the voters prompted questions about the party's future. Some post-election analyses of 'The Decline of Labour', with their demands either for more socialism or for less, seem to have overstressed the role of issues and ideology at the expense of more mundane factors. The tiny rise in the living standards over four years, and the events of the winter, were far more important than any failure to enforce planning agreements or to put through a Freedom of Information Act, or to produce a manifesto more in line with Conference sentiment. Such analyses forget that an election in 1978 might have produced a third successive Labour victory.

There are four types of explanation for Labour's reverse. First, there is the evidence that the party's position on many issues was opposed even by many Labour voters. As Anthony King remarked in the *Observer* the Sunday after the election, 'If it wants to reverse the defeat of last Thursday, the Labour Party will have to start showing greater respect for the opinions of the British electorate.' A bad defeat at the polls gives brutal emphasis to any divergence between a party's policies and the preferences of the voters. For Labour the rift had been growing for more than a decade.[3]

Secondly, there were the trade unions which many commentators made the main scapegoat for Labour's defeat. The three issues which surveys suggested were of most concern to the voters — unemployment, prices and industrial relations — all centred on the broad question of trade union power. The Conservatives had specific proposals that were popular with the great majority of voters, including trade unionists. The Labour party's traditional link with the unions meant that it could never have a free hand in this area. Policy towards trade unions presents a challenge with transcends party politics. Yet paradoxically, because Labour is so visibly close to the unions, the opinion polls show that it continued to be judged the party best capable of handling the unions, even though the actions and role of the unions were deplored.

A third source of Labour's defeat lay in its relationship with its working-class base. In 1959, Labour's reverse was attributed to its failure to retain the support of newly affluent workers. Social change in the form of higher living standards, wider home-ownership, increased public-sector employment and white-collar unionisation, had altered traditional class categories particularly among wage-earners. In 1979 the same trends were noted again. Labour had lost most ground among the skilled working class. Yet there is nothing inevitable about affluence leading to the assumption of middle-class values or to a switch to Conservative

---

[3] See I. Crewe *et al.* 'Partisan Dealignment in Britain, 1964–74'. *British Journal of Political Science* (July 1977).

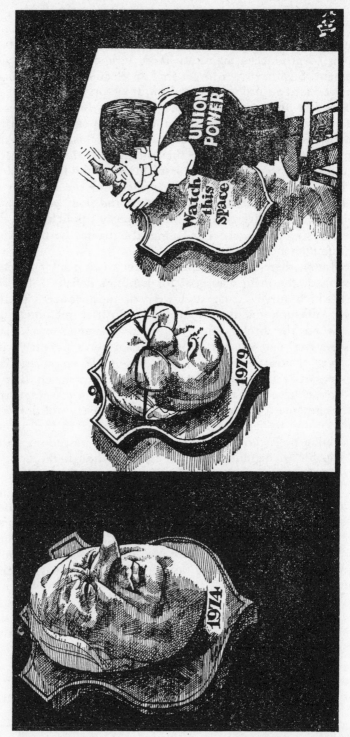

allegiance. What may have emerged is a new instrumentalism among the electorate, and with this a greater volatility in voting.[4] The number admitting a strong commitment to *any* party has declined. The skilled working class were peculiarly afflicted by pay policies and the squeeze on differentials; in 1979, as Labour candidates learned on the doorsteps, Labour's redistributive rhetoric may have combined with Conservative promises of tax cuts to shift the C2 voters. That is not to say that it turned them into life-long Conservatives.

A final type of explanation takes account of the failure of the economy to grow as quickly as our industrial competitors. Governments in Britain and elsewhere try to time the elections when incomes are ahead of prices, when the rise in real dispensable income is at its highest point.[5] In the 1950s and 1960s politicians in both main parties enhanced their prospects of electoral success by manipulating the economy, creating an electoral-economy cycle, as it were. As Richard Crossman stated with characteristic frankness in 1971, 'The main fact is that we won the 1966 election by choosing the moment of worst inflation before the prices had really been felt to rise and obviously we were seeking to do it again in 1970.'[6] But other events may cast a shadow over prosperity. Mr Heath, in 1974, held an election after an impressive rise in living standards — but he was overcome by voters' worries about his government's ability to deal with the unions and rising prices. In April 1979, living standards had been steadily improving for some 18 months, but the events of the winter took the gloss off Labour's achievements. The mood was not one of 'you've never had it so good', admitted a Labour MP.

Our questionnaire revealed interesting interpretations of the election's significance among Labour candidates. Most mentioned the winter of discontent as the main cause of the defeat. But there was also anxiety that their traditional vote, though still largely intact, was no longer sufficient; there was a feeling that the party had lost touch with middle-of-the-road voters, and

[4] According to the MORI *Sunday Times* panel, over 60% of voters mentioned 'interests' as explanations of their vote. Conservatives were more likely than Labour voters to mention policies (62% to 44%) while Labour voters more frequently mentioned leadership (33% to 25%) and tradition (49% to 33%).

[5] E. Tufte, *Political Control of the Economy*, (New Jersey, 1978).

[6] R. H. S. Crossman in 'The Key to No 10' on BBC Radio 4, April 11, 1971.

that it had to change its approach. There emerged a predictable division between the wings of the party about the way ahead. Candidates on the left blamed the leadership for losing touch with the unions and the party conference, notably over the 5% policy, and called for more 'socialist' policies of state control over the economy. But candidates on the right blamed Trotskyites and 'the looney left' for alienating voters. A number thought it was time to rethink the link with the unions; the unions immobilised the party in many areas; Labour lost popularity when unions went on strike.

Running through the answers from both left and right was the candidates' sense of how unattractive the party seemed to many of the voters who might have been expected to identify with it. An establishment MP said that Labour was now identified with bigness, bureaucracy and union bosses. A left-winger observed that many of his under-35 voters had little experience of life under the Conservatives, and saw Labour as the party of 'slums, decaying shipyards, immigrants, cloth caps and caring only for minorities and underdogs'. Neither the evidence of surveys nor the experience of candidates supported the idea that traditional Labour voters deserted the party because they wanted a more left-wing Labour party.

For the Liberals the result was a disappointment. Mr Steel had forecast the election of 20 to 50 Liberals, but in only two of their target seats, Richmond and West Aberdeenshire, did they even manage to narrow the Conservative incumbent's majority. It is true that actually to hold onto 11 seats was more than many Liberals expected but the broader strategy of winning proportional representation from a deadlocked parliament had dissolved for the time being; the Liberals held only 11 seats, and the Conservatives had a comfortable clear majority. During the campaign polls had shown two conflicting strains. There was great sympathy for the Liberals. Conservative private surveys showed that 37% of Labour voters and 33% of Conservatives thought it about time the Liberals had a chance. Yet MORI on April 17 found that only 20% of all voters actually preferred a coalition to a clear victory. David Steel had done wonders during the campaign in lifting Liberal support from 7% to 14% (granted the limited appeal of his basic party strategy), and as many as 24% of the BBC Gallup election-day sample said they would prefer him as Prime Minister to Jim Callaghan or Margaret

Thatcher. Indeed the Liberals, despite the fall from 19% in 1974, emerged from the contest with a larger percentage of the vote than in any other year since 1929, and their 11 members were widely distributed; no longer did a majority of them come from the Celtic fringe. There was a silver lining to their situation. If the Conservative government became unpopular, and if the Labour party were to quarrel, the Liberals were well placed for a new advance.

The Nationalists in Scotland and Wales had already been disappointed by the referendum of March 1. The defeat for devolution in Wales was so overwhelming that Plaid Cymru was more than ever driven back to its two strongholds, and to the three other predominantly Welsh-speaking constituencies; it was no surprise that its share of the vote in Wales fell from 11% to 9%. In Scotland, where devolution had actually won a majority of votes in the referendum, the electoral set-back was more spectacular; on May 3 the SNP lost 9 of its election seats and getting on for half its votes. But it still had 17% of the vote, and there were 8 constituencies where it was within hailing distance of victory. Like the Liberals, the Scottish Nationalists were left disappointed but still a force, with a potential for disturbing the British political scene in the 1980s. The same could be said for the politicians of Northern Ireland. The clear Conservative majority deprived their 12 MPs of the influence they had enjoyed since 1974; but they had all shown their independence from the British parties, and when, in the following parliament, they received their extra seats, they would have 17 MPs for the major party whips to worry about.[7]

The votes cast on May 3 revealed trends that were likely to have far reaching effects on British politics. Appendix II explores the continuing differences between north and south, and between rural areas and city centres, which over a generation have changed the party map of Britain, making the Labour party far more exclusively a big city and northern party than it used to be, and reinforcing the Conservative predominance in southern and rural representation. The careers of individual politicians, as well as the pressures on governments, have been transformed by the specific geographic and industrial develop-

[7] See H. Berrington 'Towards a Multi-Party Britain', *West European Politcs* (January, 1979).

ments which have changed safe seats into marginals, and
Conservative areas into Labour ones — and *vice versa*. But there
are more general trends which have occurred in recent elections
regardless of the separate issues and personalities associated
with each campaign. Also striking is the continued inversion in
the relationship between class and party. The middle class has
been shifting to Labour, while the Conservatives have increased
their strength among the working class. This tendency has been
paralleled elsewhere in the European Community.

The Conservatives have always attracted a sizeable minority
of the working class vote. Labour support in the middle class
was far lower, but it has increased sharply in the 1970s. Taking
the two main parties together, almost 40% of their support now
comes from 'deviant voters', people casting ballots against the
party that might, in an implicit way, be thought to represent their
class interest. The trend continued in 1979. The only group of
voters among whom Labour made inroads were the professional
and managerial groups, with many of the switches coming from
those who claimed to have been Liberal in 1974. But Conservative
gains among the working class were spectacular. *Table 2* shows
that among skilled workers there was an 11½% swing to the
Conservatives, with Labour's 1974 lead of 23% disappearing
altogether; the main leakage was in the 25—34 age-group. But
there was also a large swing, 9%, among the unskilled working
class, particularly among men. In 1979, Labour now held only
half (50%) of the trade-union vote and less than half (45%) of
the working-class vote. The appendix shows that there is no
simple relationship between social change and political loyalties.
We do not know how particular occupational groups in the
skilled working class moved. But such a sweeping change in
working-class electoral behaviour hardly bore out the claims of
some Labour spokesmen that the election had been a battle
between the haves and have-nots.

The Conservatives also made a striking gain among first-time
voters. Even in their 1970 victory, the Conservatives had been,
according to NOP, 5% behind Labour with the 18—24 age group,
and in 1974 they had actually come third, with less support
than the Liberals. Voting is for many a habit, and parties regard
the capture of first-time voters, with a lifetime of elections ahead
of them, as a special prize. This success was a bonus for the
Conservatives advertising campaign which, while aimed at young

voters, had been designed to impress them with the party's style rather than gain votes. On the other hand, the Conservatives were disappointed that they did not make more headway among women, towards whom they had directed their hardest sell. They were surprised that the swing was greater among men than among women. They were less surprised at the fact that Labour held its own among the over 65s; pensions were still a plus for Labour.

Labour does not seem to have suffered from special apathy on election day. Despite its poorer organisation and the disgruntlement of some of its supporters, the BBC Gallup survey found that of those who were definitely not going to vote, an almost equal number admitted to Conservative and to Labour leanings. But Labour's task in 1979 was not only to mobilise its traditional supporters, but to win new recruits; this it signally failed to do.

The votes in 1979 represented a qualified return to 'normalcy', to the two-party dominance that prevailed between 1945 and 1974. But there were still 27 MPs unattached to the two main parties — the average from 1950 to 1970 had been only 10. And the two main parties had only 81% of the total vote which, though an improvement on the 75% of the 1974 election, was far below the 92% average of 1950 to 1970. Labour's share of the votes, 36.9% was its lowest since 1931. The Conservatives' 43.9%, was only on a par with its post-war average, 43.5%. The clear Conservative victory in seats gave the party the prospect of a full five years in which to show whether its policies were adequate to master the nation's growing difficulties. It offered no assurance that the British political system was returning to the old certainties which had been so undermined in 1974.

Appendix 1: The Statistics

The House of Commons 1945–79

	1945	1950	1951	1955	1959	1964	1966	1970	Feb. 1974	Oct. 1974	1979
Conservative	213	299	321	345	365	304	253	330	297	277	339
Labour	393	315	295	277	258	317	363	288	301	319	269
Liberal	12	9	6	6	6	9	12	6	14	13	11
Plaid Cymru	–	–	–	–	–	–	–	–	2	3	2
Sc. Nat. P.	–	–	–	–	1	–	–	1	7	11	2
Others (G.B.)	20	–	–	–	–	–	1	1	2	–	–
Others (N.I.)	2	2	3	2	–	–	1	4	12	12	12
Total	640	625	625	630	630	630	630	630	635	635	635

National Results, 1945–79

	Electorate and turnout	Votes cast	Conservative	Labour	Liberal	Welsh & Scottish Nationalist	Communist	Others (mainly N. Ireland)
1945*	73.3% 32,836,419	100% 24,082,612	39.8% 9,577,667	48.3% 11,632,891	9.1% 2,197,191	0.2% 46,612	0.4% 102,760	2.1% 525,491
1950	84.0% 34,269,770	100% 28,772,671	43.5% 12,502,567	46.1% 13,266,592	9.1% 2,621,548	0.1% 27,288	0.3% 91,746	0.9% 262,930
1951	82.5% 34,645,573	100% 28,595,668	48.0% 13,717,538	48.8% 13,948,605	2.5% 730,556	0.1% 18,219	0.1% 21,640	0.5% 159,110
1955	76.8% 34,858,263	100% 26,760,493	49.7% 13,311,936	46.4% 12,404,970	2.7% 722,405	0.2% 57,231	0.1% 33,144	0.8% 230,807
1959	78.7% 35,397,080	100% 27,859,241	49.4% 13,749,830	43.8% 12,215,538	5.9% 1,638,571	0.4% 99,309	0.1% 30,897	0.5% 145,090
1964	77.1% 35,892,572	100% 27,655,374	43.4% 12,001,396	44.1% 12,205,814	11.2% 3,092,878	0.5% 133,551	0.2% 45,932	0.6% 169,431
1966	75.8% 35,964,684	100% 27,263,606	41.9% 11,418,433	47.9% 13,064,951	8.5% 2,327,533	0.7% 189,545	0.2% 62,112	0.7% 201,032
1970	72.0% 39,342,013	100% 28,344,798	46.4% 13,145,123	43.0% 12,178,295	7.5% 2,117,033	1.3% 381,818	0.1% 37,970	1.7% 486,557
Feb 1974	78.1% 39,770,724	100% 31,340,162	37.8% 11,872,180	37.1% 11,646,391	19.3% 6,058,744	2.6% 804,554	0.1% 32,743	3.1% 958,293
Oct 1974	72.8% 40,072,971	100% 29,189,178	35.8% 10,464,817	39.2% 11,457,079	18.3% 6,346,754	3.5% 1,005,938	0.1% 17,426	3.1% 897,164
1979	76.0% 41,093,264	100% 31,221,361	43.9% 13,697,923	37.0% 11,532,218	13.8% 4,313,804	2.0% 636,890	0.1% 16,858	3.2% 1,043,755

*University seats are excluded: other 1945 figures are adjusted to eliminate the distortions introduced by double voting in the 15 two-member seats then existing.

†See p. 418–20 for the votes cast for minor parties in 1979.

Regional Results

The tables on the following pages are based on the Standard Regions and the Conurbations, as defined by the General Register Office before the 1974 reorganisation of local government. Constituency boundaries in 1979 were still based on pre-1974 local government boundaries.

South-East includes Hants., Berks., Oxon., Beds., Herts., Essex, Surrey, Sussex, Kent and Greater London.

South-West includes Dorset, Devon, Cornwall, Somerset, Glos. and Wilts.

East Anglia includes Norfolk, Suffolk, Cambs., and Hunts.

East Midlands includes Lincs. (less Lindsey), Notts., Leics., Northants. and Derbys. (less the High Peak Constituency).

West Midlands includes Hereford, Worcs., Warwicks., Staffs. and Salop.

Yorkshire includes the East and West Ridings, the York constituency and Lindsey.

North-West includes Cheshire, Lancs. and the High Peak constituency.

Northern includes the North Riding, Durham, Northumberland, Westmorland and Cumberland.

Industrial Wales includes Glamorgan, Monmouthshire and the Llanelli constituency.

Industrial Scotland includes all of Ayrshire, Bute, Renfrewshire, Dunbartonshire, Lanarkshire, Stirlingshire, Clackmannan, Midlothian, West Lothian and Fife (except for the East Fife constituency).

The sub-regions are largely self-explanatory. When a city or conurbation crosses the boundary or a constituency, the constituency is included if more than half its population lies within the area concerned. The Clydeside conurbation includes Hamilton but not West Dunbartonshire.

The swing is calculated on the basis of all votes cast in each region or sub-region.

The Speaker's seat is treated as Labour.

REGIONS	Seats				% voting	Change in % voting	Con. %	Lab. %	Lib. %	Other %	Swing
	Con.	Lab.	Lib.	Other							
South-East Region	146	46	1	–	75.1	3.9	51.5	31.7	15.3	1.5	6.8
Inner London	10	25	–	–	65.9	5.8	39.9	47.2	9.6	3.3	7.1
Outer London	40	17	–	–	74.5	4.5	48.9	36.1	13.0	2.0	6.2
Rest of Region	96	4	1	–	77.5	2.8	54.9	26.6	17.5	1.0	6.9
South-West Region	37	5	1	–	79.2	2.2	51.3	24.8	22.7	1.2	6.3
Devon and Cornwall	13	1	1	–	79.1	2.0	52.8	19.1	26.5	1.6	6.3
Rest of Region	24	4	–	–	79.2	2.2	50.5	27.6	20.8	2.1	6.2
East Anglian Region	13	3	1	–	78.2	2.3	50.8	32.6	16.0	0.6	5.0
East Midlands Region	20	16	–	–	77.9	3.0	46.6	39.6	12.8	1.0	6.0
West Midlands Region	31	25	–	–	75.3	3.2	47.1	40.1	11.5	1.3	6.7
Conurbation	11	16	–	–	72.4	3.6	46.1	44.3	7.9	1.7	7.1
Rest of Region	20	9	–	–	77.6	2.7	47.9	36.9	14.2	1.0	6.3
Yorkshire Region	19	34	1	–	74.7	3.4	38.8	44.9	15.4	0.9	4.5
Conurbation	7	13	1	–	75.0	2.9	38.9	44.5	15.6	1.0	3.6
Rest of Region	12	21	–	–	74.5	3.5	38.7	45.2	15.3	0.8	4.8
North-West Region	31	45	2	–	76.2	2.9	43.7	42.6	13.0	0.7	3.2
S.E. Lancashire Conurbation	6	22	1	–	76.4	3.7	41.3	45.0	13.0	0.7	3.4
Merseyside Conurbation	6	7	1	–	73.4	3.5	42.1	43.7	13.5	0.7	4.6
Rest of Region	19	16	–	–	77.0	2.1	46.0	40.6	12.9	0.5	4.9
Northern Region	9	29	1	–	75.4	4.2	37.7	47.8	13.0	1.5	4.1
Tyneside Conurbation	2	8	–	–	73.7	4.6	35.0	53.9	10.2	0.9	3.8
Rest of Region	7	21	1	–	75.9	4.0	38.5	46.0	13.8	1.7	4.2
Wales	11	22	1	2	79.4	2.8	32.2	48.6	10.6	8.6	4.6
Industrial Wales	4	19	–	–	78.5	3.1	28.9	57.4	7.5	6.2	3.1*
Rural Wales	7	3	1	2	81.1	2.3	37.9	33.2	16.1	12.8	7.2
Scotland	22	44	3	2	76.8	2.0	31.4	41.5	9.0	18.1	0.7
Clydeside Conurbation	2	21	–	–	75.0	2.1	28.1	53.4	5.4	13.1	−0.6
Rest of Industrial Belt	6	19	–	–	78.2	1.4	29.8	46.1	7.1	17.0	0.7
Highlands	2	1	2	1	73.9	3.5	29.0	23.3	22.1	25.6	0.0
Rest of Scotland	12	3	1	1	77.5	2.5	38.3	21.7	13.3	23.7	

	Seats				% voting	Change in % voting	Con. %	Lab. %	Lib. %	Other %	swing
	Con.	Lab.	Lib.	Other							
England	306	203	7	—	75.9	3.4	47.2	36.7	14.9	1.2	5.8
Wales	11	22	1	2	79.4	2.8	32.2	48.6	10.6	8.6	4.6
Scotland	22	44	3	2	76.8	2.0	31.4	41.5	9.0	18.1	0.7
Great Britain	339	269	11	4	76.2	3.2	44.9	37.8	14.1	3.2	5.3
Northern Ireland	—	—	—	12	67.7	0.0	—	—	—	100.0	—
United Kingdom	339	269	11	16	76.0	3.1	43.9	37.0	13.8	5.2	5.2
BIG CITIES											
Greater London	50	42	—	—	71.5	+4.9	46.0	39.6	11.9	2.5	6.4
Glasgow	1	12	—	—	70.7	+2.0	25.8	58.0	4.0	12.2	−1.7
Birmingham	5	7	—	—	69.9	+4.0	44.6	46.4	7.4	1.6	6.7
Liverpool	2	5	1	—	70.0	+4.5	35.9	49.1	14.5	0.5	4.4
Manchester	1	7	—	—	73.1	+7.6	36.9	54.1	8.2	0.8	2.1
Edinburgh	4	3	—	—	75.1	+1.4	38.2	39.0	12.3	10.5	0.2
Leeds	2	4	—	—	70.6	+5.9	35.2	48.4	14.9	1.5	2.5
Sheffield	1	5	—	—	71.2	+3.5	33.9	54.3	10.9	0.9	3.5
Bristol	2	3	—	—	75.6	+3.1	42.7	43.3	12.4	1.6	5.2
Cardiff	2	2	—	—	72.3	−0.6	35.1	52.8	6.8	5.3	5.4
Coventry	1	3	—	—	76.1	+2.7	40.4	49.6	8.2	1.8	2.8*
Newcastle	1	3	—	—	71.1	+3.8	36.4	53.5	10.1	—	2.9
Teesside	—	4	—	—	73.1	+5.0	35.7	53.5	9.1	1.7	2.9
Bradford	—	3	—	—	71.4	+0.8	37.3	50.4	11.1	1.2	1.1
Kingston upon Hull	—	3	—	—	69.8	+3.2	29.8	57.7	11.5	1.0	2.3
Leicester	—	3	—	—	74.2	+4.4	39.9	48.9	8.9	2.3	0.8
Nottingham	—	3	—	—	68.9	+2.2	41.3	47.5	9.0	2.2	4.9
Plymouth	2	1	—	—	75.7	+1.0	50.7	39.6	9.2	0.5	4.4
Stoke-on-Trent	—	3	—	—	71.5	+3.4	30.9	59.4	9.5	0.2	3.3
Wolverhampton	1	2	—	—	72.3	+3.6	42.2	44.6	10.4	2.8	6.9

The Liberals fought only 577 of the 623 seats in G.B., which must affect these percentages. However they contested all but 10 of the seats in England. Only in Industrial Wales and each Scottish region were an appreciable proportion of seats left unfought. * If Cardiff West is excluded from the calculation (the Conservatives did not contest the seat in 1979), the swing in Industrial Wales is 4.3% not 3.1%: the swing in Cardiff itself is 5.4% not 2.8%. The shares of the votes in Cardiff are for all 4 seats.

Constituency Results

On the right-hand side the following tables present the election results with constituencies grouped by county (using the old administrative boundaries). A † indicates a seat won by a different party in May 1979 from October 1974. A ‡ indicates a seat that changed hands in a 1974—9 by-election.

The 'change in Lib.%' column shows the change in the Liberal % of the total vote in seats fought both in October 1974 and May 1979. A * denotes Liberal intervention in 1979. A figure in brackets indicates the Liberal % in October 1974 in a seat not fought in 1979.

Swing is presented in two forms (i) Conventional (or 'Butler') swing (the average of the Conservative % gain and the Labour % loss) is given only where the two main parties occupied the top two places in the poll, both in October 1974 and May 1979. This is the practice followed in all Nuffield Studies since 1955. (ii) Two party (or 'Steed') swing is calculated by, in effect, treating all votes not given to Conservative or Labour as abstentions; the swing is the change in the Conservative share of the Conservative plus the Labour vote.

The 'Other' column gives all individual percentage votes. The larger groups are identified

C = Communist Party (38 candidates)
E = Ecology Party (53 candidates)
N = National Front (the 5 candidates in Wales and the one in Scotland). There is a
        separate column for the 297 candidates in England.
M = Mebyon Kernow (3 candidates)
R = Wessex Regionalist (7 candidates)
S = Socialist Unity (10 candidates)
W = Workers Revolutionary Party (60 candidates).

Distribution of Census Characteristics by Constituency

On the left-hand side of these tables there are listed for the 623 constituencies in Great Britain (but not for the 12 in Northern Ireland) some of the more significant characteristics revealed by the 1971 census.

% Owner-occupiers: the proportion of households in dwellings owned or being bought by their occupiers.
% Council tenants: the proportion of households in accommodation rented from local councils.
% Non-manual: the proportion of economically active and retired persons in the Registrar-General's Occupational Categories 1, 2, 3, 4, 5, 6 and 13.
% Skilled workers: the proportion of economically active and retired persons in the Registrar-General's Occupational categories 8, 9, 12 and 14.

The last two categories are based on the more detailed questions put to 10% of the respondents to the census.

This table is designed to show the approximate rank ordering of all constituencies in the following tables as well as the range between the highest and lowest figures for any characteristic.

Ranking order in decile	Rank order in number	% Owner-occupiers	% Council tenants	% Non-Manual	% Skilled Workers
0%	1	0.7	4.0	18.3	7.2
10%	62	24.1	13.9	27.1	18.8
20%	124	34.1	17.8	30.0	20.9
30%	187	40.6	21.1	32.4	22.4
40%	249	47.8	24.3	34.5	24.0
50%	312	51.4	27.3	36.5	25.1
60%	374	54.5	31.3	38.8	26.6
70%	436	57.8	35.4	41.9	28.3
80%	498	60.8	40.9	44.8	30.4
90%	561	65.8	54.7	50.6	33.2
100%	623	82.2	96.9	69.0	45.2

In *The British General Election of February 1974* constituency data is available for (a) % over 65 (b) % with cars (c) % with New Commonwealth roots.

The British General Election of October 1974 provides constituency data for (a) % professional and managerial (b) % in manufacturing and (c) % with A levels. It also lists (pp. 326–8) the constituencies with significant numbers engaged in agriculture, mining or full-time study, as well as those with most Irish-born and most from the New Commonwealth.

The 'urban scale' divides constituencies into five categories, based on the % of the economically active population employed in agriculture (1971 census):

1. Big City   Constituencies in cities over 200,000 pop.   (137)
2. Other Urban Constituencies not in (1) with less than 3% agriculture (296)
3. Mixed   Constituencies with 3–6% in agriculture   (71)
4. Mainly rural Constituencies with 6–15% in agriculture   (77)
5. Very rural   Constituencies with more than 15% in agriculture   (40)

England

Constituency	% Owner-Occupiers	% Council Tenants	% Non-Manual	% Skilled Workers	Urban Scale	% Voting	% Change	Con. %	Lab. %	Lib. %	Nat. Front %	Others %	Change in Lib. %	Swing	Two-party Swing
Bedfordshire, Bedford	59.4	21.1	41.8	23.8	2	78.7	1.8	51.2	30.8	16.7	1.3	–	-3.3	6.6	8.0
Mid-Beds	52.5	24.9	37.2	25.1	4	81.3	3.0	56.9	25.8	17.3	–	–	-7.2	7.6	8.3
Bedfordshire South	61.3	25.6	38.7	28.0	2	79.9	1.6	56.4	28.2	14.4	1.1	–	-11.9	9.7	10.7
Luton, East†	56.6	19.0	33.1	28.0	2	77.7	4.2	43.7	41.6	13.0	1.1	C0.3, W0.1, 0.1	-4.7	5.7	6.9
West†	65.0	22.5	35.0	28.9	2	78.7	3.8	44.1	43.6	10.9	1.5	–	-10.4	7.6	9.7
Berkshire, Abingdon	53.2	24.4	42.4	20.3	3	79.5	3.7	53.7	24.7	21.1	–	0.5	-1.2	6.8	8.6
Newbury	56.8	22.7	41.7	24.1	3	79.3	3.0	52.8	10.5	36.7	–	–	-3.9	–	12.0
Reading, North	57.4	17.4	43.8	22.6	3	75.9	3.5	50.6	35.6	12.4	1.1	0.3	-7.0	7.0	8.1
South	63.5	19.4	44.5	22.4	2	76.5	1.8	53.9	25.8	19.1	–	E1.3	-10.6	–	7.1
Windsor & Maidenhead	57.9	19.8	49.0	20.2	2	75.4	3.6	59.7	20.7	17.8	1.4	0.4	-6.7	8.3	9.4
Wokingham	53.9	32.9	49.9	21.2	2	78.2	2.6	54.4	26.2	18.2	1.1	–	-9.3	7.2	7.9
Buckinghamshire, Aylesbury	50.8	29.5	40.1	22.2	3	78.0	3.6	58.2	24.2	17.6	–	–	-6.7	8.1	8.9
Beaconsfield	56.2	27.8	49.6	20.2	2	76.2	6.0	61.7	20.2	17.1	1.1	–	-9.1	–	9.9
Buckingham	50.4	32.8	34.0	28.7	2	78.6	-1.1	51.3	34.1	13.6	1.0	–	-6.6	6.3	7.2
Chesham & Amersham	67.6	17.1	53.8	19.0	3	79.7	1.6	61.4	14.3	23.0	1.3	–	-5.5	–	10.3
Eton & Slough	47.3	34.3	36.2	24.4	2	74.9	2.2	39.8	42.6	10.8	1.9	4.9	-6.9	6.9	8.7
Wycombe	62.8	22.3	42.3	26.7	2	77.6	3.3	57.3	27.0	14.4	1.3	–	-4.9	7.4	7.9
Cambridgeshire, Cambridge	41.6	28.4	48.0	18.9	2	72.0	2.5	45.7	37.1	16.6	0.6	–	-4.5	1.7	1.8
Cambridgeshire	52.9	25.9	40.8	22.3	4	78.3	2.2	56.5	24.6	18.9	–	–	-5.8	6.1	6.6
Isle of Ely	49.6	30.4	29.5	26.5	5	80.8	3.7	40.8	12.6	46.7	–	–	5.0	–	13.7
Cheshire, Altrincham & Sale	63.8	17.9	52.3	21.1	2	77.7	1.4	51.6	25.3	21.8	–	E1.4	-5.0	7.0	8.7
Bebington & Ellesmere Port	51.1	34.5	38.3	23.3	2	80.7	2.1	43.9	43.2	12.9	–	–	-1.7	5.1	6.0
Birkenhead	42.4	20.2	33.6	24.2	2	73.9	3.7	35.7	49.9	13.7	–	W0.7	-6.1	4.1	5.7
Cheadle	71.6	17.5	58.7	17.5	2	81.8	1.5	58.8	13.5	27.7	–	–	-7.8	–	5.1

4.1	3.9	−7.0	—	—	13.8	34.8	51.4	2.2	77.6	City of Chester	3	22.2	43.5	28.6	52.3
4.9	3.8	−5.7	—	0.8	11.8	48.3	39.1	4.2	77.5	Crewe	2	31.2	33.0	27.5	58.8
4.0	—	−10.5	1.5	—	29.4	15.1	55.5	1.1	83.4	Hazel Grove	2	20.3	55.7	16.2	75.2
5.5	6.6	−7.5	—	—	18.9	20.0	59.6	1.2	78.0	Knutsford	4	19.6	47.0	22.4	60.8
7.5	3.9	−3.2	—	—	17.1	24.5	58.5	−0.6	78.1	Macclesfield	3	24.8	40.8	29.2	58.8
4.3	4.4	−6.8	—	1.6	12.9	35.2	50.3	3.1	79.3	Nantwich	4	25.9	34.9	28.5	54.3
4.6	3.3	−6.5	—	—	14.4	32.9	52.8	2.3	80.9	Northwich	2	24.4	36.5	26.3	56.6
3.6	3.7	−3.2	—	—	13.7	34.8	51.5	0.2	77.8	Runcorn	2	22.9	43.3	22.9	62.0
5.1	1.8	−7.0	—	—	8.9	51.9	39.3	3.8	77.1	Stalybridge & Hyde	2	31.7	31.2	41.2	44.7
2.2	4.4	−5.2	—	0.6	12.0	44.1	43.3	1.5	79.5	Stockport, North	2	26.5	41.7	16.0	62.6
5.7	3.2	−8.3	—	1.0	11.9	45.1	42.1	3.1	77.4	South	2	27.3	34.1	31.4	51.1
3.5	5.9	−4.4	—	0.9	9.9	39.6	49.6	1.0	77.3	Wallasey	2	22.4	44.0	21.2	51.9
6.1	—	−4.6	—	—	12.9	28.1	59.0	2.3	77.8	Wirral	2	19.4	50.5	25.5	61.7
7.7	—	−8.8	E0.9, M1.7	0.5	35.2	6.9	54.9	0.2	82.5	Cornwall, Bodmin	5	25.9	34.0	19.5	59.7
7.4	9.6	−7.5	E0.9	0.5	43.7	3.2	51.7	5.5	86.1	Cornwall, North	5	26.2	33.6	15.8	58.8
11.7	—	1.2	M3.0	0.5	13.9	25.9	56.7	1.5	77.3	Falmouth & Camborne	5	28.2	34.4	18.0	62.7
7.4	—	−9.8	E1.0, M4.0	—	20.1	20.9	54.0	3.3	77.0	St. Ives	5	25.6	33.1	19.2	55.0
18.6	—	13.0	0.4	0.3	52.8	7.4	39.1	4.3	82.9	Truro	4	25.7	39.2	19.0	60.4
2.7	2.3	−1.6	—	—	11.2	49.7	39.1	1.2	80.0	Cumberland, Carlisle	2	27.4	35.0	45.1	42.5
2.6	2.4	−1.3	—	—	16.5	22.4	61.2	4.0	77.0	Penrith & the Border	5	27.2	36.6	16.7	49.9
7.9	6.3	−8.2	1.8	—	5.9	52.4	39.8	4.6	81.7	Whitehaven	3	31.8	29.2	39.2	38.8
6.8	5.6	−5.6	—	—	6.1	53.2	40.7	8.0	83.8	Workington†	3	33.3	30.8	23.1	47.4
6.6	5.6	−3.6	—	—	12.0	42.9	44.4	2.0	83.6	Derbyshire, Belper†	3	36.0	30.7	36.8	57.2
8.4	6.2	−4.5	—	0.8	8.9	66.6	24.5	3.8	78.3	Bolsover	2	45.2	21.0	36.0	37.1
5.8	4.4	−3.8	—	—	10.4	57.4	32.2	0.8	73.4	Chesterfield	2	35.6	31.9	31.9	40.6
4.0	3.3	−8.0	0.2	0.9	9.5	44.9	44.5	3.5	76.8	Derby, North	2	30.1	41.1	31.8	53.4
4.4	3.4	−4.9	W0.3, 0.2	1.1	9.6	50.0	38.7	1.9	71.4	South	2	30.2	33.2	25.2	54.2
7.3	5.4	−7.3	—	—	13.2	48.1	38.7	4.3	79.9	Derbyshire, North-East	3	35.5	34.3	33.6	49.5
7.7	6.8	−3.0	—	1.1	11.8	35.6	51.5	0.8	81.1	Derbyshire, South-East	2	31.7	35.9	22.1	58.6
6.4	—	0.0	—	—	27.6	19.9	52.5	2.2	80.7	Derbyshire, West	4	27.7	36.5	18.8	54.6
3.1	2.7	−4.6	—	—	16.9	36.6	46.4	1.3	81.8	High Peak	3	27.2	34.5	22.8	56.0
8.6	6.8	−3.8	—	—	13.4	50.6	36.0	3.2	78.1	Ilkeston	2	38.7	23.7	24.8	57.3
9.7	—	−11.4	E1.1, 0.2, 0.1, 0.1, 0.1	0.4	36.7	11.2	50.1	2.1	81.7	Devon, Devon North†	4	27.1	35.8	15.8	61.8

Constituency	% Owner-Occupiers	% Council Tenants	% Non-Manual	% Skilled Workers	Urban Scale	% Voting	% Change	Con. %	Lab. %	Lib. %	Nat. Front %	Others %	Change in Lib. %	Swing	Two-party Swing
Devon, West	57.8	15.3	34.3	27.0	5	78.6	-0.1	61.0	12.8	25.4	0.8		-11.5	—	3.4
Exeter	56.0	24.1	43.1	22.9	2	81.6	1.3	48.4	34.1	15.6	—	E1.9	-7.3	5.0	5.8
Honiton	62.3	17.2	40.6	20.0	4	77.4	1.8	62.4	14.4	20.8	—	E2.3	-9.1	—	4.5
Plymouth, Devonport	33.0	29.3	24.0	23.1	1	72.3	-1.1	44.5	47.4	6.8	0.7	0.6	-4.0	1.6	1.9
Drake	39.5	42.5	35.6	26.1	1	77.2	1.8	50.6	40.7	8.0	0.6	—	-9.5	4.9	5.4
Sutton	60.9	18.4	37.6	26.1	1	76.9	1.8	54.8	33.4	11.8	—	—	-10.3	5.0	4.9
Tiverton	54.1	21.5	38.8	25.4	5	79.3	1.8	56.7	14.0	29.2	—	E1.8	-7.6	—	6.3
Torbay	66.4	12.1	43.4	21.1	2	75.1	2.1	54.6	19.6	23.1	1.0	—	-5.4	—	6.0
Totnes	59.1	18.7	38.0	24.5	4	79.9	3.2	52.2	11.4	36.4	—	—	1.6	—	12.7
Dorset, Dorset North	62.5	16.7	41.3	21.8	4	79.7	0.5	62.2	11.7	26.0	—	—	-10.0	—	4.2
Dorset, South	57.0	19.5	36.3	21.6	3	78.3	2.9	55.7	29.5	14.9	—	—	-6.0	6.8	7.4
Dorset, West	50.1	22.6	38.5	21.3	5	79.0	1.1	58.7	17.9	21.8	1.1	R0.4	-6.5	—	8.0
Poole	65.3	16.5	39.0	23.3	3	78.1	2.8	57.0	22.4	20.5	—	—	-7.4	—	7.7
Durham, Bishop Auckland	42.0	39.5	28.8	28.4	3	74.7	3.8	37.9	48.7	13.3	—	—	-2.5	5.4	6.6
Blaydon	48.0	37.9	37.6	30.2	2	79.1	6.2	35.0	53.4	11.6	—	—	-6.3	7.0	9.4
Chester-le-Street	39.0	50.6	34.2	32.5	2	76.8	2.1	25.2	60.4	14.4	—	—	-3.7	—	9.6
Consett	38.0	39.1	28.5	34.4	2	75.8	7.1	24.9	61.3	13.9	—	—	-0.2	5.8	6.8
Darlington	58.3	23.2	39.1	29.4	2	78.4	4.0	43.4	45.5	10.2	0.9	—	-6.6	2.9	3.6
Durham	38.4	44.7	36.3	28.0	2	76.3	4.7	33.3	52.3	14.5	—	—	-2.4	7.4	9.2
Durham, North-West	38.0	42.1	24.8	30.8	3	76.0	4.9	29.6	61.3	9.1	—	—	-5.6	5.7	7.8
Easington	31.3	48.8	26.1	40.1	2	74.3	5.3	24.7	60.9	14.4	—	—	-1.5	5.7	7.1
Gateshead, East	26.3	57.9	31.5	31.9	2	75.3	5.0	29.9	61.2	8.9	0.9	—	-6.7	4.1	6.2
West	21.5	34.8	25.5	30.9	2	69.3	3.6	25.9	67.2	5.9	—	—	-3.6	2.7	3.6
Hartlepool	46.4	40.7	27.8	29.6	2	74.7	2.3	38.4	55.1	6.5	—	—	-6.8	0.0	0.7
Houghton-le-Spring	30.3	54.8	26.6	41.8	2	72.9	0.4	20.7	68.5	10.2	—	W0.7	-11.3	—	10.3
Jarrow	26.7	59.9	33.9	30.4	2	77.5	6.1	29.1	55.8	9.1	—	5.2, W0.9	-5.8	6.9	8.1

362

					Constituency										
24.1	46.4	30.7	31.7	2	South Shields	71.2	6.4	31.0	57.1	12.0	—	—	−5.3	2.7	4.6
32.1	51.9	26.7	33.7	2	Sunderland, North	69.5	2.5	32.1	57.5	10.3	—	—	−3.7	2.8	3.8
34.5	51.1	34.2	30.2	2	South	70.0	1.9	37.9	53.1	9.0	1.1	—	−6.0	4.9	6.4
39.4	56.2	39.6	26.6	2	Essex, Basildon†	78.0	4.2	46.9	40.5	11.5	—	—	−7.5	11.0	13.4
48.4	35.1	41.6	22.4	4	Braintree	80.9	1.5	52.0	31.4	16.6	—	—	−6.4	9.2	11.0
60.5	24.7	55.3	17.7	3	Brentwood & Ongar	80.6	3.4	60.4	25.3	14.3	—	—	−9.5	8.8	8.9
60.1	25.7	50.6	19.6	2	Chelmsford	81.0	1.8	49.6	8.9	41.6	—	—	6.3	—	20.7
57.4	22.2	38.7	21.6	3	Colchester	76.6	0.5	52.9	33.0	14.1	—	—	−5.8	5.6	6.1
55.3	32.4	53.0	21.2	2	Epping Forest	76.6	3.2	57.6	27.4	12.8	2.2	—	−6.3	7.9	8.9
82.2	9.0	45.3	25.1	2	Essex, South East	76.9	3.2	64.0	25.2	10.8	—	—	−7.1	11.6	12.3
19.7	75.1	41.5	27.6	2	Harlow	78.7	3.5	40.1	42.7	15.6	1.6	—	−7.4	12.9	16.9
72.3	11.1	39.6	24.0	3	Harwich	74.7	2.3	54.3	24.5	20.3	0.9	—	−3.1	6.5	7.9
71.1	14.7	41.8	24.1	4	Maldon	77.9	1.7	57.8	25.1	17.1	—	—	−9.4	9.6	10.5
54.0	23.4	39.3	23.2	4	Saffron Walden	81.6	3.5	53.8	19.9	24.9	0.6	0.8	−5.5	—	10.3
50.8	14.9	39.2	21.1	2	Southend, East	70.1	1.3	56.1	29.1	13.1	1.7	—	−6.8	7.6	8.5
66.9	9.7	51.3	19.5	2	West	76.2	3.1	57.7	16.3	24.6	1.3	—	−8.6	—	6.6
42.2	46.5	33.9	26.9	2	Thurrock	75.1	6.6	39.2	48.6	9.4	2.0	W0.4, 0.5	−10.6	10.9	14.1
					Gloucestershire										
53.3	32.7	30.2	27.5	1	Bristol, North-East	73.5	2.2	36.5	51.6	9.8	0.9	E1.3	−7.2	4.1	5.4
42.0	50.7	42.7	21.5	1	North-West†	81.3	2.1	48.6	39.8	11.0	0.5	0.1	−6.0	5.0	5.7
40.0	52.0	28.0	28.1	1	South	71.9	2.5	32.0	57.9	8.8	0.9	W0.3	−6.0	4.8	6.9
64.6	23.3	36.2	26.7	1	South-East	78.4	2.2	45.4	45.4	11.6	1.0	0.1	−5.4	7.1	9.0
43.2	4.0	53.9	15.5	1	West	71.6	6.2	52.6	22.9	21.0	0.6	E2.7, 0.2	−8.4	—	3.2
55.0	23.7	45.0	19.3	2	Cheltenham	77.6	2.6	51.0	18.3	30.0	0.7	—	1.9	—	9.5
52.2	22.9	39.0	21.4	4	Cirencester & Tewkesbury	78.7	2.0	56.0	17.2	26.8	—	—	−3.6	—	9.1
59.8	23.8	38.7	26.1	2	Gloucester	79.5	2.0	48.7	36.3	14.0	1.0	—	−1.0	2.6	3.1
66.6	20.3	45.5	24.5	3	Gloucestershire, South	82.1	2.4	51.2	29.4	18.5	—	E1.0	−4.3	7.4	9.1
61.6	21.9	33.4	27.5	4	Gloucestershire, West†	83.9	3.8	47.9	29.4	10.8	—	—	−6.5	3.9	4.5
70.3	22.3	42.2	29.2	2	Kingswood†	86.2	2.1	45.4	44.8	9.3	0.5	—	−8.1	3.0	3.6
59.8	23.7	36.8	26.2	4	Stroud	81.3	0.9	52.6	27.5	19.9	0.5	—	−4.8	6.2	7.2
58.4	19.0	43.5	21.1	3	Hampshire, Aldershot	76.5	3.6	57.5	20.7	21.8	—	—	−5.6	—	9.6
46.6	33.9	41.0	24.6	3	Basingstoke	79.5	2.6	54.1	26.5	18.5	0.9	—	−3.2	9.2	11.1
61.0	65.8	44.4	20.0	2	Bournemouth, East	73.1	2.6	62.6	18.3	16.4	—	E1.3, 1.4	−8.9	—	6.2
50.7	14.6	40.8	20.4	2	West	70.5	1.8	59.8	21.4	17.8	1.0	—	−6.4	6.5	6.8

Constituency	% Owner-Occupiers	% Council Tenants	% Non-Manual	% Skilled Workers	Urban Scale	% Voting	% Change	Con. %	Lab. %	Lib. %	Nat. Front %	Others %	Change in Lib. %	Swing	Two-party Swing
Christchurch & Lymington	69.1	14.8	47.9	20.9	2	77.6	2.9	66.0	14.9	16.9	—	E2.2	−6.9	—	6.2
Eastleigh	63.9	22.0	43.4	25.6	2	80.7	1.8	55.9	26.5	17.6	—	—	−5.5	8.2	9.4
Fareham	74.5	13.8	43.6	22.8	2	79.1	2.0	59.0	16.5	24.0	0.5	—	−9.1	—	8.1
Gosport	52.9	22.4	30.4	20.0	2	77.5	2.1	61.8	26.3	11.9	—	—	−11.7	8.4	7.9
Havant & Waterloo	53.5	36.8	40.7	22.4	2	75.6	1.9	57.3	24.5	18.2	—	—	−10.9	—	7.0
New Forest	65.5	14.9	39.9	23.6	3	77.2	3.0	59.5	19.7	20.8	—	—	−5.7	—	7.6
Petersfield	59.6	16.1	37.3	20.2	4	78.3	1.8	61.1	12.6	26.2	—	—	−8.4	—	5.3
Portsmouth, North†	48.1	31.9	31.8	24.5	2	78.7	1.8	48.6	44.4	6.2	0.6	W0.2	−3.6	3.4	3.7
South	54.5	9.8	34.6	22.8	2	72.9	3.5	54.7	31.2	13.2	0.9	—	−6.8	3.5	3.2
Southampton, Itchen	47.8	31.5	34.3	27.9	2	74.7	4.4	43.6	46.3	10.1	—	—	−5.6	5.4	6.6
Test†	43.8	31.9	40.7	23.2	2	76.3	3.2	46.4	42.7	10.9	—	—	−5.8	2.3	2.6
Winchester	44.2	27.3	40.1	19.8	4	78.0	2.8	56.0	22.5	20.9	—	R0.6	−8.8	—	8.2
Herefordshire, Hereford	50.8	28.8	37.4	23.1	4	78.4	2.6	47.7	14.8	37.4	—	—	1.0	—	15.1
Leominster	50.6	17.6	30.4	22.0	5	81.9	3.5	53.5	5.3	41.2	—	—	−2.7	—	9.7
Hertfordshire															
Hemel Hempstead†	41.0	47.7	46.3	24.7	2	84.8	3.1	48.7	42.3	8.1	0.8	—	−7.2	3.6	3.9
Hertford & Stevenage†	27.8	62.6	45.6	24.5	2	80.4	4.1	45.1	43.2	10.9	0.8	—	−7.3	8.1	10.1
Hertfordshire, East	60.9	24.7	45.5	22.8	3	77.8	3.7	55.5	26.9	15.2	2.4	—	−8.3	8.0	9.1
Hertfordshire, South	52.2	36.3	51.4	20.8	2	79.0	2.9	54.1	31.2	13.6	1.2	—	−5.5	9.2	10.6
Hertfordshire, South-West	57.7	28.6	51.1	20.9	2	79.7	2.7	54.7	27.7	16.2	1.4	—	−8.5	8.5	9.7
Hitchin	44.5	36.6	43.1	24.2	3	82.2	2.6	52.3	31.6	13.0	1.4	—	−3.3	7.7	9.2
St. Albans	61.3	20.6	53.7	18.6	2	80.4	2.4	53.1	23.1	23.8	—	—	−3.1	—	8.2
Watford†	57.5	22.6	40.9	25.1	2	81.3	3.9	47.6	40.3	11.2	0.9	—	−7.8	8.2	9.9
Welwyn & Hatfield†	35.0	57.1	50.3	20.4	2	85.0	3.7	48.6	42.8	7.9	0.8	—	−7.5	3.4	3.8
Huntingdonshire, Huntingdon	50.3	28.7	34.5	24.6	4	77.4	2.2	55.3	25.7	17.6	1.4	—	−7.7	7.1	8.0
Peterborough†	51.2	29.1	37.7	23.7	3	77.9	0.0	48.8	39.8	10.0	1.2	W0.2	−4.9	6.4	7.3

53.5	25.7	37.2	29.8	4	Kent, Ashford	76.7	2.1	55.7	26.7	16.2	1.4	—	−9.0	7.6	8.3
62.1	21.8	44.1	17.8	3	Canterbury	74.7	2.1	58.3	24.3	16.0	1.4	—	−6.3	5.1	5.0
55.9	24.8	41.9	28.4	2	Dartford†	80.4	3.8	45.9	42.9	9.5	1.0	0.7	−5.6	7.8	9.3
50.0	27.0	34.1	24.3	3	Dover & Deal	80.6	2.0	50.0	37.0	11.3	0.6	1.0	−5.3	4.5	5.1
56.3	27.5	34.4	24.4	4	Faversham	78.5	1.8	54.4	34.5	10.3	0.7	—	−8.5	7.5	8.0
56.7	19.9	42.0	14.0	3	Folkestone & Hythe	72.6	2.6	55.7	20.8	22.5	1.0	W0.2	−5.1	—	8.6
67.6	25.0	38.1	16.5	2	Gillingham	78.8	2.9	53.1	32.3	12.3	1.0	—	−13.4	6.2	6.3
56.9	26.4	43.6	27.0	2	Gravesend†	81.4	2.7	52.0	39.0	8.2	0.8	—	−6.8	8.1	9.1
57.0	22.1	36.7	23.2	3	Maidstone	77.0	3.0	52.6	23.2	23.2	1.0	—	−5.2	—	7.6
53.5	27.3	43.6	29.2	2	Rochester & Chatham†	72.7	−0.8	47.5	42.8	9.0	0.7	—	−6.4	4.4	5.1
58.0	19.8	49.4	22.1	3	Sevenoaks	79.0	3.2	57.4	22.8	18.5	1.3	—	−8.0	7.1	7.7
61.7	23.9	36.6	16.8	3	Thanet, West	72.7	1.2	57.2	28.4	13.3	1.1	—	−5.5	7.8	8.5
59.5	20.6	38.5	14.8	3	West	71.6	2.4	55.4	26.2	18.4	—	—	−7.8	6.2	6.5
56.8	24.8	42.8	23.9	3	Tonbridge & Malling	79.5	3.9	54.5	24.5	20.1	0.8	—	−3.6	6.3	7.6
50.9	19.9	45.5	20.2	2	Tunbridge Wells	74.7	2.1	59.5	21.2	18.3	0.9	—	−7.3	—	7.2
71.7	32.2	27.9	14.8	2	Lancashire, Accrington	78.7	−0.7	40.7	48.9	9.1	1.3	—	−5.0	3.6	4.7
53.8	30.7	30.4	27.4	2	Ashton-under-Lyme	76.6	4.4	36.0	54.7	8.2	1.1	—	−8.6	3.0	4.5
68.7	32.2	31.2	18.3	2	Barrow-in-Furness	78.3	1.2	35.1	53.2	11.7	—	—	−2.1	−0.3	0.0
59.4	31.5	25.2	28.1	2	Blackburn	74.0	1.0	36.6	50.7	11.3	1.5	—	−0.7	2.6	3.5
68.5	24.4	40.1	13.3	2	Blackpool, North	72.6	3.0	53.7	30.0	14.2	2.2	—	−4.5	5.3	6.1
72.3	27.6	36.4	8.5	2	South	72.1	2.2	51.5	30.6	16.7	1.2	—	−6.3	4.0	4.4
58.4	28.6	28.7	30.2	2	Bolton, East	78.7	2.1	43.6	47.6	7.8	1.0	—	−4.7	2.4	3.0
64.9	26.4	32.5	19.2	2	West	79.4	2.1	43.3	44.8	11.0	0.9	—	−2.0	0.4	0.5
26.8	24.0	31.2	46.7	2	Bootle	70.4	3.2	26.6	61.0	10.3	—	2.1	0.4	2.4	2.4
64.3	32.7	27.5	21.1	2	Burnley	77.7	3.0	35.4	50.8	12.8	—	0.9	−7.7	7.3	10.0
66.7	29.5	35.8	21.9	2	Bury & Radcliffe	82.6	1.8	45.2	45.3	8.9	0.6	—	−7.8	0.3	0.4
68.0	30.4	32.2	19.7	2	Chorley†	82.0	0.8	46.8	43.0	9.6	0.6	—	−6.3	4.1	4.8
71.0	30.5	35.7	13.8	2	Clitheroe	80.7	2.1	57.1	30.7	12.2	—	—	−8.6	4.8	4.4
68.5	18.8	56.2	12.2	3	Crosby	75.2	1.7	56.9	25.4	15.2	—	E2.4	−2.8	5.2	6.3
78.9	26.7	39.2	11.6	2	Darwen	78.0	1.4	52.6	30.4	17.0	—	—	−6.3	5.9	6.6
47.6	28.0	35.7	36.3	2	Eccles	77.5	4.6	35.8	53.6	9.8	—	C0.8	−4.9	2.2	3.1
49.2	30.3	31.4	43.6	2	Farnworth	77.8	3.0	35.5	50.1	14.4	—	—	−6.6	6.7	9.2
57.4	30.4	31.8	28.1	2	Heywood & Royton	76.6	0.0	41.6	45.2	12.1	1.0	—	−9.7	4.8	6.4

% Owner-Occupiers	% Council Tenants	% Non-Manual	% Skilled Workers	Urban Scale	Constituency	% Voting	% Change	Con. %	Lab. %	Lib. %	Nat. Front %	Others %	Change in Lib. %	Swing	Two-party Swing
34.4	56.7	36.6	24.7	2	Huyton	72.4	1.3	37.7	51.9	10.4	–	–	0.9	8.4	9.2
50.0	38.0	29.6	32.4	2	Ince	74.2	1.8	32.9	56.2	10.2	–	W0.7	–4.9	9.4	11.8
60.9	22.8	34.8	26.0	4	Lancaster	79.4	1.2	47.6	37.3	14.6	0.5	–	–3.8	3.4	3.9
56.5	31.3	27.5	30.3	2	Leigh	76.9	3.0	36.5	54.1	9.4	0.6	–	–8.6	6.4	8.8
30.1	12.9	26.8	25.0	1	Liverpool, Edge Hill‡†	69.0	7.8	12.7	34.6	52.0	–	–	24.7	–	–1.7
42.5	44.9	40.2	21.8	1	Garston†	73.8	1.8	48.1	43.3	8.4	0.7	W0.2	–1.7	5.2	5.8
30.4	17.4	27.1	26.1	1	Kirkdale	70.2	6.7	30.7	56.1	12.6	–	–	2.5	3.8	3.7
63.5	74.9	18.2	16.0	1	Scotland Exchange	57.4	3.6	12.2	75.1	10.5	–	C2.3	5.5	2.8	1.1
25.0	15.9	31.6	22.1	1	Toxteth	64.8	6.1	32.0	54.7	11.8	0.7	–	0.0	2.1	2.5
33.6	34.2	32.1	25.1	1	Walton	72.8	4.5	34.6	55.2	9.5	–	W0.5, S0.9	–2.4	3.6	4.3
53.0	22.3	47.0	19.8	1	Wavertree	73.3	4.0	50.3	34.2	15.5	–	–	0.5	4.7	5.6
19.7	73.7	31.9	24.8	1	West Derby	70.2	2.9	35.3	55.5	9.3	–	S0.9	–1.4	5.7	6.5
37.3	18.4	30.7	24.6	1	Manchester, Ardwick	68.4	9.6	32.8	56.7	9.6	0.8	–	–3.4	0.1	0.5
46.3	30.8	34.8	25.9	1	Blackley	76.4	5.7	39.2	50.4	9.6	1.8	–	–4.7	3.6	4.8
21.2	40.5	20.8	25.8	1	Central	63.7	10.3	22.1	70.8	5.3	1.1	–	–5.9	0.6	1.9
51.7	23.7	32.3	30.0	1	Gorton	77.2	6.2	38.4	53.5	6.9	–	–	–8.2	3.6	4.9
35.0	22.6	34.2	22.2	1	Moss Side	71.5	8.7	38.7	51.9	8.7	1.1	W0.7	–8.9	–0.3	0.5
46.5	21.9	25.5	32.1	1	Openshaw	72.8	7.0	36.2	62.1	0.0	–	C0.6	(14.2)	2.2	4.8
39.2	30.5	47.6	18.3	1	Withington	74.7	7.0	47.3	38.9	13.5	–	0.4	–5.7	1.7	1.7
17.6	79.0	33.4	25.5	1	Wythenshawe	75.0	6.2	32.4	59.1	8.5	0.6	–	–5.1	2.5	3.8
52.3	33.4	41.2	24.1	2	Middleton & Prestwich	78.9	3.1	44.0	45.8	9.7	–	–	–4.7	2.3	2.7
69.2	10.4	40.1	23.0	3	Morecambe & Lonsdale	76.5	3.6	55.4	25.3	19.3	–	–	–5.5	2.8	2.4
71.0	17.8	28.0	36.7	2	Nelson & Colne†	81.5	0.5	45.0	43.9	11.1	–	–	–1.3	1.4	1.6
59.3	27.9	37.3	31.1	2	Newton	78.4	1.6	37.3	51.4	10.5	0.8	–	–5.5	4.2	5.5
74.8	12.3	39.8	24.0	4	North Fylde	75.3	3.9	60.1	24.4	14.7	–	–	–6.4	1.8	0.8
47.7	38.2	28.6	30.3	2	Oldham, East	68.7	–2.5	37.8	50.7	11.5	0.8	–	–5.5	4.8	6.3

				Constituency											
56.1	28.5	25.5	29.4	West	2	72.6	0.4	35.4	52.4	10.6	1.5	—	−6.2	3.1	4.2
47.8	35.8	42.3	24.0	Ormskirk	4	76.1	3.3	48.9	50.0	0.0	—	W1.1	(11.9)	5.7	6.6
59.6	31.5	27.1	25.6	Preston, North†	2	77.8	1.1	46.3	46.2	6.7	0.8	—	−5.8	2.3	2.6
62.6	29.2	21.0	28.3	South	2	77.2	0.8	19.3	44.5	11.6	0.6	W0.3	−2.3	4.0	4.8
50.1	28.7	33.7	27.6	Rochdale	2	73.7	3.4	48.0	34.3	45.0	1.4	—	2.4	—	5.1
59.4	26.0	27.6	34.9	Rossendale†	2	83.8	2.9	31.1	43.6	8.3	—	—	−13.0	2.5	2.7
43.0	25.1	34.7	32.1	St. Helens	2	72.8	5.9	36.1	59.6	8.4	—	W0.9	−6.7	7.4	9.8
23.8	29.7	37.9	26.3	Salford, East	2	64.3	4.8	37.3	63.9	0.0	—	—	(13.2)	2.5	5.0
35.7	49.4	30.9	26.9	West	2	68.7	3.5	63.4	61.5	0.0	1.3	—	(14.2)	2.2	4.4
72.0	46.2	11.0	20.8	South Fylde	4	76.7	4.7	50.8	18.8	16.5	—	W1.3	−5.7	—	4.0
64.8	41.8	7.3	20.2	Southport	2	74.7	1.0	48.3	11.2	38.0	—	—	2.3	3.0	8.5
58.3	24.4	23.2	23.8	Stretford	2	77.7	1.1	28.8	39.9	11.8	—	—	−6.5	3.0	3.3
38.2	33.1	40.1	33.0	Warrington	2	71.3	3.3	39.6	61.7	9.0	—	0.5	−4.1	7.8	4.2
64.9	31.9	22.5	32.5	Westhoughton	2	80.1	2.2	37.5	48.2	12.2	—	—	−3.7	7.0	9.5
46.2	27.7	42.5	26.6	Widnes	2	74.2	3.3	30.1	55.2	7.4	—	—	−5.9	7.5	8.7
46.2	44.6	39.5	30.1	Wigan	2	74.1	0.1		59.8	9.4	—	W0.8	−3.8	6.1	9.2
75.4	28.5	13.5	29.4	Leicestershire, Blaby	3	83.3	5.0	58.1	22.0	16.2	3.6	—	−7.9	6.1	6.8
65.5	43.4	20.7	41.5	Bosworth	3	84.5	2.5	48.5	37.5	13.1	0.9	—	−4.4	5.3	6.2
70.8	29.9	14.4	27.3	Harborough	3	80.0	3.7	60.4	20.6	17.3	1.8	—	−7.7	—	6.2
50.0	34.0	29.9	35.3	Leicester, East	1	75.6	3.3	41.3	46.9	9.1	2.7	—	−3.2	1.3	1.9
47.6	27.9	20.4	29.5	South	1	74.8	5.9	42.6	46.4	9.2	1.8	—	−2.2	−0.8	−0.8
38.0	33.9	40.8	34.9	West	1	72.3	3.8	35.4	53.6	8.3	2.7	—	−3.3	2.2	3.3
55.8	38.5	26.1	34.8	Loughborough†	2	81.2	2.7	48.0	39.6	10.7	0.8	—	−8.2	6.3	7.5
65.7		16.7	30.6	Melton	3	78.7	1.7	58.6	23.1	18.3	—	—	−6.3	6.5	6.8
				Lincolnshire											
54.1	28.0	31.6	31.1	Brigg & Scunthorpe†	3	75.6	5.1	43.4	42.7	10.8	—	2.9, 0.1	−8.8	5.6	7.0
52.6	30.1	21.8	26.6	Gainsborough	5	78.9	4.2	46.4	19.9	32.6	—	1.1	−0.3	—	8.0
52.3	33.8	25.4	22.6	Grantham	4	78.2	4.0	55.5	28.1	16.4	—	—	−2.1	6.8	8.0
55.5	29.8	26.0	22.2	Grimsby	2	75.8	6.4	39.7	52.0	7.6	0.3	0.4	−13.0	1.4	2.9
52.1	31.3	30.2	25.1	Holland-with-Boston	5	74.6	2.4	55.5	28.1	16.4	—	—	−1.6	6.3	7.3
54.2	30.8	17.7	22.7	Horncastle	5	75.2	4.5	55.1	16.1	28.0	0.8	—	−4.8	—	6.4
44.4	33.4	36.3	26.4	Lincoln†	2	77.0	2.3	16.1	28.0	13.3	0.3	4.1, 0.2	*	—	—
64.0	35.4	17.6	24.4	Louth†	4	78.2	5.1	44.9	21.5	33.2	0.5	—	0.3	—	10.3
46.0	34.7	26.8	23.6	Rutland & Stamford	4	78.1	2.5	56.5	24.5	19.0	—	—	−5.5	7.5	8.5

Constituency	% Owner-Occupiers	% Council Tenants	% Non-Manual	% Skilled Workers	Urban Scale	% Voting	% Change	Con. %	Lab. %	Lib. %	Nat. Front %	Others %	Change in Lib. %	Swing	Two-party Swing
London, Barking, Barking	22.5	70.7	34.1	25.7	2	71.1	3.7	32.4	52.8	10.7	3.0	1.2	-4.8	13.0	18.4
Dagenham	26.6	67.2	30.2	27.2	2	69.1	4.1	31.1	52.6	11.9	3.3	C1.2	-4.7	13.4	16.6
Barnet, Chipping Barnet	67.4	16.0	58.8	17.3	2	75.6	2.0	57.1	25.3	15.6	2.0	–	-5.8	6.4	6.8
Finchley	53.5	12.2	53.8	17.3	2	71.8	2.3	52.5	32.7	13.2	1.3	0.2	-6.5	4.7	4.9
Hendon, North	52.0	31.6	51.0	18.7	2	73.8	1.6	52.1	36.0	10.3	1.6	–	-5.6	5.6	6.3
Hendon, South	51.4	10.9	61.2	13.7	2	70.2	0.4	52.8	29.7	15.3	0.8	E1.5	-5.2	4.7	5.4
Bexley, Bexleyheath	75.4	14.1	50.0	21.8	2	80.1	2.3	53.7	32.7	11.7	1.8	–	-5.6	8.0	9.1
Erith & Crayford	59.0	27.9	42.4	24.5	2	77.5	4.3	41.5	47.2	9.5	1.8	–	-7.3	6.7	8.2
Sidcup	77.3	9.6	57.9	18.4	2	79.3	3.3	59.8	25.8	12.4	2.0	–	-6.1	7.0	7.4
Brent, East	31.1	13.2	41.8	21.6	2	66.9	6.8	36.7	53.3	7.3	1.9	W0.8	-4.3	3.5	4.7
North	70.9	11.0	56.0	19.2	2	76.7	4.8	53.8	34.0	10.6	1.6	–	-5.1	2.9	2.7
South	42.6	14.4	34.0	24.2	2	68.2	7.0	30.9	59.4	7.0	2.0	W0.7	-3.5	0.5	1.4
Bromley, Beckenham	55.4	10.8	57.8	17.0	2	74.7	4.9	56.9	25.1	14.9	1.4	E1.8	-10.6	5.5	5.4
Chislehurst	54.1	32.1	54.4	17.8	2	79.0	2.8	54.5	31.6	12.6	1.3	–	-4.4	6.7	7.6
Orpington	73.2	17.9	61.4	16.1	2	81.7	2.6	58.0	11.9	29.0	0.9	0.3	-8.4	–	8.0
Ravensbourne	68.6	13.3	63.2	15.3	2	77.6	3.6	60.9	18.5	19.3	1.3	–	-8.1	–	4.9
Camden, Hampstead	18.8	13.0	63.3	11.2	1	67.4	4.3	47.3	38.8	13.3	0.6	–	-0.4	2.1	2.5
Holborn & St. Pancras South	3.5	38.1	44.0	13.7	1	60.4	6.6	39.8	49.3	9.0	1.4	W0.5	-5.0	8.1	9.7
St. Pancras North	15.6	30.6	43.6	19.8	1	63.7	5.6	33.9	54.2	9.9	1.3	W0.6	-4.3	5.5	6.7
Croydon, Central	42.5	35.4	47.9	22.3	2	75.7	3.1	52.5	36.7	10.1	–	0.5	-6.0	7.7	8.6
North-East	55.5	12.6	51.1	19.9	2	74.1	3.1	51.0	35.0	12.9	1.1	–	-4.5	5.4	6.1
North-West	57.4	11.7	49.2	19.6	2	72.5	3.3	49.4	40.1	10.5	–	–	-6.7	2.7	2.8
South	75.0	9.0	68.8	12.4	2	76.7	2.8	64.9	13.1	21.0	1.0	–	-4.9	–	5.1
Ealing, Acton	34.1	13.7	51.6	18.4	2	71.4	2.4	51.9	37.6	8.7	1.2	0.6	-2.9	6.1	6.8
North†	57.6	22.2	49.9	22.2	2	77.8	4.0	46.0	43.6	8.6	1.8	–	-6.7	3.9	4.5

56.3	12.7	36.2	24.0	2	Southall	71.7	8.1	32.9	54.4	7.5	2.9	S0.9, 1.2, 0.2	−7.1	0.3	0.6
58.0	25.1	36.6	26.6	2	Enfield, Edmonton	74.6	7.6	42.6	47.1	7.5	2.8	—	−6.4	6.0	7.6
57.1	26.0	37.6	27.1	2	North†	78.1	7.6	48.1	41.3	9.0	1.6	—	−10.9	8.4	10.2
68.6	9.7	61.3	15.1	2	Southgate	76.3	8.5	61.6	22.6	14.1	1.7		−6.6	4.0	3.0
27.1	37.2	41.7	20.2	1	Greenwich, Greenwich	70.6	5.3	33.3	52.1	10.6	2.6	1.3	−6.3	5.0	6.4
38.5	40.7	36.7	22.4	1	Woolwich East	70.1	5.7	30.5	58.9	8.1	2.4	—	−6.0	4.7	7.0
43.5	40.1	50.0	17.7	1	Woolwich West‡‡	79.6	5.7	47.3	41.5	9.7	1.4	—	−4.6	7.2	8.2
12.4	40.0	27.7	27.1	1	Hackney, Central	60.2	7.4	27.6	59.0	6.6	5.1	C1.2, W0.5	−5.8	9.4	10.5
16.0	33.1	37.1	24.5	1	North & Stoke Newington	60.9	8.1	33.2	51.6	10.6	3.0	C1.5	−3.0	9.7	12.6
5.8	56.3	25.1	27.5	1	South & Shoreditch	60.1	5.4	28.2	54.1	9.2	7.6	W0.8	−2.5	11.6	15.4
20.2	15.0	46.3	18.8	1	Hammersmith, Fulham†	76.1	5.2	46.7	43.2	8.9	1.2		−2.1	8.2	9.3
15.4	24.9	40.7	18.9	1	North	70.4	5.8	38.4	48.2	11.6	1.3	W0.5	−3.8	7.1	8.8
32.7	8.5	52.9	18.1	2	Haringey, Hornsey	70.1	1.6	49.4	39.5	9.9	0.8	0.4	−3.3	3.9	4.4
39.3	15.1	30.8	26.6	2	Tottenham	61.2	5.0	32.0	56.9	7.6	2.9	W0.3, 0.2	−1.0	4.8	6.8
34.3	35.6	37.6	24.7	2	Wood Green	67.4	5.1	39.8	46.9	10.4	2.8		−4.3	9.1	12.3
66.1	7.9	51.9	19.0	2	Harrow, Central	75.9	2.9	49.0	35.7	14.1	1.3		−2.8	3.5	4.0
68.1	15.5	53.7	20.3	2	East	77.8	2.9	54.3	33.8	10.4	1.5		−6.6	5.5	6.0
75.3	9.6	60.7	15.8	2	West	78.7	4.3	58.1	24.1	16.4	2.1		−7.1	3.2	2.7
70.3	18.4	44.5	25.6	2	Havering, Hornchurch†	78.1	5.4	44.9	43.3	9.8	1.4		−6.8	8.5	10.4
68.6	18.7	47.5	25.6	2	Romford	76.6	5.1	53.8	32.9	11.4	1.9		−8.0	7.1	7.8
60.3	32.2	49.3	22.8	2	Upminster	80.4	4.2	52.7	35.6	9.8	1.8		−6.1	7.8	8.8
54.4	29.9	40.3	26.5	2	Hillingdon, Hayes & Harlington	75.0	5.5	40.5	48.3	9.3	1.4	C0.6	−7.0	8.2	10.7
70.8	14.1	59.5	17.0	2	Ruislip-Northwood	78.6	4.0	61.3	21.9	15.7	1.1		−5.6	7.0	7.3
51.6	33.6	43.5	22.5	2	Uxbridge	78.9	3.7	52.5	35.7	10.6	1.3		−5.2	6.0	6.7
45.3	17.9	50.4	19.3	2	Hounslow, Brentford & Isleworth	78.1	4.8	49.4	40.4	7.6	1.3	0.5	−4.0	4.3	4.7
53.5	30.4	41.0	24.0	2	Feltham & Heston	74.3	6.4	41.4	48.3	8.5	1.5	W0.3	−5.6	5.1	6.5
14.4	27.1	35.9	22.5	1	Islington, Central	63.7	8.3	35.6	51.5	8.6	3.1	E1.2	−6.5	10.8	14.4
17.8	21.2	37.0	20.1	1	North	61.2	7.0	33.6	52.6	8.9	2.1	W0.9, S1.9	−3.3	5.7	6.8
7.7	38.5	34.4	21.5	1	South & Finsbury	62.9	6.9	34.1	52.0	8.2	3.4	C1.4, 0.9	−7.2	11.3	14.2
					Kensington & Chelsea										
16.0	5.9	64.1	7.2	1	Chelsea	57.3	7.3	66.1	18.5	13.8	1.0	0.4, 0.1	−4.1	3.4	3.0
15.8	9.6	54.7	12.1	1	Kensington	64.6	8.2	51.3	35.1	10.4	1.1	E2.1	−4.8	5.3	6.1

% Owner-Occupiers	% Council Tenants	% Non-Manual	% Skilled Workers	Urban Scale	Constituency	% Voting	% Change	Con. %	Lab. %	Lib. %	Nat. Front %	Others %	Change in Lib. %	Swing	Two-party Swing
					Kingston upon Thames										
60.5	15.4	55.1	18.0	2	Kingston	74.9	3.1	57.9	26.4	15.7	–	–	−6.8	5.8	5.9
62.9	10.4	55.3	17.7	2	Surbiton	75.5	2.6	56.6	26.1	17.2	–	–	−9.4	6.3	6.2
13.7	33.2	37.4	18.8	1	Lambeth, Central	63.2	10.6	33.1	54.7	8.5	3.0	W0.6, 0.2	−4.1	6.1	7.3
26.4	23.7	44.7	19.3	1	Norwood	70.4	8.5	41.7	47.4	8.9	2.1	–	−4.5	4.5	5.3
31.3	19.2	55.4	16.7	1	Streatham	71.5	7.4	51.4	37.0	9.9	1.4	0.3	−3.9	3.2	3.4
5.3	49.4	34.2	19.5	1	Vauxhall	62.5	9.7	33.6	52.4	7.4	3.5	W0.6, 2.3, 0.2	−6.1	10.5	12.0
24.3	35.9	36.0	22.3	1	Lewisham, Deptford	63.8	5.1	32.5	54.2	7.8	4.2	W0.6, S0.8	−6.0	7.3	9.8
35.6	39.1	46.1	20.6	1	East	74.3	5.6	42.8	46.0	8.6	2.3	0.4	−8.3	7.8	9.5
36.9	29.2	46.7	20.8	1	West	76.0	5.9	44.1	46.4	7.4	2.0	–	−6.2	5.2	6.3
50.9	30.8	42.7	25.2	2	Merton, Mitcham & Morden	76.9	5.8	43.9	45.2	8.9	2.0	–	−7.1	6.0	7.3
58.1	8.5	55.5	16.7	2	Wimbledon	76.4	7.6	55.1	28.5	15.2	1.2	–	−5.6	4.4	4.6
46.5	20.2	35.3	24.2	2	Newham, North-East	63.1	3.9	30.5	54.5	9.6	4.2	W0.4, 0.8	−2.9	5.4	7.8
27.9	25.4	30.7	24.5	2	North-West	55.4	3.8	26.5	61.5	7.9	4.1	–	−7.3	6.8	8.7
21.2	44.8	26.4	23.9	2	South	57.1	3.6	22.5	64.4	6.8	6.2	–	−4.9	–	12.0
66.0	19.9	49.3	21.8	2	Redbridge, Ilford North††	79.0	4.5	51.3	37.3	8.9	1.6	0.9	−7.8	7.8	8.9
59.1	12.9	50.1	20.8	2	Ilford South†	75.9	6.1	46.8	42.7	8.9	1.5	–	−5.7	4.3	4.9
67.3	13.5	60.4	17.1	2	Wanstead & Woodford	73.7	5.4	62.2	20.1	15.5	2.3	–	−5.3	7.4	8.4
					Richmond upon Thames										
42.9	15.3	60.1	14.3	2	Richmond	81.4	6.3	46.7	11.3	40.5	0.6	0.8, 0.1	7.8	–	13.7
59.1	11.5	54.9	18.2	2	Twickenham	80.3	5.9	52.2	16.7	29.9	1.2	–	5.6	–	14.0
1.4	68.2	27.3	23.6	1	Southwark, Bermondsey	59.3	2.9	24.9	63.6	6.8	3.9	W0.8	−1.3	10.5	12.4
29.1	33.5	43.1	21.5	1	Dulwich	70.4	5.3	42.8	43.0	11.0	2.1	E1.1	−6.9	8.3	10.2
5.4	55.5	30.2	24.3	1	Peckham	57.7	3.5	28.1	59.8	7.7	4.4	–	−3.9	11.5	13.0
52.4	32.5	49.6	21.9	2	Sutton, Carshalton	76.8	2.5	51.3	31.2	15.7	1.8	–	−1.0	6.3	7.7
74.7	5.5	59.1	18.5	2	Sutton & Cheam	78.8	1.9	58.0	14.3	26.4	0.9	0.3	−10.1	–	4.5

Constituency	No.															
Tower Hamlets, Bethnal Green & Bow	1	3.3	60.1	22.9	26.5	55.5	2.4	19.5	49.8	23.4	6.1	W0.6, S0.5	10.4	—	14.9
Stepney & Poplar	1	1.6	74.0	25.3	22.9	53.3	1.8	21.0	62.6	7.1	5.0	C1.3, W0.8, 2.1	−3.1	12.9	13.5
Waltham Forest, Chingford	2	64.2	19.7	47.6	25.0	78.4	4.9	56.1	27.9	11.9	2.6	E1.5	−8.3	8.5	9.8
Leyton	2	40.2	17.2	36.0	25.5	69.4	6.7	37.4	51.4	8.3	2.9	—	−5.1	7.3	9.7
Walthamstow	2	34.3	28.0	33.0	28.4	71.2	5.0	37.7	50.2	8.9	3.2	—	−6.1	9.1	12.3
Wandsworth, Battersea North	1	13.6	37.2	36.5	23.0	68.0	6.4	33.2	56.2	7.2	2.7	W0.4, 0.2, 0.1	−3.9	8.7	11.2
Battersea South	1	29.3	13.9	46.1	19.4	70.9	6.7	44.0	45.1	9.0	1.8	—	−4.4	4.2	4.9
Putney†	1	26.1	38.2	51.3	18.3	76.1	4.3	46.8	41.5	10.3	1.4	—	−4.7	5.6	6.5
Tooting	1	31.5	20.2	43.5	21.4	70.5	7.0	37.4	51.9	8.1	1.9	C0.6	−5.5	4.3	5.3
Westminster, C. of London & W'ster S.	1	9.3	22.5	49.0	8.4	55.1	2.0	60.7	25.4	12.2	1.7	—	−2.7	7.2	7.9
Paddington†	1	8.3	21.8	49.6	13.5	63.3	1.7	45.5	45.2	7.9	1.1	W0.3	−2.5	3.4	3.8
St. Marylebone	1	13.0	14.9	61.8	8.6	60.8	3.8	59.9	26.5	9.9	1.0	E2.8	−6.5	3.6	3.7
Norfolk, Norfolk North	4	64.3	14.7	37.6	25.7	78.7	2.2	56.9	28.6	13.8	0.7	—	−6.1	6.1	6.5
Norfolk, North-West	5	47.6	28.1	31.6	22.9	79.2	0.7	51.0	39.0	9.9	—	—	−4.2	4.9	5.4
Norfolk, South	4	53.8	25.5	36.3	24.4	78.3	2.1	54.5	30.2	15.3	—	—	−6.0	5.8	6.2
Norfolk, South-West	5	48.3	24.7	28.1	24.5	78.1	1.2	54.8	31.1	14.1	—	—	−2.0	5.9	6.7
Norwich, North	2	27.0	49.2	27.1	35.7	75.6	4.4	34.9	50.8	12.0	0.7	E0.9, C0.3, W0.3	−4.7	6.4	8.0
South	2	35.2	43.8	39.3	28.0	80.2	1.7	41.6	44.9	12.8	0.7	—	−2.7	3.2	3.8
Yarmouth	3	58.3	25.2	35.8	22.7	77.1	3.5	50.4	37.4	11.0	1.1	—	−6.8	4.3	4.8
Northamptonshire, Daventry	4	57.1	28.0	38.5	26.9	80.5	3.4	56.6	27.3	15.4	0.7	—	−5.8	7.6	8.5
Kettering	2	41.4	48.1	28.7	38.4	79.3	6.1	42.9	45.0	12.0	—	—	−7.1	7.8	9.8
Northampton, North†	2	54.2	34.3	33.0	33.6	76.0	0.3	48.2	36.1	14.7	1.0	—	−1.9	8.1	9.6
South	2	63.3	13.3	33.0	32.1	75.3	0.0	49.7	40.2	9.0	1.1	—	−5.4	4.5	5.0
Wellingborough	3	55.0	30.1	30.9	40.9	81.3	1.6	52.3	34.9	11.8	0.7	0.3	−5.2	7.4	8.4
Northumberland, Berwick-upon-Tweed	5	32.7	33.3	32.7	24.9	83.8	2.4	38.4	7.3	54.3	—	—	11.2	—	8.6
Blyth	2	34.8	46.7	28.8	35.8	78.3	4.0	22.7	40.1	8.3	—	28.8	−6.5	—	—
Hexham	4	45.2	31.8	40.9	22.8	79.5	1.4	48.0	31.9	20.1	—	—	−1.5	1.7	2.0
Morpeth	3	34.5	36.5	31.2	36.3	77.4	4.1	25.7	56.3	18.0	—	—	4.4	5.3	5.2

% Owner-Occupiers	% Council Tenants	% Non-Manual	% Skilled Workers	Urban Scale	Constituency	% Voting	% Change	Con. %	Lab. %	Lib. %	Nat. Front %	Others %	Change in Lib. %	Swing	Two-party Swing
9.1	48.4	22.0	28.1	1	Newcastle-upon-Tyne, Central	65.3	6.8	19.3	67.3	13.4	—	—	1.7	3.6	3.6
34.7	40.6	38.6	28.2	1	East	74.5	2.8	36.4	55.1	8.5	—	—	−4.9	0.2	0.8
34.0	18.8	42.0	19.7	1	North	68.0	3.0	47.6	41.2	11.2	—	—	−4.9	2.3	2.5
33.8	56.0	37.4	24.9	1	West	72.4	3.6	35.9	54.5	9.6	—	—	−5.4	4.9	6.4
51.3	25.6	43.4	23.2	2	Tynemouth	77.7	3.4	51.6	38.5	9.9	0.7	—	−9.3	3.8	3.8
32.7	45.1	38.4	27.7	2	Wallsend	75.9	5.0	31.3	55.1	12.3	0.6	W0.6	−4.1	4.7	6.2
50.6	33.3	22.2	44.9	4	Nottinghamshire, Ashfield‡	80.6	5.0	40.4	52.8	6.2	—	—	−8.0	14.3	17.3
40.7	22.4	29.8	34.3	4	Bassetlaw	79.4	5.0	38.0	50.2	11.8	—	—	−2.9	5.3	6.5
60.7	22.4	37.1	30.8	2	Beeston	81.3	0.8	52.6	36.5	11.0	1.0	—	−5.2	8.0	8.9
59.7	21.1	42.1	31.8	2	Carlton	78.9	1.2	52.6	31.4	15.0	0.5	—	−2.7	6.4	7.4
48.5	27.8	27.4	41.2	2	Mansfield	77.3	4.8	31.9	52.3	15.4	—	—	−3.2	6.9	9.1
41.2	28.8	31.4	31.8	4	Newark†	79.9	2.1	45.8	42.9	11.2	1.4	S0.8	−3.4	6.6	7.7
22.8	23.2	23.2	27.5	1	Nottingham, East	63.9	3.9	39.9	50.5	7.4	0.9	C2.0	−6.3	3.9	5.1
31.2	39.6	30.1	29.3	1	North	67.6	0.5	41.1	46.5	9.2	1.3	W0.3	−5.4	3.8	4.8
25.0	65.7	31.2	28.9	1	West	73.2	2.3	42.1	46.5	9.7	—	—	−7.7	6.2	7.7
61.1	15.6	49.7	21.2	3	Rushcliffe	81.7	4.3	62.2	21.3	16.5	0.9	—	−4.3	5.4	5.4
45.7	29.8	35.4	21.9	4	Oxfordshire, Banbury	78.3	2.6	54.7	29.2	15.2	—	—	−1.1	6.7	7.9
58.4	20.4	44.7	18.9	3	Henley	77.5	3.9	58.7	18.5	22.9	—	—	−3.8	—	9.1
56.5	18.8	37.8	20.9	3	Mid-Oxon	79.1	2.7	56.9	26.0	16.7	—	0.3	−7.4	7.4	8.1
44.6	24.2	42.2	20.0	2	Oxford†	74.2	3.4	45.3	42.8	10.3	0.9	1.5, 0.1	−5.0	2.2	2.5
50.1	20.3	33.1	26.0	5	Shropshire, Ludlow	78.6	3.8	52.8	14.4	31.6	—	0.3	1.7	—	11.3
47.4	27.2	32.6	26.2	5	Oswestry	73.9	2.0	54.6	23.5	21.8	—	—	−4.4	5.2	5.8
55.2	25.4	40.4	25.0	4	Shrewsbury	76.6	3.2	48.6	23.8	27.6	—	—	−3.3	—	4.7
43.8	41.9	29.4	27.6	3	The Wrekin†	77.4	2.0	45.6	44.2	10.2	—	—	−3.3	6.2	7.1
50.2	23.4	45.5	22.1	2	Somerset, Bath	78.1	−0.6	46.4	23.0	28.0	0.4	E2.2	−5.3	—	10.0

Constituency															
Bridgwater	55.2	34.1	24.4	25.0	4	79.1	1.8	54.1	29.1	16.8	—	—	-5.6	6.8	7.6
Somerset, North	64.3	46.6	25.6	23.4	3	82.2	1.8	54.3	27.8	16.2	—	—	-6.7	6.6	7.5
Taunton	52.4	42.8	21.8	28.7	4	80.7	1.3	53.2	29.4	14.8	—	—	-8.9	5.1	5.5
Wells	51.7	33.9	29.4	25.8	3	79.2	0.3	51.3	16.9	30.7	—	E1.6	1.1	—	11.9
Weston-super-Mare	62.0	43.3	21.8	18.7	3	77.5	2.7	56.9	20.2	22.9	—	E2.6	-5.7	—	5.0
Yeovil	53.0	34.5	28.2	28.9	4	81.0	1.6	47.9	21.6	30.5	—	0.7, R0.3	1.5	—	10.2
Staffordshire															
Aldridge-Brownhills†	61.0	38.3	33.0	32.2	2	82.5	2.8	50.3	39.4	10.3	—	—	-7.4	8.0	9.2
Burton	55.0	33.5	30.7	24.6	3	78.7	0.8	54.0	36.3	9.7	—	—	-5.3	6.9	7.5
Cannock	46.2	30.1	35.6	37.2	2	79.8	3.7	37.3	52.8	10.0	—	—	-7.4	6.5	8.6
Dudley, East	39.0	27.4	34.7	53.0	2	70.1	1.8	35.5	53.8	8.7	2.0	—	-3.4	5.6	7.1
West†	55.5	34.2	34.3	37.5	2	76.3	1.1	51.0	49.0	0.0	—	—	(12.9)	8.5	9.7
Leek	65.9	31.9	33.1	19.9	4	80.4	1.9	51.9	36.9	9.2	—	2.1	-3.9	4.2	4.7
Lichfield & Tamworth†	55.0	37.0	31.8	31.7	3	81.3	3.1	50.3	40.1	9.0	0.6	—	-6.3	5.4	6.0
Newcastle-under-Lyme	54.2	34.3	31.3	32.2	3	81.6	3.5	41.3	48.5	9.9	—	0.3	-3.4	2.9	3.5
Stafford & Stone	54.8	42.3	23.1	25.8	3	78.8	2.8	52.4	32.3	15.3	—	—	-3.9	4.8	5.3
Staffordshire, South-West	60.5	43.6	28.6	25.4	3	79.0	3.6	60.4	27.6	10.3	1.7	—	-7.9	8.2	8.6
Stoke-on-Trent, Central	47.9	22.4	41.7	33.8	1	69.0	3.8	29.5	60.2	10.4	—	—	-5.4	3.0	4.7
North	55.0	23.6	44.1	32.7	1	72.8	3.1	30.6	59.4	9.2	0.8	—	-5.7	3.7	5.3
South	50.0	25.2	40.5	34.4	1	72.5	3.4	32.3	58.8	9.0	—	—	-1.5	3.2	3.8
Walsall, North‡	26.3	22.8	37.5	63.6	2	72.3	5.7	39.8	50.9	7.2	2.1	—	-6.2	11.1	13.4
South	42.0	33.1	30.0	36.8	2	76.7	3.2	47.3	50.9	0.0	1.8	—	(11.6)	3.6	4.4
West Bromwich, East	43.1	32.2	31.1	48.7	2	71.1	3.4	42.2	47.0	7.9	2.9	—	-5.9	7.1	8.9
West	25.7	21.6	33.9	64.9	2	67.1	4.3	36.3	60.3	0.0	3.4	—	(9.6)	7.7	10.8
Wolverhampton, North-East	32.1	27.3	34.0	60.2	1	70.7	4.5	37.4	50.0	9.9	2.7	—	-5.7	9.6	12.6
South-East	33.3	24.5	34.2	54.7	1	69.1	3.1	34.5	55.7	6.7	3.1	—	-3.2	5.4	6.9
South-West	58.4	44.1	23.4	19.8	4	76.6	2.9	52.5	31.2	13.7	1.8	0.8	-5.8	5.0	5.4
Suffolk, Bury St. Edmunds	42.9	32.2	23.2	32.7	4	76.3	3.1	56.8	29.0	14.2	—	—	-2.4	5.2	5.8
Eye	51.2	31.9	22.3	21.4	5	79.1	1.7	52.0	24.8	22.2	—	—	-6.4	—	6.1
Ipswich	53.7	34.6	27.7	28.5	2	80.8	1.3	43.0	48.2	8.1	0.6	0.6, 0.5	-3.8	-1.4	-1.5
Lowestoft	62.2	32.1	26.2	17.6	4	80.0	1.8	50.5	38.6	10.3	—	W0.2	-8.3	4.2	4.5
Sudbury & Woodbridge	56.8	36.6	21.5	20.1	4	78.7	3.6	55.0	26.4	18.7	—	E0.7	-5.4	4.8	5.0
Surrey, Chertsey & Walton	63.8	50.3	20.2	16.4	2	76.5	3.1	49.0	23.2	26.2	—	—	7.7	—	5.0
Dorking	60.3	49.5	19.6	18.4	3	77.9	2.9	61.4	19.0	19.6	1.6	—	-7.8	—	6.6

Constituency	% Owner-Occupiers	% Council Tenants	% Non-Manual	% Skilled Workers	Urban Scale	% Voting	% Change	Con. %	Lab. %	Lib. %	Nat. Front %	Others %	Change in Lib. %	Swing	Two-party Swing
Epsom & Ewell	73.2	12.3	59.9	13.9	2	76.9	3.2	61.9	17.9	20.2	—	—	−6.5	—	3.9
Esher	69.7	13.0	59.3	15.4	2	77.5	3.2	65.1	15.2	19.7	—	—	−5.4	—	6.5
Farnham	60.0	19.6	47.3	18.1	2	77.6	1.3	58.3	14.5	26.4	—	0.4, 0.3	−6.2	—	5.9
Guildford	56.1	21.5	49.6	19.0	2	75.3	3.5	57.2	21.2	21.2	—	0.4	−7.1	—	4.4
Reigate	59.3	24.2	55.0	17.0	2	78.2	2.9	59.8	22.1	18.2	—	—	−4.8	6.5	6.9
Spelthorne	65.8	16.0	52.0	21.9	2	76.9	2.4	57.4	27.8	13.9	1.0	—	−5.9	9.1	10.0
Surrey, East	64.1	17.6	54.0	17.0	2	78.4	2.2	62.8	16.4	19.7	1.0	—	−9.5	—	5.2
Surrey, North-West	59.8	21.4	47.5	18.6	2	75.6	4.7	63.7	18.9	15.9	1.4	—	−7.4	8.5	9.0
Woking	62.7	19.7	49.6	19.5	2	76.5	3.6	57.0	24.0	18.0	1.0	—	−10.4	—	4.4
East Sussex															
Brighton, Kemptown	42.6	28.7	36.2	22.7	2	74.2	1.8	53.6	36.8	8.8	0.8	—	−4.4	5.6	6.0
Pavilion	49.9	10.1	45.4	18.7	2	72.6	4.0	53.7	29.3	14.4	1.1	E1.5	−7.6	2.8	2.6
Eastbourne	60.2	15.8	46.7	16.9	2	76.7	2.1	63.0	17.2	18.8	0.9	—	−7.1	—	4.8
East Grinstead	65.8	12.4	47.5	18.7	4	77.1	2.5	62.0	13.6	24.4	—	—	−6.4	—	5.2
Hastings	49.4	15.4	39.8	20.9	2	71.7	0.1	51.5	30.0	15.7	0.8	2.0	−5.9	5.1	6.0
Hove	44.7	11.9	44.9	17.5	3	71.6	1.8	60.1	21.5	17.4	1.0	—	−7.0	—	2.7
Lewes	65.5	15.7	47.6	18.8	3	76.3	2.4	58.4	19.2	21.1	1.3	—	−4.7	—	5.4
Mid-Sussex	66.5	13.7	52.2	17.3	3	78.0	1.6	61.2	15.5	22.0	—	1.3	−6.1	—	4.8
Rye	64.5	13.4	43.9	17.2	4	77.1	2.9	62.7	12.1	22.0	1.0	E2.2	−5.7	—	5.2
West Sussex, Arundel	66.1	13.9	42.8	18.7	4	73.9	0.9	65.0	15.5	19.5	—	—	−5.8	—	5.5
Chichester	53.1	20.3	40.7	17.6	4	75.6	2.0	62.3	15.4	19.6	—	E1.2, 1.5	−10.8	—	4.7
Horsham & Crawley	43.5	43.8	47.4	22.0	2	81.4	3.3	52.2	33.8	13.4	0.6	—	−6.1	6.6	7.4
Shoreham	67.2	19.2	42.8	22.1	3	78.0	3.3	60.9	15.7	22.6	0.7	—	−6.3	—	7.5
Worthing	68.4	9.4	47.7	15.6	2	73.3	2.2	61.2	13.0	24.1	1.6	—	−0.5	—	5.3
Warwickshire															
Birmingham, Edgbaston	39.4	31.5	40.9	21.0	1	67.8	4.6	54.1	33.5	9.4	0.0	1.2	−8.1	7.6	8.5

39.7	44.6	28.8	29.2	1	Erdington	67.9	2.4	44.4	46.0	8.0	1.6	—	-6.2	9.4	11.5
52.7	37.5	43.2	26.5	1	Hall Green	73.3	3.1	54.5	35.3	8.9	1.2	—	-9.2	6.8	7.3
53.5	14.5	30.6	25.6	1	Handsworth	68.4	1.9	44.8	55.2	—	—	—	(10.6)	1.2	2.2
29.5	40.1	19.3	27.6	1	Ladywood	62.3	5.4	26.9	63.5	9.6	—	W0.3	-3.8	2.9	4.2
34.9	53.3	34.0	27.0	1	Northfield†	70.6	2.7	45.4	45.1	8.1	1.1	—	-6.8	10.2	12.2
55.8	37.2	30.1	33.3	1	Perry Barr	75.8	2.4	46.3	47.6	4.6	1.5	—	-6.4	3.5	4.1
49.0	18.1	41.1	23.0	1	Selly Oak†	73.7	6.5	48.7	38.6	11.4	0.8	0.4	-7.2	5.4	6.2
28.6	51.6	18.5	27.3	1	Small Heath	62.9	5.3	21.4	60.5	15.2	1.7	S1.2	0.9	4.2	3.8
39.5	31.7	23.2	28.0	1	Sparkbrook	65.0	4.8	34.9	62.7	—	—	C2.4	(9.8)	0.3	1.8
34.9	55.0	26.1	30.0	1	Stechford‡	71.6	7.4	47.6	48.4	5.4	1.6	—	-9.2	13.0	15.4
50.0	38.3	32.8	29.8	1	Yardley	73.8	0.6	47.6	44.8	5.9	1.8	—	-4.6	6.2	7.0
55.1	29.0	26.3	30.7	1	Coventry, North-East	72.7	2.7	35.0	57.3	4.9	1.2	C0.8, W0.8	-10.5	6.8	9.5
69.7	17.2	34.6	30.7	1	North-West	79.2	4.0	39.9	50.1	8.8	0.9	0.3	-6.9	5.0	6.4
45.4	30.7	28.4	27.7	1	South-East	69.9	2.2	34.0	55.0	8.4	1.4	W1.2	-6.0	7.1	8.8
68.4	20.8	42.9	25.7	1	South-West†	81.5	2.1	49.3	39.3	10.4	0.9	0.1	-5.5	7.0	8.0
43.8	43.7	33.7	32.4	2	Meriden	77.0	1.9	48.8	43.3	6.5	1.4	—	-11.0	8.8	10.4
59.4	27.0	27.2	36.1	2	Nuneaton	78.5	4.5	37.7	49.9	9.8	1.6	1.0	-8.8	9.3	12.0
65.3	19.5	41.5	26.0	3	Rugby†	83.9	4.1	47.3	42.0	9.6	1.1	—	-4.7	8.1	9.4
75.6	13.3	58.7	20.4	2	Solihull	77.2	1.9	66.2	16.6	15.7	1.5	—	-10.6	—	8.4
54.6	23.3	42.6	21.1	4	Stratford-on-Avon	76.7	2.6	60.4	17.6	22.0	—	—	-5.3	—	7.3
72.1	15.5	60.5	17.1	2	Sutton Coldfield	77.3	2.8	68.9	13.1	16.1	0.9	0.9	-11.3	5.5	5.2
57.5	22.7	44.3	21.2	2	Warwick & Leamington	77.7	2.9	54.3	29.3	15.0	—	E1.4	-4.8	—	6.2
52.9	20.5	39.6	27.8	5	Westmorland	74.5	2.1	56.6	14.6	28.8	—	—	-2.9	—	5.0
64.1	12.5	40.4	22.2	3	Isle of Wight	81.8	5.1	47.7	4.0	48.2	—	E0.9	3.2	—	15.8
50.2	26.3	35.0	23.4	4	Wiltshire, Chippenham	80.0	1.6	49.2	8.6	41.3	—	E1.1, R0.2	2.2	—	14.3
52.2	22.6	34.8	23.5	4	Devizes	79.6	4.4	50.9	25.7	22.1	—	—	-5.0	6.6	8.3
45.6	22.6	36.9	19.1	3	Salisbury	77.4	2.7	49.9	12.6	37.4	—	—	2.7	—	12.9
53.6	36.6	31.4	27.9	3	Swindon	76.4	2.4	38.4	50.2	11.4	—	—	-6.6	5.2	6.9
56.2	24.7	36.5	24.4	4	Westbury	79.7	1.0	47.2	19.8	25.2	—	E0.9, R3.0, 4.0	-6.2	—	9.7
					Worcestershire										
58.9	27.1	40.8	24.4	2	Bromsgrove & Redditch	78.7	-0.9	54.3	35.0	9.8	0.9	—	-4.0	8.2	9.1
59.0	29.9	38.3	28.4	2	Halesowen & Stourbridge	79.3	3.1	49.6	36.2	12.8	1.4	—	-10.6	6.0	6.9
58.0	26.1	34.7	28.5	4	Kidderminster	77.6	2.6	53.7	28.6	15.9	1.7	—	-9.0	6.8	7.6

Two-party Swing	Swing	Change in Lib. %	Others %	Nat. Front %	Lib. %	Lab. %	Con. %	% Change	% Voting	Constituency	Urban Scale	% Skilled Workers	% Non-Manual	% Council Tenants	% Owner-Occupiers
5.3	4.0	(12.1)	—	3.1	—	55.0	41.9	3.3	70.5	Warley, East	2	29.8	28.1	40.0	42.1
8.9	6.4	−8.4	—	—	6.6	58.4	35.0	3.8	70.8	West	2	34.1	22.9	48.4	37.8
6.4	5.3	−2.8	E1.2	0.8	15.1	31.6	51.3	1.6	75.4	Worcester	2	25.2	38.5	29.2	53.8
6.2	—	−8.7	E2.8	—	23.3	16.7	57.1	2.2	77.3	Worcestershire, South	4	23.1	41.8	25.9	53.4
										Yorkshire, East Riding					
0.0	—	−6.1	—	—	20.3	24.9	54.8	6.3	74.2	Bridlington	4	22.9	38.8	19.6	61.5
3.5	—	−5.3	—	—	23.6	20.6	55.8	2.4	77.3	Haltemprice	3	20.9	51.5	18.9	64.9
2.4	—	−10.1	—	—	25.3	18.6	56.0	1.8	74.4	Howden	5	24.0	34.1	21.0	52.6
3.8	2.6	−6.4	S0.6	1.0	11.8	52.1	34.4	2.7	70.4	Kingston upon Hull, Central	1	23.9	33.8	33.2	34.5
5.2	2.9	−6.6	—	0.6	12.0	62.5	24.9	3.7	70.8	East	1	25.4	27.8	55.8	25.7
3.5	2.1	−7.2	—	1.2	10.3	55.8	32.7	2.9	67.5	West	1	25.5	29.3	26.2	37.7
										Yorkshire, North Riding					
5.4	4.9	−5.7	W2.3, 1.9	—	11.2	37.8	51.0	3.9	80.0	Cleveland & Whitby	4	26.5	35.6	21.9	59.0
6.8	5.8	−4.7	0.7	—	9.1	56.2	30.4	6.7	67.9	Middlesbrough	1	28.3	26.4	55.1	30.5
5.1	3.6	−7.6	—	—	8.9	53.7	36.7	6.8	75.9	Redcar	1	29.3	29.6	40.1	49.3
3.7	—	−2.2	—	—	21.2	17.4	61.5	6.4	72.1	Richmond	5	22.2	34.2	21.1	48.3
1.0	—	−5.1	1.1	—	20.3	25.5	53.2	5.0	73.1	Scarborough	4	21.2	37.2	20.3	61.2
4.6	3.8	−2.4	C0.4, 0.5	0.6	9.2	53.1	36.2	4.6	73.7	Stockton	1	28.7	35.3	40.4	49.2
3.6	—	−4.3	—	—	19.2	21.7	59.2	3.6	76.5	Thirsk & Melton	5	21.8	36.3	16.0	56.2
−0.8	−0.8	−2.9	—	0.5	9.2	51.1	39.1	2.4	74.7	Thornaby	1	26.8	35.9	19.0	64.6
										Yorkshire, West Riding					
5.3	5.2	−8.6	E2.5	—	11.0	30.2	56.2	2.3	78.1	Barkston Ash	4	24.9	41.9	23.3	61.5
5.8	3.7	−6.6	W0.6, 1.1	—	10.1	64.0	24.1	4.5	72.9	Barnsley	2	37.5	24.9	42.9	41.0
5.5	3.9	−10.2	E1.0, 1.8	1.2	10.5	49.0	37.6	5.0	74.5	Batley & Morley	2	32.1	29.1	31.3	48.3
2.8	1.6	−8.5	W0.3	0.8	11.8	50.9	35.7	1.4	71.8	Bradford, North	1	27.8	31.0	23.3	60.7
5.3	4.0	−6.9	—	1.4	12.8	47.1	39.4	1.6	73.2	South	1	29.8	32.5	29.2	59.6
−2.9	−2.9	−5.4	—	—	8.1	53.8	36.7	−0.4	69.1	West	1	23.3	29.1	24.2	55.5
4.5	3.8	−2.6	—	—	13.9	41.4	44.7	1.6	80.2	Brighouse & Spenborough†	2	30.4	33.6	20.3	62.1
18.3	—	−5.9	0.2	—	38.4	33.9	27.5	0.1	81.9	Colne Valley	2	34.4	33.6	17.6	64.0

					Constituency										
34.4	46.6	23.1	42.7	2	Dearne Valley	72.0	0.9	19.6	68.8	11.6	—	—	−0.8	5.7	6.8
49.5	34.3	31.7	30.6	2	Dewsbury	77.1	4.2	37.8	46.7	15.5	—	—	−9.0	3.2	4.9
44.7	38.1	34.1	28.2	2	Doncaster	75.0	2.2	42.4	48.9	8.0	0.7	W0.6, 1.0	−6.6	5.3	6.5
38.8	31.8	26.3	37.6	2	Don Valley	74.7	1.4	31.2	55.6	11.6	—	—	−4.0	8.9	10.9
38.6	41.0	25.6	33.6	3	Goole	72.8	3.5	34.2	57.6	8.3	0.9	—	−3.5	4.0	5.1
57.1	28.5	29.1	28.2	2	Halifax	76.7	2.1	41.3	43.8	14.0	1.1	—	−4.3	3.1	4.0
63.3	12.3	48.6	16.7	3	Harrogate	74.3	3.8	59.5	16.0	23.4	—	—	−1.3	—	3.5
27.3	43.2	20.3	44.4	2	Hemsworth	73.3	3.1	20.0	69.6	10.4	—	—	−1.0	7.4	8.7
47.0	37.4	29.9	33.1	2	Huddersfield, East	74.3	1.9	39.7	47.5	12.2	—	0.6	−6.7	7.0	9.3
66.2	15.3	37.0	31.5	2	West†	76.0	−0.3	44.2	40.6	14.9	0.5	0.2	−3.5	3.5	4.2
67.0	19.3	28.9	31.8	1	Keighley	80.5	−2.5	44.8	45.0	9.3	0.9	E0.5	−4.3	3.5	4.2
31.9	62.5	32.7	29.9	1	Leeds, East	70.9	5.2	33.3	55.4	9.7	—	E0.4, 0.2	−5.9	2.8	4.1
59.0	16.6	46.1	21.7	1	North-East	70.1	4.6	49.0	36.0	12.9	—	E2.0	−4.6	−0.8	−1.2
48.9	32.0	48.0	22.6	1	North-West	73.1	6.8	47.5	35.1	15.7	1.2	E1.7	−4.4	1.5	1.7
32.0	45.4	23.5	33.1	1	South	68.7	4.9	23.4	65.0	10.4	0.6	—	−6.2	1.9	3.7
27.0	37.5	21.7	30.1	1	South-East	65.0	8.7	23.2	56.3	19.2	1.1	—	3.4	3.1	2.8
42.1	40.2	28.3	33.6	1	West	73.3	4.4	27.0	49.4	22.6	—	C0.7	−8.8	—	7.7
50.2	33.9	30.6	37.5	2	Normanton	76.8	6.3	30.6	56.4	13.0	—	—	−4.8	4.7	6.6
45.5	38.3	32.9	36.1	2	Penistone	78.9	4.2	32.1	49.1	18.9	—	—	−2.9	6.6	8.9
37.6	46.5	39.8	33.1	2	Pontefract & Castleford	73.9	2.7	23.8	68.2	8.1	—	—	−4.2	4.9	7.1
66.1	23.7	43.3	26.3	2	Pudsey	80.3	2.2	45.1	25.2	29.1	—	E0.6	−1.5	—	7.3
59.1	20.0	44.4	22.2	4	Ripon	78.8	−0.1	60.3	16.1	21.7	1.1	E1.9	−12.7	—	−0.5
36.2	49.0	29.2	31.9	2	Rotherham	72.1	6.7	29.9	60.5	8.4	—	—	−5.0	6.0	7.6
37.9	40.9	29.8	39.2	2	Rother Valley	74.6	2.4	27.0	62.2	10.7	1.0	—	−4.1	7.1	9.3
38.8	34.4	29.4	34.7	1	Sheffield, Attercliffe	72.7	5.5	25.3	64.9	8.8	0.9	—	−3.5	5.3	6.7
22.8	67.6	25.5	33.2	1	Brightside	68.8	1.4	21.3	68.5	9.3	0.5	—	0.3	—	—
60.4	13.0	55.5	19.6	1	Hallam	72.5	3.7	54.9	28.8	15.7	0.6	—	−6.3	3.0	2.7
48.2	35.6	39.3	30.0	1	Heeley	77.3	3.8	40.1	49.8	9.5	0.9	—	−5.4	5.0	6.4
38.4	31.3	29.1	32.6	1	Hillsborough	70.8	4.2	33.7	56.8	8.5	0.8	—	−5.6	6.2	7.9
18.1	61.5	20.2	33.6	1	Park	64.4	2.0	17.9	68.6	11.8	—	C0.7, W0.3	−2.7	—	5.1
63.7	27.3	41.4	24.8	2	Shipley	80.5	−0.5	52.6	53.1	13.2	—	E1.1	−6.1	6.1	6.9
61.2	16.9	31.3	31.5	4	Skipton	84.1	1.9	51.2	10.2	38.6	—	—	−1.3	—	14.6
58.5	21.6	25.3	32.7	3	Sowerby†	80.7	1.6	42.2	39.3	18.5	—	—	−5.2	2.3	2.9
41.2	45.6	34.8	31.2	2	Wakefield	75.6	5.3	36.7	50.9	11.4	1.0	—	−6.4	6.6	8.6
52.4	29.8	35.4	22.1	2	York	77.7	2.4	42.6	44.7	11.3	0.4	1.0	−1.4	2.1	2.5

Wales

% Owner-Occupiers	% Council Tenants	% Non-Manual	% Skilled Workers	Urban Scale	Constituency	% Voting	% Change	Con. %	Lab. %	Lib. %	Plaid Cymru %	Others %	Change in Lib. %	Swing	Two-party Swing
48.1	28.4	34.2	27.1	4	Anglesey†	81.2	5.0	39.0	31.7	9.0	20.3	—	−6.4	12.5	18.8
51.9	26.7	30.5	29.4	5	Brecon & Radnor†	84.2	2.8	47.2	40.9	9.7	2.1	—	−7.7	6.6	8.0
55.6	22.4	33.2	25.1	4	Caernarvonshire, Caernarvon	81.5	0.6	19.9	24.8	5.7	49.7	—	−5.0	—	17.5
53.4	25.3	38.7	21.7	3	Conway	79.0	2.8	44.7	29.7	16.9	8.6	—	0.8	3.9	5.1
58.1	17.3	36.1	29.8	5	Cardiganshire	81.5	1.0	29.7	20.2	35.6	14.5	—	−6.5	—	38.4
59.3	21.3	28.2	35.2	5	Carmarthenshire, Carmarthen†	84.4	−1.2	23.6	35.8	8.0	32.0	N0.3, 0.2	−2.4	—	26.6
56.4	31.7	25.9	33.2	2	Llanelli	79.4	2.5	20.5	59.5	11.4	7.4	C1.2	−3.0	—	8.4
57.8	19.1	38.7	24.3	5	Denbighshire, Denbigh	80.0	3.5	44.9	17.6	28.1	9.3	—	−1.1	—	6.2
38.7	48.0	29.4	30.5	2	Wrexham	78.4	4.2	29.5	49.2	18.4	2.8	—	−3.7	—	7.7
57.1	29.2	31.8	28.8	3	Flintshire, East Flint	81.7	2.1	38.1	48.3	11.1	2.0	—	−5.2	3.6	4.9
63.5	19.1	36.0	25.1	3	West Flint	78.6	3.2	49.0	31.0	16.8	3.2	C0.5	−5.7	4.0	4.4
48.5	41.5	29.0	29.9	2	Glamorgan, Aberavon	79.2	6.1	24.7	61.7	9.0	3.8	—	−2.0	4.5	7.5
60.5	23.1	24.3	34.7	2	Aberdare	78.6	−0.5	17.3	71.5	—	9.8	C0.8	(5.5)	—	9.2
59.2	29.5	45.8	21.8	2	Barry	80.3	2.6	50.9	36.3	10.1	2.1	C1.4	−6.0	4.6	5.0
51.8	9.0	28.2	35.0	2	Caerphilly	78.8	3.2	18.9	58.8	7.4	14.9	N0.5	−0.1	—	7.5
60.0	25.1	50.2	18.2	1	Cardiff, North	75.7	2.4	47.3	36.2	13.6	3.0	—	−4.3	2.5	2.7
65.6	32.2	57.6	18.5	1	North-West	80.6	1.6	51.0	33.2	13.7	2.1	—	−4.5	2.6	2.5
44.0	38.7	32.8	25.4	1	South-East	73.8	3.1	37.7	59.3	—	1.6	C0.3, 0.9, 0.3	(19.9)	2.4	5.9
40.1	37.3	37.3	24.4	1	West	60.8	−9.0	—	85.6	—	10.4	N4.1	(12.9)	—	—
65.8	32.9	25.0	31.5	3	Gower	80.8	3.9	30.5	53.2	9.1	7.2	—	−3.4	7.2	10.3
53.1	32.2	25.0	33.5	3	Merthyr Tydfil	79.1	3.3	14.1	71.3	4.1	9.4	C0.7, W0.4	−0.3	—	5.7
57.4	29.3	27.7	32.7	2	Neath	81.2	3.3	20.2	64.5	—	15.3	—	(9.2)	—	8.2
58.6	27.1	31.8	35.8	2	Ogmore	79.7	4.3	24.6	53.4	17.5	4.4	—	1.5	7.3	10.3

Constituency													
Pontypridd	58.4	31.8	30.4	29.7	2	78.1	4.3	29.2	56.0	10.6	3.8	N0.4	−4.9	4.7	7.9
Rhondda	67.8	15.8	23.5	35.5	2	79.8	3.6	12.9	75.1	—	8.4	C3.6	(4.3)	—	5.8
Swansea, East	52.6	35.0	28.6	29.5	2	75.6	4.3	23.4	69.9	6.6	6.0	C0.7	(12.3)	1.5	6.7
West	55.5	25.9	41.5	23.2	2	79.6	4.6	45.3	46.1	12.1	1.9	—	−7.3	4.6	5.6
Merionethshire	55.4	21.8	30.7	26.3	5	83.4	−0.6	23.6	23.5	—	40.8	—	−3.3	—	23.6
Monmouthshire, Abertillery	56.9	29.9	21.9	38.0	2	80.2	5.1	16.2	76.0	—	7.9	E1.4	(6.5)	—	7.3
Bedwellty	42.6	39.1	25.5	36.5	2	79.6	2.5	20.7	71.3	10.7	6.6	—	(9.3)	4.2	8.2
Ebbw Vale	54.5	36.8	23.2	34.8	2	79.9	3.8	13.6	69.2	12.8	6.5	—	−0.4	—	7.2
Monmouth	50.8	35.4	40.4	24.7	4	83.0	3.5	50.5	35.8	10.5	1.0	N0.8	−4.2	5.4	6.1
Newport	52.7	30.8	34.1	28.8	2	79.7	4.1	36.3	51.7	12.3	0.8	—	−5.8	4.5	6.2
Pontypool	37.1	52.6	27.0	28.8	2	78.4	5.7	23.2	61.9	—	2.6	—	−2.1	4.0	6.4
Montgomeryshire†	48.7	26.0	30.7	32.3	5	81.4	3.5	40.3	16.3	34.9	8.5	—	−8.2	—	11.6
Pembrokeshire	51.9	29.8	33.0	26.2	5	81.3	1.8	49.2	37.1	10.1	2.5	E1.1	−5.8	5.3	6.1

Scotland

% Owner-Occupiers	% Council Tenants	% Non-Manual	% Skilled Workers	Urban Scale	Constituency	% Voting	% Change	Con. %	Lab. %	Lib. %	S.N.P.	Others %	Change in Lib. %	Swing	Two-party Swing
16.1	64.7	29.9	25.3	2	Aberdeen, North	69.7	0.0	17.0	59.3	10.8	12.8	—	2.7	—	4.1
43.7	33.9	46.5	20.2	2	South	78.6	2.2	40.7	39.2	11.5	8.5	—	1.9	0.4	0.4
36.7	39.0	29.6	24.2	5	Aberdeenshire, East†	72.4	1.9	42.8	15.8	—	41.4	—	(6.6)	—	−5.9
41.8	31.7	36.8	25.9	5	Aberdeenshire, West	75.9	−0.6	40.9	15.3	35.5	8.3	—	5.7	—	−1.7
					Angus & Kincardine,										
36.2	33.5	33.8	21.5	5	Angus North & Mearns	73.8	1.5	57.5	19.3	—	23.2	—	(9.9)	—	−3.0
33.3	43.9	35.1	26.9	4	Angus South†	79.9	5.4	43.6	10.1	4.8	41.5	—	−1.7	—	2.4
36.5	35.4	35.1	21.7	5	Argyll†	76.1	4.1	36.8	15.9	15.4	31.8	—	*	−0.7	−3.1
41.7	49.2	42.3	24.4	3	Ayrshire & Bute, Ayr	79.8	0.4	43.3	36.9	10.7	9.1	—	4.3	−0.7	−1.1
25.3	66.7	35.0	28.5	3	Ayrshire Central	79.8	0.5	29.3	51.1	9.1	10.4	—	3.5	—	1.0
19.1	69.3	26.8	36.4	3	Ayrshire South	79.9	2.6	25.4	35.2	—	8.0	31.4	(5.4)	—	−0.3
39.0	45.7	35.6	23.9	3	Bute & North Ayrshire	75.9	4.6	45.7	34.3	6.0	13.9	—	−0.3	0.7	6.3
23.8	68.1	32.1	31.4	3	Kilmarnock	81.1	0.7	29.1	52.6	—	18.3	—	(5.2)	—	−8.0
41.9	37.0	31.5	26.3	5	Banff†	72.5	0.0	44.6	14.2	—	41.2	—	(8.9)	—	1.6
25.6	52.0	32.8	25.4	5	Berwick & East Lothian	82.9	−0.1	40.2	43.5	9.8	6.5	—	3.9	1.2	7.6
33.5	41.6	33.4	24.6	5	Caithness & Sutherland	82.9	0.3	30.5	41.5	28.0	—	—	(22.0)	—	—
33.3	44.5	34.3	27.9	4	Dumfries	78.1	1.4	45.2	27.3	14.3	13.2	—	5.9	2.8	2.9
23.1	68.2	38.0	29.4	2	Dunbartonshire, Central	80.6	0.2	21.6	51.9	7.8	15.3	C2.6, 0.8	3.0	—	−0.7
39.5	56.5	54.4	21.8	2	East†	83.9	3.2	34.1	37.9	7.5	20.6	—	0.2	—	−3.3
29.4	54.0	36.0	24.4	2	West	80.2	1.9	33.7	48.4	—	17.9	—	(5.0)	—	3.2
22.6	56.6	33.7	24.1	2	Dundee, East	77.7	4.3	18.2	36.0	4.6	41.0	0.1	1.8	—	−0.4
18.0	62.4	32.8	23.5	2	West	78.4	4.0	25.8	47.3	—	26.4	0.6	(4.6)	−2.0	4.2
46.8	11.4	39.8	22.8	1	Edinburgh Central	67.5	0.0	29.6	47.8	12.2	9.8	0.7	3.2	—	−1.0
34.4	56.2	41.4	25.1	1	East	76.1	−0.1	33.5	53.7	—	12.1	C0.4, W0.3	(5.9)	—	4.5

L1	L2	L3	L4	No.	Constituency	J	I	H	G	F	E	Code	C	B	A
44.8	25.0	39.5	24.9	1	Leith	75.2	0.4	32.0	46.3	12.1	9.7	—	5.9	−1.3	−0.5
57.8	9.8	53.8	19.9	1	North	71.8	2.5	43.6	30.1	15.5	10.8	—	4.3	0.0	−1.1
39.2	46.0	50.1	19.5	1	Pentlands	76.8	1.2	39.3	36.3	13.1	11.0	E1.2	2.5	−0.2	−0.6
49.0	35.8	53.9	19.5	1	South	77.3	3.1	39.7	34.3	16.3	8.4	—	2.1	−1.2	−2.4
53.1	37.3	57.3	18.7	1	West	77.8	1.3	45.4	28.2	17.2	9.2	—	0.8	2.2	1.5
38.6	35.7	34.2	21.2	5	Galloway†	81.2	4.1	8.5	44.3	8.5	37.1	—	−1.9	—	2.7
25.4	60.0	35.7	29.2	2	Fife, Dunfermline	79.3	3.4	30.1	58.0	11.3	14.3	C2.5	3.0	—	4.0
10.4	81.5	28.5	35.2	3	Central Fife	77.4	3.5	20.2	19.9	—	19.3	—	—	—	6.6
38.6	39.7	38.3	22.7	4	East Fife	79.0	5.3	43.0	53.9	23.0	14.1	—	10.4	—	−1.3
21.3	64.6	32.1	31.9	2	Kirkcaldy	77.4	2.4	26.2	45.9	—	19.9	—	(6.1)	—	6.0
36.4	48.4	46.5	24.7	1	Glasgow, Cathcart†	78.6	2.0	41.8	72.5	5.3	6.9	—	2.6	−4.4	−5.2
14.9	44.2	20.8	27.4	1	Central	59.5	2.6	16.4	59.9	—	11.1	—	(4.2)	—	1.6
16.0	75.6	41.7	25.6	1	Craigton	75.2	−0.6	28.5	61.5	—	11.7	—	(5.1)	—	3.8
5.7	90.6	33.8	30.4	1	Garscadden	73.2	2.3	21.9	67.9	—	15.7	C1.0	(5.0)	—	6.0
26.2	33.0	26.7	26.7	1	Govan	69.1	−2.6	18.5	34.4	—	13.6	—	(1.9)	—	9.0
46.9	22.7	58.7	18.4	1	Hillhead	75.7	3.3	41.0	50.3	14.4	10.1	—	2.5	−1.1	−2.4
32.0	8.9	42.0	23.3	1	Kelvingrove	65.6	2.3	28.8	66.2	10.9	9.9	—	4.5	−3.1	−2.8
9.7	77.0	24.9	28.5	1	Maryhill	67.7	1.8	15.0	49.2	6.8	11.2	C0.8	3.7	—	4.5
30.6	52.5	44.1	24.4	1	Pollok	73.7	1.3	29.7	69.5	9.1	9.6	N0.2, 2.1	3.8	−1.5	−0.7
0.7	96.9	26.2	31.7	1	Provan	66.0	2.0	15.1	64.5	—	13.8	C1.1, W0.6	—	—	3.5
27.5	38.7	34.4	27.8	1	Queen's Park	68.3	1.3	24.1	64.1	—	9.7	C1.1, W0.4, S0.4	(3.7)	—	3.9
21.1	47.9	25.1	27.8	1	Shettleston	68.2	3.9	22.0	66.1	—	13.9	—	(2.8)	—	4.6
21.0	56.5	28.5	28.1	1	Springburn	67.8	1.3	21.4	20.6	—	12.6	—	(2.7)	—	4.9
37.3	41.9	37.1	24.1	4	Inverness	74.4	4.0	24.8	55.0	33.7	20.6	0.2	1.4	—	−3.8
24.5	69.3	33.5	29.6	2	Lanarkshire, Bothwell	78.6	2.1	23.4	60.9	10.8	10.8	—	1.9	—	3.0
11.1	85.0	31.3	30.1	2	Coatbridge & Airdrie	75.3	0.8	27.5	53.9	—	11.6	—	(3.3)	—	6.1
14.0	83.0	44.1	25.4	2	East Kilbride	79.7	0.6	29.4	59.6	—	15.6	C1.1	(5.1)	—	7.2
26.0	68.1	34.3	28.9	2	Hamilton	79.6	2.4	23.8	43.2	7.1	16.6	—	(4.0)	—	11.9
25.6	62.8	32.4	31.8	4	Lanark	81.8	−0.4	30.9	55.5	—	18.8	—	3.6	—	3.6
34.1	58.1	38.4	28.1	2	Lanarkshire, North	79.7	0.3	31.5	56.9	—	13.1	—	(4.4)	—	3.5
12.7	83.2	37.2	29.2	2	Motherwell & Wishaw	77.8	2.4	28.9	46.7	18.4	12.3	C1.9	(2.9)	—	4.7
35.6	55.3	42.1	25.7	2	Rutherglen	80.4	1.6	26.5	47.8	9.0	8.4	—	12.1	—	1.1
21.5	65.7	39.0	30.3	3	Midlothian	77.8	0.3	26.4	47.8	9.0	16.8	—	2.1	—	7.7

% Owner-Occupiers	% Council Tenants	% Non-Manual	% Skilled Workers	Urban Scale	Constituency	% Voting	% Change	Con. %	Lab. %	Lib. %	S.N.P.	Others %	Change in Lib. %	Swing	Two-party Swing
35.2	34.5	28.9	18.5	4	Moray & Nairn†	77.5	2.8	40.1	8.7	12.3	38.9	—	3.1	—	1.6
51.6	22.3	29.9	28.9	5	Orkney & Zetland	67.2	0.4	21.3	17.4	56.4	4.8	—	0.2	—	1.6
41.1	26.2	39.8	19.3	5	Perthshire, Kinross & West	79.6	4.5	50.5	8.4	11.6	29.4	—	2.5	—	1.2
33.4	41.9	41.4	21.5	4	Perth & East†	77.3	3.5	41.9	13.4	9.2	35.5	—	2.5	—	1.8
					Renfrewshire,										
15.7	69.9	28.2	31.4	2	Greenock & Port Glasgow	73.7	2.6	10.9	53.0	28.2	7.6	W0.4	8.7	—	-1.9
20.6	65.7	32.7	25.8	2	Paisley	72.8	0.6	26.2	55.8	—	15.7	C0.3, W0.3, 1.7	(6.5)	—	6.1
67.0	27.5	59.3	17.7	2	Renfrewshire East	80.6	2.9	49.9	24.4	18.0	7.7	—	3.4	—	0.7
28.9	59.4	41.4	24.7	2	Renfrewshire West	81.2	1.1	31.0	44.5	11.4	13.1	—	5.3	—	0.0
43.8	32.5	33.7	24.2	5	Ross & Cromarty	76.4	6.9	42.4	20.1	13.9	23.6	—	5.4	—	-2.0
33.8	42.7	33.3	28.2	4	Roxburgh, Selkirk & Peebles	82.0	2.8	31.3	8.5	53.1	7.2	—	9.4	—	3.2
					Stirlingshire,										
21.4	71.3	32.3	31.4	2	Clackmannan & East†	81.7	-0.1	18.0	41.9	—	40.1	—	(2.5)	—	7.7
23.6	67.6	36.4	27.4	2	Stirling, Falkirk & Grangemouth	78.9	-0.4	26.6	56.5	—	17.0	—	(2.9)	—	7.5
20.6	70.0	35.2	29.4	3	Stirlingshire West	82.0	1.2	25.8	47.7	8.3	18.3	C0.6	3.9	—	3.0
15.4	76.8	30.1	29.2	2	West Lothian	78.1	-0.7	19.7	54.9	—	24.9	—	(3.4)	—	8.4
71.3	19.8	21.5	30.1	4	Western Isles	67.5	4.1	10.6	32.3	4.6	52.5	—	-0.9	—	-0.4

Northern Ireland

Constituency	% voting	change in % voting	OUP	DUP	Other U	UPNI	Alli-ance	SDLP	Other Rep	Other
Antrim, North	64.2	6.8	23.4	51.7	—	—	11.9	7.4	5.6	—
South	58.2	0.2	69.0	—	—	—	16.2	10.1	2.2	2.6
Armagh	70.1	1.4	48.5	8.6	—	—	3.2	36.1	3.5	—
Belfast, East †	67.6	0.4	31.2	31.4	—	4.0	29.5	—	—	3.9
North †	65.1	−0.8	25.3	27.6	—	10.0	9.7	18.5	4.5	4.5
South	67.9	0.2	61.7	—	—	3.8	25.1	7.9	—	1.5
West	56.5	−10.6	24.8	11.2	—	—	6.1	49.5	6.9	1.6
Down, North	62.2	1.3	18.9	—	59.6	—	21.5	—	—	0.3, 0.1
South	72.0	−0.4	50.0	—	—	—	6.8	37.3	2.9 2.6	—
Fermanagh & S. Tyrone	87.0	−1.7	28.0	—	17.0	—	1.7	17.3	36.0	—
Londonderry	67.1	−2.3	49.7	—	—	—	9.2	30.2	8.6, 1.4	1.0
Mid-Ulster	80.4	1.4	—	—	44.7	—	5.3	29.4	18.4, 2.2	—
Northern Ireland	67.7	0.3	36.6	10.2	11.0	1.2	11.9	19.7	8.3	1.1

TURNOUT

10 Highest		10 Lowest		10 Largest Increase		10 Largest Decrease	
%		%		%		%	
87.0	Fermanagh & S.T.	53.3	Stepney & P.	+10.6	Lambeth C.	−10.7	Belfast W.
86.2	Kingswood	55.1	C. of Lon. & Westminster S.	+10.3	Manchester C.	−9.0	Cardiff W.
86.1	Cornwall N.	55.4	Newham N.W.	+9.7	Vauxhall	−2.6	Gl. Govan
85.0	Welwyn & H.	55.5	Bethnal G. & B.	+9.6	Man. Ardwick	−2.5	Keighley
84.8	Hemel Hempstead	56.5	Belfast W.	+8.7	Man. Moss Side	−2.5	Oldham E.
84.5	Bosworth	57.1	Newham S.	+8.7	Leeds S.E.	−2.3	Londonderry
84.4	Carmarthen	57.3	Chelsea	+8.5	Southgate	−1.7	Fermanagh & S.T.
84.2	Brecon & Radnor	57.4	Liv. Scotland-Exch.	+8.5	Norwood	−1.2	Carmarthen
84.1	Skipton	57.7	Peckham	+8.3	Islington C.	−1.1	Ply. Devonport
83.9	Dunbarton E.	58.2	Antrim S.	+8.2	Kensington	−1.1	Buckingham

EXTREME SWINGS

10 Highest Swings (total vote)		10 Lowest Swings (total vote)	
%		%	
14.3	Ashfield	−4.4	Gl. Cathcart
14.0	Barking	−3.1	Gl. Kelvingrove
13.4	Dagenham	−2.9	Bradford W.
13.0	B'ham, Stechford	−2.0	Edin., C.
12.9	Harlow	−1.5	Gl. Pollok
12.9	Stepney & P.	−1.4	Ipswich
12.5	Anglesey	−1.3	Edinburgh Leith
11.6	Essex S.E.	−1.2	Edinburgh, S
11.6	Hackney S.	−1.1	Gl. Hillhead
11.5	Peckham	−0.8	Thornaby

CLOSE RESULTS

10 Closest Results	
% votes	
0.1 (29)	Preston N. (Con.)
0.1 (38)	Bury & Rad. (Lab.)
0.2 (64)	Belfast E. (D.U.P.)
0.2 (78)	Keighley (Lab.)
0.3(106)	Paddington (Con.)
0.3(122)	Dulwich (Lab.)
0.3(214)	Derby N. (Lab.)
0.4(204)	B'ham North'd (Con.)
0.5(246)	Luton W. (Con.)
0.5(352)	Isle of Wight (Lib.)

MINOR PARTIES

10 Liberal nearest misses

%	
-5.4	Aberdeens. W.
-5.4	Montgomery
-6.2	Richmond (Sy)
-7.9	Chippenham
-8.0	Cornwall N.
-8.0	Chelmsford
-10.3	Hereford
-11.7	Louth
-12.3	Leominster
-12.5	Salisbury

10 most improved Liberals

% incr.	% vote	
+24.7	(52.0)	Liv. Edge Hill*
+13.0	(52.8)	Truro*
+12.1	(18.4)	Rutherglen
+11.2	(54.3)	Berwick-upon-Tweed*
+10.4	(23.4)	Bethnal G. & B.
+10.4	(23.0)	Fife E.
+9.4	(53.1)	Roxburgh, S&P*
+8.7	(28.2)	Greenock & PG
+7.8	(40.5)	Richmond (Sy)
+7.7	(26.2)	Chertsey

10 best SNP

% vote	% maj.	
52.5	(+20.2)	W. Isles*
41.5	(-2.1)	S. Angus
41.4	(-1.4)	Aberdeens. E.
41.2	(-3.4)	Banff
41.0	(+5.0)	Dundee E.*
40.1	(-1.8)	Stirling E. & Cl.
38.9	(-1.2)	Moray & Nairn
37.1	(-8.7)	Galloway
35.5	(-6.4)	Perth & E.P.
31.8	(-5.0)	Argyll

10 best PC

% vote	% maj.	
49.7	(+24.9)	Caernarvon*
40.8	(+17.2)	Merioneth*
32.0	(-3.8)	Carmarthen
20.3	(-18.7)	Anglesey
15.3	(-49.2)	Neath
14.9	(-43.9)	Caerphilly
14.5	(-20.1)	Cardigan
10.4	(-75.2)	Cardiff W.
9.8	(-61.7)	Aberdare
9.4	(-61.9)	Merthyr

10 Best 'Other' Votes (GB)

%	
31.4	Ayrshire S. (Sc. Lab. Party)
28.8	Blyth (Ind. Lab.)
5.2	Jarrow (Ind. Lab.)
4.9	Eton & Slough (Ind. Con.)
4.1	St. Ives (Mebyon K.)
4.1	Lincoln (Dem. Lab.)
4.0	Westbury (Ind.)
3.6	Rhondda (Comm.)
3.1	Falmouth & C. (Mebyon K.)
3.0	Westbury (Wessex Reg.)

Next 10 'Other' Votes (GB)

%	
2.9	Brigg & Scun. (Dem. Lab.)
2.8	Worcs. S. (Ecol.)
2.6	Taunton (Ecol.)
2.6	Dunbarton C. (Comm.)
2.5	Barkston Ash (Ecol.)
2.5	Fife C. (Comm.)
2.4	Crosby (Ecol.)
2.4	Bm. Sparkbrook (Comm.)
2.3	Middlesbrough (WRP)
2.3	Honiton (Ecol.)

10 Best National Front

%	
7.6	Hackney S. & S.
6.2	Newham S.
6.1	Bethnal G. & B.
5.1	Hackney C.
5.0	Stepney & P.
4.4	Peckham
4.2	Deptford
4.2	Newham N.E.
4.1	Cardiff W.
4.0	Newham N.W.

* Elected

BY-ELECTIONS 1974—9

		Turnout %	Con. %	Lab. %	Lib. %	NF %	Others %	Swing (Total Vote) (a) 1974 – by-elec. (b) by-elec. – 1979 (c) 1974–1979
Woolwich West CON. GAIN	1974	73.9	38.6	47.1	14.3	–	–	(a) 8.4
	26.6.75	62.3	48.8	42.1	5.3	2.4	(4) 1.4	(b) –0.5
	1979	79.6	47.3	41.5	9.7	1.4	–	(c) 7.9
Coventry NW	1974	75.2	31.6	51.9	15.7	–	–	(a) 5.0
	4.3.76	72.9	37.4	47.7	11.3	2.8	(3) 0.8	(b) 0.1
	1979	79.2	39.9	50.1	8.8	0.9	0.3	(c) 5.1
Carshalton	1974	74.3	45.4	37.9	16.7	–	–	(a) 8.4
	11.3.76	60.5	51.7	27.5	15.0	4.6	(3) 1.2	(b) –2.1
	1979	76.8	51.3	31.2	15.7	1.8	–	(c) 6.3
Wirral	1974	75.5	50.8	31.6	17.6	–	–	(a) 13.7
	11.3.76	55.5	66.8	20.3	11.4	–	(2) 1.5	(b) –7.8
	1979	77.8	59.0	28.1	12.9	–	–	(c) 5.9
Rotherham	1974	65.5	22.1	64.6	13.3	–	–	(a) 13.3
	24.6.76	46.8	34.7	50.7	7.8	6.0	(2) 0.8	(b) –7.3
	1979	72.1	29.9	60.5	8.4	1.1	–	(c) 6.0
Thurrock	1974	68.6	24.4	55.6	20.0	–	–	(a) 10.2
	15.7.76	54.1	35.4	45.3	12.2	6.6	(2) 0.5	(b) 0.2
	1979	75.1	39.2	48.6	9.4	2.0	(2) 0.8	(c) 10.4
Newcastle Central	1974	58.4	16.5	71.8	11.7	–	–	
	4.11.76	41.0	19.7	47.6	29.0	1.8	1.9	
	1979	65.3	19.3	67.3	13.4	–	–	(c) 3.7

Walsall North	1974	66.0	26.1	59.5	13.4	—	1.0	(a)	22.5
CON GAIN	4.11.76	51.5	43.4	31.6	3.2	7.3	(5)14.5	(b)	−11.5
LAB RECOVERY	1979	72.3	39.8	50.9	7.2	2.1	—	(c)	11.0
Workington	1974	75.8	32.3	56.0	11.7	—	—	(a)	13.1
CON GAIN	4.11.76	74.2	48.2	45.6	6.2	—	—	(b)	−7.6
LAB RECOVERY	1979	83.8	40.7	53.2	6.1	—	—	(c)	5.5
Cambridge	1974	69.6	41.2	36.0	21.1	—	1.7	(a)	9.9
	2.12.76	49.2	51.0	26.0	18.3	1.8	(2)2.9	(b)	−8.7
	1979	72.0	45.7	37.1	16.6	0.6	—	(c)	1.2
City of London	1974	53.2	51.7	30.9	14.9	2.5	—	(a)	9.3
& Westminster, South	24.2.77	39.6	59.1	19.7	9.8	5.2	(6)6.2	(b)	−2.1
	1979	55.1	60.7	25.4	12.2	1.7	—	(c)	7.2
Birmingham,	1974	64.1	27.8	57.6	14.6	—	—	(a)	17.5
Stechford	31.3.77	58.8	43.4	38.0	8.0	8.2	(2)2.4	(b)	−4.6
CON GAIN	1979	71.6	44.6	48.4	5.4	1.6	—	(c)	12.9
LAB RECOVERY									
Grimsby	1974	69.4	31.9	47.1	20.6	—	0.4	(a)	7.1
	28.4.77	70.2	45.7	46.9	6.7	—	(3)0.7	(b)	−5.6
	1979	75.8	39.7	52.0	7.6	0.3	0.4	(c)	1.5
Ashfield	1974	74.7	63.4	22.3	14.3	—	—	(a)	20.9
CON GAIN	28.4.77	59.7	43.1	42.5	9.6	3.8	1.0	(b)	−6.5
LAB RECOVERY	1979	80.6	40.4	52.8	6.2	0.6	—	(c)	14.4
Saffron Walden	1974	78.1	43.7	26.0	30.3	—	—		
	7.7.77	64.8	55.7	14.6	25.2	—	4.5		
	1979	81.6	53.8	19.9	24.9	0.6	0.8		

		Turnout %	Con. %	Lab. %	Lib. %	NF %	Others %	Swing (Total Vote) (a) 1974 – by-elec.	(b) by-elec. – 1979	(c) 1974–1979
Birmingham, Ladywood	1974	56.9	22.1	64.5	13.4	–	–	(a) 11.9		
	18.8.77	42.6	28.4	53.1	4.9	5.7	7.9		(b) –6.0	
	1979	62.3	26.9	63.5	9.6	–	–			(c) 5.9
Bournemouth East	1974	70.5	51.7	21.0	25.2	2.1	(2) 4.9			
	24.11.77	42.6	63.4	15.3	13.4	3.0	(2) 2.7		(b) –1.9	
	1979	73.1	62.6	18.3	16.4	–	–			
Ilford North CON GAIN	1974	74.5	40.9	42.5	16.6	–	–	(a) 6.9		
	2.3.78	69.1	50.3	38.0	5.0	4.8	(4) 1.9		(b) 0.8	
	1979	79.0	51.3	37.3	8.9	1.6	0.9			(c) 6.1
Glasgow, Garscadden	1979	70.8	12.9	50.9	5.0	–	(N) 31.2			
	13.4.78	69.1	18.5	45.4	–	–	(N) 32.9, (3) 3.2			
	1979	73.2	21.9	61.5	–	–	(N) 15.0, (1) 1.0			
Lambeth Central	1974	52.6	26.2	60.1	12.5	–	(2) 1.2	(a) 9.5		
	20.4.78	44.5	34.4	49.4	5.3	6.2	(7) 4.7		(b) –3.0	
	1979	63.2	33.1	54.7	8.5	3.0	(2) 0.7			(c) 6.5
Epsom & Ewell	1974	73.7	54.1	19.3	26.6	–	–			
	27.4.78	54.9	63.6	16.5	12.8	1.8	5.3			
	1979	76.9	61.9	17.9	20.2	–	–			
Wycombe	1974	74.3	46.3	30.8	19.4	3.5	–	(a) 8.0		
	27.4.78	59.0	60.0	28.5	7.4	4.1	–		(b) –0.6	
	1979	77.6	57.3	27.0	14.4	1.3	–			(c) 7.4

Constituency	Date								
Hamilton	1974	77.2	9.5	47.5	4.0	—	(N)39.0	1.0	(a) 3.5
	31.5.78	72.1	13.0	51.0	2.6	—	(N)33.4	1.5	(b) −3.7
	1979	79.6	23.8	59.6	—	—	(N)16.6	0.7	(c) −0.3
Manchester, Moss Side	1974	62.9	34.3	47.1	17.6	—	—	—	(a) 8.9
	13.7.78	51.6	40.6	46.4	9.2	2.3	—	—	(b) −2.2
	1979	71.5	38.7	51.9	8.7	—	—	—	(c) 6.7
Penistone	1974	74.7	24.0	54.2	21.8	—	—	—	
	13.7.78	59.8	32.9	45.5	21.6	—	—	—	
	1979	78.9	32.1	49.1	18.9	—	—	—	
Pontefract & Castleford	1974	71.2	16.2	70.4	12.3	—	—	1.1	(a) 7.8
	26.10.78	48.9	27.3	65.8	6.9	—	—	—	(b) −3.1
	1979	73.9	23.8	68.2	8.1	—	—	—	(c) 4.7
Berwick & E. Lothian	1974	83.0	37.6	43.3	5.9	—	(N)13.2	—	(a) −0.8
	26.10.78	71.2	40.2	47.4	3.6	—	(N)8.8	—	(b) 2.0
	1979	82.9	40.2	43.5	9.8	—	(N)6.5	—	(c) −1.2
Clitheroe	1974	78.6	48.0	31.2	20.8	—	—	—	(a) 9.9
	1.3.79	66.1	65.0	28.4	6.6	—	—	—	(b) −4.8
	1979	80.7	57.1	30.7	12.2	—	—	—	(c) 5.1
Knutsford	1974	76.8	51.0	22.6	26.4	—	—	—	
	1.3.79	59.6	67.1	15.6	15.8	—	—	1.5	
	1979	78.0	59.6	20.0	18.9	—	—	1.5	
Liverpool, Edge Hill LIB GAIN	1974	61.2	20.8	51.9	27.3	—	—	—	
	29.3.79	56.6	9.4	23.8	64.1	—	—	2.7	
	1979	69.0	12.7	34.6	52.0	0.6	—	—	

Appendix 2: An Analysis of the Voting

by John Curtice and Michael Steed

The 1979 election produced an overall majority of 43 seats. This was amply sufficient to withstand likely government by-election losses for a full five-year parliament, and was the first such clear-cut victory for either major party since 1970. Moreover it also reduced the representation of third parties from 42 at the dissolution to 27. On the face of it, the two-party system came back into favour.

The overall votes tell a different story. In the first eight post-war elections (1945–70), the Conservative and Labour share of the total vote cast had averaged 91.3%, and had never fallen below 87.5% (1964). In the two 1974 elections it dropped to 75.0%; in 1979 it only rose to 80.8%. The two-party system was restored in the House of Commons, but not among the people.

There are further reasons to question whether the 1979 election signified a return to the pre-1974 pattern. In the 1950s and 1960s, the operation of the British two-party system depended partly on the exaggeration of the winning party's lead in votes into a far larger one in seats, and partly on one feature of British electoral behaviour – the uniformity of swing throughout the country. In this analysis we question whether the 1979 election signifies a return to the previous situation by examining the evidence for the continued existence of these underpinnings of the two-party system.

A summary of the result in Great Britain is presented in Table 1.[1] The rise in the two-party vote reflected several distinct changes. In Scotland the SNP vote plummeted, while in England

---

[1] The Northern Ireland results confirmed the province's total departure from the British party system; we consequently look at those results separately. The change in the Northern Ireland situation by itself accounts for about 1½% of the drop in the two-party share of the UK vote compared with pre-1974 figures.

Table 1. Voting by Type of Contest in the October 1974 and 1979 General Elections

Type	England & Wales 3-cornered		Lib withdrawal		Scotland 4-cornered		Lib withdrawal		All GB	
	Votes (000s)	%	Votes (000s)	%	Votes (000s)	%	Votes (000s)	%	Votes (000s)	%
October 1974										
Con	9,590	38.5	162	24.3	482	29.1	172	18.0	10,465	36.7
Lab	9,992	40.1	393	59.1	524	31.7	407	42.7	11,457	40.2
Lib	5,029	20.2	73	11.0	179	10.8	48	5.0	5,347	18.8
SNP	–	–	–	–	467	28.2	324	34.0	840	2.9
Other	287	1.2	38	5.7	4	0.2	3	0.3	379	1.3
Total	24,899		666		1,656		954		28,487	
May 1979										
Con	12,510	46.8	231	34.0	604	33.8	275	28.2	13,698	44.9
Lab	9,809	36.7	417	61.3	638	35.7	502	51.5	11,532	37.8
Lib	4,037	15.1	–	–	257	14.4	–	–	4,314	14.1
SNP	–	–	–	–	283	15.8	194	19.8	504	1.7
Other	399	1.5	32	4.7	4	0.2	4	0.4	477	1.6
Total	26,755		680		1,786		975		30,525	

3-cornered: The 531 constituencies in England and Wales with Conservative, Labour and Liberal candidates at both elections.

Liberal withdrawal (England and Wales): The 17 constituencies where Liberals withdrew in May 1979.

4-cornered: The 42 constituencies in Scotland with Conservative, Labour, Liberal and SNP candidates at both elections.

Liberal withdrawal (Scotland): The 25 constituencies where Liberals withdrew in May 1979.

Eight seats are excluded from those categories, but included in the final column: Cardiff West (no Con candidate May 1979); Blyth, Sheffield, Brightside and South Ayrshire (split Lab vote at one or both elections); Lincoln (split Lab vote; Lib vote; Lib vote; Argyll (Lib intervention in May 1979); Glasgow Provan, Central Fife (no Lib candidate both elections).

and Wales the Liberal vote dropped on a more modest scale. To these voluntary voting movements from the smaller to the larger parties was added the effect of the Liberal party failing to nominate candidates in 44 constituencies where a Liberal had stood in October 1974. Table 1 distinguishes the four situations. In Scotland the Liberal withdrawals constitute a significant group, and so are treated separately. But in the 17 constituencies in England and Wales where 1974 Liberal voters had to choose in 1979 between abstention, Conservative, Labour and maybe a minor party, the absence of a Liberal had no clear effect on swing or turnout.[2] We can therefore safely include these seats in our analysis of swing and turnout, though whenever the change in the Liberal vote is involved, our analysis is restricted to the 531 strictly comparable English or Welsh three-cornered contests, or the 573 in the whole of Great Britain.

Table 2 presents the electoral change between October 1974 and 1979 in several different ways. Each party's gain or loss is shown together with two measures of swing. Total vote swing is the average of the change in the Conservative and Labour shares of the total vote; '–' indicates a swing to Labour. Two-party swing is the change in the Conservative share of the vote cast for Conservatives and Labour only. All references to swing in this appendix are to two-party swing unless otherwise stated. Both the two-party swing and total vote swing in each constituency are listed on pp. 360–82. In the circumstances of 1979, for most of the analyses the measure of swing used would not make a great difference to the findings, but two-party swing enables us to take better account of the impact of the movement to and from the Liberals and the SNP on the relative fortunes of the two major parties.

By any of the measures of swing, the Conservatives secured the biggest net movement between the two largest parties at any election since 1945. This substantial swing produced the decisive outcome of the election; it gave the Conservatives as large a plurality of votes (7.0%) over the next largest party as any party

[2] These seats are a small, unrepresentative group – all in the North-West, South Wales or the West Midland conurbation, and all held by Labour in 1974. In previous elections, Liberals without a candidate have been shown to have a higher abstention rate, and to boost the vote of minor parties such as the National Front. In 1979 these effects, if present at all, were slight. In the 17 constituencies the swing was lower than the national average, but detailed inspection suggests that this reflects location rather than Liberal preference for Labour.

Table 2.   Changes in Voting 1974 (October)—1979 (GB only)

	Seats included	Mean change	Overall change
Change in turnout	all (623)	3.1	3.2
Change in Con vote	618	7.9	8.2
	573	7.7	8.0
Change in Lab vote	618	−2.0	−2.5
	573	−2.7	−3.0
Change in Lib vote	573	−4.4	−4.6
Total vote swing	618	4.9	5.3
Two-party swing	618	6.4	6.6

618: all but Cardiff West and four seats (see Table 1) with a split Labour vote.
573: those of the 618 with a Liberal candidate in both 1974 and 1979.

had enjoyed since Labour's 1945 land-slide — larger, in fact, than the 1955 and 1959 Conservative victories which produced bigger parliamentary majorities. Yet Mrs Thatcher took office with a smaller share of the national vote than any Prime Minister enjoying a secure parliamentary majority since Bonar Law in 1922.

For Labour the result was an unmitigated setback. Although their share of the popular vote fell by only 2½%, this brought the party to its lowest level of support since the debacle of 1931. For both the Liberals and the Nationalists it was a mixed outcome. Their support dropped in 1979, but, on a longer view, both the Liberal party and the SNP held on to approximately one-third of the electoral ground they had gained between 1970 and their respective peaks in February and October 1974. The SNP's support remained well ahead of that in any pre-1974 general election. While, after allowing for the differences in the number of candidates, Liberal support was below its 1964 level, it was a better Liberal result than in any of the other six elections in the 1950—70 period, and was a substantial improvement on the 1951 and 1970 results, the two previous elections ending a period of Labour government.

We examine first the movement between the two largest parties and particularly its most arresting feature — the variation in swing. We then turn to the change in support for the smaller parties, and the impact this had on the relative fortunes of the Conservative and Labour parties.

Variations in Swing

The 1974–9 swing was not uniform: it varied more from seat to seat than in any other election since 1950. Table 3 shows the standard deviation of the constituency swings at each election since 1955. However, most of the variation can be attributed to factors working systematically throughout the country rather than to the eccentricities of individual seats.

Table 3.   Variation in Swing

	Mean Swing	Standard Deviation	No. of months since previous election
1955–9	1.3	2.7	52
1959–64	−3.5	3.1	60
1964–6	−3.5	2.1	17
1966–70	4.7	2.6	50
Feb–Oct 1974	−3.3	2.4	8
Oct 1974–9	6.4	4.1	53

1970–Feb 1974 is omitted because of the distortions produced by the general revision of boundaries.

The most striking difference in swing was the marked contrast between the North and the South of Great Britain. As can be seen from the tables on pp. 356 the swing to Conservative in each of the five southernmost regions of England and in Wales was higher than in any of the three northernmost regions of England and in Scotland. The line drawn just south of the Humber to the Mersey, which is the boundary in these regional tables, is very close to the actual boundary between high southern swings and lower northern ones. The boundary can be plotted more precisely on the ground. To the west of the Pennines it dips south to include Stoke-on-Trent and some nearby constituencies. Towards the North Sea, Lindsey (Lincs.) except Grimsby, nearly the whole of South Yorkshire, and the Wakefield area of West Yorkshire had higher swings, partly reflecting the mining character of many constituencies in this area (see p. 400); lower swings started sharply with Huddersfield, Dewsbury and Leeds.

The impact of this North-South variation shows up in a chart of the individual swings. The distribution comes close to a bimodal distribution with Southern British and Northern British

Variations in Constituency Swings Oct. 1974–1979.

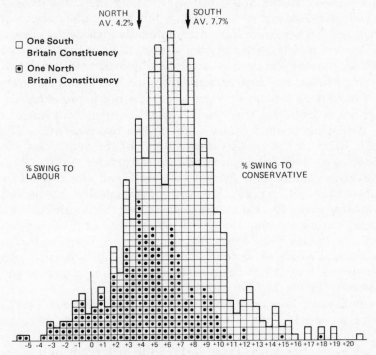

This diagram is based on two-party swing. The extreme cases are not marked (Banff (−8.0), Merioneth (+23.6), Carmarthen (+26.6) and Cardigan (+38.4).

peaks. Post-war British elections have always previously produced unimodal distributions. The variation is genuinely regional, as it is not possible to account for it by differences in urbanisation or any other compositional characteristics. North Britain swung to the Conservatives by little more than half the amount (mean 4.2%) that South Britain did (mean 7.7%).[3]

[3] We use the following definitions in this appendix:
South & Midlands: the five southernmost regions of England.
North of England: the three northernmost regions of England.
South Britain: South & Midlands plus Wales.
North Britain: North of England plus Scotland.
For consistency we have used the regions in the tables on pp. 355–7. These are the pre-1974 standard regions, since constituency boundaries have yet to be brought into line with the 1974 local government reorganisation. On the post-1974 standard regional boundaries High Peak, Horncastle, some of Louth and most of Gainsborough would be switched to South Britain.

Within North Britain, the swing was still lower in Scotland (see p. 414). Within South Britain, the table on p. 356 shows a low regional swing in East Anglia, but this is more apparent than real.[4] There were some extraordinarily high swings in rural Wales (see p. 403), affecting the voting statistics for Wales as a whole, but for the most part the Welsh voted with the rest of South Britain. For these reasons all the analysis in this appendix has been done separately, even where it is not so presented, for the South & Midlands, North of England, Scotland and Wales.

Within the South & Midlands there were two areas of notably high swing to the Conservatives, a part of the South-East and some West Midland conurbation constituencies. In the West Midlands conurbation, the pattern was varied and there were substantial differences between geographically contiguous constituencies. The distinctive segment of the South-East is a large, continuous zone focussing on the East End of London and on South-West Essex, but bearing no resemblance to traditionally-defined regions in the South-East — it cuts right across the boundaries between Inner and Outer London, and between Greater London and the Home Counties.

In Greater London itself, the highest swings (mean 14.2%) were recorded in ten constituencies stretching from Islington Central through the East End along the north bank of the Thames to Dagenham. These formed the high point of a wider area of consistently high swings. This area, containing 31 constituencies, comprised all the seats in the 7 north-easternmost boroughs, plus 4 constituencies, from Tottenham to Enfield North, along the Lea valley, 2 divisions of Islington, the borough of Southwark and three other Labour strongholds on the south bank of the Thames. Within this well-defined group of constituencies, the swing averaged 11.1% and only dropped below 7.5% in one seat, the Labour marginal, Ilford South. In the remaining two-thirds of Greater London the swing was consistently much lower (mean 6.2%) and only rose above 10% in Hayes & Harlington and, as a result of tactical voting, in the two Richmond-on-Thames seats.

---

[4] There was no consistently lower swing throughout East Anglia. The 17 constituencies include one strongly university influenced town, Cambridge (see p. 400); two fishing ports, Lowestoft and Yarmouth (see p. 399); and the very unusual swing in Ipswich (see p. 413). The average swing in the remaining 13 was 6.8%.

The high North-East London swing extended out into Essex where, averaging 11.2%, it varied rather more; it was highest in the 7 south-western constituencies clustered close to the GLC border (mean 13.1%). But in a whole arc of 34 constituencies North and West of London, stretching from East Herts to Basingstoke and Spelthorne the swing was above average at 8.6%; here it was extremely consistent, with low swings only in 3 seats Labour gained in October 1974 — Hemel Hempstead, Oxford and Welwyn & Hatfield. In the southern Home Counties (Kent, Sussex and most of Hampshire and Surrey) it was lower, averaging 6.3%.

Certain of the high swings within these areas, notably the Dagenham swing (16.6%), and those leading to the unexpected Labour losses in Birmingham Northfield, Basildon, and Hertford & Stevenage attracted considerable attention immediately after polling day. These results encouraged the notion that the Conservatives had made special advances among car workers and among New Town dwellers. Both ideas fitted a more general hypothesis that certain parts of the electorate were responding directly to particular election pledges. Car workers could have been reacting against Labour's incomes policy, while New Town dwellers might have been registering their approval of the Conservative promise on the sale of council houses. Closer examination suggests the need for caution about such conclusions. Constituencies containing New Towns and major car plants did, more often than not, have above average swings. But in neither case was there a consistent pattern — the three unusually low swings in the northern Home Counties were in two New Towns and a major motor manufacturing town (all marginal seats, see p. 408) — and in only a handful of seats, such as Dagenham and Harlow, was the swing above that in nearby but dissimilar constituencies. In the rest of the country, there were some identifiable high swings in New Towns such as Ince (which contains Skelmersdale and had the highest swing in the North-West) and Kettering (which contains Corby and had the second highest East Midland swing). But again the pattern is not consistent, and is complicated by several constituencies containing both New Towns and coal mining activity.

Three Essex constituencies, all composed largely of Londoners decanted outwards, may offer an important clue to the geography of the 1979 swing. Each had a swing of more than 12%.

In Essex South-East these Londoners' homes were built and owned privately (82% were owner-occupied in the 1971 census), Harlow (75% council tenant) is a New Town and Dagenham (67% council tenant) is dominated by a massive former London Country Council estate. This suggests that the movement in this area was not a simple response to the housing issue. Furthermore because they lie on the north-eastern perimeter, these areas all drew their populations very disproportionately from the old East End, whose remaining voters were swinging sharply to the right at this election. East End dwellers, exiled East Enders and the children of former East End dwellers all moved together. This suggests that underlying developments in the history of social structures and political attitudes in East London may be behind this area's swing in 1979.

Another part of the explanation could lie in the higher movement to the Conservatives which survey evidence shows among skilled manual workers (see p. 343). Overall, there is a positive but very low correlation (0.14) between the 1974–9 swing and the proportion of skilled manual workers (which is given for each constituency in the tables on pp. 360–82). Several constituencies with high proportions of skilled manual workers, such as the Potteries area or Barrow, had low swings. So any relationship is far from simple. It may be that there were some occupational groups within the skilled working class which did swing markedly more heavily to Conservative at this election, and that their behaviour was reflected in the higher swings in some manufacturing areas. But swing and the market researcher's C2 category are instruments which are too crude to identify the groups precisely.

The high swings to Mrs Thatcher in North-East London probably also reflected one more factor. This is the area which has given the National Front some of its highest support in the past, and the indications that a Conservative government would take a more restrictive line on coloured immigration could have had most appeal here. Within north-east London the rank order correlation between the 1974–9 swing to Conservative and the NF's level of support in the 1977 Greater London Council elections, 0.62, is strong evidence for such an interpretation.

However it is clear that the immigration issue worked both ways. Two of the only 6 English swings to Labour in seats where Conservative and Labour shared first and second places occurred in Bradford West (−2.9%) and Leicester South (−0.8%), turning two pre-1974 Conservative seats into relatively safe Labour ones. Both have substantial Asian communities, as does Southall, which produced the lowest swing in the South-East (0.8%). Constituencies in Greater London with large numbers of black people did not behave distinctively (possibly because those blacks who vote were already strongly Labour). But in Birmingham the 4 most black constituencies, where the 1971 population contained more than one-sixth born in the New Commonwealth, had low swings (mean 3.0%) whilst the remaining 8 (all with less than one-tenth New Commonwealth born in 1971) had much higher swings (mean 9.0%); there were signs of a similar pattern in some other parts of the West Midlands conurbation and also in Manchester and Leeds (in the Ardwick, Moss Side and Leeds North-East results).

It is not possible to deduce from these figures anything precise about ethnic voting. Apart from the problems of discerning individual behaviour from ecological evidence, the fact that most London constituencies now have significant coloured communities limits any conclusions. But it seems most likely that the following four changes were taking place in most urban areas with significant ethnic minorities. Firstly, the already strong preference of black and brown voters for Labour was strengthened at the 1979 election; a CRE survey suggested that Labour got 85%—90% of their votes. Secondly, the increasing proportion of coloured voters in certain constituencies has been steadily altering their political character in Labour's favour. Thirdly, outside North-East London at any rate, white voters with black or brown neighbours showed no marked response to the Conservative party's appeal. Fourthly, again outside the NF's North-East London territory, the Conservative party gained most in areas which are overwhelmingly white, but are near immigrant concentrations. These divergent movements were most sharply illustrated in Birmingham where adjacent constituencies differed very sharply in the number of coloured people living in them, and where the swing varied substantially.

There was a consistently lower swing in constituencies with fishing interests, especially on the east coast of England, and particularly on Humberside, presumably in response to John Silkin's stance as Agriculture and Fisheries Minister in Brussels.

Another group of constituencies with consistently lower

swings comprised those with the highest number of students, as Table 4 shows. Apart from Cardigan, these seats generally showed a better performance for Labour of around 2—3%. Once again, explanations must be offered with caution. Though changes in the student vote may have played some part, the phenomenon could just as easily have reflected the behaviour of university teachers and other professional people, who tend to cluster in these constituencies.

But whilst some of these swings may be evidence of short-term responses to policy pledges or of the behaviour of certain social groups in the light of the 1979 party images, it is important to stress how much of the variation in the movement in opinion between 1974 and 1979 represents not a new departure, but the continuation, and in some cases an acceleration, of trends which have been evident since the 1959 general election. Previous appendices in this series have picked out, in addition to regional variations, distinctive long-term electoral trends in large cities, mining areas and more rural constituencies. This time, rural areas did not behave differently from urban areas outside the big cities, but mining constituencies did throughout Britain and, with the very striking exceptions of parts of Inner London and the West Midland conurbation, so did big cities:

Table 4.   Swing since October 1974 in Special Groups of Seats

	All Seats	Big Cities	Mining Seats	Student Seats
South & Midlands	7.6 (344)	7.3 (71)[a]	8.9 (14)	3.5 (10)
North of England	5.1 (169)	3.5 (41)	7.7 (19)	1.5 (7)
Wales	9.4 (35)[b]	3.7 (3)	8.0 (11)	b
Scotland	2.0 (70)	1.6 (20)	6.1 (4)	−1.5 (6)

Definitions: Mining — constituencies with at least 6% engaged in mining at the 1971 census.

Student — the 25 constituencies with the most students at the 1971 census.

[a]Excluding London and the West Midland conurbation, this figure becomes 5.3 (21).
[b] Excluding the 8 most rural constituencies, the figure for Wales becomes 6.8 (27); one of the two student seats in Wales is in Cardigan, where the rural Welsh swing masked any university effect in Aberystwyth.

Table 5. Swing since 1970 by Region and Big City

	All seats		Big Cities	
South-East	4.5	(192)	1.5	(35)
South-West	7.3	(43)	1.3	(8)
East Anglia	4.6	(17)	—	
East Midlands	4.3	(36)	−2.5	(6)
West Midlands	0.9	(56)	−2.1	(22)
South & Midlands	4.2	(394)	0.1	(71)
Yorkshire	1.7	(54)	−2.9	(18)
North-West	−1.2	(78)	−6.0	(16)
Northern	0.6	(38)	−2.7	(8)
North of England	0.1	(170)	−4.0	(42)
Wales	7.6	(34)	0.8	(3)
Scotland	−2.8	(69)	−6.8	(20)
All seats	2.5	(617)	−2.2	(136)

Merthyr Tydfil, Blyth, Greenock & Port Glasgow, Southampton Itchen, Cardiff West and South Ayrshire are not included because independent Labour candidates or lack of Conservative candidates in 1970 or 1979 make them non-comparable.
Calculations are derived from notional bases as though the 1970 election was fought on 1974–9 boundaries. See *British General Election of February 1974*, p. 284.

The extent and importance of these trends can be seen in Tables 5 and 6. Table 5 provides evidence of how the regional and urban/rural variation in swing has accumulated since 1970. With the exception of Inner London, Bristol and Cardiff, the big cities in the rest of the country have actually swung to Labour, strongly so in the case of the North-West and Scotland, while the country as a whole has swung Conservative. The North/South pattern of 1974–9 does not fit the movement since 1970 so well. The swing in the West Midlands more closely matches that in the North of England, despite the particularly high swing there between October 1974 and 1979. This suggests that part at least of the 1974–9 swing to Conservative in this region reflects a compensating movement for the large swing to Labour recorded in February 1974.[5]

But, for the most part, the areas which showed the lowest swings in 1979 — Scotland, the North of England and large cities — were the areas which had been drifting steadily towards Labour for over 20 years, whilst the South & Midlands and mining areas were confirming their long-term rightward movement by their bigger swings to Conservative in 1979. This broad pattern suggests that we have witnessed, at each election since 1959, stages in a long-term shift in regional voting behaviour, and in the political character of different types of constituency, which owe more to social changes and to the geography of affluence in Britain than to issues specific to a particular election. The peripheral areas of Britain, with their higher unemployment, and the declining inner parts of conurbations, have become steadily more Labour; while the expanding, more prosperous areas have become more Conservative. Table 6 shows the impact these long term trends have had on the composition of the Conservative and Labour parliamentary parties. The Conservative party is now distinctly more southern (and Welsh), and weaker in the big city seats, than it was in 1955, when it had a majority of a comparable size.

Table 6.   Parliamentary Representation — 1955 and 1979

	1979 (change from 1955 in brackets)					
	Big City		Remainder		Total	
	Con	Lab	Con	Lab	Con	Lab
South & Midlands	20(−8)	47(−5)	227(+42)	48(−24)	247(+34)	95(−29)
North of England	7(−11)	30(+7)	52 (−9)	78 (+9)	59(−20)	108(+16)
Wales	2 (+1)	2 (−)	9 (+4)	20 (−5)	11 (+5)	22 (−5)
Scotland	5 (−6)	15(+4)	17 (−8)	29 (+6)	22(−14)	44(+10)
Total	34(−24)	94(+6)	305(+29)	175(−14)	339 (+5)	269 (−8)

[5] The large swing to Labour in February 1974 was confined to the conurbation seats in the region. Outside the West Midland Metropolitan County there was a swing of 4.8% to Conservative since 1970, more in line with the rest of the South & Midlands.

One part of Britain, however, broke with its long-term trend. Throughout the 1955–74 period, whenever North Britain voted differently from the South & Midlands, Wales had tended to go the same way as Scotland and the North of England; the cleavage used to be North-West/South-East Britain. This time, however, Wales behaved like the rest of South Britain – a normal level of South Britain swing in most of Wales, with a higher swing in the mining valleys and a lower one in the largest city, Cardiff. There were signs that Wales was swinging more in line with South Britain in February but not in October 1974. In 1979, however, the switch was unmistakable and in consequence, with 11 seats, the Conservatives won their highest Welsh parliamentary representation since 1874 and, having lost 12 deposits in October 1974, they saved every one this time.

But the really dramatic reversal of the past pattern was concentrated in the most Welsh-speaking constituencies of north and west Wales, where the Conservatives took two seats they had not won for a century: Anglesey from Labour, and Montgomery from the Liberals. The Conservative increase was greater the more rural and the more Welsh-speaking the constituency. It was greatest in seats where the Conservative vote had been squeezed tactically in October 1974; this produced extraordinary notional swings in Cardigan (a jump from a badly-lost deposit to a good second place) and Carmarthen (where the loss of tactical support helped lose Plaid Cymru their leader's seat). The influx of English settlers also helped the Conservatives in these seats, especially in Anglesey where the electorate had risen by 8.4%.

The result of the devolution referendum should have helped the Welsh Conservatives. With less than one-quarter of the 1974 vote, they alone had unitedly championed the 'No' case which won four-fifths of Welsh votes. To that extent, the 1979 Conservative upsurge in Wales may only be short-term. But the concentration of the rise in rural Welsh-speaking areas argues rather for a more significant, long-term political change – these areas, after all, showed the highest 'Yes' votes. It certainly looks as if the political culture of rural Celtic Wales, which for a century regarded Conservatism as an alien political creed, has undergone a sea-change of far-reaching consequence.

Liberal Performance
The Liberal vote fell by 5.1% in the 531 comparable constituen-

cies in England and Wales. The pattern of this movement did not correspond with the pattern of swing. There were more exceptions to the Liberal decline than to the swing against Labour. Whereas there was a swing to Labour in only 8 seats in England and Wales, the Liberals increased their vote in 62 seats. This advance was concentrated in seats where they were strongest (see p. 406). But apart from that, the fall in the Liberal vote tended to be directly proportional to their strength in October 1974. This was unlike the pattern of swing. In 1979, as in previous elections, swing was unrelated to the size of the losing major party's vote.[6]

While much of the variation in swing seems attributable to differences in socio-economic structure and interest, most of the regional variation in Liberal performance appears related to autonomous factors of local political history and personality. The Liberals' best performance in England and Wales was in the area comprising Liverpool and the two immediately adjoining metropolitan districts where, excluding Edge Hill, their vote increased by an average of 0.3%. This movement, while in part compensation for a low Liberal vote in 1974, also probably reflects a response to the Liberals' local government record in Liverpool, and was encouraged by the Edge Hill by-election victory.

The rise and fall of Liberal personalities had a divergent effect on the Liberal vote at opposite ends of the country. The only other geographical cluster where the Liberals did relatively well was along the Anglo-Scottish border, on both sides of which the Liberal performance was about 3% better than the respective English or Scottish averages. In this area, which forms an Independent Television region, the two Liberal MPs, David Steel and Alan Beith, had acquired national standing since 1974 as leader and chief whip. But in the Liberal heartland of Devon and Cornwall, the publicity which had recently surrounded the former leader, Jeremy Thorpe, and former Cornish Liberal MP,

---

[6] The non-proportionality of swing means that the probability of an elector moving from one party to another varies according to the strength of those parties in his constituency. One possible reason for this is that where a party is relatively strong, the local political messages in the area will, on balance, be in that party's favour, and help to counteract any national movement against it. (See D. Butler & D. Stokes, *Political Change in Britain* (London, 1974) pp. 140–151.) The proportionality of the Liberal fall suggests that their prior strength did not produce this benefit to the same extent.

Peter Bessell, appears to have had an adverse effect.[7] In five contiguous seats in this area — Bodmin, North Cornwall, North Devon, West Devon and Tiverton — the Liberal vote plummeted by an average of 9.4%. The Liberal party saw its breakthroughs in these seats during the period between the gain of Torrington (now split between West Devon, North Devon and Tiverton) in 1958 and North Cornwall in 1966, and the Liberal strength had been closely associated with Jeremy Thorpe and Peter Bessell. In contrast, in the two seats further from North Devon — Truro and Totnes — where the Liberal strength had only been established in 1974, the Liberal vote rose.

Only two regional differences appear to be unrelated to the Liberals' recent political history. There were above-average falls in the West Midland Metropolitan County (−6.9%) and the South-East (−6.4%) which were particularly concentrated in the more suburban parts of these areas.

These limited exceptions exhaust the regional variation in the Liberal performance. In contrast to the North/South variation in swing there was little clear geographical variation in the change in the Liberal vote. Nor was there any consistent variation in Liberal performance when we look at types of constituency on the urban/rural scale, or according to other social or economic characteristics. But the change in the Liberal vote (standard deviation 3.6%) varied rather more in the 531 comparable English and Welsh constituencies than the change in the Conservative (3.2%) or Labour (3.1%) vote. There remains a substantial variation in Liberal performance to be explained.

Liberals and swing

The coincidence of a large fall in the Liberal vote and a substantial swing to Conservative leads one to the question whether there was any causal relationship between the two. In the 471 constituencies in England where the Liberal vote fell, the correlation coefficients both for the North of England (0.06) and the South & Midland (−0.09) suggest that there was no significant relationship, and this lack of relationship holds, however we examine the question. But there is one exception.

[7] Because of this factor we exclude these seats from the analysis of tactical voting on p. 406. On the events leading to the trial of Jeremy Thorpe, see p. 92.

In places where the Liberal vote remained stable or rose in the South & Midlands,[8] the swing to Conservatives was generally higher. Most of the constituencies concerned were traditionally Conservative ones in Southern England, and include many where it had been hoped that the Lib-Lab pact of March 1977 would entice Labour supporters to vote Liberal. Table 7 examines the Conservative- or Liberal-held constituencies in the South & Midlands (excluding the five seats in the Liberal heartland of Devon and Cornwall, but including three in Lindsey) according to their tactical situation.

Table 7.   Tactical Voting

| Oct 1974 situation | Change in share of vote | | | |
	Con	Lab	Lib	Swing
Lib 1st. or 2nd. (a)	6.3	−8.7	2.2	13.3 (15)
Lib 2nd. (b)	9.7	−3.8	−6.7	7.8 (11)
Lib 2nd. (c)	9.0	−3.2	−6.7	6.3 (48)
Lib 3rd.	8.7	−3.8	−5.6	7.0 (133)

Lib 2nd. (a) seats where the Liberals were within 9% of the Conservative; or where there had been a clear improvement in their credibility either through in October 1974 both reducing the February 1974 majority by at least 2½% and increasing the Liberal lead over Labour by at least 2½% (Ludlow, Totnes), or through subsequent substantial local election progress (Richmond, Sy.).
Lib 2nd. (b) those seats not included above in which the Liberal was within 15% of the Conservative.
Lib 2nd. (c) remaining seats in which the Liberals were second.

Table 7 shows that there is a very clear division between those constituencies where the Liberals were credible contenders, and those (including most second-places) where they were not. Among the 192 South & Midlands constituencies outside the first category in Table 7 only a handful of Liberals improved their shares of the vote.[9]

The Liberal success in the first category could reflect two separate types of movement. It might have been occasioned by

[8] Among the handful of North of England constituencies where the Liberals and Conservatives were in close contention a similar pattern, within the lower level of swing, can be observed.
[9] These were from second place in Cheltenham and Wells, and from third place in Chertsey & Walton, Twickenham and Yeovil.

the local appeal of the Liberal candidate, in which case one would expect the Liberal to draw his support from both Conservative and Labour. On the other hand, the cause could have been a tactical switch from the third-placed Labour candidate to the better-placed Liberal; this movement would have no effect on the Conservative's performance. Table 7 suggests that both influences were at work. Both the Conservative and the Labour performances were below average in the first group of constituencies, but Labour suffered most, losing on average 2½% more of their vote than the Conservatives.

This limited tactical switch from Labour to Liberal was in addition to previous gains which many Liberal candidates had made in 1974 at the expense of third-placed Labour candidates. Therefore, the table also shows that, even where second-placed Liberals were not close to winning, Labour did not recover this support.[10] It may be that the Lib-Lab parliamentary agreement did thereby assist some of the better-placed Liberals to hold their 1974 vote.

However, fresh tactical Labour support only clearly saved one Liberal seat, the Isle of Wight. In Berwick-on-Tweed, Isle of Ely and Truro, sitting Liberal MPs were returned by performing better at the expense of both rival parties. There were also the three Liberal MPs facing Labour opponents, who had in October 1974 clearly squeezed Conservatives. Although all these retained their seats, only Cyril Smith, the one Liberal MP to publicly oppose the pact, appears to have retained most of that tactical support; in Cardigan and Colne Valley the return of previous tactical voters produced extremely high two-party swings to Conservative.

Thus in constituencies perceived as being marginal between the Liberals and another party, voters were prepared to behave according to the local situation. The same can be shown, as we shall see, in the Nationalist-held seats in Scotland. But the largest number of marginal seats at this election were, of course, those which Labour was defending against the Conservatives.

Marginal Seats
The outcome of an election is primarily decided in marginal seats: the Conservative advance in 1979 depended on what

[10] The main exceptions were those seats in which past by-elections had induced an exceptionally strong squeeze on Labour (See p. 410).

Table 8.   Swing in Labour-held Seats

Swing required for Con gain	Change in % share of vote			Swing	
	Con	Lab	Lib		
a) South & Midlands					
up to 2%	6.0	−0.2	−5.7	3.8	(12)
2–6%	7.8	−2.5	−5.2	6.0	(23)
6–10%	9.9	−3.9	−6.2	8.3	(17)
over 10%	9.6	−4.8	−5.4	9.1	(75)
All	9.0	−3.7	−5.5	7.9	(127)
b) North of England					
up to 2%	4.5	1.7	−5.8	1.6	(5)
2–6%	5.1	−1.0	−3.9	3.6	(15)
6–10%	5.8	1.2	−7.4	3.3	(10)
over 10%	6.5	−2.6	−4.4	5.9	(78)
All	5.8	−1.8	−4.9	5.2	(108)

This table is confined to constituencies in England won by Labour in October 1974, with Conservative in second place, and contested by Liberal in 1979. The vast majority of marginal Labour seats were in England.

happened in Labour marginals. Table 8 summarises the results in those seats.

It is clear that Labour kept down the swing in its marginal constituencies, particularly in those with less than a 2% two-party majority. Table 8 rules out one possible cause: the Liberal performance was not generally worse in marginal seats than elsewhere, and so did not contribute to the lower swing. The lack of a squeeze on Liberal voters in two-party marginals probably reflects two factors – the long interval since the previous elections (see below p. 422), and the fact that the Liberal vote in such constituencies had already been squeezed (in the Conservatives' favour) in October 1974. A major reason for the low swing, particularly the very low swing in the most marginal seats, is the effect of a change in incumbent MP since 1974. Because of the greater attention he can command in the media and the constituency services he can render, an incumbent

MP is more likely than a prospective parliamentary candidate to be able to establish a personal vote, consisting of those who support him as an individual rather than as a party representative. Where an MP does build such a personal vote in his favour, that vote will be lost if he is defeated. If he does lose, by the time of the next election the new incumbent MP may have acquired his own personal vote. The combined effect of these two personal votes would be a lower swing against the second incumbent at the following election.

In 1979 these conditions were most clearly fulfilled in the 12 seats which, in October 1974, an incumbent Conservative MP defended against a Labour candidate who had not represented the constituency before, and which, following that Conservative MP's defeat in October 1974, was defended in 1979 by an incumbent Labour MP against a new Tory candidate. In these seats the swing was 1.3% (4 seats) in the North of England, and 3.8% (8 seats) in the South & Midlands; in both cases about 4% less than the average swing in the region. These account for most of the seats with Labour two-party majorities of under 2% in October 1974.

But in a second set of constituencies, the effect of an incumbency change was only slightly less apparent. These were the 6 seats in which an incumbent Conservative MP lost in February 1974, which he tried to regain (and failed) only 7 months later in October (probably still reaping some of the personal vote he could have acquired as MP, while his opponent had had little time to gain one) and which the Labour MP first elected in February 1974 defended against a different Conservative candidate in 1979. In these seats the swing in the North of England was 2.2% (4 seats) and in the South & Midlands 4.5% (2 seats).

These 18 clear cases amount to strong evidence of the personal vote that an MP can build up. The low swing in them is consistent and appears to be independent of location or type of constituency. For the period from 1974 to 1979, it would appear that the double effect amounted to around 1500 votes in an average sized constituency — an incumbent Conservative or Labour MP could attract about 750 votes which would have otherwise gone to his opponent. It is, of course, in marginal seats that MPs have the greatest incentive to work for such personal votes.

In the remaining marginal constituencies, less clear-cut

examples of change in incumbency can explain some of the lower swing. However, in the limited number where the Labour MP did not stand again or had held the seat, without boundary change, for a long period, the swing nevertheless tended to be lower. Inspection of these cases suggests that they may be explained by location or character of constituency and that a small Labour majority in itself therefore had no systematic effect on voting behaviour. We cannot, however, conclusively disprove such an effect.

The recent political history of a constituency also had an impact on the election results in certain seats in which a by-election held since 1970 had seen the constituency change hands. The swing to Conservative was above average in all 6 of the seats which the Conservatives had gained from Labour in by-elections during the 1974—9 parliament (mean 11.7%). It was especially high in the 4 seats (Ashfield, Birmingham Stechford, Walsall North and Workington) which had previously been regarded as very safe Labour. The sites of past Liberal by-election success followed divergent paths. The Liberals lost support heavily, to the clear benefit of the Labour candidate, in the two seats they gained in 1972 and 1973 and subsequently lost (Ripon and Sutton & Cheam), suggesting that Labour voters who had previously cast a tactical vote for the Liberals felt that it was no longer worthwhile doing so. But David Alton succeeded in retaining Liverpool Edge Hill which he had dramatically won only a few days before the dissolution. His support, while just over 12% below that in the by-election, was still a massive 24.7% increase on that in October 1974, the largest achieved by any candidate in a comparable seat in 1979.

Constituency voting

This appendix has so far examined two possible sources for the large variation in swing in England and Wales. It has explored how much of the pattern seems explicable by the dissimilar behaviour of different groups of people, defined by geographical or social situation, and it has also established that there was some systematic variation between constituencies according to their type of contest. But was the large variation in swing also caused by an increase in behaviour peculiar to individual constituencies?

Table 9 examines this question by listing the ten best, and

Table 9.   Deviant Results

In 531 three cornered contests in England and Wales

Change in Conservative % of Vote

Cardigan	RW	20.3	*Liv. Edge Hill	BE/MS/BC	−8.1
Ashfield	BE	18.0	*Berwick-on-Tweed	CL	−4.5
Carmarthen	RW	17.8	Chertsey & Walton		−1.7
B'm. Stechford	BE	16.8	*Bradford W.	NC/BC	−0.5
Barking	SE	16.8	Truro	CL	0.1
Fareham		15.8	Ipswich	EP/LI/LF	0.2
Harlow	SE	15.8	*Thornaby	LI/BC/EP	0.3
Anglesey	RW	15.2	*Liv. Scotland-Ex.	BC/MS	0.4
S.E. Essex	SE	15.2	*Leeds N.E.	NC/BC	0.4
S. Beds.	SE/HC	15.1	*Barrow		1.2

Change in Labour % of Vote

*Bradford W.	NC/BC	5.3	Bethnal G. & Bow		−19.1
*Grimsby	EP/LF	4.9	*Liv. Edge Hill	BE/MS	−17.3
*Mcr. Moss Side	NC/BC	4.9	Cardigan	RW	−15.0
*Rossendale	LI/LF	4.0	Stepney & Poplar	SE	−15.0
*Hartlepool	EP	3.4	Chelmsford	CL	−14.4
*Bury & Radcliffe	LI	3.3	Truro	CL	−13.1
Leicester S.	BC/LI/NC	3.2	Dagenham	SE	−12.7
Ipswich	EP/LI/LF	2.9	Twickenham		−12.1
*Ripon	BE	2.6	Peckham	SE	−11.8
*Bridlington	EP	2.6	Barking	SE	−11.1

Change in Liberal % of Vote

*Liv. Edge Hill	BE/MS	24.7	Gillingham	HC	−13.4
Truro	CL	13.0	*Grimsby		−13.0
Berwick-on-Tweed	CL	11.2	*Rossendale		−13.0
Bethnal G. & Bow		10.4	*Ripon	BE	−12.7
Richmond, Sy.	CL	7.8	S. Beds.	HC	−11.9
Chertsey & Walton		7.7	Gosport	HC/LF	−11.7
Chelmsford	CL	6.3	W. Devon	DC	−11.5
Twickenham		5.6	N. Devon	DC	−11.4.
*Liv. Scotland-Ex.	MS	5.5	Sutton Coldf'd.	WM	−11.3
Isle of Ely		5.0	*Houghton-le-Spring		−11.3

BC	Big City Seat (outside London and W. Midlands).	MS	Merseyside area of good Lib performance.
BE	Impact of past by-election gain.	NC	High concentration of New Commonwealth born.
CL	Seat with Lib in close contention.		
DC	Seat in Lib heartland in Devon and Cornwall.	RW	Seat in rural Wales.
		SE	Seat in high-swing area of South-East.
EP	East coast port.		
HC	Home counties seat with poor Lib performance.	WM	West Midlands area of poor Lib performance.
LF	Local factors important in addition.	*	Indicates a seat in the North of England.
LI	Marginal Seat with Lab MP first elected in 1974.		

the ten worst, changes in the share of the poll achieved by each of the three main parties in the 531 comparable contests in England & Wales. Two contrasts are immediately evident when it is compared with a similar table for the October 1974 election. (See *The British General Election of October 1974*, p. 343.) Firstly, the wider variation in swing is clear; the difference between the Conservatives' single best and single worst performance in Table 9 is 28.4% (Oct 1974, 8.6%) and Labour's 16.4% (11.0%). Secondly, tactical voting accounts for fewer of the entries in 1979. In October 1974, in 21 of the 44 listed seats, the exceptional result could be clearly attributed to tactical voting; but in 1979 no more than 10 out of 43 could in any way be so attributed.

But despite these differences, only 10 entries are not immediately explicable by the systematic factors already discussed. In only 6 cases does the result seem totally out of line when compared with the result in similar constituencies, while in another 4 the extent of the deviation is rather greater than might anyway have been expected from the general characteristics of the seat.

In 3 cases the deviant result in May 1979 reflected a return to normal, following deviant October 1974 results. There were then especially good Liberal performances drawn from one of the major-party candidates in Fareham (unpopular Conservative) and Gosport (Labour candidate under a cloud); in 1979 these candidates were no longer present. Houghton-le-Spring did not figure in the October 1974 list because it was a case of Liberal intervention; it was the highest Liberal vote in such a situation, and unexpectedly high for a mining constituency; the 1979 vote represents a more typical level of Liberal support.

Of the 7 remaining cases, 5 are primarily the consequence of an unusual Liberal movement. In Grimsby and Rossendale there was a large and uncharacteristic fall in the Liberal vote.[11] The

---

[11] In Rossendale the local Liberal association withdrew its candidate at the outset of the campaign, intending not to fight; a new Liberal candidate was adopted, under pressure from the Liberal party, two weeks before polling day. In Grimsby, the Liberal's poor performance in the 1977 by-election may have affected their support in 1979.

The presence of both these seats in the Labour column is the combined effect of the low swing which constituencies of the same type shared, plus the Liberal fall. The Liberal vote does not appear to have gone disproportionately to Labour in either case.

Liberal increase in Chertsey & Walton was an outstanding reversal of the general tide, and was not presaged by local government success or any other obvious cause; it seems to have been disproportionately at the sitting Conservative MP's expense. However, the especially good Liberal performance in Bethnal Green & Bow and Twickenham were clearly foreshadowed in the striking Liberal advances in these areas in the 1978 London borough elections.

The results in Ipswich and Barrow stand out as the two most exceptional so far as the movement between the two major parties is concerned. The failure of the Conservatives to dislodge Ken Weetch in Ipswich was perhaps the most surprising result of the election. The result may be interpreted as signifying the acquisition of a personal vote by Ken Weetch as a new Labour incumbent — but the extent of his success goes far beyond that of any other candidate in a similar position. Interestingly, the local election results in Barrow in 1977 showed a strong swing to Labour from the previous year; this was well against the national trend.

Ipswich and Barrow share a characteristic which predominated amongst those constituencies that produced a deviant result in October 1974 — that is their boundaries enclose a self-contained town. Each of them also has its own local evening newspaper, maximising the chances of an MP to secure publicity and to encourage the growth of local political consciousness. Four of the other individually deviant results, Fareham, Gosport, Grimsby (also with its own evening newspaper) and Rossendale are also constituencies enclosing one self-contained community. In such constituencies candidates do seem to be more likely to win or lose votes on account of their personal popularity or unpopularity. But the results at this election do not provide any strong evidence that, in general, local constituency factors have become more important in affecting the electorate's behaviour, at least so far as the movement between Conservative and Labour is concerned.

Previous elections have suggested a reluctance amongst the electorate to vote for coloured candidates. In 1979 two Asian Conservative candidates, in Glasgow Central and in Greenwich, achieved a typical result for their kind of seat. But larger falls in their votes than those in neighbouring constituencies were experienced by an Asian Liberal in Coventry North East

(−10.5%), and a black Liberal in Nuneaton (−8.8%), while the Guyanese Labour candidate in the City of London & Westminster South suffered one of the largest swings in west London (−7.9%).

Local Elections[12]

A full comparison of the parliamentary election results with those of the local government elections held simultaneously throughout England and Wales outside Greater London is beyond the scope of this appendix. However, it is worthwhile recording that the simultaneous elections provided substantial evidence of the willingness of the electorate to vote differently in national and local elections. Most of the ticket-splitting would appear to have favoured the Liberals at local level, most noticeably in Liverpool where they acquired approximately twice as many votes at local level. But in Rochdale, the local Liberal candidates were unable to match Cyril Smith's parliamentary vote; their lower vote and the higher Conservative local vote confirms the importance of tactical voting in Cyril Smith's success. There were also reversals of the parliamentary result in a few Conservative/Labour marginals. For instance, the Conservatives outpolled Labour in the local elections in York, while Labour reversed the parliamentary result in the Cambridge council elections.

Scotland

Having precipitated the confidence vote which led to the May 1979 general election, the Scottish National Party lost more ground than any other party. Its share of the Scottish vote dropped from 30.4% to 17.3%, and its parliamentary representation from 11 MPs to 2. Its vote fell everywhere except in Caithness & Sutherland.[13] However the drop was significantly less (mean −6.2%) in the seats, apart from Argyll,[14] which the

---

[12] For a more detailed analysis see R. Waller, 'The 1979 Local and General Elections in England and Wales', *Political Studies* (1980).

[13] Caithness & Sutherland was the only constituency in 1979 with a large previous Liberal vote (22.0% in October 1974), in which no Liberal stood. More of the Liberal voters appear to have voted Conservative or Nationalist than Labour, and caused (in conjunction with the better SNP performance in the Highlands) the only increase in the SNP vote in 1979.

[14] In Argyll, the only constituency with a significant previous Liberal vote where no Liberal stood in October 1974 (the local Liberal association indicating support for the SNP MP), the intervening Liberal vote of 15.4% in 1979 was clearly largely responsible for the abnormal 17.9% drop in the SNP vote.

SNP were defending. In most constituencies the drop was clustered between 12% and 21%. It was higher in the three constituencies, Glasgow Govan, Hamilton and Stirling, where Nationalist support had been boosted by an earlier by-election. It was generally lower in two regions, Highland and Tayside (where the regional effect on top of a sitting member's vote enabled the SNP to retain its single remaining mainland seat in Dundee East) and also in constituencies where the SNP had done markedly less well in October 1974.

This fall in nationalist support dominated the results in Scotland, producing a rise in the Conservative, Labour and Liberal vote in almost every constituency. There is, therefore, some difficulty in interpreting whatever movements may have taken place between the other three parties. There was a mean swing of 2.0% to Conservative but, as Table 10 shows, this varied markedly according to both the nature of the contest and the scale of the SNP fall:

Table 10.   Swing in Scotland

Type of contest: Size of SNP Fall	Lab/SNP	Con/Lab	Con/SNP
Above 13.1%	5.4 (24)	−0.5 (8)	−0.3 (2)
Below 13.1%	3.6 (9)	−0.8 (8)	−0.3 (9)
All seats	4.9 (33)	−0.7 (16)	−0.3 (11)

In this table 60 Scottish seats are classified by the top two parties in October 1974. Three Liberal-held seats, West Aberdeenshire, Greenock & Port Glasgow (tactical support for well-placed Liberal candidates), Argyll and Caithness & Sutherland (see footnotes 13 and 14), South Ayrshire, Central Dunbartonshire (8.7% Communist vote, October 1974) and two three-way marginals, East Dunbartonshire and West Renfrew, are excluded.

This table shows very clearly that the swing to the Conservatives was a phenomenon of constituencies where the Conservatives were in third place by October 1974, and more particularly of those constituencies in which the SNP vote dropped heavily in 1979. In this, the commonest electoral situation in Scotland and mostly found in the Strathclyde region, it is evident that the SNP gained more than average in October 1974 by biting into the Conservative vote, and then lost more — disproportionately back to the Conservatives — in 1979.

In the other half of Scotland, Table 10 suggests that there was actually a slight swing to Labour. This movement to Labour, however, was mostly confined to Glasgow and Edinburgh — in the 10 Conservative/Labour seats in these two cities the swing averaged 1.5% to Labour. Elsewhere there may have been a slight net movement to the Conservatives, illustrated particularly by the Conservatives' holding their most marginal seat, Aberdeen South (despite its fishing and university character) and by the drop in Labour's majority in its most marginal seat, Berwick & East Lothian. Thus in Scotland as a whole, if we can exclude the effect of the drop in SNP support, there was probably no significant net movement between the two major parties. However, the difference between the swing in the two large cities and in the remainder of Scotland is understated in Table 4 above, due to the number of Labour/SNP seats in Glasgow.

The Conservatives recovered from their October 1974 nadir in parliamentary representation in Scotland. They gained seven SNP seats and increased their vote, principally by regaining support from the nationalists in Labour strongholds. But they are at as low a level in relation to Labour as they have ever been. Labour took two constituencies where the Conservatives had previously been ahead of them, East Dunbartonshire[15] and Glasgow Cathcart, while the Conservatives held only one Scottish seat that had ever been Labour, Aberdeen South (in 1966). Twelve of their 22 MPs are very vulnerable, with majorities of less than 7%, and there are now only two completely safe Tory seats in Scotland — East Renfrew (25.5% majority) and North Angus & Mearns (34.3%).

The swing to Conservative in Scotland also appears slightly to have been enhanced by the decision of the Liberals to withdraw in 26 constituencies. Of these, 23 were constituencies where Labour and SNP shared first and second places in October 1974, and most of them had large falls in the SNP vote, including all the biggest falls. If we allow for this coincidence by comparing

---

[15] Labour gained East Dunbartonshire from the SNP, having been third in October 1974. The Conservatives won the seat in February 1974, and within its 1974 boundaries it would probably have previously been a Conservative seat.

constituencies with comparable drops in the SNP vote, a Liberal withdrawal appears to have added about 1% to the swing to Conservatives. This is the net effect of the behaviour of the probable 7% of voters who would have voted Liberal in these constituencies in 1979, if a candidate had been available. In the three Conservative/SNP seats where a Liberal withdrew, the erstwhile Liberals seem to have moved disproportionately to Labour, producing especially sharp swings to Labour in Banff and East Aberdeenshire.

In the 42 seats where the Liberals maintained their presence, their vote rose by an average 3.7%. This is rather more than they would have achieved if they had simply acquired the support of former Nationalist voters in proportion to their previous share of the three-party vote. As with the fall in the SNP vote, the rise in the Liberal vote was generally even throughout Scotland. The Liberal vote only fell in 4 cases; only in another 4 did it rise by more than 6%.

Most of the Scottish results which appear exceptional after taking account of the factors discussed so far are in seats where the Liberals and SNP had their best performances. They suggest that in Scotland, as in England and Wales, the tactical situation in a constituency could induce some people to vote according to the local situation rather than follow the general pattern of behaviour. Labour and Liberal voters in Scotland appear, at this election, to have been more susceptible to these considerations than Conservative voters. The Labour vote fell in five seats — the four most marginal seats which the SNP were defending against the Conservatives, plus Roxburgh, Selkirk & Peebles, where the Liberal leader's personal success (+9.4%) came particularly at Labour's expense. Three of the four falls in the Liberal vote occurred where SNP MPs were defending their seats, and the slight swing to Labour in the two seats which the SNP retained reflects a failure by the Conservatives to regain as much of their 1974 losses to the SNP as they did elsewhere. Greenock & Port Glasgow, where there was a local Liberal victory in the 1977 district council elections, also exhibited tactical behaviour: a large rise in the Liberal vote (8.7%), was accompanied by one of the only two falls in the Conservative share of the vote in Scotland. However, it is notable that, with the exception of Kinross & West Perthshire (October 1974 Conservative majority over SNP only 0.2%; 1979 rise in Labour vote only 0.8%), the many seats where the SNP came close to victory in 1974 show no signs of tactical behaviour in 1979.

After taking account of the tactical situation, four other results stand out as representing deviant local behaviour. Three of these involve the Liberals. Their vote fell in North Ayrshire & Bute (−0.3%), while they achieved two large increases in their vote at Rutherglen (+12.1%) and East Fife (+10.4%). The only example involving the movement between the Conservative and Labour parties is Glasgow Cathcart. Here, Teddy Taylor, Shadow Secretary of State for Scotland, was the only Conservative MP to lose his seat. The result was the largest swing to Labour in Great Britain (−5.2%) in a Conservative/Labour contest. This was probably a compensatory movement for Labour's poor performance in October 1974, when the swing to them was 3% lower than in any other seat in Glasgow.

Minor Parties

Like the Liberals and the SNP, almost all the smaller parties lost ground at this election. In Wales, Plaid Cymru fell back from 10.8% to 8.1%, its lowest share of the Welsh vote since 1966. Apart from the special case of Cardiff West, where there was no Conservative, its share of the poll rose in only four constituencies. The biggest was in Caernarvon, where Dafydd Wigley (+7.1%) seems to have gained at the expense of all three other parties. Plaid Cymru did worst of all in Carmarthen, where its leader Gwynfor Evans lost his seat. Elsewhere it slumped most in the South Wales valleys, particularly in three of the four Mid-Glamorgan seats where it had been strongest, and saved only two deposits, in Caerphilly and Neath, in industrial South Wales. Its limited strength became more concentrated than ever before in rural, Welsh-speaking West Wales — essentially the arc of five constituencies stretching from Anglesey to Carmarthen. It is this concentration which allows it to retain parliamentary representation, despite its falling support in Wales as a whole.

The National Front secured 191,719 votes by fighting with 303 candidates, the largest number ever fielded by so small a party. This confirmed the National Front's position as England's fourth party. But it was a double edged achievement. In each of the 80 constituencies fought by the National Front in October 1974 its share of the vote dropped (mean, 1.4%) — the most uniform of all the voting changes at this election. In all the constituencies it fought the mean National Front vote was 1.4% compared to 3.6% in 1970, 3.3% in February 1974 and 3.1% in October 1974.

This drop was more pronounced in its areas of greatest success in the past, particularly in North-East London[16] (−2.4%) and Leicester (−2.8%). The National Front failed to find any new areas of strength; their candidates fared slightly worse in the seats where they intervened than those in which they fought both times. North-East London still provided the National Front with its greatest support, most notably in the boroughs of Tower Hamlets, Newham and Hackney (mean 5.2%). In North-East London as a whole, the National Front vote averaged 3.8%, in the Leicester area 2.4% and in the Black Country boroughs (Dudley, Sandwell, Walsall and Wolverhampton) 2.5%. These three areas account for almost all the 49 seats in which the National Front acquired 2% or more of the poll. These three regions are among those containing the largest number of immigrants. However, it is clear that the percentage of immigrants within any constituency is less important than the percentage of working class, in determining the size of the National Front's support. Its best performance in the country, in Hackney South & Shoreditch (7.6%), was in the most working-class seat in London.

The Ecology Party put up 53 candidates polling 39,918 votes and an average of 1.5%. Its choice of constituencies was heavily-weighted in favour of Conservative-held seats in the south of England, and it fought in only 8 Labour constituencies. Its two best performances at 2.8% were in St Marylebone and South Worcestershire, typical of the more rural and middle-class residential areas where its appeal was greatest. On its first substantial electoral venture in Britain, the Ecology Party failed to find the level of support that similar parties have found in France and Germany in the 1970s. But for a British minor party, its vote could have been worse: the five Ecologists who stood in October 1974 had averaged only 0.8%; Ecology candidates beat the National Front in two-thirds of the constituencies in which they competed; and the Ecology Party clearly did better than any of the parties of the far left.

---

[16] For the National Front vote in North-East London, see Michael Steed, 'The National Front Vote' *Parliamentary Affairs*, Vol. XXXI, pp. 287−9.

Of these, the Communists, with 16,858 votes for 38 candidates (a mean vote of 1.1%), polled better than the newcomers,[17] the 60 Workers' Revolutionary Party candidates (12,631 total; 0.5% mean) and the 10 Socialist Unity ones (2,834 total; 0.9% mean). This miniscule level of support is the more significant for coming on top of a period of steady decline in the Communist vote, as Table 11 shows.

Table 11.   Communist Share of the Vote Since 1964

	Mean % Vote		Change in Mean % Vote
	(a)	(b)	
1964	3.4	4.8	−0.0
1966	3.0	3.8	−0.5
1970	1.8	2.4	−1.3
1974 (F)	1.8 (1.4)	2.1	−0.4
1974 (0)	1.7 (1.4)	1.6	−0.5 (−0.3)
1979	1.1	1.5	−0.5 (−0.2)

Column (a) refers to all seats fought at that election; column (b) to the 12 seats fought at each of the last 6 elections; the third column refers to seats fought at that and the preceding election. Bracketed figures exclude Dunbartonshire Central, where Jimmy Reid polled a high personal vote in 1974.

Two regionalist groups, which had fought in 1974, also mounted a stronger challenge this time. Mebyon Kernow (Sons of Cornwall) fought three of the five Cornish seats, averaging 2.9%, compared with an average vote of 1.4% on previous occasions. Altogether including another Cornish Nationalist candidate, 4,391 votes (1.7% of the total Cornish vote) went to nationalists. Seven Wessex Regionalists together polled 3,098, but more than half of these were won in Westbury, where the Wessex Regionalist took 3.0%.

Among the other candidates, the outstanding performance by far was that of Jim Sillars in South Ayrshire, who polled 31.4%, and nearly succeeded in retaining the seat he had won as a Labour candidate in 1974. His vote confirmed what previous

[17] Norwich North (Ecologist 334, NF. 250, Communist 106, WRP 92) nicely illustrated the relative strength of the minor parties.

examples in the 1970s had shown[18] — that a very substantial proportion of the Labour vote may follow an MP who splits with his party. The two other candidates who stood under his 'Scottish Labour Party' colours won only 1.7% and 0.7% of the poll. Another Labour ex-MP, Eddie Milne in Blyth, failed to regain the seat he lost in October 1974, but polled a very creditable 28.8%. Otherwise only five[19] of the remaining 104 candidates who stood as Independents or for some minor party polled more than 2.5%.

Turnout

Turnout, at 76.2%, increased by just over 3% compared with October 1974. The increase may be entirely attributable to the fact that the register used in 1979 was five months younger. The formula suggested by Richard Rose for adjusting overall turnout for differences in the age of the register produces adjusted figures of 78.8% for October 1974 and 78.9% for May 1979.[20] However, the change in turnout at constituency level produces a pattern of variation that points to other factors besides the age of the register.

Mean turnout rose in England (3.3%) and Wales (3.0%),[21] substantially more than in Scotland (1.8%). However, this brought the overall turnouts in England (75.9%) and Scotland (76.8%) back into line with each other, leaving Wales (79.6%), as usual, the country with the highest participation rate. In October 1974 Scottish turnout had moved 2.3% ahead of English turnout, reflecting the excitement which the February 1974 Nationalist surge had added to that election; five years later this excitement had ebbed. Within England there was no significant regional variation, but turnout did rise more in big city seats (4.6%) and also in Outer London (4.4%).

---

[18] S. O. Davies (Merthyr Tydfil, 1970), D. Taverne (Lincoln, 1973 and Feb 1974) and Eddie Milne (Blyth, Feb 1974) initially succeeded in retaining their seats.

[19] All but one were party rebels. They were two Taverne-inspired Democratic Labour candidates in Lincoln (4.1%) and nearby Brigg & Scunthorpe (2.8%), an Independent Labour candidate in Jarrow (5.2%); a rebel Conservative local councillor who had recently held office as mayor in Eton & Slough (4.9%); and an Independent in Westbury (4.0%) who had been campaigning for the previous four years. The Conservative ex-MP, Tom Iremonger, only secured 0.9% in his old seat, Ilford North.

[20] See Richard Rose *Electoral Behaviour*, (London, 1974), p. 494.

[21] Figures in this section exclude Cardiff West.

One would expect a greater increase in turnout in inner city seats when an election is fought on a newer register. Inner city seats generally have a higher rate of population mobility, so that the register ages more quickly. However, a comparison of the May 1979 turnout with that in both the 1974 elections suggests that turnout in big-city seats has increased, relative to other constituencies, by about 1%. It is possible that the completion of schemes of slum clearance and rehousing, has led to more stable inner-city populations, and thus a higher turnout.

In all previous post-war elections, Liberal withdrawal has clearly depressed turnout and Liberal intervention increased it. But at this election, within England and Wales, there was no clear relationship between Liberal withdrawal and turnout change.[22] However, in Scotland the increase in turnout was 0.8% lower in seats where the Liberals withdrew than in those they fought both times, which suggests that approximately one in seven of 1974 Scottish Liberal voters preferred to abstain rather than vote for an alternative candidate where a Liberal candidate did not stand in 1979.

In previous elections, the willingness of the electorate to participate has also been influenced by the marginality of the constituency in which they were eligible to vote. The impact of the marginality of a contest upon the level of turnout varies according to the time-span between elections. While the level of turnout always tends to be higher in marginal seats, the difference between turnout in marginal and non-marginal seats is greater at elections which have followed closely upon the previous election, as in 1951, 1966 and October 1974, and less when an election has been held towards the end of the full length of the parliamentary term, as in 1970. This pattern results in the increase in turnout being greater (or the decrease less) in marginal seats than non-marginal ones in a closely-following election but less (or decrease greater) in a later-timed one.

The 1979 election, coming over 4½ years after the previous election, fits this pattern. Amongst those seats in which the Conservatives and Labour parties shared first and second place in October 1974, where the Conservative share of the two-party vote lay between 45% and 55%, turnout rose by only 2.4%. In other seats it rose by 3.7%.

---

[22] One exception was Aberdare, where there was also a large fall in the Plaid Cymru vote.

Of the seats with unusually large declines or increases in turnout, only a few are not encompassed by the factors so far mentioned. The absence of a Conservative or a Liberal candidate in Cardiff West, the Speaker's seat, produced a 9.0% drop in turnout. The next biggest fall was in Glasgow Govan (−2.6%) where the effect of the 1973 by-election in boosting the 1974 turnout did not last, and a similar effect could be seen in Ripon and Sutton & Cheam. There was also a noticeable drop in turnout in certain northern constituencies such as Keighley (−2.5%), Shipley (−0.5%) and Accrington (−0.7), where traditionally electoral participation has been high.

In general, there is no clear evidence that differences in change in turnout as between constituencies benefited one party rather rather than another. There is a hint that the SNP performed better where turnout rose more — if constituencies affected by Liberal withdrawals are excluded, turnout in the 6 constituencies in which SNP held its 1974 vote best rose by 4.0% compared with 1.9% in other Scottish seats.

Northern Ireland
Westminster elections are now the only ones in Northern Ireland with the single member seat, relative majority system; in all others the single transferable vote form of proportional representation is used. Table 12 overleaf, therefore, compares elections held under both systems. Northern Ireland voters show awareness of the difference involved — above all that, whereas proportional systems ensure that all votes cast may matter, under the British system the effectiveness of voting varies greatly.

Northern Ireland's 12 constituencies, for instance, produced the highest turnout in the United Kingdom, in evenly divided Fermanagh & South Tyrone (87.0%), but the lowest for a non-city seat in utterly-safe South Antrim (58.2%), and the biggest drop in turnout (−10.7%) in Belfast West, where population movements during the troubles have made a once marginal constituency fairly safely Catholic.

The biggest change in 1979 occurred within the Unionist block, although its overall strength remained very constant. With the break-up of the 1974 United Ulster Unionist Coalition, the Official Unionists were in competition with Ian Paisley's Democratic Unionist Party or other strong Loyalist candidates in 7 constituencies — and lost to them in 4. This gave the DUP two

Table 12. *Voting in Northern Ireland 1974—9.*

Election:	Oct 1974 Westminster	May 1975 Convention	May 1979 Westminster	June 1979 Europe
DUP		14.7 (12)	10.2 (5)	29.8
OUP	58.4 (12)	25.4 (12)	36.6 (11)	21.9
Other Loyalist		14.7 (12)	11.0 (3)	6.7
UPNI	3.6 (2)	7.7 (11)	1.2 (3)	0.6
Alliance	6.4 (5)	9.8 (12)	11.9 (12)	6.8
Other Centrist	1.8 (7)	1.5 (5)	1.2 (7)	2.9
SDLP	22.0 (9)	23.7 (12)	19.9 (10)	24.6
Republican	7.8 (6)	2.5 (8)	8.3 (9)	6.7

Figures show percentage of total Northern Ireland vote and (in brackets) the number out of the 12 constituencies in which the party or tendency put forward candidates. For the European election, the whole of Northern Ireland formed one constituency. In the Convention and European elections, voting was by the single transferable vote, and the figures refer to first preference votes. In this Table 'Other Loyalist' is mainly Vanguard Unionist Party (1975), James Kilfedder (Independent Unionist, May and June, 1979) and the United Ulster Unionist Party (5.7% May 1979); 'Other Centrist' includes all other non-sectarian candidates, mainly Northern Ireland Labour Party; SDLP includes Independent SDLP in Fermanagh (May 1979); Republican includes all other Republican or Nationalist candidates, including Irish Independence Party (3.3% May 1979).

gains from Official Unionist, on a mere 31.4% of the vote in East Belfast and on 27.6% in North Belfast (the lowest share of the vote to elect a Member of the House of Commons since 1922, Portsmouth Central 26.9%). In May the once dominant monolith of the Official Unionist party was thereby reduced to only five Westminster MPs; in the European election in June the loss of its traditional position was emphatically confirmed, suggesting that the OUP's higher vote in May in part reflected a sitting MP's tactical advantage (in Armagh) or the absence of Unionist competiton in four constituencies.

In the centre, the late Brian Faulkner's pro-power sharing Unionists (UPNI) were clearly eliminated as a significant force, their vote partly returning to the main Unionist camp and partly feeding what, in the May 1979 results, seemed to be growing support for Alliance. However the European voting suggested that some of the Alliance vote was due to the lack of alternative candidates in certain Westminster constituencies — the Catholic Alliance vote seems to have switched to John Hume, who stood for the SDLP in June 1979.

Within the Catholic camp there was solid support for the SDLP, in stark contrast to the evaporation of pro-power sharing Unionism, and the drift from Official to extreme Loyalism. Apart from Fermanagh & South Tyrone where, right on the border, a more intransigent attitude showed through in the return of the Republican Independent, despite unofficial SDLP opposition, Republican and traditional Nationalist groups (now appearing under the Irish Independence Party label) failed significantly to dent Catholic support for the more conciliatory Social Democratic and Labour Party.

The Electoral System
This appendix has so far examined the ways in which the electorate behaved in 1979; the behaviour of the electoral system in translating votes into seats presents different problems. The outstanding feature of the distribution of seats remained the massive over-representation of the two largest parties — their electoral preponderance of 80.8% was turned into a parliamentary preponderance of 95.7%. But if we confine our attention to the relative strengths of the Conservative and Labour parties, the most important feature of the electoral system is that it gave the Conservatives a parliamentary majority of only 43 for a lead of 7.0%. The largest post-war Conservative majority over Labour in votes was not translated into the largest Conservative majority in seats.

A part of the explanation for this is that short-term factors, associated with the October 1974—79 swing, lost the Conservatives some 10 seats. A uniform 6.4% two-party swing thoughout Great Britain would have transferred 61 seats from Labour to Conservative; in fact, the Conservatives gained only 53 and effectively lost 2.[23] The regional divergences in swing do not explain this shortfall, but make it more remarkable. On a uniform

---

[23] In this section, we treat East Dunbartonshire, where Labour overtook the Conservatives from third place to gain the seat from the SNP, as notionally Conservative-held.

basis, the mean regional swings actually observed in each of the
North of England, the South & Midlands, Wales and Scotland,
would have produced 15, 46 and 2 Conservative gains respectively
in the first three areas, and no change in Scotland – a total of
63 gains. In fact, only Wales conformed to this pattern, with
one unanticipated gain (Anglesey) compensating for one narrow
failure to gain (Swansea West). Labour held 7 seats in the North
of England and 12 in the South & Midlands that it should have
lost, and it gained 2 seats in Scotland; it lost only 2 seats in the
North of England and 7 in the South & Midlands, which required
above average swings for them to change hands. Why was the
number of seats Labour were able to save because of a below-
average swing, twice the number the Conservatives were able to
gain with an above average swing? The principal reason lies in the
effect of a change in incumbency discussed on p. 408–10.
Because of the boundary changes between 1970 and February
1974, it is not always clear where the effect should be evident.
But an examination of the 20 seats that Labour saved suggests
that the personal vote established by a Labour MP new to the
constituency in 1974 explains 5 of the cases – and possibly 10.
There is only one Conservative gain which the loss of a Labour
incumbent's personal vote could have caused, Anglesey.[24]

Therefore, without this incumbency effect, the Conservatives
would probably have a parliamentary majority of 60–65. This
is still far short of their 1959 majority (100), based on a smaller
(5.4%) popular lead over Labour. For an explanation of this
difference we must look into longer term changes in the working
of the electoral system.

Table 13 explores the operation of the electoral system by
examining the effect of various uniform total-vote swings from
the 1979 results. (Total vote swing is used to maintain comparability with previous tables in this series.) This table is unlikely
to offer an accurate guide to the possible outcomes of the next
general election as new constituency boundaries are due to
come into force and these will be more favourable, though to
an extent as yet unknown, to the Conservatives. But Table 13

[24] The 1979 Conservative plurality (7.3%) is much larger than the normal personal
vote. But the widely-attested personal popularity of Cledwyn Hughes (Labour MP
1951–79), which corresponds to the electoral record both during his years as a
Member and with the results on his retirement, was probably exceptionally large in
this rural, Celtic, island constituency.

*Table 13.   Effect of Uniform Total Vote Swing from May 1979
            Election Result*

Swing	Seats changing hands			% lead in votes	Lead in seats	Overall majority
to Con	Lab to Con	Con from Other	Lab to Other	Con	Con	Con
None	0	0	0	7.1	70	43
1%	14	1	0	9.1	99	73
2%	33	1	1	11.1	138	111
3%	43	1	1	13.1	158	131
4%	50	1	3	15.1	174	145
5%	59	1	3	17.1	192	163
to Lab	Con to Lab	Lab from Other	Con to Other	Lab	Lab	Lab
1%	15	0	0	−5.1	−40	−13
2%	28	0	2	−3.1	−12	none
3%	39	0	3	−1.1	11	none
4%	49	0	4	0.9	32	1
5%	63	1	5	2.9	62	31
10%	128	2	13	12.9	201	163

does illustrate the relationship between seats and votes, as it
existed in 1979. Two features stand out from this table. Firstly,
there is currently a bias in the system against the Conservatives;
secondly, the number of seats changing hands for any given
swing is substantially lower than it once was. Each of these
features helps to explain the Conservatives' relatively low
majority.

The bias can be seen if we assume a 3.5% total vote swing to
Labour from the 1979 election result, uniformly applied. This
would result in Conservative and Labour receiving equal shares
of the vote, but Labour would have 26 seats more than the
Conservatives. Labour now receives as large a bonus from the
operation of the electoral system as it did in 1970 before the
last constituency redistribution. In October 1974, by contrast,
equality of votes would have given the Conservatives an advantage of 9 seats.

This transformation is the consequence of the way in which
the swing varied between October 1974 and 1979. First, the
principal cause of the bias to Conservative in October 1974 was
removed: at that election the low swing to Labour in many
Conservative marginals enabled the Conservatives to save a

number of seats they would not otherwise have done, and they won far more seats than Labour by small majorities. Consequently, their vote was more effectively concentrated than Labour's. Because, in general, as Table 8 above shows, Labour did better than average in its marginal seats (principally because of the change in incumbency effect) and worse than average in its safe ones, that advantage was reversed; Labour won slightly more seats than the Conservatives by small majorities.[25]

But, in addition, Labour received an increased advantage from a factor from which they also benefited in October 1974 — their ability to concentrate their vote in smaller sized constituencies. This was where the regional variation in swing did have an impact on the electoral system. Scotland, with the smallest swing, also had the lowest electorates (mean swing 2.0%; mean electorate 53,463); in the North of England (mean swing 5.1%) the average electorate was 63,594; while in South Britain (mean swing 7.7%), it rose to 67,636. This correlation of size of swing with electorate size was accentuated by the lower swing in smaller inner-city seats, and the very high swing on the north eastern perimeter of London, where the seats have some of the highest electorates in the country. Overall, in Great Britain, the 31 constituencies with electorates below 40,000 had a mean swing of 4.1%; in the 388 with electorates between 40,000 and 70,000 the swing was 6.2%, and in the 204 with more than 70,000 electors the swing rose to 7.1%. This explains the differences between the various measures of electoral change derived from averaging the individual constituency changes, and those calculated from the same change in the overall votes cast, as shown in Table 2 above.[26]

But the more important and unexpected change is the reduction in the number of marginal constituencies. The figures in Table 13 show that, on average, about 12 seats would change hands for each 1% swing. However, the equivalent tables produced after the 1964 and 1966 elections showed that about 18 seats would change hands for each 1% swing.[27] This dramatic

[25] In October 1974, the Conservatives won 51 seats by less than a 6% majority, Labour 35. In 1979 the figures were 39 and 43 respectively.

[26] This correlation therefore overrode the impact of the above average increase in turnout in big city seats which were predominantly Labour.

[27] *The British General Election of 1964* p. 359 and *The British General Election of 1966* p. 294.

reduction in the number of seats liable to change hands has undermined the 'cube law',[28] which, if it holds, does result in practice in about 18 seats changing hands for each 1% swing.

How has this situation arisen and is the change permanent? The full answer to these two questions requires an analysis of several successive elections and is beyond the scope of this appendix.[29] But it does appear to result from two independent features of recent British electoral behaviour whose impact has lasted beyond a single election.

The first cause is the cumulative variation in swing by geography and urbanisation. This has steadily been making the bulk of Labour seats more Labour, and the bulk of Conservative seats more Conservative. Only mining constituencies stand out as clear exceptions; otherwise the Conservatives (gaining in the more rural and more southern constituencies) and Labour (gaining in more metropolitan and in northern and Scottish constituencies) have each been strengthening their hold on their own territory; this has made a number of their seats less likely to change back.

The second reason for the demise of the 'cube law' is the pattern of the rise in Liberal and Scottish Nationalist support in 1974. Their increased vote was often more at the expense of the weaker of the two major parties in a constituency. In particular this phenomenon left Labour strikingly weaker in many Conservative-held seats (some of which used to be Conservative-Labour marginals), especially in the South of England. Despite the fall in the Liberal vote in 1979, Labour did not regain much of this lost support (see p. 407 above); it remained strikingly weaker in these seats than in 1970 or 1959.

The combined effect of these two movements has been that between 1970 and 1979, Conservative-held seats[30] have swung 5.0% to Conservative, while Labour seats have swung 0.1% to Labour. An essential assumption behind the 'cube law' was that such non-uniform behaviour as exists should be randomly distributed. When variation in behaviour is as great as this, and

[28] This stated that if the two major parties' share of the total poll was divided between them in the proportion A:B, then the total of seats they won would be divided in the proportion $A^3:B^3$. See M. G. Kendall and A. Stuart 'Cubic Proportion in Election Results', *British Journal of Sociology*, 1 (1950), p. 183.
[29] We hope to publish such an analysis in the near future.
[30] Those seats won by the Conservatives in February 1974.

is as systematically distributed, the working of the electoral
system is profoundly altered. The divergence in swing (from
both sources) was particularly strong in February 1974, and the
decline of the 'cube law' can be dated from that election.

This change could have considerable political impact. If the
number of marginal seats remains reduced, it becomes more
likely, for any given number of third-party representatives, that
neither of the major parties will acquire an overall majority. For
example, as Table 13 shows, if the electorate's support for third
parties merely remains at its current level, then, on the current
boundaries, any uniform swing to Labour within the range 1.4%
to 4.0% would produce a hung parliament.

These changes will inevitably lead to the continued discussion
of the merits of alternative electoral systems. Table 14 suggests
what might have happened in 1979 under three different kinds
of proportional representation.

Table 14. 1979 Election under Different Systems

| | Votes | Actual result | | Proportional Systems | | | | | |
	Actual %	Seats	%	Dutch Seats	as %	Hansard Seats	as %	STV Seats	as %
Con	43.9	339	53.4	282	44.4	281	44.3	289	45.5
Lab	36.9	269	42.4	238	37.5	239	37.6	238	37.5
Lib	13.8	11	1.7	89	14.0	87	13.7	80	12.6
SNP	1.6	2	0.3	10	1.6	10	1.6	10	1.6
P. Cymru	0.4	2	0.3	2	0.3	2	0.3	2	0.3
N. Front	0.6	0	0.0	3	0.5	0	0.0	0	0.0
Others (GB)	0.5	0	0.0	0	0.0	0	0.0	0	0.0
N. Irish	2.2	12	1.9	9	1.4	16	2.5	16	2.5

The Dutch system is the purest form of PR in which the whole country is treated as a
single constituency and seats are allotted in strict proportion to votes. This would mean
that in the UK a party would have secured one seat for every 49,167 votes.

The Hansard Society enquiry of 1976 recommended single-member constituencies, but
with seats added in each Standard Region to make the result more proportional (for
parties which pass a 5% threshhold).

The Single Transferable Vote system is used for most Northern Irish elections: for this we
have regrouped the 635 constituencies into multi-member ones of about half a dozen
members each. We have assumed for each system that each part of the UK would have the
number of seats to which its electorate currently entitled it: 529 seats for England, 58 for
Scotland, 32 for Wales, and 16 for Northern Ireland. Because of the splintering of Northern
Irish votes between so many parties only nine members would have been elected under
the Dutch system; in reality the discipline of such a party list system would have produced
fewer parties and more seats there.

Table 14 does not, of course, show what the 1979 general election would have produced under a system of proportional representation since (as our evidence of tactical voting shows) voting behaviour would clearly differ with a different electoral system.

Furthermore, as the smaller parties would have had candidates available to many more voters with a single UK-wide constituency, they would have won a handful more seats under the Dutch system; but Table 14 also shows that there would be very little difference in outcome between this extremely proportional system and the fairly high threshold which the Hansard Society inquiry recommended. With the Liberal and Nationalist votes at their 1979 levels, the single transferable vote operating in six-member constituencies would produce a nearly proportional result; but with a slightly lower level of support or smaller constituencies it would underrepresent those parties.

The principal beneficaries under proportional representation, as compared with the present system, would clearly be the Liberals; they would acquire a pivotal role in Parliament, being able to create an overall majority in combination with either of the two larger parties.

Conclusion
Despite the return of a government with a safe overall majority for the first time since 1970, some of the traditional underpinnings of the two-party system have not returned. There was a substantial systematic variation in the swing between October 1974 and 1979, most notably from the North to the South of the country, which nullified the assumption of uniformity of swing. The 1979 election did not provide a united national verdict on the merits of the two major parties. Although there was a fall in the third-party vote, two interrelated legacies of the 1974 elections remain. The electoral system has lost some of its ability to provide the winning party with a safe parliamentary majority, and avoid a hung parliament. The success of the Liberals in retaining much of their tactical support in the seats in which they were second, has transformed the electoral geography of Southern England and profoundly altered the pattern of the distribution of the Conservative and Labour vote.

Index